AN AMERICAN PRINCESS

AN AMERICAN PRINCESS

The Remarkable Life of Marguerite Chapin Caetani

LAURIE DENNETT

McGill-Queen's University Press
Montreal & Kingston • London • Chicago

ISBN 978-0-7735-4818-3 (cloth)
ISBN 978-0-7735-9992-5 (ePDF)
ISBN 978-0-7735-9993-2 (ePUB)

Legal deposit fourth quarter 2016
Bibliothèque nationale du Québec

Printed in Canada on acid-free paper

This book has been published with the help of funds provided by the Fondazione Camillo Caetani, Rome, and the Fondazione Roffredo Caetani, Latina, Italy.

McGill-Queen's University Press acknowledges the support of the Canada Council for the Arts for our publishing program. We also acknowledge the financial support of the Government of Canada through the Canada Book Fund for our publishing activities.

Library and Archives Canada Cataloguing in Publication

Dennett, Laurie, 1946–, author
An American princess : the remarkable life of Marguerite Chapin Caetani / Laurie Dennett.

Includes bibliographical references and index.
Issued in print and electronic formats.
ISBN 978-0-7735-4818-3 (cloth).–ISBN 978-0-7735-9992-5 (ePDF).–ISBN 978-0-7735-9993-2 (ePUB)

1. Caetani, Marguerite. 2. Commerce (Paris, France : 1924). 3. Botteghe oscure. 4. Periodical editors–France–Biography. 5. Periodical editors–Italy–Biography. 6. Princesses–France–Biography. 7. Princesses–Italy–Biography. 8. Giardino di Ninfa (Italy). 9. Europe–Intellectual life–20th century. I. Title.

PN5183.C217D45 2016 070.92 C2016-904528-5
C2016-904529-3

For Esme Howard:
his book as well as mine, in memory of Marguerite

CONTENTS

Acknowledgments • ix

1 A Girl from New England • 3

2 A Young Heiress in the Making • 24

3 One Life, Two Worlds • 43

4 Prince Roffredo and the Caetani • 69

5 A Strained Courtship with a Happy Outcome • 99

6 A Family in War and Peace • 122

7 Villa Romaine and the Genesis of *Commerce* • 140

8 A Unique Vocation: Fostering the *Commerce* of Ideas • 160

9 The Move to Rome, and Ninfa • 191

10 War and Tragedy • 222

11 New Beginnings: *Botteghe Oscure* • 243

12 The Fullness of Time • 281

13 A Legacy for the Future • 315

Notes • 335

Select Bibliography • 383

Image Credits • 395

Index • 397

ACKNOWLEDGMENTS

It is a pleasure to be able to express my appreciation to those who have had a part in bringing this long project to fruition. First among them is Esme Howard, with whom the idea of writing about Marguerite originated. Merely to say that he has been a constant source of encouragement from beginning to end would be an understatement, since he has been so much more than that. With characteristic goodwill, he has given unstintingly of his time, his knowledge, and his memories of the Caetani family, provided essential introductions, facilitated my research, and given endless practical help. The dedication of this book to him is a mark of respect and gratitude that goes beyond words.

I would also like to thank the Fondazione Camillo Caetani, Rome (its former chairman, the late Avv. Giacomo Antonelli, and its current chairman, Dr Bruno Toscano), and the Fondazione Roffredo Caetani, Latina (and its chairman, Pier Giacomo Sottoriva), for their generous contribution towards the costs associated with my research in their archives, and for allowing me the use of their photographic collections. I am especially grateful for the advice and practical assistance of the staff of the archives of the Fondazione Camillo Caetani, especially the late Dott. Luigi Fiorani, the current archivist, Dott. Caterina Fiorani, and Dott. Massimiliano Tortora. My visits to the Natural Monument of Ninfa, and the conversations with its director, Lauro Marchetti, brought Marguerite Caetani and her husband Roffredo's generation of that extraordinary family alive for me. The International Friends of Ninfa (UK), (Philip, Lord Howard of Penrith, chairman, and Esme Howard, coordinator) has also contributed generously to this project, and I hope that its members will find a reflection of their own love of the garden in what is said in this book about Ninfa and its creators.

The staffs of the following institutions and foundations also gave valued assistance: the Fondazione Leone Caetani, Accademia Nationale dei Lincei, Palazzo Corsini, Rome; the Bibliotèque nationale de France, Paris; the Booth Family Center for Special Collections, Joseph Mark Lauinger Memorial Library, Georgetown University, Washington, DC; the British Library; the Fitzwilliam Museum, Cambridge; the Harry Ransom Research Center for the Humanities, University of Texas at Austin; the Imperial War Museum, London; the Institut Catholique, Paris; the Archives of the LSA (Little Sisters of the Assumption) Family in Mission, New York City; the New York City Department of Records and Information Services, Commissioner of Records, Surrogates' Court, County of New York; the New York City Vital Records Department and Health Department, Municipal Archives; the Schlesinger Library, Radcliff Institute, Harvard University, Cambridge, Massachusetts; the Vernon Museum, Vernon, British Columbia.

I am grateful to the following for permission to use extracts from unpublished or published sources of which they are the copyright holders:

The Accademia dei Lincei Library for quotes from Leone Caetani's letters;

Stephen G. Biddle of Quakertown, Pennsylvania, for permission to quote from the unpublished papers of Katherine Biddle;

Theodore (Ted) Chapin and the late Schuyler Chapin for permission to quote from the Cornelia Chapin Papers;

Katherine Clark, for permission to quote from her oral biography of Eugene Walter, *Milking the Moon: A Southerner's Story of Life on This Planet.* Crown Publishers, New York, 2002 [and Untreed Reads (ebook), San Francisco, 2011];

The Estate of T.S. Eliot, administered by Faber & Faber, for permission to quote unpublished letters from Eliot to his cousins, Marguerite Caetani and Katherine Biddle;

Garry O'Connor, for permission to quote from his biography of Dame Maggie Teyte, *The Pursuit of Perfection*;

Mrs Helen Tate, for permission to quote unpublished letters of her late husband, Allen Tate, to Katherine Biddle;
The Booth Family Research Center for Special Collections, Georgetown University, Washington, DC, for permission to cite the letters of Harold H. Tittmann and the copy of Sir D'Arcy Osborne's diary, included in the Harold H. Tittmann Papers;
The Estate of Dylan Thomas, administered by David Higham and Associates, London, for permission to quote his unpublished letters to Marguerite Caetani.

In addition, I would like to thank the following people, who have provided information in response to my queries, given help with translations, or taken the time to read early drafts: Dott. Piero Craveri, Diane Howard, Dr Sophie Levie, Pier Giacomo Sottoriva, Sister Maryalice Spencer, Dott. Massimiliano Tortora, Miranda Jones, the late Dr Anita McConnell, the late Noella Terrail, and Emma Vickers.

Photographs have been considered an essential accompaniment to Marguerite's life story, although, given the riches available, it has sometimes been difficult to make choices among them. I am deeply grateful to Stephen G. Biddle, Ted Chapin, and the Howard family for providing family photographs, and equally so to Jonathan Biddle, to Robbie Cannon of Quarry Printing, in Uckfield, and to Esme Howard for enhancing many of them for reproduction. The collaboration of the Fondazione Camillo Caetani and the Fondazione Roffredo Caetani in providing images has been outstanding. To Charles Quest-Ritson, Lino Rizzi, Heidi Thompson, and others who have generously made photographs available, I express my thanks.

No biographical research on a recent subject would be complete without the recollections of those who knew the person, the places, and the period. I was fortunate to have been able to record such accounts from a number of people who knew Marguerite, or who had known others who played a part in her remarkable life: the late Avv. Giacomo Antonelli, Paola Bassani Pacht, the late Anthony Burton, the late Schuyler Chapin, Theodore (Ted) Chapin, Dott. Piero Craveri, the late Dott. Luigi Fiorani, Maria Luisa Fiorenza Tompkins, Florence

Hammond Phillips, Esme Howard, the late Mrs Henry Howard, Benedetta Origo, Lauro Marchetti, Arturo Osio, Sophie Palmer, Contessa Desideria Pasolini dall'Onda, the late Peter Tompkins, and the late Gore Vidal.

It remains only to thank Linda McKnight of Westwood Creative Artists, Toronto, Philip Cercone, Ryan Van Huijstee, and the staff of McGill-Queen's University Press, and Patricia Kennedy, copy editor, for their respective contributions to producing this book. May it in turn help to gain for Marguerite Caetani the wider recognition she deserves.

Laurie Dennett,
La Laguna de Tablas, Pedrafita do Cebreiro, Lugo, Spain
30 May 2016

AN AMERICAN PRINCESS

1

A GIRL FROM NEW ENGLAND

One day late in April 1954, two American writers visiting Rome were invited to lunch at Ninfa, the country estate belonging to Prince Roffredo Caetani and his wife, Princess Marguerite. In the unique setting of a ruined medieval town some forty kilometres southwest of the Italian capital, three generations of Prince Roffredo's family had created what has sometimes been called the most romantic garden in Europe. Any garden is at its best in spring, but Ninfa is particularly enchanting. Drifts of narcissus charm the eye, the delicate tones of lilacs and wisterias soften the broken walls, and the orchards are heavy with blossom and scent. On that April day, the experience of so much beauty left the visitors lost for words – a rare occurrence for the translator and professor of French literature, Wallace Fowlie, on leave from Duke University, and the poet Allen Tate, a Fulbright Professor who was spending that year at the University of Rome.

Princess Marguerite was an expert guide to Ninfa, since she was one of its creators, but once her visitors had recovered their powers of speech, there was much to talk about besides the garden. Her literary review, *Botteghe Oscure* (which the critic Edmund Wilson had recently deemed "the best thing coming out of Europe"), was well-known to Tate and Fowlie, since their work had appeared in it. What many of its readers – and even some of its contributors – didn't know was that, like her visitors, the princess was American: born Marguerite Gibert Chapin in Waterford, near New London, Connecticut, and raised just steps from Fifth Avenue in New York City. On that spring day in 1954, she was nearly seventy-five years old, but neither looked her age nor left her guests in any doubt about her intellectual vitality. News from the

United States was always welcome, and as the conversation touched upon the current work of one American poet or novelist after another, Tate and Fowlie were impressed by how up-to-date she was about what was being written on the other side of the Atlantic.

After a buffet lunch, taken on a terrace outdoors with Prince Roffredo as host, the visitors had a few more moments of conversation with Princess Marguerite. Fowlie later observed that she was "totally unpretentious, totally dedicated to her work, totally indifferent to polemical literary discussion." What he and Tate wanted to convey to her in that brief interlude was "how appreciative we were of her efforts on behalf of the writer in so many countries, of the encouragement she had given to so many young writers, of the help she had extended to so many established writers ... She smiled faintly as she listened to us, and then said quite simply, 'I live with the belief that the artist is the most important person alive.'"[1]

By 1954, this was a declaration that Marguerite Caetani had become used to making. *Botteghe Oscure* was attracting admiration worldwide – from reviewers, from readers, and above all, from writers – while Marguerite, somewhat to her surprise, was at last garnering what many who knew her judged to be some long-overdue and well-deserved recognition. Not that it had mattered to her, over the years, whether she received accolades or not, since she did not regard herself as central to the scheme of things, as most of us do. Personally self-effacing, avoiding the limelight whenever possible, she spent her time, energy, and resources on winning that limelight for countless writers, most of them young. Asked how she viewed her position in relation to them, she would reply that she was privileged – not for being titled or rich, but because she was able to use her resources to bring them and their work to the notice of a world that needed to hear what they had to say. She seldom, if ever, mentioned her personal and particular qualifications for such a task: a mind well-furnished through a lifetime's reading, complete fluency in four languages, and an unerring editorial eye and ear for what was perennial but freshly stated, the authentic voice.

Marguerite Caetani has been called "the Diaghilev of modern letters,"[2] but she was no showy impresario. She was not herself a writer, but she was the friend of writers, championing their essential role in society all her life. Along the way she acted as catalyst, patron and promoter, talent scout, counsellor, and mentor, but unlike the great force behind the Ballets Russes, she was never demanding, possessive, or histrionic. Always, she showed the strength of her convictions through generous personal support, both financial and moral. As she intended it should, such support made a difference: some of the best-known and best-loved authors of the twentieth century have acknowledged as much. If today, half a century after her death, she is less well-known – especially in her native United States – than she deserves to be, that is a reflection on an age that has come to value show above substance, rather than on the value of her contribution to the literary history of the twentieth century.

It is obviously a very long way from New London, Connecticut, to a uniquely beguiling twenty-acre garden in the shadow of the Lepini mountains south of Rome. However dissimilar these two places are, Marguerite Caetani's story links one to the other, and each of them to other places still. Like everyone, she has a "back story": an ancestry, context, and early life that were the preparation for what came later. Even the basic facts of this early period have sometimes been difficult to trace. An intensely private person, Marguerite seems never to have written a memoir or kept a diary, and on only a few occasions deigned to give interviews where notes were taken by someone else. Perhaps it was simply that, once left behind on the other side of the Atlantic, her childhood and youth ceased to have much importance for her in the life she created for herself elsewhere. For those seeking to understand her – not just "who was she, and where did she come from?" so much as "how did she come to be the person she was, and do the things she did?" – that ancestry and background, that context, may provide essential clues. Clues are necessary, because although Marguerite Caetani valued simplicity and directness, she was herself a complex and sometimes contradictory personality: easily moved to compassion, yet finding overt sentiment abhorrent; generous of spirit and equally generous in her dealings, yet, when disappointed, capable of abrupt and chilly endings, without (or so it seemed) a backward glance. Such inconsistencies may not yield to purely rational analysis or a single interpretation. Perhaps the best a biographer can do is present what has been learned through sifting the evidence, be honest about where the gaps are, try to be aware of personal bias, and indicate when and where the evidence leaves off and the attempts at guesswork begin.

Fortunately, although finding documentary evidence has sometimes been difficult, enough has been discovered to reconstruct for Marguerite that all-important "context" of ancestry and background. This in turn may indicate some of the ideals that helped to forge the characters of her ancestors and, possibly, her own. Two such ideals were those of rectitude and sturdy independence, embodied by the first of her forebears to set foot on American soil: Deacon Samuel Chapin, "The Puritan," whose statue stands today in the middle of Springfield, Massachusetts. Born in Devonshire, England, in 1595, Samuel Chapin was a Protestant Nonconformist, finding the English church created by the Elizabethan Settlement far too "Catholicke" for his liking. In 1635, Samuel, his wife, Cicely, and their five children left England, seeking freedom of worship in the New World. They settled first in Roxbury in the Massachusetts Bay Colony, but after seven years moved to Agawam on the Connecticut River, a clutch of homesteads that became the nucleus of the town of Springfield. Samuel Chapin was a pillar of this community from the time he arrived there, serving as a Selectman (an office combining the duties of elder, moral guardian, magistrate, and surveyor) for several terms, and as a deacon of the Congregational church from 1650 until his death in 1675.

The Chapins' seven sons and daughters (two more children were born in Massachusetts) produced a total of seventy-two offspring.

Over the next two centuries, successive generations of Chapins populated the area around the Connecticut River that became known as "Pioneer Valley," of which Springfield became the chief town. They intermarried, cousins marrying cousins to create a dense network of family, landowning, and business relationships. They prospered, not only as farmers, but also as tradesmen, artisans, teachers, and clergymen: active members of a community that valued initiative and hard work.[3] In 1862, a Chapin family gathering organized in Springfield was attended by hundreds of the descendants of Samuel and Cicely Chapin. By 1880 the names of the Chapins resident in Springfield and the townships around it took up two full columns in the Springfield and Chickopee directory.

The first member of the family to acquire a position of influence on more than a local scale was Marguerite Chapin's great-grandfather, Chester William Chapin, born in Ludlow, Hampden County, Massachusetts, in 1798. He started his working life as part owner of a dry-goods business in Chickopee Falls, near Springfield. By the time he was twenty-five, he was driving a stagecoach to carry provisions to the store. As the population of Pioneer Valley increased, he created a passenger stagecoach service, then purchased a steamship franchise to establish a monopoly of land and river transport in and around Springfield.

This formative part of Chapin's career, during which he became one of Pioneer Valley's most prosperous residents, coincided with the rise of railroad development in New England. The railways threatened his transport business, but at the same time the ambitious Chapin saw that they represented a once-in-a-lifetime opportunity. He became a leading investor in the construction of the new rail lines joining the major towns of Massachusetts and Connecticut. Since railroad concessions depended on legislative approval, he went into local politics, the better to lobby for the railroad interest. In 1842 he persuaded the Massachusetts legislature to fund the Northampton and Springfield line, which soon merged with another local line to become the Connecticut River Railroad, with Chapin as its first president. He became president, too, of the Agawam Bank of Springfield, as a means of joining a group of Boston investors in financing more railroads. Alongside all this, he and

1.1
Chester W. Chapin I (1796–1883), railway magnate: the first of his family to achieve wealth and influence.

other Springfield entrepreneurs set up the Springfield Car and Engine Company to manufacture railway carriages and rolling stock.

The growing demand for rail transport throughout New England meant that local companies were quickly bought up and merged with others to create larger entities. The opening up and settlement of the West was another factor in the rapid expansion of the American railroad network in the mid-nineteenth century. Within a short time, Chapin was president (1854–57) of the Western Railroad Corporation, and then of the Boston and Albany Railroad Company (1868–78). He became increasingly wealthy and influential, known for his forceful pursuit of new business. The railway expert Edward Chase Kirkland cites the following commentary about him:

> Chapin ... was one of the great railroad capitalists of New England, indeed of the nation. A former stage driver and steamboat man, he ... became a large investor in the New York, New Haven and Hartford, the Connecticut River Road [*sic*], and the New York Central (at least 3,400 shares and sat [*sic*] on the board after 1867), as well as the Boston and Albany. Characterised by one of his associates as "one of the hardest men I ever knew,"

> he exemplified the policy of presidential management, if not dictation. He determined the composition of the board of directors, assembled it at his pleasure "when anything happened," and secured the successor to the throne.[4]

In the aftermath of the American Civil War, railroad construction accelerated to keep pace with an economic boom that altered the face of the nation. The boom was centred on the port city of New York, already the most important nucleus of population on the eastern seaboard. The influx of immigrants, mainly from Ireland and continental Europe, soon made it the fastest-growing city in the western hemisphere. The fact that so many of them were poor and illiterate, with ties only to others who spoke their language, set the stage for the development of the ethnic slums and the contrast between prosperity and poverty that characterized New York City during its so-called "Gilded Age" in the last thirty years of the century. This pool of unskilled labour, coupled with technological advances and the availability of cheap raw materials, fuelled the industrialization of manufacture. Goods for export poured out of New York, while imports to satisfy the tastes of the newly prosperous poured in. By the 1870s, the city was said to be "literally awash" with new money. When the New York Stock Exchange came into being in 1869, following the merger between two existing exchanges, membership doubled within months. It was the era when the term "millionaire" came into its own,[5] and soon fell short of describing the fortunes amassed by such domineering individuals as Cornelius Vanderbilt (railroads and shipping), Andrew Carnegie (steel), John Pierpoint Morgan (finance), James Duke (tobacco), Jay Gould (shipping and communications), John D. Rockefeller (oil), and James Gordon Bennett (newspapers). In an era when corporate and labour law was in its infancy and political influence easy to manipulate, the new breed of competitive, ruthless businessmen, later given the unflattering name of "robber barons," carried all before them.

Chester William Chapin was not rich or powerful enough to be considered a "robber baron," though he made a fortune through his railroad dealings. The Boston and Albany, as its name suggests, linked

1.2
"The Puritan": Augustus Saint-Gaudens' evocation of Chester W. Chapin's pioneering ancestor, Deacon Samuel Chapin.

Boston, Massachusetts, and Albany, New York. As a major shareholder in the small companies absorbed by it (there were no concerns about conflict of interest in those days), he made money on each acquisition, and enhanced his status as president of the company at the same time. In 1875, when the Boston and Albany built a huge side-wheel steamship at the port of New London, Connecticut, the vessel – not surprisingly – was given the name *Chester W. Chapin*. By then, Chapin had been elected to Congress as a Democrat, the culmination of a lifelong ambition to represent Massachusetts in national politics.[6]

In 1881, Chapin – by then eighty-three years old – commissioned Augustus Saint-Gaudens, the foremost American sculptor of the day, to create a statue to commemorate his pioneer ancestor Deacon Samuel Chapin. This statue of "The Puritan," mentioned above, was cast in bronze and depicts the deacon in mid-stride, wearing a flowing cloak and carrying a Bible and staff. Saint-Gaudens acknowledged having used a bust of Chester William Chapin as the model for the figure's head. Since 1887, "The Puritan," standing first in Stearns Square and later in Merrick Park in the centre of Springfield, has embodied the enterprising spirit that created "Pioneer Valley" and the city itself. Marguerite Chapin must surely have known this statue, and to have been presented, as a very small child, to her great-grandfather, whose legacy it was.

Chester William Chapin's marriage to a cousin, Dorcas Chapin, produced two sons and three daughters. Observations such as Kirkland's, above, about Chapin's dictatorial nature may in part explain the disinclination of his elder son, Abel Dexter Chapin, born in 1829, to take up a position in his father's railroad empire. In contrast, the younger son, Chester William, Jr, born in 1842, inherited his father's ambition and drive, and succeeded him as president of the Connecticut Railroad. In addition, he was a true entrepreneur and transferred his knowledge of railways, steamships, and urban planning to a range of other ventures. These included canal-building, paper mills, the manufacture of electric trolley cars, and the founding of the Chapin Bank in Springfield. He also spent much of his time in the faster-paced atmosphere of New York. In partnership with an equally enterprising cousin, the lawyer Alfred Clark Chapin, Chester William Chapin, Jr, set up the Securities Corporation, with its headquarters on Broadway, to finance and launch new companies. Like so many of the outstanding businessmen of the era, both he and Alfred Chapin used their personal fortunes to ensure that the Chapin name lived on through a variety of philanthropic projects – perhaps the best known being the Chapin Library of Rare Books at Williams College, Williamstown, Massachusetts, where Alfred studied before attending Harvard Law School.[7] Like his father, the younger Chester William Chapin had a ship named after him: the New Haven Steamboat Company's 312-foot passenger steamer, built in 1899. He also developed an eighteen-thousand-acre tract of land in the Catskill Mountains into a huge private estate, which today is a residential community bearing his name.[8]

But it is Abel Dexter Chapin, the elder, lesser-known, son of Chester William Chapin, Sr, who is of primary interest here, since he was Marguerite's grandfather. The few surviving details of his life suggest a man who was more interested in learning and cultural pursuits than his father and brother, and who perhaps possessed a gentler nature. Rather than moving to New York, as his brother Chester did, Abel chose to remain in the family seat of Springfield, where he practised law, married Julia Irene Clark, and produced eight children, the eldest being Lindley Hoffman Chapin, born in 1854, Marguerite's father. His second son, Robert Williams Chapin, would also play an important part in her life.

Abel seems to have been the first of the Chapins to use his money for personal cultural enrichment. He took his family to Europe for several months in the summer of 1859, when Lindley was five years old. Like so many well-to-do Americans of his time, Abel was captivated by Paris, the French way of life, and the French countryside. Back in Springfield at the outbreak of the Civil War, he enlisted as a Private in the Massachusetts Regiment (his profession is noted as "armourer"), but was mustered out after ten months, probably because of wounds or ill health. Thereafter, he and Julia returned regularly to Paris for extended stays, and their children received much of their education in Europe. In the case of Lindley, this meant attendance at a private academy in Dresden, where he became fluent in French and German and acquired a love of serious music. Lindley was a handsome and highly eligible young bachelor by the time he returned to the United States to enter Harvard Law School in 1874, in what was becoming a family tradition. At some point – perhaps in Paris or back in New York – he met brothers of about his own age, Frederick and Audinet Gibert, graduates of Cornell University and members of a wealthy Franco-American Roman Catholic family that moved in the highest echelons of New York society. It was not long before he met the Giberts' sister, Leila Marie, to whom he became engaged.

Abel and Julia Chapin were still in Paris, and it was there – possibly because of the coronary heart disease that would claim several of his male descendants in middle age – that Abel died, aged only forty-nine, on 24 November 1878. He must have had a premonition that all was not well, for he left instructions that he should be buried in Paris, and that his death should not interrupt the plans for his eldest son's wedding, due to be celebrated on 30 November in New York.[9] Lindley Hoffman Chapin, aged twenty-four, was duly married on that day, as his father had wished, having already been received into the faith of his bride. (It would be interesting to know how his conversion was

1.3
Lindley Hoffman Chapin (1854–1896), grandson of Chester W. Chapin I, and father of Marguerite Chapin.

viewed by his parents, and by the rest of the Chapins, staunchly Protestant since the days of Deacon Samuel, but no comment on the subject has come to light.) St Ann's Roman Catholic Church on East Twelfth Street was, according to the *New York Times*, "filled with a brilliant assemblage" of relatives and friends on the morning of 30 November,[10] even though Lindley and his immediate family were in mourning, and his mother was still abroad. Members of the Chapin clan who attended included those now prominent in New York's business and political life, and others who had remained in Pioneer Valley as farmers and shopkeepers. Lindley Chapin by this time had graduated from Harvard and joined a Manhattan law firm, though he would never have to depend upon his earnings as a lawyer to maintain his standard of living. Leila Gibert was not yet twenty-one, the co-heiress, with her brothers, to a fortune in Manhattan and Long Island real estate.

On their return from their honeymoon, Lindley and Leila Chapin moved into an apartment at 49 Fifth Avenue, on what was becoming New York's most fashionable thoroughfare. From his father and grandfather, Lindley had inherited properties in Springfield and a magnificent summer mansion called Rock Lawn, built by the elder Chester William Chapin on some 240 acres of land on Goshen Point, Waterford, near the old shipping port of New London, Connecticut. The young couple spent much of their time at Rock Lawn, and it was there that their first child, Marguerite Gibert Chapin, was born on 24 June 1880.

Marguerite grew up as an only child, but it was clearly not her parents' intention that she should lack siblings. In February 1882 Leila gave birth to another little girl, Julia Irene, named after Lindley's mother. The couple suffered a devastating blow when this baby died in July of the same year. Marguerite would have been too young to retain any memory of this tiny sister, or of her mother's illness following a miscarriage in 1883. By Christmas 1884, Leila was once more pregnant. This time, husband and wife chose to remain in New York, so as to be close to the best of medical care. Despite this precaution, Leila again miscarried, this time late in the fifth month. After two weeks of suffering, she died of puerpural septicaemia on 1 April 1885, aged just twenty-six.[11]

Marguerite was not yet five years old, unable to grasp that her mother would not suddenly reappear. In his grief, Lindley Chapin withdrew from professional and social life. Father, daughter, and servants, including the French-speaking nurse insisted upon by Leila, abandoned the Fifth Avenue apartment for the mansion at Waterford. The widowed Julia Chapin came from Springfield to help her son through this difficult time and to care for her granddaughter.

Though so few traces of Leila Gibert remain, she could hardly have been so ephemeral a figure to Marguerite. To a small child, a mother is everything, and the sudden removal of such an essential figure produces overwhelming emotional pain. Such a psychological trauma is often the subject of specialized counselling today, but no such support existed in 1885. Bereavement at such a young age was bound to leave a scar. In later life, Marguerite's tendency to retreat into herself in the face of painful events was noted by others. This, and the similarly self-protective trait of abruptly withdrawing emotionally from those who hurt or offended her, may have been part of the legacy of maternal loss. Leila was deeply loved by her husband: he built a private chapel at Rock Lawn in her memory, dedicated to Our Lady of Good Counsel, and is reputed to have provided it with a chalice designed by Benvenuto Cellini and altar linen and vestments bordered with the lace from Leila's wedding dress. What of the shadowy recollections that must have lingered in Marguerite's memory? Did her preference for simplicity rather than adornment in dress and furnishings, for freshness and naturalness rather than artifice, her directness, her love of music, her delight in rhyme and word play – all of which were characteristic of her as an adult – owe anything to her memories of her mother? If anything definite can be attributed to Leila, it may be her identification with her French heritage, shown in her determination to pass on to Marguerite the Catholic faith, the French language, and the love of French culture. These were not material gifts, but as will become apparent, they were formative and lasting, and in time they gave Marguerite another perspective from which to view and experience the world.

Leila's marriage to Lindley Hoffman Chapin does not seem to have resulted in the merging of her personal wealth with his. Perhaps – since she married before she legally became of age – her parents preferred that both she and they retain a measure of discretion concerning the disposition of her inheritance. Whatever wealth Leila was due to inherit from her parents was transferred to a trust set up for Marguerite, either at the time of Leila's own death or perhaps later, when Lindley remarried: we simply do not know. However the matter was legally arranged, the fortune that came to Marguerite through her mother was even more important than her Chapin inheritance in guaranteeing her financial independence when she came of age.

Because Leila died so young, the Gibert family has received comparatively little attention in previous accounts of Marguerite's life. Who were her mother's relations, where did they come from, and – to repeat the question that was all-important in the drawing rooms of Gilded Age New York – how had they made their money?

Leila's grandfather, and Marguerite's great-grandfather, was Nicholas Gibert, born in about 1770 in the French Caribbean island of Martinique. He married Catherine Audinet, the daughter of the governor of another French possession, the nearby island of Guadeloupe. The couple arrived in Newport, Rhode Island, in 1793, fleeing the revolutionary violence that had spread from France to her colonies. Nicholas Gibert may already have had some familial mercantile connection with

Newport. At that time, it was a centre for trade with the West Indies, especially in the commodities produced by the colonial plantations, such as sugar, jute, indigo, and rum. Nicholas prospered, and moved to New York sometime around 1811. Wisely, he invested in property. By the time of his death in 1851, in addition to a handsome house in Newport, he owned various commercial premises and warehouses dotted around Manhattan and Brooklyn, and at least one house on Long Island. His will indicates that he was able to provide handsomely for his two sons and their families, for the young daughters of a third son who predeceased him, and for a friend and business associate who had fallen on hard times.[12]

Nicholas's surviving sons were Frédéric Edouard Gibert (later known as Frederick), who carried on his father's business as a merchant at Newport, and Jean-Jacques Nicholas Gibert, who, as a doctor in New York City, adopted the name of James Thevigny Gibert. Their close ties with France, in an era when wealthy Americans regularly crossed the ocean to spend months at a time in Paris, gave them an additional boost up the New York social ladder. French continued to be the language spoken in the Gibert family circle, English outside it, just as the brothers retained their Roman Catholic allegiance in a milieu that was predominantly Protestant. James's four daughters, Clara, Eugenie Mathilde, Marie Josephine, and Anna Marie, were the subjects of childhood portraits that suggest this dual cultural identity.[13] The paintings were done by an unknown nineteenth-century French artist, and are now in the Frick Collection in New York City. One picture shows two of the little girls, Clara and Anna Marie, playing with a lamb and a rabbit in a pastoral setting that evokes both childhood innocence and the material comfort associated with land ownership. Its companion piece, depicting Eugenie Mathilde and Marie Josephine dancing to the music played by a Black woman in the background, may refer to former plantation – and slave – ownership in Martinique or Guadeloupe.

Nicholas Gibert's third son, William Nicholas, brought his family a valuable connection through his marriage to Elizabeth Schermerhorn. She belonged to an influential family descended from Dutch Calvinist burghers who settled in Albany, New York State, in about 1640. The Schermerhorns became commercially powerful in New York, and by the 1840s were one of the city's most prominent families. Thus, within a generation of Nicholas Gibert's arrival in the United States, his son William's marriage linked the Giberts to New York's "Knickerbocracy" of long-established, Dutch-descended families with "old money." Before his death in 1848, William Gibert appointed his brothers, Frederick and James, as guardians of his young daughters, Elizabeth and Julia – still minors at the time of their grandfather Nicholas's demise in 1851. The $50,000 legacies left to each girl by Nicholas made them desirable heiresses, though the funds were held in trust for them by their guardian-uncles until they came of age.[14] When Julia Gibert married her cousin George Stevens Schermerhorn in 1859, she strengthened the existing relationship with his powerful family.[15] Further reinforcement of the Giberts' social position came through the marriages of two of James Thevigny Gibert's daughters. In becoming the wife of the lawyer James Bliss Townsend, Eugenie Mathilde linked her family to an Anglo-American dynasty that traced its English titles and landholdings back to Norman times. The marriage in 1885 of Marie Josephine (1853–1916) to Chevalier Hugo Otto de Fritsch, the Austro-Hungarian consul to the United States, brought further European and diplomatic connections.

The Gibert fortune, ever-increasing as New York property values skyrocketed after the Civil War, eventually passed to James Thevigny Gibert's four daughters and to the three children of his brother Frederick's marriage to Margaret Reynolds of Rhode Island. These were two sons, Frederick Edward, junior, born in 1851, and Nicholas Audinet, born in 1852. There was also a daughter, born in 1859: Leila Marie, Marguerite's mother. In time, the Gibert money, together with the family connections mentioned above, would provide the young Marguerite Chapin with an automatic entree to the ballrooms of Fifth Avenue and the grand residences of the Champs-Elysées. A much older second cousin was none other than Caroline Webster Schermerhorn, better known as Mrs William Astor (mother of John Jacob Astor), the matriarch who dominated the New York social scene during the Gilded Age.

Impeccable Dutch and English ancestry, great wealth, and an indomitable character were her credentials as spokeswoman of the New York establishment. Her famous address book contained the names of everyone she considered worth knowing in New York, and reputedly determined the social fortunes of three generations of debutantes. Nothing has come to light regarding her relationship with the Chapins, but the family relationship with the Giberts would certainly have operated in Marguerite's favour.

In June 1885, three months after his wife's death, Lindley Chapin took Marguerite, together with valet, nursemaid, and tutor, to Paris for the summer. It was Marguerite's first direct exposure to the French way of life. The American Giberts had maintained contact down the generations with the descendents of Nicholas Gibert's brothers, several of whom were painters of note. In Paris, Marguerite met young cousins, played with them in the Bois de Boulogne, and was taken to see the major monuments. It would be another three years before Joseph Gibert, a retired professor of Classics at the Sorbonne, set up his few stalls of textbooks at the top of the boulevard Saint-Michel, but the young Marguerite may well have met this distinguished elderly relative in 1885. Years later, when she was living in Paris as a young woman, Gibert Joseph – the vast book emporium that occupies the same (but greatly extended) site today – would be one of her favourite haunts.[16]

Whether in Paris or back in New York and Waterford, no child could have been more lovingly and carefully attended than was Marguerite Chapin in the years following her mother's death. Lindley Chapin sought to counterbalance the loss of her mother by providing pretty clothes, toys, pets, and excursions, but most of all by spending time with her and ensuring that family ties were maintained. Julia Chapin and Margaret Gibert, in the way of grandmothers, probably indulged her. Lindley's brothers, Robert and Henry, and other Chapin relatives in Springfield, were close and familiar figures. Her Gibert uncles, "Uncle Fred" and "Uncle Audie," told her stories and – in the way of uncles – no doubt included some about themselves when young that made her laugh. The servants did their best. On Lindley's orders, Marguerite was never to be left alone, so it was as well that her nursemaid, twenty-

1.4
Marguerite Chapin, aged three, photographed by J. Ludovici of New York.

four-year-old Kate Clancy, was young enough to be playmate as well as caregiver. Her tutor spoke and read to her in French, her governess in English, so that she conversed easily in either language.[17]

Lindley Chapin remained a widower for nearly three years, during which he and Marguerite lived mainly at the Waterford estate. At any time of the year they could enjoy the sea views and the sunsets, but from April to late October the place was particularly delightful. Rock Lawn included an expanse of prime Long Island Sound shoreline. The mansion, with gabled windows and a wide veranda, was surrounded by century-old oaks and maples, and by gardens that invited exploration. In front of the house, the lawn sloped down to a private beach, while behind it stood greenhouses, where the gardeners raised exotic fruits such as pineapples and avocados. Farther off, there were outbuildings that housed horses and carriages, a dairy herd, a poultry run, and a colony of rabbits. Farther off still, there was an orchard, and a vegetable plot that provided seasonal produce for the table. Dogs were a feature of life at Waterford, and in later years Marguerite would always have one or more of them around her.

1.5
"Rock Lawn," the summer mansion built by Chester W. Chapin I at Goshen Point, Waterford, near New London, Connecticut.

Rock Lawn must have been paradise to Marguerite, the best thing about it being the simple fact of having Lindley's unrivalled love and attention. They spent hours together every day, the sorrowful father and the bereft child finding comfort in each other's company. In summer, Lindley's brothers, Robert and Henry, and their families came to stay, providing an extensive web of Chapin cousins and second cousins. Among these were Mary and Grace Britton Miller, twins a little younger than Marguerite herself. Their parents had died in an accident when the twins were just two, and they and their brothers and sister were being raised by Chapin relatives in Springfield. Mary later became a writer, using the pseudonym "Isabel Bolton." In her memoir of life as a twin, *Under Gemini*, she described how she and Grace regarded Lindley and Marguerite on their summer-afternoon visits to the beach below Rock Lawn:

> Mr Lindley Chapin, such a very decorative gentleman with his wonderful dark beard and the turquoise rings upon his fingers and such a high-pitched voice and nearly always laughing ... And there was Marguerite ... oh, so very handsome with her long dark curls and her perfectly beautiful dresses ... She had a donkey and a donkey cart. We'd rather be Marguerite Chapin than anybody on the earth.[18]

Lindley Chapin emerges from such impressions, and from his surviving letters, as a good-humoured and fun-loving man and a doting father. On the weekdays during the autumn and winter when he commuted to New York, he sometimes took Marguerite with him. One of her Gibert uncles would accompany her to dancing class, then take her back to the home they shared with their mother at 93 Fifth Avenue for supper, before Lindley reclaimed her. The domestic situation of Lindley's brothers-in-law was somewhat unconventional. In 1878 they too had married. Their brides were sisters: Alice and Annie Reed, the daughters of Edgar Reed, a New York banker and president of the prestigious New York Club. Within a few years, both marriages were under strain. The couples spent lengthy periods in Paris, but whether there or in New York, each pair sometimes lived apart. Audinet Gibert seems to have been Marguerite's favourite relative, given that she kept three of her childhood letters to him all her life. In one of them, written when she was five, she inquires whether "Uncle Odie" [*sic*] is coming to collect her from dancing class, while in another, composed when she was seven, she reports having as a pet "a squiril [*sic*], he is very tame he takes nuts out of my hand."[19] Marguerite was dearly loved by her grandmother, Margaret Reynolds Gibert, who left her several Manhattan apartments on her death in 1905.

On the basis of ancestry and length of residency in New England, and in New York itself, both the Chapins and the Giberts represented "old money." That meant that they belonged to a pre–Civil War social aristocracy that valued its European heritage and its descent from the early settlers. By the late-nineteenth century, members of "old money" families were already several generations away from manual toil, and their prosperity derived from land, property, investments, and rents. In contrast, the energetic, home-grown entrepreneurs who made their fortunes through trade after the Civil War were viewed by "old money" as brash parvenus, vulgar in their attempts to gain social acceptance through the conspicuous display of wealth. Much has been written about the excesses of this new class of industrialists and entrepreneurs, whose material ostentation supplied much of the "gilding" to the Gilded Age. Some of their New York residences had proportions more suitable to railway stations than private homes, and sported turrets, buttresses, and gargoyles in imitation of French châteaux. William Kissam Vanderbilt's house, for instance – one of five houses belonging to the family that turned upper Fifth Avenue into "Vanderbilt Alley" – had a dining room eighty feet long, with a renaissance-style fireplace at each end and an imported stained-glass window depicting the meeting of kings Henry VIII and Francis I at the Field of the Cloth of Gold. From the entrance hall, a spiral staircase in Caen stone brought from France ascended to the upper floors, while the ballroom could hold more than a thousand guests. Mrs William Astor's ballroom, on the other hand, became legendary for being able to hold only four hundred – but they were, she claimed, the four hundred that counted: they comprised New York's "old money" and, with it, the city's links with the culture of Europe and the earliest history of the United States.

Marguerite's first twenty years coincided with the period when social relations between "old" and "new" money were being worked out, not always comfortably. Few events better illustrate this than the origins of New York's Metropolitan Opera House:

> The cultural mecca of the old establishment was the Academy of Music. The new rich had attempted to buy their way into this exclusive circle, offering as much as thirty thousand dollars for a box, but had been turned down. So they set up, in direct competition, the Metropolitan Opera House. In October 1883 the opening night was held. It was reported that: "the Goulds and the Vanderbilts and people of that ilk perfumed the air with the odour of crisp greenbacks."[20]

The distinctions really came down to education, and the leisure available to pursue other aims than mere money-making. Those who possessed "old money" had learned over the generations what it could buy and what it couldn't. It could not, as Lindley Chapin found, protect him from tragedy, but it could buy material well-being and the leisure to pursue his interests seriously, to travel without time constraints, and explore the avenues of the mind. To those with inherited wealth, money represented liberation, the means to an end, which was self-fulfillment. This tacit understanding must have been absorbed early by the young Marguerite. In a child of less character, it might have bred aimlessness and a sense of entitlement. Thanks to healthy doses of the puritan ethic of personal responsibility from the Chapin side of her family and the Catholic idea of stewardship from the Giberts, self-discipline was also instilled in her early on, and would prove invaluable.

2

A YOUNG HEIRESS IN THE MAKING

In September 1887, two and a half years after his wife's death, Lindley Chapin attended the wedding of a friend from his Harvard days, James Tremenheere. The bride was Jessie Van Auken, the daughter of Barret Van Auken, a New York financier, and his wife, Catherine Garrison Van Auken.[1] At this event Lindley met the bride's younger sister Cornelia – and was instantly captivated.

Cornelia Garrison Van Auken was brown-haired and blue-eyed, with a rosy complexion and a lively, expressive manner. As Lindley soon discovered, she was not merely pretty, but was also a match for him intellectually. Well-educated and well-travelled, she spoke excellent French and was a talented actress. Since the stage was not an option for a girl of her social position, her parents had built a private theatre for her in their home at 421 Fifth Avenue.

Within days Lindley had called upon Cornelia. After another week, during which he visited her again and was given permission to write to her, he decided to cancel a projected trip to Europe and spend the winter in New York. He was relieved not to be going, and to Cornelia confessed that he felt "quite like a school boy again, who has gotten out of a severe punishment." Lindley began the search for a house to rent in Manhattan, telling Cornelia that it might be "rather hard to find what I want, but I will not mind hunting for it" with the prospect before him of "having an occasional one of your lovely evenings" during the coming months.[2]

Lindley's letters to Cornelia leave no doubt of his feelings. He poured out his admiration for her, and his conviction that the burden of his loneliness was lifting for having met her. He longed to share with her the beauties of Rock Lawn ("from my desk I can see the sun just about to sink into the sea, in the most gorgeous splendour … how I am longing to have you here by my side, to enjoy it too") and to have her see him at his best, in his own surroundings. She would be for him, as he assured her repeatedly, the perfect companion. He portrayed Marguerite as a much-loved and lovable child in need of a mother:

> This morning Marguerite asked me if I had seen Miss Van Auken in New York and wanted me to talk about you – she is too cute for anything. She waits to talk to me until there is no one by – and she told me she had said two little prayers for "papa's friend" and that she knew who she was … You know … what happiness that all was to me. As much as I loved that child before – to have her appreciate my feelings so clearly makes me even [*sic*] love her more.[3]

For her part, Cornelia admitted her attraction to Lindley, but also expressed her misgivings. She considered herself a very young and inexperienced twenty-three-year-old in comparison to Lindley's worldly thirty-four, and feared that his feelings might be a passing fancy. She was a Presbyterian, and knew nothing of Lindley's Catholic faith, in which he was raising Marguerite. In any case, she was not sure she was capable of taking on a child of seven, as yet sight unseen.

Little by little, such fears were assuaged. Lindley reassured her that she could take her time, but urged her "not to think of yourself as a weak timid woman … Your 'wings' will grow stronger. They are stronger now than you think, all they need is exercise." Most of all, he dissuaded her from thinking too much about the responsibility she might take on: "Trials if they come we will meet together."[4]

By Christmas 1887, after what was really a very short acquaintance, Lindley and Cornelia were engaged. Throughout the intensely personal correspondence that charts the development of their relationship runs the sense that, for Lindley, Cornelia represented a reawakening to the simple delights that life could hold, after a long period of sadness and aridity. Some years later, a press report would describe Cornelia as "one of the wittiest women in New York society," with "a talent for relating anecdotes, which are told so well that even the dreariest luncheon or dinner is made enjoyable at once."[5] This gift for entertaining clearly salvaged a dinner given by Lindley to introduce his fiancée to some of his friends. It took place at his temporarily rented apartment at 8 Washington Square North, which may explain why the meal was not up to standard. Cornelia's vivacity nonetheless "made what was positively the poorest dinner I have ever had at my own table the happiest and most enjoyable to me individually. Charlie Harris said to me 'No one can meet her without understanding your infatuation.'"[6]

Lindley and Cornelia were married on 14 February 1888 at the bride's Fifth Avenue home. The out-of-church ceremony was celebrated by no less a dignitary than the Roman Catholic Archbishop of New York, Michael Corrigan, who was a friend of Lindley's. The mansion's main salon was converted into a temporary chapel, with an altar and seating for two hundred guests.[7] The whole house was lavishly decorated with early tulips, and a sumptuous array of wedding gifts was on display. Following a reception in the ballroom of the Van Auken home, Lindley and Cornelia travelled by train to Montreal for their honeymoon. Marguerite stayed behind, in the care of Julia Chapin.

When Lindley and Cornelia returned to New York, they moved into Lindley's newly purchased and decorated brownstone house at 5 West Thirty-seventh Street, just off Fifth Avenue, in the residential district of Murray Hill. Prominent residents of the area at the time the Chapins moved there included John Pierpoint Morgan, whose palatial dwelling (today the Morgan Library) at the corner of Madison Avenue and East Thirty-sixth Street rivalled the Vanderbilt mansions in opulence. Lindley Chapin chose Murray Hill for the family connections he already had there: his cousin George Clark and his family, including two daughters, Edith and Julia, of about Marguerite's age, lived next door at number seven, and his brother Robert, with his wife, Adele, were around the corner on West Thirty-eighth Street. Lindley also valued the proximity of his new home to Grand Central Terminus (the future Grand Central Station), and to the various clubs to which he belonged.[8] New York's Metropolitan Opera House was also conveniently close by, at

Broadway and Thirty-ninth Street. As Marguerite grew older, she accompanied Lindley and Cornelia to the opera. Afterwards the three would be collected by their carriage or even walk home, humming and singing the arias they had just heard. Among the singers who impressed the young Marguerite was the dashing Polish tenor Jean de Reszke, who made his American debut at "the Met" in 1891.

Number five, West Thirty-seventh Street no longer exists, but must have been similar to the numerous brownstone houses surviving in the same area. Such townhouses, built for the wealthiest members of the middle class in an era of burgeoning prosperity, were designed to allow free rein to the social pretensions of the inhabitants. These houses were fitted out with salons, dining rooms, drawing and smoking rooms, libraries, conservatories, nurseries, schoolrooms, and the vast kitchen, scullery, and storage areas needed to support the provision of meals for varying and often large numbers of people. If a family kept a carriage, there would be a carriage house and stables to the rear of the house. At least some of the staff needed to service such a lifestyle lived in. According to the census returns for 1890, Lindley and Cornelia Chapin had seven servants living under their roof by that date.[9] By 1894, the births of the Chapins' own three children had brought to thirteen the number of people residing at number five. These, of course, included Marguerite.

Years later, Marguerite would allege that her relationship with her stepmother had been strained, and it is not hard to understand why, despite the initial goodwill on both sides. For three years Marguerite had enjoyed her father's undivided attention. Then someone else had entered the circle, someone whose every expression of interest or preference her father leapt to fulfill, and whose every move he followed with adoring eyes. Cornelia glowed with the robust health of her Dutch ancestors; Marguerite was slight and dark, a pretty child, but not blessed with the vivaciousness that had captivated Lindley. On the matter of religion – at least at this point in their lives – there is room for doubt. Where there is no doubt, since there is much evidence to confirm it, is in the matter of Cornelia's outgoing personality, her gift for telling stories and making others laugh. Marguerite may well have

2.1
Lindley and Cornelia Chapin: A studio portrait from the early years of their marriage, possibly taken as a Christmas greeting.

felt overwhelmed by such extroversion, especially when it was linked to the very accomplishments – speaking French, playing the piano, or singing for guests – for which she herself had up until now been the centre of attention. In reaction, did she become retiring and shy, since she felt she could not compete? Then there is the suspicion that Cornelia did not really approve of her stepdaughter's good-natured Gibert uncles, wealthy young men-about-town, separated from their wives and living with their mother, enjoying the life of New York to the full and in no apparent hurry to resolve their marital situations. Their influence over Marguerite was suspect, too: they gave her books that were too advanced for a child of her age (she devoured them), and they took her to exhibitions and theatres and restaurants where she might see and experience … heaven knew what. As a new and inexperienced stepmother, Cornelia may have felt she had much to contend with.

It cannot have helped that she became pregnant almost at once, and perhaps spent much of the first year of her married life feeling less than at her best. In the circumstances, she may have had limited patience with a child who constantly sought to reclaim her father's attention. Whatever the underlying causes, the seeds were sown, in this early period of living together, for the distance that reportedly gradually grew up between Marguerite and her stepmother. The birth of Lindley Hoffman Paul Chapin, on 30 December 1888, was a momentous event, but – as all attention focused on her new half-brother – did it confirm for Marguerite the sense of being relegated to the sidelines? Cornelia came under further strain when, barely a month after the birth of her son, her parents separated. Barret Van Auken had become mentally ill, and was divorced by his wife in April 1889, and subsequently committed to an asylum. Three months after her divorce, Catherine Van Auken married George Pierce Andrews, a justice of the Supreme Court of the State of New York. In the aftermath of all this family turmoil, the only glimpse of Marguerite is an alarming one, conveyed in a letter to Cornelia from her sister Jessie Tremenheere in November 1890: Marguerite and another child had accidentally made themselves ill by eating dogwood berries,[10] and had required the services of a doctor. This may suggest that ten-year-old Marguerite was not now as closely supervised as she had once been.

The Chapin family increased twice more, with the births of Katherine Garrison Chapin on 4 September 1890 and Cornelia Van Auken Chapin on 7 August 1893. All three of the children born to Lindley and Cornelia were baptized in the private chapel at Rock Lawn by Archbishop Corrigan.[11] By the time the younger Cornelia arrived, Marguerite was thirteen, and entering adolescence. No evidence survives regarding her relationship with her half-brother and half-sisters at this early age, but since she remained close to them, and especially to Katherine, all her life, it was perhaps not as limited as the disparities in age might suggest.

It was probably less the difference in age than the kind of education the four children received that really distinguished Marguerite's upbringing from that of her half-brother and half-sisters. Cornelia's views on education – and especially the education of girls – were advanced for her time and social position, and all three of her children would attend fee-paying schools. Paul would be sent to a Manhattan preparatory school and then to the prestigious St Mark's, an Episcopalian foundation. Katherine and Cornelia would attend less-expensive and more socially inclusive girls' schools, which Katherine later characterized as "somewhat experimental," in that they encouraged creativity and the development of a social conscience. As schoolgirls, she and the younger Cornelia wrote and acted in theatricals and engaged in debating. They also did charity work, as Cornelia herself did in acting as a "Lady Servant," or helper, to the Little Sisters of the Assumption in their work among the poor of Harlem.[12] Even the celebrations organized for her children by Cornelia had some didactic purpose, such as the "bird party," at which some fifty young guests listened to a lecture on birds (illustrated with stuffed specimens), and then enjoyed games and a tea structured around the theme of birds.[13]

Marguerite, on the other hand, had always been tutored at home, very likely with a similar intensity to that experienced by her slightly older contemporary, Consuelo Vanderbilt, who later recalled, "In the eighties the foundations of education were laid young. We were not encouraged to consider self-expression more important than the acquisition of knowledge ... At the age of eight I could read and write in French, German, and English."[14] Unlike Marguerite, Consuelo later attended classes organized for half-a-dozen wealthy girls at the home of Mrs Frederick Bronson, at Madison Avenue and Thirty-eighth Street. The sheer amount of instruction was demanding: "Mr Rosa managed to cram such various [*sic*] subjects as English, Latin, mathematics, and science into two hours ... and he was ... especially successful with history and literature," Consuelo reported, and considered an essay on the Punic Wars the best of her many long written assignments.

2.2
Marguerite Chapin, aged twelve.

Music lessons, further language classes, and an hour's exercise rounded off a gruelling daily schedule.[15]

Marguerite's day would have been no less taxing, but studying at home may have suited her temperament, if the shyness reported of her as a young woman was already manifest. The only activity she is known to have attended outside her home were the dancing classes already mentioned, possibly given by the same "elderly and elegant" Mr Dodsworth who taught Consuelo and "generations of New Yorkers how to dance and how to behave in company."[16] These at least ensured that she met other children, both girls and boys, and also that she learned the manners and deportment that governed every aspect of life in the upper echelons of New York society.

If in her teens Marguerite became a girl for whom reading became an escape as well as an intellectual pursuit, that is hardly surprising, given the series of events that rocked the foundations of her life between 1892 and 1897. The first of these was the scandal surrounding the divorce proceedings brought against Audinet Gibert by his wife, Annie, in January 1892. Annie Gibert's allegations – refusal to support her, physical violence, and the use of "opium and intoxicants" – were particularly lurid, and the case dragged on for nearly two years. Audinet's counter-accusation of adultery as the grounds of his non-support was fruitless, and the much-publicized duel to which he challenged the rival for his wife's affections, one "Señor Manuel de Santa Maria," did nothing to slow the descent of his reputation into the social abyss. Press reports of all this kept readers in New York and Paris agog, and appeared within days in the local papers of places as far-flung as British Columbia and Tahiti.[17]

The divorce was made final in the autumn of 1893, after which Audinet decamped to Paris. He first took an apartment in the elegant avenue de Ièna in the sixteenth arrondissement, close to the avenue des Champs-Elysées, an area frequented by many wealthy Americans. His cousin Marie Josephine ("Cousin Minnie") de Fritsch was already living in the same street. Chevalier de Fritsch had died in 1889, and Minnie had moved to Paris to give her son, Hugo, a French upbringing. After Audinet's departure from New York, Marguerite's grandmother Margaret Reynolds Gibert took to spending several months of the year in the French capital. Life in Paris suited Audinet, although he returned to New York from time to time. On one such visit, in 1896, he donated his collection of Mexican sculptures and artifacts to the Metropolitan Museum of Art. Back in Paris, he moved to a larger apartment in the avenue Niel, though he did not marry again until 1907 –

and when he did, he and his Canadian second wife, Margaret McLaren, continued to live in the avenue Niel. As for Audinet's brother, Frederick, in 1895 he and his wife, Alice, were also divorced. After a time apart, during which Frederick became engaged to someone else who then fell ill and died, the two were reconciled, and remarried in 1898 ("the Roman Catholic church recognising neither the divorce nor the remarriage," as the *New York Times* waspishly remarked).[18] Frederick Gibert was appointed United States consular agent at Biarritz that same year, and lived there or in Paris with Alice and his son, also named Frederick, until his death in 1913.

Audinet's divorce and the scandal surrounding it was bad enough, but the departure from New York of her favourite uncle was bound to have left a gulf in Marguerite's life. How Lindley and Cornelia viewed the matter remains a mystery. In the short term, the loss of Audinet's company was Marguerite's private sorrow, stoically borne, but in the long term his move to Paris came to have its positive aspects. His presence there, along with that of Cousin Minnie, and from time to time that of her grandmother Gibert, may well have ignited in Marguerite's mind the idea that Paris might one day be an alternative to New York as a place to live. The tolerance of the unconventional behaviour of others later attributed to her may well have owed something to the worldly influence of her francophile Gibert uncles.

The events that next occurred fell like hammer blows upon the entire Chapin family. In November 1894 the stately Rock Lawn, the pride of three generations of Chapins, burned to the ground, leaving only the stable block, the chapel, and a few outbuildings intact. The fire was caused by a lightning strike during a thunderstorm, and is reported to have forced those staying in the house at the time to flee in their nightclothes in the small hours of the morning. The event left Marguerite with a paralyzing dread of thunderstorms that lasted for the rest of her life.

Lindley Chapin immediately set about rebuilding Rock Lawn, modernizing it to include electric light, flush toilets, and a telephone. In view of the size of the project, it is doubtful whether it could have been finished in less than a year, and thus indeed whether Lindley himself ever spent a night in the new mansion. What is certain is that the destruction of the original house prompted him to draw up or revise his will. The greater part of his assets, including his Chapin railroad inheritance and Rock Lawn, was left to Cornelia (except for the chapel, which was specifically left to Paul), with the right to sell if she wished. On her death, everything was to pass to Paul, Katherine, and Cornelia, in equal shares. The Springfield real estate left to Lindley by his father and grandfather was allocated to Marguerite. Lindley also set up various bequests to Roman Catholic charities in New York and New London.[19]

By the time he drew up this will, Lindley Chapin was not in good health. Even at the time of his son Paul's birth in December 1888 he had been incapacitated by gout.[20] This was a condition that required careful monitoring, but in addition, Lindley suffered a bizarre accident in the summer of 1895 that had disastrous consequences. With the new Rock Lawn still under construction, he rented a summer place nearby, farther up the River Thames, so that the family could escape the heat of New York in the accustomed surroundings. One afternoon, while swimming with friends, he jumped into the water and "alighted on some sharp stones in the bed of the river ... cutting his feet severely and severing several arteries and nerves," as the *New York Daily Tribune* later reported. Due to his existing circulatory problems, Lindley's injuries did not heal, and blood clots developed in the veins of his legs. From mid-October he was confined to 5 West Thirty-seventh Street with severe phlebitis, unable to leave his bed.

On the evening of Saturday, 25 January 1896, Cornelia was reading aloud to Lindley when he had a massive heart attack. Three doctors struggled to revive him, without success. At his bedside when he died were the priest who gave him the last rites, his wife, Cornelia, his mother, Julia, and "other relatives." Did these include Marguerite, now aged fifteen, eight-year-old Paul, Katherine, five, and Cornelia, just two? The children are not specifically mentioned as having been present at their father's death, but they would certainly have attended his funeral, which took place at St Patrick's Cathedral on Park Avenue, on the morning of Tuesday, 28 January. It was conducted by Archbishop Corrigan, who only a few years earlier had celebrated his friend's marriage

2.3
The second Rock Lawn, almost twice the size of the first.
Note the chapel to the right.

and baptized his children. Accompanied by a large crowd of mourners, Lindley's body was then conveyed in procession the few blocks to Grand Central Terminal, taken by train to New London, and given burial in the Roman Catholic cemetery there, next to Leila.[21]

Lindley Chapin's death at just forty-two years of age echoed the premature demise of his father, Abel Chapin.[22] It left Cornelia a widow two weeks short of her thirty-first birthday, and Marguerite technically an orphan, though Lindley very likely made provision for someone – possibly his brother Robert, in the light of the socially tarnishing effect of the Gibert divorces – to act as her guardian until she came of age. Three partners from the Manhattan legal firm of Cadwalader, Wickersham, and Taft were appointed as the trustees of Marguerite's inheritance.

Her father's death marked a watershed for Marguerite: her childhood was behind her, the time when she could be independent still far distant. Nor could the present have offered much in the way of consolation, unless it lay in the realm of the imagination. She had always read serious fiction in both English and French, but now took up the great Russian authors in translation and began to study German. She eagerly devoured the classic works of history and philosophy – Herodotus and Thucydides, Plato and Aristotle. Marguerite, as young people so often do, was seeking answers to the central problems of human existence, a quest made urgent by recent personal experience. Perhaps that was why narratives of travel and exploration fascinated her, not just for the journeys they described, but also for what they could reveal about the mental resilience needed to face danger and survive hardship. It was poetry, however, that most absorbed her, since it engaged her imagination as well as her intellect. The classical poets, the Anglo-Saxon epics, the work of the Elizabethans and Donne, of Milton, Wordsworth, and Browning became particular favourites. Her love of American "romantic" authors such as Poe and Hawthorne led her naturally to French poets such as Baudelaire, Verlaine, and Mallarmé.

And then there was music, to which she was increasingly drawn as something not merely to be listened to, but as a channel for the expression of feelings that were impossible to put into words. Like most well-to-do girls, Marguerite had taken piano lessons from an early age, but now, perhaps inspired by her enjoyment of the opera, she began to study singing. Somewhat to her surprise, she found that she had a fine mezzo-soprano voice. In this period marked by grief and uncertainty, music – and especially singing – was less a pastime than an important emotional outlet that gave her confidence and helped to counterbalance her shyness.

One last, terrible event was still in store. By the summer of 1897 Rock Lawn was rebuilt, and Marguerite, with Cornelia and the younger children, joined other members of the Chapin family at Waterford's Goshen Point. It was there that they received the news that Marguerite's second cousin, fourteen-year-old Grace Miller, had drowned while swimming from a rowing boat with her twin, Mary, off the resort of Quogue on the south shore of Long Island.[23] Grace's death left Mary permanently traumatized and plunged the Chapins once again into mourning. Did Marguerite's Catholic faith, her reading, her music, help her to weather such a tragedy? She never alluded to her young cousin's death, though she kept in touch with Mary, who shared her childhood memories and whose writings she would publish many years later.

Despite the harrowing events that marred her adolescence, it does not seem that Marguerite's personality was irrevocably blighted by them. She was still only seventeen. She had lost three people close to her in quick succession, as well as Rock Lawn, the idyllic setting for so much of her childhood. Nonetheless, the way she would be described only a few years later suggests that she had a positive and energetic approach to life, and an exceptional degree of personal charm. Nor was she as isolated from her peers as the fact of having been privately educated might suggest. She had a large extended family, including cousins of her own age, some of whom were also close friends. It seems that she was blessed with emotional toughness and a firm will, and with the traits of generosity and humour, without which the first two qualities might have deteriorated into the mere determination to survive. Marguerite was also strikingly attractive. For her time, she was tall, standing about five feet six inches in height, a very slender girl with large brown eyes, a mass of wavy, dark-brown hair, and the kind of complexion that tanned easily and gave the impression of freshness and health. Her features were regular – her nose straight and neat (although it would become slightly aquiline in old age), her mouth well-formed. She had a particularly direct, intense manner of looking at people: she seemed, in the words used by an acquaintance many years later, "to look right through you." Her smile, when it came, revealed perfect teeth and illuminated her whole face.[24]

Well-to-do young people like Marguerite had plenty of occasions to socialize at the many at-homes, parties, and teas organized for them during the autumn and winter months. From the late 1890s come a few brief glimpses of her, attending a theatre party as one of a group of young people, or at Cornelia's side to "pour" at the teas and luncheons given by her stepmother.[25] She was now on the threshold of adulthood – ready, in the terminology of the time, to be "presented" to society through the coming-of-age ritual of making her debut. This marked a girl's entry into the adult world, and usually took place when she was considered to have completed her education, which could mean at any age between sixteen and twenty.

Introducing a girl into the New York social scene involved weeks and even months of preparation on the part of her mother, aunts, and other female relatives, as gowns were commissioned, venues secured, the guest list compiled, and plans for the catering set in motion. Teas and receptions were given for the debutante, at which she "received" next to her mother, assisted by her women relations and closest friends. The culmination of all this was usually a sumptuous dance and dinner, either in her own home, if her parents had a dining room and ballroom they wished to show off, or at one of the better hotels. The subtext to "coming out," as making a debut was termed, was the recognition on the part of everyone present that the gorgeously attired young woman leading the dance on the arm of her father was available for marriage. Her entry into society signified that she was taking, and being granted, her place among people of the same social class, that she was now bound by its rules, and that, eventually, she would marry within it.

Marguerite's debut, on 1 December 1898, did not involve a ball, possibly because Lindley was no longer there to lead the dance with her, but possibly too because she favoured a more informal celebration, with genuine friends rather than a sea of acquaintances invited for the sake of their parents' connections with hers. As one social column described it,

> On Thursday afternoon Mrs Lindley Hoffman Chapin introduced her handsome, fresh-looking charming stepdaughter, Miss Marguerite Chapin, who was in a simple but beautiful gown of white silk tissue with garniture of white roses. The young debutante was assisted in receiving by several of her girl friends and also by her stepmother, Mrs Chapin, who was in a gown of cherry velvet; the latter's sister, Mrs Tremenheere, of India, in cream satin, and Mrs Abel Chapin … After the reception there was a dinner party for the young people.[26]

With entry into society came the freedom to go out and about with a chaperone or with female friends and their mothers. Travel to another city or abroad was also possible, as long as an older woman or family relations shared the journey.

Marguerite was twenty at the turn of the century. On her first return to France since her visit there with Lindley when she was five, she sailed to Cherbourg with her uncle and aunt, Robert and Adele Chapin. They left New York on board the SS *Kaiser Friedrich* on 10 May, the Chapins then going on to London, where Robert was taking up a banking position.[27] In Cherbourg, Marguerite was met by her Gibert relations and travelled with them to Paris for a four-month stay. The Paris Universal Exhibition (much bigger and grander than the exhibition of 1889, for which the Eiffel Tower had been built) supplied the motive for many Americans to cross the Atlantic that year, but an additional one for Marguerite was surely the chance to spend time with her grandmother Gibert, "Uncle Audie," and Cousin Minnie. In their company – perhaps from the *terrasse* of a café on the Left Bank, or strolling in the Tuileries Gardens – she observed the naturalness that governed social relations between Parisians, even among the upper classes, and "the warm humanity of French lives, so simple and gay ... the frank acceptance of life's joys."[28] Life in Paris was characterized by the pleasure and amusement that could be found everywhere and at any moment, simply by paying attention to one's surroundings. It was not only the city's beauty that won Marguerite's heart; what she came to feel for it on this visit went far deeper than an appreciation of its beauty. Her life in New York was hedged round with social constraints and expectations; Parisian life, in contrast, felt free of them. Everywhere there were open-air entertainments and music, flower stalls and street markets, universal in their appeal. Everyday pastimes – browsing the booksellers' stalls near Nôtre Dame, watching children play in the Jardin du Luxembourg, or halting on the Pont Neuf to see the swallows skimming over the waters of the Seine – produced a feeling of joie de vivre. Best of all, thanks to the graciousness of her relatives in helping her rediscover her maternal heritage, she was coming to see that a life in Paris could one day be open to her, should she choose it.

She returned to New York at the end of September, this time travelling with Cornelia's sister, Jessie Tremenheere. Once on board ship, the social conventions closed around her once again. On arrival in New York, she found the autumn and winter "season" about to begin, with its at-homes, receptions, "pink teas" and "coming out" parties, supper dances, formal dinners, cotillions, and balls. Since it went without saying that every such gathering required a gown not previously worn, it was a fortunate girl who could bring back from a visit to Paris a few dresses in the latest fashion, or the fabric and patterns for her own seamstress to make up at home. Marguerite was such a girl, though after a summer exploring the French capital with the Giberts, she may well have found the regimentation of the New York social scene unappealing. If private, these occasions took place in the homes of wealthy families. "Public" events were the balls organized by committees for subscribers and a certain number of discretionary guests, and held in the ballrooms of the better hotels. The protocol surrounding them was rigidly formal, enforced by tradition and the writings of such self-styled arbiters of taste as Ward McAllister, the great ally of Marguerite's relative Mrs Caroline Astor in her attempt to maintain "old money" standards.[29] "The committee," composed of matrons whose wealth and influence was unquestionable, was on hand to receive, and to ensure that proper form and the rules established for a particular event were adhered to. It was they who determined where a reception or ball was to be held, together with the menu, musical offerings, and, most important of all, the guest list. These women were as all-powerful in the social sphere as their husbands were in finance, industry, or politics. It was rumoured that they could make or break a young person's chances of contracting an advantageous match, either by ensuring that he or she was or was not invited, or through some purposeful tinkering with the seating plan. These occasions were, after all, a sophisticated form of the marriage market, and the exclusivity imparted by wealth and class had to be upheld.

Formal dances began late, and ended in the small hours. A "Cinderella" dance attended by Marguerite (so-called because the dancing ended at midnight, at which hour supper was served) was described in the society pages the following day as "a large and brilliant affair," held in the ballroom at Sherry's. It was the custom at such dances, rather as at childrens' parties, to provide each guest with a "favour," and on this occasion the little gifts were reported to be "flower fans for the girls and fancy leather pen wipers of a new design for the men."[30] The balls often bore a strong French influence, but one seemingly inspired by the frivolity of the *ancien régime*, rather than the contemporary Parisian ambience that Marguerite had just left. The following notice, typical of many that appeared in the social columns of the New York papers, gives an idea of the tone of some of these gatherings: "The second meeting of Mrs Schuyler Quakenbush's dancing class, otherwise known as the 'Five Cotillions,' which will be held at Sherry's next Friday evening, will be a *bal poudré*. Fancy dress will not be obligatory, but the committee insists that the girls shall have their hair powdered."[31]

Whether Marguerite considered such trifles fun, or merely absurd, the fact remained that once she had made her debut she could no longer regard the balls and dinner-dances as entirely innocent entertainments. Attending them was a tacit announcement of her availability, while her prospects as an heiress, not to mention her good looks, made her highly desirable. Unless she welcomed the inevitable consequence of all this, her future, should she stay in New York, must have begun to seem oppressively predetermined.

In contrast, there was the memory of Paris, with its uncomplicated sense of well-being, its openness, and its particular enchantments, especially in springtime: "When I think of spring it is of Paris, with its sweet scent of budding chestnut trees and flowering lilac, and of the lilies the hawkers used to vend in the streets, those little sprigs of *muguet* one wears on the first of May."[32]

The writer of these lines was Consuelo Vanderbilt in late middle age, not the twenty-year-old Marguerite, but for the latter, after six months in New York, the longing to be once again in the French capital in spring was irresistible. She set off as soon as the weather permitted a calm crossing, this time with her cousins Edith and Julia Clark as travelling companions. The three young women sailed on board the SS *Kaiserin Maria Theresa* on 20 April 1901, and arrived back two months later, on 18 June, on the SS *Augusta Victoria.*

On 24 June 1901, a week after her return to New York, Marguerite celebrated her twenty-first birthday. On that day she came into her mother's fortune in New York properties, and the income from the Chapin properties in Springfield as well. She could begin to plan her own future, but planning took time, and she did not immediately act on her new-found freedom. She was still in New York on 9 April 1902, since she helped Cornelia to receive at a reception and "musicale" (an event featuring recitations, imitations, and musical offerings) held by her stepmother at Sherry's on that date.[33] On 18 June 1902, the social column of the *New York Daily Tribune* announced that Cornelia had left the city to spend the summer in New London, where she planned to give "a few informal entertainments for her stepdaughter, Miss Marguerite Chapin." This is an intriguing comment: was Cornelia creating such occasions to matchmake, or to dissuade her stepdaughter from a decision that had by then been made? If so, it was to no avail. It would be four years before Marguerite's name again appeared in the society columns of the New York papers. Late in the summer of 1902, she once again crossed the Atlantic, this time with a view to a longer Parisian stay.

3

ONE LIFE, TWO WORLDS

The few published accounts of Marguerite's life allege that she departed New York for good when she came of age, as though she had literally shaken its dust from the soles of her elegant shoes.[1] Her subsequent movements back and forth across the Atlantic tell a rather different story. Like most people who have ever voluntarily moved from one country to another, Marguerite kept her options open, living most of the time in Paris, but also making periodic visits to New York. She travelled extensively in Europe as well, but as late as September 1909 she was still claiming New York City as her permanent residence, and the duration of her stay abroad as "temporary." As for the assumption that she cut herself off from her stepfamily, that too should be modified. On their trips to Europe with their mother, Katherine and Cornelia kept diaries that indicate that they spent time with Marguerite whenever they were in Paris.[2]

When Marguerite arrived there in the autumn of 1902, it was with steamer trunks and a French-speaking Canadian *dame de compagnie*. She was there to study singing at the school established a year earlier by the operatic tenor Jean de Reszke following his retirement from the stage. News of the school had created a flurry of interest among aspiring young singers, especially in the United States. Marguerite, who had seen de Reszke perform in many Metropolitan Opera seasons between 1891 and 1901,[3] found the possibility of studying with him – and in Paris, of all places – irresistible. Quite what her ambitions were at this point remains a mystery. Did she really want to sing professionally? Or, knowing that she had a good voice but suspecting she lacked the temperament to become a performer, did she regard her training as a serious but purely personal project? His fees were high – but she was now a wealthy woman, and could afford them. Since de Reszke demanded that prospective pupils audition for him, it can be assumed that Marguerite did so (though she never revealed where or when), and that he considered her voice worth training.[4]

Simply wanting to be in Paris, close to the Giberts and immersed in a way of life that delighted her, must surely have counted as much as any other motive. Paris drew her like a magnet, and always would. The city had long been a byword for all that was culturally new and exciting, and at the time Marguerite arrived there, the leisurely opulence of the *belle époque* was giving way to fast-moving modernity. The new public transport system known as the *Métro*, whose distinctive station entrances by Hector Guimard established art nouveau as the dominant artistic style of the era, was the most visible innovation. It was a city where fashions originated, where food, wine, and conversation were taken seriously, where, on any given evening, public and private musical events, plays from the classical repertoire, opera, and experimental theatre vied for an audience.

Marguerite came to know other great cities, but Paris would always be the place where she felt most alive, and most surrounded by the things that mattered to her. Even at twenty-two, she prized books and music (art came later), and the company of like-minded people with whom to discuss and enjoy them. Her Gibert relations were important in providing her with an address and a ready-made niche in their social circle. During her first decade in Paris, she lived mainly with her widowed second cousin, fifty-three-year-old Marie Josephine de Fritsch ("Cousin Minnie") and her son, Hugo Gibert de Fritsch, who in 1902 was a lad of a fifteen, at 101, avenue des Champs-Élysées in the eighth arrondissement. Marguerite's grandmother, Margaret Reynolds Gibert, may also have lived there when she was in Paris. Audinet Gibert's bachelor establishment in the avenue Niel, on the other side of the Place d'Étoile, was a quarter-of-an-hour's walk away.

Today the avenue des Champs-Élysées, lined with expensive designer shops and thronged with tourists, is a byword for luxury the world over.

In 1902 it was still a residential street lined with stately chestnut trees. From the tall, mansard-roofed dwellings that lined the avenue, well-to-do Parisians emerged each afternoon in their carriages – and increasingly, in the first decade of the century, their motor cars – on their way to the gardens of the Tuileries or the Bois de Boulogne. On the ancient hill of Chaillot stood the Arc de Triomphe, with its friezes celebrating Napoleonic victories, visible from anywhere along the twelve broad thoroughfares radiating from the Place d'Étoile.

The area between the Arc de Triomphe and the Louvre, laid out during the Second Empire, was the showpiece of the development plan for a model Paris devised by Baron Georges-Eugène Haussmann at the behest of Napoleon III. During the 1850s, an enormous program of public works created new infrastructure to provide water and sanitation. Warrens of alleys and slums were swept away, to be replaced by boulevards that facilitated the circulation of traffic and streets that were inviting to stroll along. Two huge new public parks, the Parque de Vincennes in the east and the Bois de Boulogne in the west, encouraged healthy recreation and family life. The enlightened theory behind all this reform was that dignified living conditions were a safeguard against social unrest. What this meant in practice was that Paris became the most modern city in Europe: a confident metropolis, open to innovation and technological advance. The introduction of gas lighting during the 1860s was a case in point, prompting its popular designation as "the City of Light." The ease with which Paris made the transition from horse-drawn to motor-powered vehicles around the turn of the century was exemplary when measured against the transport chaos of other capitals, such as London or Rome.

From the de Fritsch apartment, Marguerite and her lady companion made their way each weekday morning to the de Reszke residence at 53, rue de la Faisanderie, a quiet street twenty minutes' walk to the west in the sixteenth arrondissement. Years later, Marguerite related how she had been the "*benjamine*" of her class: the youngest of the students who began a two-year course of study sometime late in 1902 or early in 1903.[5] She came to know Jean de Reszke and his family well, and to admire her teacher's human qualities as well as his professional ones.[6]

Born in Poland in 1850, de Reszke made his operatic debut in Venice in 1874. Like Placido Domingo in our own day, he began his career as a baritone, but, realizing the limitations of his voice in that register, deliberately set out to retrain as a tenor. This required a sustained period of private study, and in 1876 de Reszke retired temporarily from operatic life. Apart from isolated performances, he spent the next eight years working on repositioning his voice. Following his return to the stage in 1884, he achieved even greater fame as a lyric tenor than he had as a baritone. Strikingly handsome, with the physique of an athlete and a stage presence that held audiences spellbound, he was that rare operatic phenomenon, the singer who was also an outstanding actor. His appearance guaranteed a full house, especially when he sang with his equally imposing younger brother Edouard, a leading bass. The romantic roles of the French and Italian repertoire, such as Gounod's "Romeo" and Verdi's "Otello," were considered de Reszke's particular strength, until he surpassed them with his interpretations of the Wagnerian heroic tenor roles such as Siegfried, Tristan, and Lohengrin. By the time he made his New York debut in 1891, he was universally acclaimed as the greatest living tenor, credited with having revived almost single-handedly the fortunes of London's Royal Opera House. He had a decade of fame on both sides of the Atlantic before the damage done to his vocal chords through overuse forced his retirement from public performance in 1901.

De Reszke and his wife – the Countess Marie de Goulaine, so fine a singer that the composer Reynaldo Hahn always referred to her as "The Voice" – chose to settle in Paris with their young son rather than return to Poland, though de Reszke kept a stable there. As an extension to the house in the rue de la Faisanderie, he built an auditorium seating a hundred people, where he could teach and stage private operatic performances. The English soprano Maggie Teyte, who enrolled with him in 1904, the year after Marguerite, recalled the place well, and left a colourful account of her time there. The de Reszke household was somewhat eccentric, and the morning ritual, as Jean and his retinue descended a spiral staircase to the hall where the students awaited him, made a lasting impression upon her. First came the *valet du chambre*,

3.1
The great Polish tenor Jean de Reszke as Siegfried in Richard Wagner's opera of the same name.

bearing the cage belonging to Jean's parrot, Coco. Then came Jean himself, not now the Tristan who had once set hearts aflutter, but "portly and bald" in his fifties, with the large green parrot perched on his shoulder. The enchantingly lovely Mme de Reszke hovered protectively around the great man, ready to envelop him in a shawl at the slightest sign of a cough. Jean greeted each student by name and bestowed a paternal kiss on the cheek. Maggie Teyte recalled that "His smell was clean and beautiful: a combination of soap and very expensive hair tonic." Jean's personal valet brought up the rear, ceremoniously carrying the de Reszkes' dachshund. Once inside the auditorium, "Coco was more often than not put on his cage, not in it. Some of the students were terrified of this parrot, and he would stroll or flap about, happily taking nips at their ankles. The accompanist would sit at the piano, the valet would kiss the master's hand and withdraw. 'Maintenant, chantons' de Reszke would say, and they would begin."[7]

The students, in groups of four, started off with a series of physical exercises designed to strengthen the diaphragm and position the voice. There would follow six or seven vocal exercises of the fourteen developed by de Reszke himself:

> There was one for scales, long sustained phrases for breath control, taken from well-known passages in opera; there was one for pianissimo, the famous aria from Don Carlos in which Elizabeth recalls past happiness ... which they sang moving it upwards in semitones, as high as they could go; there was one for staccato, one for pianissimo and head voice. Then they practiced from Vaccaj's *Metodo Pratico*, de Reszke allowing them to imitate the quality of tone he was putting into his own voice. Then they would tackle various extracts, arias, and recitatives from operas.[8]

De Reszke was famed as a linguist: he sang perfectly in German and Italian, but it was his French that was outstanding, which was why he had set up his school in Paris, and not in London or New York. The music critic Camille Bellaigue wrote of him in *La Revue des Deux Mondes* that "The French language has never been pronounced and accented with such accuracy and force, or if need be with such charm and tenderness, as in the mouth of this foreigner,"[9] and as a result, his students – among them many Americans in the early years – returned home "singing more perfect French than most French singers, even though their conversational abilities were still halting."[10]

Marguerite's French diction must have pleased de Reszke, since she took part in the matinee concerts performed for the master's guests.

Many of these were fellow operatic singers, some were critics, but others still were members of royalty, such as King Carlos I of Portugal, the Duke of Connaught, and Grand-Duke Vladimir of Russia. Marguerite recalled the "marvelous musical parties" given by the de Reszkes, to which anybody who was anybody in the world of the arts in Paris was invited – "writers and painters and all."[11] Maggie Teyte was surprised to find that younger students such as herself "were assigned Dukes to dance with." De Reszke was famed for his comic imitations (a cork being drawn from a bottle being one of the better ones), his bountiful table, and the quite astonishing breadth of his friendships. Stars of the theatre such as Sarah Bernhardt also attended these gatherings, which provided the students – mainly young women – with the chance to meet creative and famous people in a socially acceptable setting.

The musical life of the French capital was vibrant and varied, and included such offerings as the Bon Marché concerts for working people. There were the subscription concert series, such as the Concerts Lamoureux and the Concerts Colonne, providing a number of events over a given season. There were also the public concerts organized by the various music societies, whose boards of directors took the calculated risk that ticket sales would cover the cost of engaging the orchestra, the principals, and the venue. The greatest of these was the Société des Grands Auditions Musicales, founded and directed by the Countess Élisabeth Greffulhe, who championed the music of Berlioz, Wagner, Debussy, and other composers considered avant-garde.[12] Then there were the private concerts, foremost of which were the recitals organized by the American sewing-machine heiress and patroness of the arts, Winnaretta Singer – the widowed Princesse de Polignac. These musical salons were showcases for established composers and musicians, but they were also an opportunity for those who were less well-known to perform before an audience of serious music lovers. The Princesse de Polignac's house in the rue Henri Martin in the sixteenth arrondissement had a concert room, where guest musicians or works commissioned by the princess were presented to an invited audience. The aim was not just to provide entertainment, but to offer those who attended something they might not hear elsewhere, and so to provoke interest and discussion.

Rather as Gertrude and Leo Stein made known the work of Cézanne, Matisse, and Picasso through their "Saturday evenings" at 27, rue de Fleurus,[13] Countess Greffulhe – in addition to her leading role in the Société des Grandes Auditions Musicales – brought composers such as Gabriel Fauré, Paul Dukas, and Vincent d'Indy to a wider acquaintance through the concerts at her house in the rue d'Astorg, a town dwelling so imposing (being several knocked together) that it was locally known as "the Vatican."[14] The de Reszkes were frequent guests and occasional performers at such events, and sometimes took students along. A further link between the salon concerts and the de Reszke school was the composer Reynaldo Hahn, who taught some of the opera classes and sometimes acted as accompanist. With his wide social circle, he was a frequent performer at private events, or even in the more intimate setting of someone's drawing room. Hearing him sing his own songs while accompanying himself on the piano was an unforgettable experience for the students, not least because the beauty and melancholy of his voice sometimes moved them to tears. Hahn was as much poet as musician, and was admired for the way his melodies supported so perfectly the poems he chose as subjects. His settings for poems by Hugo and Verlaine were among the pieces given to de Reszke's students to learn.

Marguerite left no indication of how she spent her time outside the school in the rue de la Faisanderie, and therefore what follows can be no more than reasonable conjecture. She very likely made friends with some of her fellow students, attended the kinds of concerts mentioned above, as well as the theatre, the opera, the Opéra-Comique, and the Comédie-Française, and spent hours in the Louvre and parks in the company of her *dame de compagnie*. This was the period when the Sorbonne and the College de France offered programs of evening lectures that were open to the public, those given by the philosopher Henri Bergson at the latter being among the best attended. Whether Marguerite sought to broaden her horizons in this way, or whether she merely read as voraciously as ever, she frequented Gibert Joseph and the bookshops of the Left Bank. She lived comfortably and harmoniously with Cousin

Minnie and Hugo, and saw Audinet and her grandmother Gibert often. Perhaps she travelled with her relatives, leaving Paris in August for the Normandy beach resorts that were among her favourite holiday destinations some years later. She visited Robert and Adèle Chapin at their London home at 34 Kensington Square, which gave her the chance to know another of Europe's capitals, and probably took in literary pilgrimage sites such as Stratford-on-Avon and the Lake District. Frederick and Alice Gibert's Villa Zarbias in Biarritz – a suitably dignified residence for a United States consular agent – is also likely to have welcomed her from time to time.

One upsetting piece of news from home came in the summer of 1903. The rebuilt Rock Lawn was again struck by lightning on 14 July, and – as on the occasion of the first strike nearly a decade earlier – was completely destroyed.[15] This time, rebuilding it became a kind of mission for Cornelia Chapin, who employed the architectural firm of Lord and Hewlett to design a new house in a Classical Revival style. Escalating costs dogged the project, which by the time of its completion in 1906 had seriously reduced Cornelia's financial means. The forty-two-room mansion, together with the estate around it, was sold the following year to the philanthropist Edward Harkness, heir to a fortune in shares of the Standard Oil Company. Renamed "Eolia" by Harkness and his wife, Mary, the new mansion became their summer residence and the centrepiece of a magnificent botanical garden created around it.[16]

Presumably Marguerite finished her time at the de Reszke school midway through 1904. Whether she ever sang before an audience again, she certainly did not pursue either a musical career or further training, though she kept in touch with the de Reszkes and continued to see them socially. It is hard, in fact, to suggest what she did with her talent and her time. September 1904 yielded the first surviving depiction of her since her childhood portrait. She was back in New York and Waterford, and posed with her stepmother, Cornelia, and her two half-sisters in the grounds of Rock Lawn, where the new mansion was, quite literally, rising from the ashes. The younger Cornelia and Katherine are still schoolgirls, with calf-length skirts and beribboned

3.2
Marguerite (standing, back right) with her stepmother, Cornelia Garrison Chapin, and half-sisters, Katherine (right) and Cornelia, September 1904.

hair, but Marguerite, aged twenty-four, and her stepmother, aged forty, wear their hair in similar matronly styles above high-necked, billowy blouses with ample sleeves.

At some point, probably in 1906, the de Fritsch household moved around the corner from 101, avenue des Champs-Élysées to a mansion block apartment at 44, avenue d'Ièna in the sixteenth, one of the broad, tree-lined streets running off the Place d'Étoile. Perhaps it was a smaller apartment; by 1906 Hugo de Fritsch was at Harvard, and Marguerite's beloved grandmother, Margaret Reynolds Gibert, had died. This building, erected in 1890, would be Marguerite's home until early in 1910, and remained her postal address for some time after that.[17]

She still had, metaphorically speaking, one foot on each side of the Atlantic. In June 1906, her two worlds came together when her step-family came to Europe.[18] Cornelia Chapin, with sixteen-year-old Katherine, and thirteen-year-old Cornelia junior, arrived in Antwerp on 6 June, and Paul, aged eighteen, joined them from London soon after. Cornelia intended to spend the next three months travelling through Belgium, France, Switzerland, and Germany, taking in museums and monuments at every stop and hiring a car and driver to visit places not served by the railway network. By 17 June the Chapins were in Paris for a two-week stay, during which they saw Marguerite several times. On one occasion, she and Katherine dined together and went on to the Opéra-Comique for a much-enjoyed adaptation of Henri Murger's *La Vie Bohème*.[19] On another, the party lunched with Marguerite. Following the lunch, as the young Cornelia recorded in her travel diary, "Mrs Mason came for Kate and me," and the three went off to visit Napoleon's tomb.[20]

Here, in passing, is the first reference to someone who had come to play an important role in the lives of Cornelia Chapin and her children. This was Charlotte Osgood Mason, the wealthy fifty-four-year-old widow of the eminent surgeon and pioneering parapsychologist Rufus Osgood Mason. His writings focused on the beneficial applications of hypnosis (*Hypnotism and Suggestion in Therapeutics, Education, and Reform*) and on psychical research, one of his theories alleging that there was a "subliminal self" common to all human beings, through which the living could communicate with the dead, or "disincarnated," on "the other side." Until his death in 1903, Rufus Osgood Mason was also well-known as a spiritualist in the upper echelons of New York society.[21] Spiritualism, immensely popular in the United States since the 1850s, emphasized the possibility of ongoing relationships with the dead, often through "spirit guides" or mediums, who claimed that their own highly developed "spiritual" qualities could bring the living into contact with the departed.

Charlotte Osgood Mason is acknowledged today as the generous-but-controlling patron of some of the Black writers who gained recognition during the "Harlem Renaissance" of the 1920s. By then Katherine and Cornelia would be acting as her secretaries, helping her to administer the support she provided as "Godmother" (as she insisted on being called) to writers such as Zora Neale Hurston, Langston Hughes, and Alain Locke.[22] In 1906, however, her prevailing interests were psychical research, along the same lines as her late husband's, and anthropology, a field of study that was currently taking shape under the influence of the Masons' friend Franz Boas at Columbia University. She shared Rufus Osgood Mason's conviction that the cultures of "primitive" peoples, such as Native Americans and the Inuit, were superior, in the sense of being more vital and natural, to those of the industrialized populations of Europe and North America. Charlotte Osgood Mason was travelling with the Chapin party as Cornelia's friend, but it is clear that she was close to Katherine and the younger Cornelia as well. How had Cornelia Chapin met the Masons? Perhaps it is not too fanciful to imagine that the drawing-room spiritualism in vogue among wealthy New Yorkers had attracted her, bereft in the aftermath of Lindley Chapin's death. Whether Marguerite remained an observant Catholic or not (and there is no evidence either way), she was certainly raised as one, and would have known – and expected Cornelia, as a convert, also to know – that the practices engaged in by spiritualists, such as seances, table-tapping, and the use of Ouija boards, were forbidden. Perhaps for this reason, she found Mrs Mason's presence in the family group somewhat disquieting. That Katherine and Cornelia continued to travel with Mason, and were still participating in the seances organized by her as mature women in the 1930s, reinforces the idea that her influence with them remained strong.[23]

On 27 June 1906, although the Chapin party was still in Paris, Marguerite sailed back to the United States – she must have arranged her journey in advance, since she spent the rest of the summer in the fashionable resort of Newport, having rented the "Weaver cottage" on Berkeley Avenue, near "Le Chalet," the summer home of her Gibert relatives. This was a chance to renew some long-standing friendships, and to enjoy the life of the town that had been her mother's childhood home. Despite the presence of New York's super-rich and all the ostentatious rivalry they brought with them, Newport was still a town where, in quieter circles, literary conversation reigned. It was even supposed to be possible to conduct a dinner party entirely in French.[24] Marguerite enjoyed the experience enough to rent the "cottage" – in reality, a fairly large house – again for the following summer. Nonetheless, after spending the nine months from September 1906 to June 1907 back in Paris, she decided not to return to Newport that summer, and sublet the cottage to a fellow New Yorker.[25]

It is interesting to speculate what might have made Marguerite change her plans for the summer of 1907. Her life in Paris was full and satisfying: she had the support of an extended family, she was blessed with good looks, health, and a personal fortune. With her paid companion, she could travel independently and as she wished, perhaps to some part of Europe as yet unexplored. She was probably not lonely – her relatives saw to that – but from the evidence of what her life later became, her situation in Paris, despite its many satisfactions, still lacked an emotional centre. Did still being single at the age of twenty-seven concern her? Did she long to fall in love, marry, have a family of her own? The social round of New York that was the conventional route to marriage had clearly not interested her enough to keep her there. Had she hoped that in Paris she might meet someone with whom she could share her interests, someone for whom the life of the mind and the arts were essential, not optional or peripheral? And if she did meet her intellectual match, would it matter if he were rich or poor, foreign or American, a professional man or an artist living from day to day? The most likely reason for staying in Paris in the summer of 1907 may simply have been that she had discovered a new interest, or made some amusing and like-minded friends – perhaps even one who might supply that missing dimension.

One of her neighbours in the apartment block at 44, avenue d'Ièna was Henri Bernstein, a controversial but extremely popular playwright in the decade before the First World War.[26] Bernstein was not only talented, but immensely rich, as the grandson and heir of the banker

William Seligman.[27] As a playwright he was considered daring, his outspoken treatment of themes such as anti-Semitism linking him to liberal circles in a society still divided over the Dreyfus affair.

But Bernstein was more than a banking heir and polemical playwright: he was also a discerning collector of modern painting. He owned works by contemporary masters such as Monet, Renoir, Fantin-Latour, Cézanne, Matisse, Signac, Redon, Bonnard, and Vuillard, the latter two artists also being personal friends. Marguerite and her relatives lived only metres from Bernstein and his wife. After they had become acquainted, it would have been surprising if an invitation to see the paintings did not follow. Just as important in awakening Marguerite's interest in modern art were the introductions Bernstein provided to his friends, two of whom would also become hers.

These were the Bibesco brothers, Prince Emmanuel, aged thirty, and Prince Antoine, aged twenty-nine. They were heirs to vast estates in Romania, but they were born in Paris and nurtured in the intellectual milieu created by their mother, Princess Hélène Bibesco, a leading hostess and *saloniste* during the 1890s. As the American writer Edith Wharton observed, "In France, where politics so sharply divided the different classes and coteries, artistic and literary interests unite them,"[28] and Princess Hélène's house in the rue de Courcelles attracted public figures and talented people from across the political spectrum. She herself had trained as a pianist, and composers such as Charles Gounod, Jules Massenet, Camille Saint-Saëns, Claude Debussy, Gabriel Fauré, and Georges Enesco were frequent visitors. She also brought together writers as diverse as Pierre Loti, Jules Lemaître, Anatole France, and the young Marcel Proust. Over the years, she befriended and commissioned work from many painters, including some, such as Aristide Maillol in the years before he took up sculpture, who were struggling to survive.

The Bibesco brothers thus grew up in a cosmopolitan, highly charged atmosphere, where ideas were debated freely and sparkling conversation was the norm. They were related to much of the nobility of Europe, including, in their immediate circle in Paris, the Countess Greffulhe, and her cousin (and theirs), the flamboyant aesthete Count Robert de Montesquiou. They were fluent and well-read in several languages, urbane and witty, with friends that ranged from aristocrats like themselves to penniless artists who had yet to achieve recognition. Both princes were among Marcel Proust's close friends, and he invented a secret language for his correspondence with them, in which he was "Lecram" and they, collectively, were "Ocsebib." Prince Antoine knew Henri Bernstein through the theatre, since he too had ambitions as a playwright, but both he and Emmanuel had common ground with Bernstein through an interest in modern painting. Like him, they commissioned works from Pierre Bonnard, and in 1908 they ordered a set of very large decorative wall paintings from Edouard Vuillard for their apartment on the Île Saint-Louis.[29]

Marguerite and the Bibesco princes soon became friends. Each of the brothers was handsome and temperamental in his own way, but the two were close and devoted to each other. Emmanuel was known to be homosexual: tall, dark, and fine-featured, he moved so gracefully that he had acquired the nickname "L'Almée" ("the dancing girl"). Prince Antoine was very different. Fairer and more angular in build and features, he had a face that was inscrutable one minute, alive with feeling the next, as he probed and tested the intellectual mettle of others. Marguerite's relationship with him was platonic, though whether it was always so is a shadowy matter: perhaps she learned about his string of affairs with actresses, or sensed the emotional instability underlying his very considerable charm. Prince Antoine's feelings for Marguerite, on the other hand, apparently came to include the idea of marriage.[30]

For the moment, the brothers were good company, and Marguerite (with her lady companion) began to attend the theatre and the opera with them. Their enthusiasm for the new developments in painting, like Bernstein's, was contagious, and through them she was introduced to dealers such as Gaston and Joss Bernheim of Bernheim Jeune and Ambroise Vollard, in whose galleries new work could be viewed and discussed. The Impressionists and the Nabis were already slightly passé, the Fauves and the Pointillists were astonishing and scandalizing the public by equal turns, and from the study of Cézanne and of African art, Pablo Picasso and Georges Braque were already devising the analytical system that would shatter existing conceptions of space and perspective. "Cubism," as it came to be known, encapsulated the fragmented, multi-faceted nature of modern existence, and Paris was soon full of artists finding ways of dealing with its powerful influence.

The princes knew many artists, and visited them in their studios to look at work in progress. Did Marguerite go along on such visits? Their example encouraged her to see herself as someone who could use her wealth constructively as a patron: someone who, by buying and surrounding herself with the work of artists she admired, could assist those artists in becoming better known. Her first commission was very likely Pierre Bonnard's half-length portrait of her with her little dog (a painting today known as *Femme au Canapé Bleu*) executed in 1908 just before she sailed back to New York in May to attend a cousin's wedding.[31] Sometime after her return in June, Marguerite commissioned from him the large, square canvas entitled *En Barque* (*In the Boat*), a composition with an arresting perspective, showing a rowboat and its occupants advancing along a stream bordered by colourful foliage.[32]

From the summer of 1908 come photographs that reveal the change in prevailing fashions, and in Marguerite's appearance, that had taken place in the four years since that family portrait at Rock Lawn. They were taken at the recently opened Waldhaus Hotel in Sils Maria (the village frequented by Friedrich Nietzsche in the 1880s) in the Engadine region of the eastern Swiss Alps, and depict Marguerite at the age of twenty-eight.[33] Gone is the matronly hairstyle and the billowy blouse. In these photos, her abundant dark hair is braided and coiled in a smooth crown around her head, above a fitted lace blouse that emphasized her slenderness and left her neck, wrists, and forearms bare. With this she wore a gored, ankle-length skirt of some flannel-like material, and low-heeled shoes: in all, an understated but stylish and modern costume. In the photograph most often reproduced, in which she is shown standing outdoors, while a moustached elderly man removes her suitcase from a car, she wears a broad-brimmed hat that casts her face into shadow, held on by a gauzy veil tied under her chin, and carries a parasol against the midday sun. Two more photographs were taken indoors, and show her standing or sitting, looking out of an open window with her back to the camera. The window was evidently too high up to show any physical features outside, such as trees or other buildings. A further photograph was taken at a distance, as Marguerite relaxed on the grass under some trees.

These photographs, reproduced individually, have had dates ranging from 1900 to 1914 attributed to them. The evidence supplied by a strong magnifying glass, however, reveals that Marguerite is dressed identically in all the pictures, suggesting that they were taken within the same brief space of time – by whom, of course, we shall never know. The photo in which she wears the large hat bears a pencil inscription in Marguerite's hand on the back: "Sils Maria 1908." To hazard a guess, it may well show her arrival at the hotel, and the removal of her suitcase from a vehicle by a porter, while a third person – usually cropped from the photo, but perhaps her *dame de compagnie* or a female relative – looks on. It follows that the interior photographs were taken in Marguerite's room, while the last-mentioned photo seems likely to show her in the grounds of the hotel, somewhat later in the day. Her relaxed poses in these pictures, together with her simple-yet-elegant attire, suggests the self-containment of a person who feels no need to impress or draw attention to herself. This is a new, more confident and sophisticated, Marguerite.

Late in the autumn of 1908 Cousin Minnie made one of her periodic visits to New York, and Marguerite accompanied her, not returning to Paris until March 1909. Perhaps it was during the summer of 1909 that she became acquainted with the playwright Tristan Barnard (who later appeared in a painting she commissioned from Edouard Vuillard), with Thadée Natanson, one of three brothers who had owned the leading intellectual journal *La Revue Blanche*, and with Jeanne Muhlfeld, the widow of Lucien Muhlfeld, a leading critic who had written for it. Madame Muhlfeld was a literary *saloniste* in whose drawing room at 12, rue Galilée an artistic and intellectual coterie met every afternoon. If – and it is an "if" – Marguerite attended these gatherings (but since Mme Muhlfeld was soon to be among Marguerite's luncheon guests, it makes sense to suppose she did), it would explain how she met some of the people who became her friends, such as Paul Valéry, André Gide, Léon-Paul Fargue, Jacques-Émile Blanche, Valery Larbaud, Paul

3.3
A typically elusive pose: Marguerite seated at her hotel room window, Sils Maria, summer 1908.

Claudel, Alexis Saint-Léger Léger, Anna de Noailles, Natalie Clifford Barney, and the writer Princess Lucien Murat.

Marguerite's freedom from domestic ties meant that she was living more or less according to her own lights. She could even resume her study of German by moving to Munich for several months, and engaging a German lady companion with whom to converse. On 11 September 1909, from the American consulate in Munich, she obtained an emergency passport via the United States embassy in Berlin, for the purpose, so the entry reads, "of traveling in Turkey." The consular official noted that Marguerite "swears she was born in New London, Connecticut, on 24 June 1880; states her permanent residence to be New York City. She left the US on 23 March 1909 and is temporarily sojourning in Munich, Bavaria, and intends to return within two years" and that the passport was for herself; he also provided a physical description of her: "height 5′ 6″, eyes and hair brown, complexion dark, nose straight, face oval, mouth small."[34]

In addition to visiting the archaeological sites that presumably provided the motive for such a journey, might it also have been made at the invitation of Prince Antoine, in order that she might visit, en route, the Bibesco estates in Romania? Since, in an interview years later, Marguerite confided that Prince Antoine had wanted to marry her, when did this prospect become apparent? And when did she firmly decide, as she also declared in the interview, "I didn't want to marry him"? Possibly – just possibly – after visiting his homeland, and realizing that (even had she returned the prince's feelings) Romania was a very long way from Paris and all that she held dear. This is a hazy area, though Marguerite was clearly tactful enough to retain Prince Antoine's friendship, since she and the Bibescos continued to socialize and attend the theatre together.[35]

The winter of 1910 was particularly wet, and in mid-January water began to rise through the sewers and cellars in the streets bordering the Seine. The river rose some eight metres above its normal level, reaching its maximum height on 28 January, as the many plaques still to be seen on nearby buildings attest. For a week the Parisians moved about in boats, or traversed the flood waters by means of wooden walkways erected by the municipal authorities. Almost as quickly as it had risen, the water abated, leaving behind the immense task of drying out, clearing up, and restoration.

Where Marguerite was during the dramatic few weeks of the floods can only be guessed at, but by March she was installed in a rented apartment at 11, rue de l'Université on the Left Bank, in an area that only weeks earlier had been under water. The apartment was situated on the ground floor of an eighteenth-century *hôtel*, at the back of a brick-paved courtyard reached from the street through a private entrance and carriageway. The building and the apartment still exist, although surviving plans of it predate Marguerite's time there. Assuming that the disposition of the rooms did not change radically between 1850, when they were made, and Marguerite's tenancy, it would seem that the apartment was spacious and high-ceilinged, with a large salon, dining room, and library, and at least two bedrooms, a bathroom, and a kitchen. From the rooms at the back, one of which was the salon, French doors opened onto an attractive, sunlit formal garden designed by the landscape architect Le Nôtre.[36]

The painter Edouard Vuillard had been a friend of Pierre Bonnard's since the 1890s, when both belonged to the group of painters who claimed the name of the *Nabis*, or "prophets." He was also a friend of the Bibescos[37] and of Henri Bernstein, each of whom had commissioned work from him. He finally met Marguerite on 11 March 1910, when he, Bonnard, and Emmanuel Bibesco were her guests for lunch. In his journal he described Marguerite's apartment as "almost bare" – perhaps because it had just been redecorated after the floods, or because she had not yet had time to acquire many furnishings of her own – and Bonnard's portrait of her with her terrier, one of the few objects already in place, as "classic," in being full of light and nicely composed.[38]

On this occasion Vuillard received his first commission from Marguerite. The setting of *Interior with a Lady and Her Dog* was a comfortable sitting room or study, very likely the one at 44, avenue d'Ièna rather than any room in Marguerite's new and barely furnished apartment at 11, rue de l'Université. Like Bonnard's initial work for Marguerite, this too was a portrait, but with a difference, in that the setting draws as much of the viewer's attention as its human subject. Marguerite herself is shown full figure, with her back to an elaborate fireplace and her gaze averted, bending to stroke her small dog – the same terrier as in the Bonnard portrait. The vivid greens and golden-browns of the furnishings suggest comfort, even a degree of opulence, while the books and decorative objects that adorn every surface point to a life of the mind and a settled, socially established existence. It is a delightful picture, and Vuillard by his own admission enjoyed painting it, not least because he found Marguerite attractive and her company enlivening. Having made his preliminary sketches during a visit to her on 14 April, a month after meeting her, he delivered the finished work to her on 4 May, once again staying to lunch.[39] For her part, Marguerite must have been pleased with the picture, for within a few months she had again commissioned Vuillard, this time to paint the much more ambitious work known as *The Library*.

Though her living arrangements were somewhat unconventional – it was still rare for a young unmarried woman to set up house on her own – she was evidently happy in them, and wealthy enough to allay criticism by always maintaining a paid live-in companion. Her social circle was widening; she could entertain, and be entertained in turn, with her German lady companion as chaperone. The diplomat and diarist Count Harry Kessler noted the presence, at a lunch with friends on 16 November 1910, of "a very pretty and very jolly American, Miss Chapin, who has allowed herself to be painted by Bonnard."[40]

As well as having the liberty to pursue her interest in painting, Marguerite was also now able to indulge her longing to create a garden of her own, a legacy of her childhood summers at Rock Lawn. She began to order trees and plants to counterbalance the rather stark planting she found on moving into the apartment. As one of her several guests on 28 May 1911, Count Kessler noted in his diary:

> Lunch at the beautiful Miss Chapin's, the American, 11, rue de l'Université: old Louis XV hotel. The salon and the study, which had been painted by Vuillard, leads to a pretty, square, architectonically laid-out garden, where Miss Chapin has had yews planted in a strictly old-fashioned English style, also many irises and roses. This mixture of Louis XV and English Tudor gardening offers a very curious harmony, especially where the garden is reflected in the large Louis XV mirrors in the salon.

Marguerite's rented apartment clearly came with some furnishings, such as these large, ornate mirrors, which were in keeping with the building's grand style. On this occasion, as Kessler recorded, the other guests were on the grand side too – "Princess Lucien Murat, a daughter of the Duchess of Rohan, Chambrun, who had been earlier part of the embassy in Berlin, an English attaché, May, and Mme Muhlfeld … an intriguer and obsessed with her salon" – but all were adept conversationalists, and Kessler enjoyed his visit.[41]

The works by Vuillard that Count Kessler saw that day were *The Library*, executed between October 1910 and March 1911, which hung in the salon, and *Place Vintimille: A Five-Panel Screen for Miss Marguerite Chapin*, painted in the spring of 1911 and evidently on view in Marguerite's study before the end of May. *The Library* is a complex and somewhat challenging work.[42] As Vuillard's *Journal* reveals, his feelings for Marguerite had taken a romantic turn by the time she commissioned it, and he put an immense amount of time and thought into the painting. The theme seems to be that of the earthly paradise, where civic, creative, and intellectual life can coexist harmoniously. The painter set himself the task of finding antique models to support this idea, and only then, when he had spent months studying the paintings and sculpture in the Louvre, brought his versions of them together in what became an audacious composition. In *The Library*, classical motifs and allusions dominate the decor of a comfortably furnished modern interior, where a gathering of contemporary people, some of whom – such as the bearded figure of playwright Tristan Barnard, the wives of art dealers Joss and Gaston Bernheim, and Vuillard's twelve-year-old niece Annette – have been identified, is observed by the slight figure of Marguerite herself. She is shown in profile, outlined by the glow from the fireplace behind her, wearing a simple, dark-green dress and buckled shoes: an appropriate outfit for the New England descendant of Puritan forebears, and a deliberate contrast with the elaborate costumes, hats, and feather boas worn by two of the other women in the picture. For the lovesick Vuillard, Marguerite was "a modern Venus who all by herself is sufficient justification for this brilliant collage of an antique marble sculpture, a tapestry inspired by Titian and small columns and cabochons from the Italian Renaissance, the whole rendered in a rough, fabric-like pictorial surface."[43]

If *The Library* is a singular and demanding work, it is also extremely large – nearly twelve feet tall and nine feet wide – and its density of elements conveys a brooding presence that recalls the intensity of the painter's feelings while he was executing it. It was probably never an easy painting to live with, despite Marguerite's initial liking for it. The screen depicting the Place Vintimille, on the other hand, has a light-hearted spontaneity, befitting a picture that was begun and completed within weeks. The subject was one of Vuillard's favourites: he had recently painted a version of it for Henri Bernstein, the viewing of which very likely prompted Marguerite to commission her own. In it, the square at the heart of a Parisian *quartier* is shown as it looked in springtime, exuberantly alive with colour and movement.[44]

Marguerite's paintings became a talking point, particularly as, in June 1911, pictures from Henri Bernstein's collection were on sale at the Hôtel Druout as a result of one of his periodic clear-outs. In his diary entry for 14 June, Count Harry Kessler reported suggesting to the Italian poet Gabriele D'Annunzio that they visit Marguerite together the following day to see her Vuillard paintings. This they did, and Kessler left a vivid account of the occasion. The garden, as before, pleased him ("At Miss Chapin's the gardeners were in the midst of planting the lilacs in the garden, the roses were in full bloom"), but what charmed him even more was Marguerite herself, "especially slender and girlish in a flowing dark blue dress." Kessler was homosexual, but the forceful and charismatic D'Annunzio was not, and as Marguerite led the pair from room to room the Count noticed how his companion "observed how she moved" and "allowed his gaze to slide over her whole figure," while Marguerite remained unruffled.[45] Finally, having viewed the paintings, D'Annunzio took one of his own works from a nearby shelf and engaged Marguerite in conversation about it. Then, as Kessler recorded:

> Out of the blue he then said suddenly, "But truly, what a charming woman you are! One of those women of whom you retain a delicious memory. And we will never see each other again.

> Perhaps, later, seeing each other more often, one would discover faults, but, like this, it will be one of those memories you have in life, the memory of something exquisite that you will never see again." He insisted that they would never see each other again, with that light, half-ironic melancholy peculiar to him.[46]

D'Annunzio's negative prediction did not in fact hold true, since before too long he did meet Marguerite again – although her circumstances by that time were very different.

Kessler was an exceptionally intelligent and cultured man, and found himself at ease in Marguerite's company. On 19 July he recorded, "Visited Miss Chapin. I feel strongly the charm of her personality and the entire atmosphere around her."[47] In this he echoed Vuillard, who had confided to his journal a few months earlier, when preparing to hang *The Library*, "Miss Chapin – charming. Feel her at a distance from my ladder."[48] This impression of charm and personal magnetism would be mentioned by countless people in the course of Marguerite's life, particularly by those whose dealings with her grew out of a shared love of painting, music, or literature. What is singular about this is that Marguerite was not herself a painter or a poet, but seemed, to those who were, to grant their creative effort the same supreme importance they gave it themselves. If her own creative impulse found an outlet, it was still through music: she had a piano, and continued to sing for her own enjoyment. It was through music that her life was about to change forever.

Marguerite was thirty-one in 1911: an attractive single woman seemingly content to reside in a city she loved, to follow her interests, and surround herself with people who shared them. If she felt her life incomplete in any way, she seems to have given no sign of it to anyone who recorded an impression of her – except, perhaps, to Prince Antoine Bibesco, whose response to being turned down was to insist "I'll find someone for you to marry – you *should* marry."[49] It was as if he grasped that, at the heart of Marguerite's life, as at the centre of his own, there was a great solitude, and one that he, as a friend if not as a lover, could possibly help to remedy.

3.4
Roffredo Caetani, Prince of Bassiano, 1903.

He had long known the composer Prince Roffredo Caetani through the circles in which they both moved, and they had numerous friends in common. Whether he engineered the couple's first glimpse of each other or not hardly matters. One evening, having escorted Marguerite to a play, Prince Antoine caught sight of the exceedingly tall Prince Roffredo, with his dark hair and deep-set eyes. "Who is that?" Marguerite asked, following his gaze with her own, and received the reply,

"That's Prince Caetani, the composer." Some secondary comment claims he also told her that Prince Roffredo was just the person for her, though he knew his friend had decided not to marry. (Perhaps, indeed, he hastened to tell Prince Roffredo much the same about Marguerite.) Her account is slightly different: having seen her at the theatre, "Prince C. found out who I was from a cousin of his, an English girl who happened to be my friend – and he made her bring him to present him. We became engaged in about a minute – just like that."[50]

At the time of his introduction to Marguerite, Prince Roffredo was forty years old, and still in the process of establishing himself as a serious composer. Like Marguerite, he belonged to a social class that moved with the seasons around Europe, that spoke several languages, that had family ties in more than one country. He was as much at home in Paris as in his native Rome, but he had spent time in London, and knew Berlin and Vienna well through having lived for several months in each. His musical compositions up to this point reveal the influence of Richard Wagner (though it would be hard to find a composer of the period of whom the same could not be said), and he loved the magnificent four-part music drama, *Der Ring des Nibelungen*. That was why, when he called on Marguerite for the first time, her lady companion's declaration that "*Ich bin Fafner*!" ("I am Fafner!"), as she met him at the door, was not lost on him. Fafner is the dragon who guards the treasure in Wagner's *Ring*, and is eventually slain by the hero, Siegfried. As Marguerite recalled, Prince Roffredo ever after referred to the German woman as "Fafner" – though he was far too self-effacing to compare himself to Siegfried.[51]

4

PRINCE ROFFREDO AND THE CAETANI

Having braved the "dragon" once, Prince Roffredo became a frequent visitor to number 11, rue de l'Université. One of the earliest discoveries that Marguerite made about him was that he was an expatriate, as she was, for whom Paris was the centre of the cultural universe, as it was for her. She soon found that she had much else in common with this distinguished-looking man, whose handmade suits and shoes were unobtrusively elegant, whose dark hair was worn swept to one side above a fine, smooth brow, and whose eyes, dark too, were full of intelligence and warmth. He was so tall that she had to tilt her head back to address him, and, when he sat down, his angular frame seemed constrained by her armchairs, but neither of them felt awkward on that account. Conversation flowed easily between these two superbly well-read and well-travelled people, for whom music was one of life's chief joys and the latest plays and exhibitions an endless source of discussion. In repose, Prince Roffredo's features sometimes bore a melancholy expression, but with Marguerite he could be as animated as he felt, in whichever language seemed appropriate. Marguerite as yet spoke no Italian, and when she did eventually learn it, her American accent would remain far more noticeable than it was in French. Roffredo, on the other hand, spoke English with an upper-class English accent, French like a French aristocrat, and German far better than Marguerite did – or so "Fafner" lost no time in telling her.

Marguerite and Roffredo could not have conversed for long without realizing that they shared two characteristics more essential for a deeper relationship than mere tastes and interests – or even the powerful attraction each felt for the person of the other. Firstly, despite their different backgrounds, they viewed the world in the same way. What they found of interest in it had nothing to do with nationality or the conventions of privilege. Neither of them could be summed up by their respective social positions – his as an Italian nobleman, hers as a wealthy American. They were both members of an international elite, but each had a sensitive temperament that shunned the often coarse protocol that prevailed in that exclusive caste. Secondly, there was the inner solitude that each had accepted, perhaps as the price of directing their lives as independently as they had so far. Neither Roffredo at his age nor Marguerite at hers had expected to encounter another person so compatible, someone who sought and valued authenticity in life in quite the same way. For each of them, the gradual recognition of emotional kinship brought surprise, then the joy of affirmation. So convinced were they of each other that Prince Roffredo's proposal of marriage and Marguerite's acceptance came within weeks of their first meeting,[1] as the most natural thing in the world. What they knew of each other, they had learned in that brief time – but it was enough.

Who was Prince Roffredo Caetani, apart from being a composer with a number of chamber pieces to his credit? The answer to this question must have occupied many an hour, as Roffredo recounted to Marguerite something of his life and the history of the ancient and extraordinary dynasty of which he was part. In legal and genealogical terms, he was the second son of Onorato Caetani, the 14th Duke of Sermoneta, one of the largest private landowners in Italy. While Roffredo's elder brother, Leone, had enjoyed the title of "Prince of Teano" from birth as the first-born son, his own title of "Prince of Bassiano" was bestowed upon him only in 1903 by his childhood friend, now King Victor Emmanuel III of Italy, and derived from the name of a hill town in the Pontine Marshes belonging to the vast Caetani estates. Roffredo could trace his ancestry back to about 750 AD, when there were "Gaetani" in the area around the peninsula and port city of Gaeta, halfway between Rome and Naples. In that shadowy period of history, a number of them emerged from local power struggles as individual overlords associated with specific towns. The monumental genealogy *Domus Caietana* later compiled by Roffredo's younger brother Gelasio identified a powerful man called Anatolio as lord of Gaeta in the ninth century. Around that time, too, the family name was Latinized or softened to "Caetani."

The first member of the family to achieve greater prominence was Giovanni Caetani, born in 1060, who became a monk at the Benedictine mother-house of Monte Cassino and served as papal chancellor from 1089. He reformed the central administration of the Roman Church by establishing a staff of educated clerics and introducing a uniform minuscule script for the easier recording and understanding of papal documents. He was elected pope, taking the name Gelasius II, on 24 January 1118. It was a particularly conflictive time for the papacy, and this first Caetani pope died after a tumultuous reign lasting precisely one year and five days.

Not until 1294 did the Caetani again exercise such influence, but with the election of Benedetto Caetani as Pope Boniface VIII in that year, the family's fortunes altered radically. Boniface is chiefly remembered today as the founder of the University of Rome (*La Sapienza*, "the Wisdom"), the institution (in 1300) of the Roman Jubilee, and the place in the seventh circle of Hell accorded to him by Dante Alighieri, who had cause to hate him.[2] He was indeed one of the most ambitious popes in history. Through the bull *Unam Sanctam* of 1302, he advanced the claim of papal supremacy in the temporal sphere as well as the spiritual, and backed it up through edicts of excommunication and armed conflict. His enemies were many, from locally powerful families like the Colonna, whose stronghold at Palestrina he destroyed with the loss of six thousand lives, right up to king Philip IV of France and the Holy Roman Emperor. In his nine-year reign he amassed vast wealth – admittedly using some of it to restore and beautify the basilicas of Rome and the Vatican library – but he was nothing if not nepotistic. In 1297 he bestowed upon members of his family the hill towns of Sermoneta, Norma, Bassiano, and San Donato, and the extensive lands around them, and created his brother Marquis of Ancona. Through arranged marriages, the Caetani acquired further territories, so that, by the time of Boniface's death in 1303, they controlled an enormous area south of Rome that extended right across the Italian peninsula and halfway to Naples. The westernmost part of this territory became less and less productive as the centuries went by. This was because the drainage to the sea of local streams and mountain run-off was slowly being blocked by coastal dunes, over time converting the whole area into the malarial swamps that acquired the name of the Pontine Marshes.

During the fifteenth century, the Caetani dynasty divided, a cadet branch establishing itself separately from 1454 as the Gaetani dell'Aquila d'Aragona, linked by marriage with Naples. Roffredo Caetani's lineage derived from the senior branch, associated with the hill town of Sermoneta and the Papal States. Its influence, both in the Roman *campagna* and in the city of Rome itself, brought it into armed conflict with other feudal overlords, such as the Colonna, Frangipane, Aldobrandini, and Orsini families. In 1500, the ambitious and nepotistic Pope Alexander VI sought to dominate the Caetani by stripping them of their fiefdoms and awarding them to his own family. Soon, however, the Caetani were more powerful than ever, thanks to Pope Julius II, who restored their lands and awarded them the duchy of Sermoneta in 1504. Pope Sixtus V rewarded the valour of Onorato Caetani IV, captain general of the papal infantry at the Battle of Lepanto in 1571, by making him Duke of Sermoneta, and added the marquisate of Cisterna to the family's titles in 1585.

Between the sixteenth and the nineteenth centuries, the Caetani had few rivals in Rome. They produced some fifty cardinals and countless collectors of works of art, enlightened patrons, military figures, diplomats, men of letters, and scientists, one after another, in a stream of outstanding ability and creativity. For two centuries the Caetani seat in the Eternal City was the fortified and strategically situated palace of San Bartolomeo on Tiber Island, but between 1557 and 1569 they moved to, and enlarged, the Palazzo all'Orso, which stood on the east bank of the Tiber. Like the palace on Tiber Island, the Palazzo all'Orso was subject to flooding, which may have prompted the move to the imposing Palazzo Rucellai on the Corso, purchased in 1638. In the early eighteenth century, outstanding debts prompted the sale of the Rucellai palace (now Palazzo Ruspoli), and, in 1725, the move to the Villa

Caserta, set in extensive gardens on the Esquiline Hill, near the basilica of Santa Maria Maggiore. In 1776 the Serbelloni family of Milan sold their grand Roman house in the Via delle Botteghe Oscure – part of the sprawling, interconnected group of buildings known as the Isola de Mattei – to Francesco V, the 11th Duke of Sermoneta. This duke was the epitome of the "new man" of the Enlightenment: cultivated and open to the ideas emerging from scientific discovery. He set up a chemical laboratory and a printing press in the old Serbelloni palace, which he renamed Palazzo Caetani, and mounted Rome's first astronomical telescope on the roof, later publishing his observations as *Effimiridi astronomichi*. He was greatly interested in botany, and developed the area given over to the cultivation of medicinal plants in the gardens of Villa Caserta.[3]

Michelangelo Caetani (1804–1882), the 13th Duke of Sermoneta and third Prince of Teano, was Roffredo's grandfather. In him the family's intellectual and artistic tendencies combined to produce a man of outstanding versatility,[4] who made the consolidation of the Caetani patrimony his life's work. In childhood he read widely, in classical history and archaeology, literature, and art. Even in his twenties he was recognized among the Roman nobility as a polymath, a formidable historian and literary scholar, and a very fine craftsman in wood,[5] who in later life amused himself by making his own furniture. He was also "a character," genial and eccentric by turns. He and his brother, Filippo – an artist and brilliant caricaturist, who as a priest was popularly known as "Don Pippo" – gave legendary fancy-dress parties for the nobility of Rome, and dinners at which they treated the guests to meals that they cooked themselves. Michelangelo is reported to have had a wit that was dry, to say the least, and to have been notoriously parsimonious. The saying attributed to him by a visitor to the castle of Sermoneta – "I'd invite you to lunch, dear man, but my cook died ... in the sixteenth century" – illustrates both attributes at once.

Michelangelo was a gifted artist in several media – he painted in watercolour, carved and sculpted in wood and marble, and drew thousands of designs for ceremonial items. Most importantly, he became the friend and patron of Fortunato Pio Castellani, the founder of the Castellani dynasty of goldsmiths. Many of Duke Michelangelo's designs for jewellery and decorative objects were based on Greek, Etruscan, Roman, and Byzantine motifs, and executed by Castellani and his sons. The resulting masterpieces, in gold set with precious stones or decorated with enamel, found their way into the hands of discerning buyers all over Europe.[6] Michelangelo was also a highly respected scholar of Dante Alighieri, and the author of several books on his works. He is said to have known the entire text of *The Divine Comedy* by heart – having memorized it from daily readings from a manuscript of the poem which bore the annotations of the Renaissance humanist philosopher Marsilio Ficino and had been in the Caetani family since the fifteenth century. The duke's drawing room rivalled the best Paris salons for the intellectual quality of those attending and the breadth of discussion to be found there. Roman thinkers of a liberal persuasion mingled with such figures as the historians Ferdinand Gregorovius and Theodor Mommsen, the political writers Hippolyte Taine and Alexis de Touqueville, and the novelists Sir Walter Scott, Honoré de Balzac, and Marie-Henri Beyle, better known under his pen name of Stendahl (who apparently claimed that the entire Roman aristocracy were imbeciles, except for the Duke of Sermoneta). Franz Liszt, by this time in holy orders, was resident in Rome from 1861 and was a frequent guest. He no longer gave public recitals, but, in the more intimate setting of Palazzo Caetani, he could sometimes be persuaded to take his place at the piano. Whether the great man played his own compositions, or those of Schubert, Chopin, and other contemporaries, the resulting display of technical virtuosity enthralled the assembled company, and inevitably drew tears from some.[7]

Despite his family's long allegiance to the Church, Michelangelo Caetani was a freethinker. Outspoken in his dislike of the papal domination of Rome (his observation that "temporal power isn't dead, it's alive and well and living in the Vatican" was a typically trenchant comment[8]), he was one of the few political liberals among the Roman aristocracy. As such, he had a part to play in the *Risorgimento* that led to the creation of a united Italy. This rise of nationalist sentiment followed decades of domination of the Italian peninsula by France and Austria. Following the series of revolutions that took place in Europe and in some of the Italian states in 1848, the political and cultural strands that would lead to unification began to come together. Guided by Count Camillo Cavour of Turin (representing the Kingdom of Sardinia, which included the region of Piedmont), it was a process beset by shifting alliances and popular uprisings. By 1860, when a degree of stability had finally been achieved, a series of plebiscites was held in the various regions of the peninsula – the Grand Duchy of Tuscany, the Marches, Umbria, and other parts of the Papal States. These voted to join a new Italy, with Victor Emmanuel II of the House of Savoy as king. The election of a parliament was anathema to Pope Pius IX, who continued to assert supremacy in temporal matters as in spiritual, in a manner reminiscent of the claims made by Boniface VIII. In this he was supported by Rome's "black" nobility, while the liberal, or "white" aristocracy, of which Michelangelo Caetani was a leading figure, favoured a secular monarchy. This was the option overwhelmingly endorsed by the plebiscite held in Rome. Duke Michelangelo, as a member of the new parliament, was given the task of making the journey to Florence, the recently designated capital, to present King Victor Emmanuel II with the results. That he did so enraged Pope Pius IX, who apparently pronounced the legendary "Pio Nono's curse": for its disloyalty, the proud and mighty Caetani family would become extinct within two generations.

Duke Michelangelo was probably unperturbed by this malediction, as the Caetani succession seemed secure. In 1840 he had married Polish countess Calixta Rzewuski-Lubomirski, an autodidact and intellectual like himself, and an exceptionally fine pianist. She was the daughter of Wenceslas Severin Rzewuski, author of important studies of the Islamic world, and heir to large estates located near Kiev, in the Polish territory of Galicia that eventually became part of Ukraine. The Rzewuski, like the Caetani, produced many eminent male representatives over the centuries, as well as one woman whose name has also passed into history: Calixta's cousin Eva, who was Honoré de Balzac's beloved "L'Etrangère," and eventually became his wife.[9] Michelangelo and Calixta had two children: Ersilia, born in 1840, and Onorato, born in 1842. Michelangelo's happiness with his young wife was short-lived: she died six months after the birth of her son, aged only thirty-one, leaving in Rome little trace of her presence save the genetic legacy of her exceptional height – she was apparently six feet tall.

Duke Michelangelo was married twice more, both times to English women. His second wife was Margaret Knight, whom the writer Augustus Hare, resident in Rome in the late 1850s, characterized as "a most ghostly and solemn woman to outsiders, but much beloved by those who knew her intimately."[10] Among the latter were the duke's children, Ersilia and Onorato, to whom she was devoted. By the time Margaret died, Michelangelo was losing his sight, and indeed was totally blind for the last seventeen years of his life. In May 1875 he married Harriet Ellis, daughter of the 6th Lord Howard de Walden. She was by all accounts a briskly energetic woman of considerable charm, whose dedication and gifts as a hostess enabled Michelangelo to continue his gatherings of intellectual and accomplished friends. His admiration for the English constitution and liberal values, and the influence exercised by two English wives, meant that his son and daughter were perfectly bilingual from childhood and, as adults, anglophile in outlook.

It was unfortunate, therefore, that on Michelangelo's death in 1882 an ugly lawsuit arose which irrevocably soured relations between his widow, the dowager Duchess Harriet, and her stepson Onorato, now the 14th Duke of Sermoneta. Lawyers for Harriet claimed that, according to Italian law, she had the right to the interest on a third of her late husband's property. It was then discovered that, years earlier, Michelangelo had transferred the whole of his inheritance to Onorato, keeping only an annuity for himself. This had taken place at the time when the newly formed Italian parliament was debating the abolition of the law vesting the whole of a family's patrimony in the eldest son. In the event, the law was not abolished – but neither, following his father's death, did the new duke recognize his stepmother's claim. The matter went to court, and a verdict was awarded in Onorato's favour. On appeal, the result was radically different, with the dowager duchess

4.1
Michelangelo Caetani, 13th Duke of Sermoneta (1802–1883), polymath, jewellery designer, and renowned scholar of Dante. Blind for the last seventeen years of his life, he kept mind and spirit alight by memorizing the entire *Divine Comedy.*

being awarded interest on half of Duke Michelangelo's entire estate, that half being valued at some 3,500,000 lire:[11] about $700,000 US in pre-1914 monetary value.[12]

By the time he became duke in 1883, Onorato Caetani had turned forty, and was at the height of his very considerable intellectual powers. He and his sister, Ersilia, were largely self-taught, having had the run of their father's library from an early age. As they got older, they were tutored by the best specialists available, and each spoke, read, and wrote several languages. Ersilia grew up to be a woman of great wit and presence, able to converse on an equal footing with the many intellectuals she met through her father's salon. Her first love was the study of ancient languages – Greek, Latin, and Sanskrit – and the surviving traces of ancient civilizations. In 1859 she married Giacomo Lovatelli, and with him had a son, Filippo, who became a sculptor, and a daughter, Calixta. Alongside family life she continued her study of antiquity, maintaining a wide scholarly correspondence and becoming renowned as an archaeologist, specializing in epigraphy. In 1879

4.2
Onorato Caetani (1842–1917), Prince of Teano, and from 1883, the 14th Duke of Sermoneta.

she became the first – and for many years, the only – woman member of the Accademia Nazionale dei Lincei, Italy's foremost scholarly institution. This was followed by numerous other honours, many from institutions in Germany and France. Ersilia's own writings[13] are still read today, while her salon, at the Lovatelli-Caetani palace only steps away from Palazzo Caetani, was one of the most advanced intellectual circles in Rome for fifty years.[14]

Having been close in childhood, Ersilia and Onorato remained so all their lives. Ersilia had the stronger constitution, Onorato having inherited his father's tendency to poor sight and his mother's great height (he stood six feet six inches tall without shoes), which over time resulted in chronic back pain. His abiding interest was geography, which he studied assiduously from boyhood; from 1879 he served as president of the Società Geografica Italiana. He had other interests, including a deep love of music (he was president of the Filarmonica Romana from 1879 to 1883), and of the outdoors, especially the natural world of the rural, feudal, virtual principality that he would inherit. As a political liberal, though a less dogmatic one than his father, he believed that it was his duty to contribute to the betterment of the new Italy. In 1870 Rome supplanted Florence as its capital, and when elections were held, Onorato was elected to parliament as deputy, or member, for Velletri, a town in the nearby Alban hills. He held this seat until he became mayor of Rome in 1890. He also served briefly under Prime Minister Rudinì as minister of foreign affairs in 1896, and in 1911 was made a senator. He was outspoken in his opposition to colonialism and financial chicanery – both of which were rife in the politics of the 1890s – to the point of resigning his post in 1896 when he felt he must.

These are the public details of a singularly interesting and fruitful life, at the heart of which was Onorato's family. In 1867, during a long stay in London as a twenty-five-year-old bachelor, he met and married Ada Constance Bootle-Wilbraham, the fourth daughter of the Honourable Colonel Edward Bootle-Wilbraham (the second son of the first Baron Skelmersdale). Ada was a pretty but serious-looking girl, just twenty-one when she married, but her appearance was deceptive: she had an independent, even slightly eccentric, spirit. She was already an avid traveller with a love of the Mediterranean, but she was also unconventional in preferring hunting and shooting (she was an expert horsewoman and a good shot) to the drawing room or the card table. She grew up at Rode Hall, a rambling house in Cheshire set in lakeside gardens, amidst a family with a strong interest in the theatre. At Rode

Hall, an ancestor, Mary Bootle, had created one of the finest collections of porcelain in the country. The Bootle-Wilbraham children spent much time at the Skelmersdale seat of Lathom House, a Palladian country villa set in one of the best garden parks in Lancashire. Laid out by Sir Humphrey Repton, this park possessed a magnificent avenue of trees – beech, oak, plane, Japanese maple, and others – known as "The Line," which, at more than two kilometres in length, was the longest such avenue in Britain. There were also rose plantations in abundance, and areas dedicated to exotica such as palms, camellias, rhododendrons, and orchids. Not surprisingly, Ada brought with her to Italy not only a love of gardening and horticulture, but also a knowledge of how plantings could create effect and mood.

The marriage of Onorato and Ada was a love match: the two were inseparable, and as the years went on, if and when circumstances forced them to be apart, they wrote to each other daily. In the 1870s and 1880s, as Prince and Princess of Teano, they were one of the most attractive couples among the Roman aristocracy of the new Italy, renowned for being accomplished and cosmopolitan, and for having a link with the royal family. Duke Michelangelo's support for King Victor Emmanuel II led to friendship between Onorato and Ada and the heirs to the throne, Prince Umberto of Piedmont and his wife, Princess Margherita. A collection of photographs from a fancy-dress ball held at Palazzo Caetani on 8 February 1875 shows each of the four in splendid historical costume. This kind of entertainment was often held in the palaces of the Roman nobility, but the participation of heirs to the throne was rare, and indicates the degree of confidence that existed between them and the Caetani. When Prince Umberto became king in 1878, Ada was one of the first noblewomen in Rome to be appointed a lady-in-waiting to the queen. Even the fact that she found court life tedious (she apparently developed a reputation for lateness and for seldom being where she was supposed to be) did not tarnish the royal couple's affection for her.[15]

By this time, she had the excuse of having five children to attend to. The first, Leone, was born on 12 September 1869; the second, Roffredo – whom we have already met – on 13 October 1871; the third, Livio, on 9 October 1873; the fourth, and the only girl, Giovanella, on 24 September 1875; and the fifth, Gelasio, on 7 March 1877. While it was true that she and Onorato derived immense satisfaction from their growing family, it was also true that Ada was bored by inactiv ity and always had to be "up and doing."

A partial solution to this was close at hand. Early on in their marriage, Onorato took Ada to see Fogliano, an eighteenth-century palace on a Caetani estate bordering the sea and its lagoon near Circeo, on the edge of the Pontine Marshes. As a boy, Onorato had planted beech seedlings on visits there. Twenty years later they were sizable trees, thanks to the sheltered and temperate growing conditions that prevailed. The park surrounding the palace was overgrown with dense vegetation, but Ada was captivated by the untamed atmosphere. Creating a garden there fitted in well with her wish that the family should spend part of the year in the country, away from the heat of the Roman summer. From the mid-1870s, she and Onorato took to spending the months from April to October at Fogliano. Such a long, unbroken period every year allowed her to reclaim marshland, clear undergrowth, and turn the park into a garden that reflected the family's dual Italian and English heritage. She chose plants that flourished in the humid conditions: palms and giant bamboo to give structure, pampas grass, yuccas, and acanthus to supply points of interest. There were already plenty of umbrella pines and birches, most of which were preserved. Fogliano became a beloved family retreat, dubbed "the Congo" by the children, for the clumps of jungle-like vegetation that seemed reminiscent of Africa. Over the years, Onorato and Ada entertained many friends there, the king and queen among them, while by the end of the century it had become "one of the most important gardens in Italy for Mediterranean vegetation."[16] Fogliano was also reminiscent of the English gardens of Ada's youth. Daffodils, planted in their hundreds at the bases of palm trees, heralded the spring, and hundreds of old roses brought from England, the summer.

Ada also loved the moors and marshlands of the Caetani estates farther inland, and explored them thoroughly. She came to know the tenant farmers and peasants who worked the land, the mounted buffalo herdsmen in their blue jackets bearing the family crest, and the shepherds that looked after the flocks. The Caetani were considered enlightened in the management of their estates and the treatment of their tenants, but Ada found the incidence of malarial sickness among the latter disturbing. Malaria had been endemic in the marshes for centuries, but Ada soon saw to it that, on the Caetani estates, "The sick and fever-stricken are cared for and supplied with remedies and drugs which they would have to travel miles to obtain."[17] For her kindness, Ada came to be much loved by the local folk. Indeed, in the area around Fogliano, she was apparently addressed by them using the familiar "tu" rather than the polite "voi," because they thought of her as a sort of local "Madonna."[18]

Ada was above all a practical person, with interests that were unusual for a woman of her era and rank. At Cisterna, the Caetani palace and estate nearest to Rome, she established a stud farm, cross-breeding the tough little mares that inhabited the marshes with stallions imported from England, to produce animals that were rugged, agile, and fast. These she broke and trained herself, selling them on to the army as cavalry mounts. She was always eager for new challenges, and after the birth of Gelasio in 1877, took up mountaineering. In 1882, the year in which Onorato succeeded his father as Duke of Sermoneta, Ada climbed in the Dolomites above Bolzano. On that occasion she became the first woman to scale the Cima Piccola di Lavarelo, one of the three most difficult peaks in the Lavarelo region. The wife of the British ambassador in Rome, Lady Walburga Paget, confided to her diary that she thought Ada was driven by a love of adventure, and left a colourful impression of her:

> As long as she was replenishing the house of Caetani … she was sufficiently quiet, but from the moment that she thought she had done her duty in that respect, nothing could hold her. She rode and hunted; she went to live for weeks in wretched shanties in the Pontine Marshes, whilst her husband was sitting in a tub shooting wildfowl; she climbed impossible mountains in Switzerland, passing the ridges *à califourchon*. She went up in balloons, telling her

husband he must stay below, because it would not do if something happened to both of them, on account of the children.[19]

Both Ada and Onorato were loving parents, but it was Ada who provided the children with the broadening experiences of outdoor activity. As soon as they could keep up with her, whether at Fogliano or on holiday in the Alps, she thrust long walking sticks into their hands and took them hiking, seeing to it that they learned about weather conditions, plants, and wildlife. Sometimes, as though to reinforce the lessons, she took their tutor too, and one of the large Bernese mountain dogs that so often appear in the photographs of Roffredo and his family. She instilled in her children a hardy self-confidence and self-reliance that complemented, in each of them, the intellect and aptitudes they had inherited, and the weight of the family history and expectations that came with being a Caetani. She was close to them in ways that were unique to each, instinctively responsive to what he or she required, as if to the needs of rare orchids. In return, her children adored her. As they grew up and went their separate ways, each would correspond with her in terms that left no doubt that she was not only the repository of family confidences, but the central figure in each of their lives. It is interesting to note that her daughter, Giovanella, continued to live for much of the time with her parents, even after her marriage at age twenty-five, and that, of Ada's sons, none married under the age of thirty, and two did not marry at all. She was, it would seem, a hard act to follow.

From the summer residence of Fogliano, Onorato and Ada sometimes took visitors on excursions to yet another Caetani possession, the ruined and abandoned town of Ninfa. It was situated not far from Cisterna, in the lee of the Lepini mountains, but on the marshy plain, below the town and castle of Sermoneta. Dating from Roman times (its lake, crystalline river, and particular variety of trout are mentioned in one of Pliny's epistles), Ninfa's chequered and ultimately tragic history became entwined with that of the Caetani in 1298, when Boniface VIII purchased it for his nephew, Pietro Caetani. The eighty tumultuous

4·3
Ada, with her three eldest sons (Leone, Roffredo, and Livio) and their tutor, hiking in the Pontine Marshes, about 1885.

4·4
Onorato Caetani, with his three eldest sons and their tutor, near Pontresina in the Swiss Alps, about 1885.

years that followed covered the period of the Great Schism. One of its many unforeseen consequences was a wave of local conflicts, such as the one that arose between rival members of the Caetani family. In 1382 the Caetani of Sermoneta utterly destroyed Ninfa, killing or driving away its inhabitants. In the years when Onorato and Ada were taking their guests to see the ruins of Ninfa, its walls, streets, town hall, and seven churches had lain open to the elements for six centuries. The place was so densely overgrown that (according to Leone, who experienced the effect himself on what was possibly his first trip there in 1883, at the age of fourteen), once inside what was left of the walls, visitors were sometimes hard put to find their way out again.[20] Despite having become a mosquito-infested swamp, it combined the sense of being haunted with a beauty that was itself haunting. Numerous nineteenth-century visitors fell under the spell of Ninfa, and recorded their impressions of it. Edward Lear went there to sketch, and found the lake and ruins "one of the most romantic sights in Italy."[21] The abandoned town was one of those places that captured the imagination and demanded a personal response. Onorato and Ada, who created their second great garden there, certainly felt this. Roffredo and Gelasio, who would each devote a considerable part of their lives to restoring it, must, on that evidence, have felt it too.

4.5
Arthur Glennie, watercolour view of Santa Maria Maggiore, Ninfa, dated 1880.

By the late 1880s, the five Caetani offspring were rapidly growing into the people that they would become. In appearance, they were all exceptionally tall, like their father and grandmother. Of the boys, Gelasio would be the shortest at six feet two inches, and even Giovanella would marginally exceed six feet in height. They were all dark-haired, but Gelasio was the exception in having blue eyes like his mother. The family resemblance, as photographs of them together show, was marked, but not overly so: they would each become as individual in appearance as in personality and interests.

And then, unexpectedly, from being five, they were suddenly six. At the ages of forty-four and forty-eight respectively, Ada and Onorato found that they were again to become parents. Their fifth son, Michelangelo, was born on 8 August 1890, in London – a good place to escape Rome's summer heat. The entire family doted on this little boy, twenty-one years younger than his eldest brother, Leone, and thirteen years younger than his nearest one, Gelasio. In height and intellect he would come to resemble his siblings, but because of the difference in age, he would grow up almost as an only child, rather than as a member of a close-knit group.

The challenging intellectual climate of the Caetani household came to fruition as the next generation reached adulthood. They had all been educated by tutors (although Gelasio at fourteen insisted on attending the equivalent of a public secondary school). They also benefited from the conversation of the scientists and explorers, academics, politicians, and literary figures whose presence regularly enlivened the Caetani dinner table. The interest in their studies taken by their grandfather Michelangelo, and the encouragement of their parents and their Aunt Ersilia, motivated them to undertake serious intellectual work as soon as they were able.

Leone, for instance, began to teach himself Sanskrit and Arabic at fifteen, inspired by the interest in the Muslim world shared by Onorato and Ersilia, and by the example of his great-grandfather Rzewuski, the renowned Islamic scholar. By the time he entered the University of Rome to study oriental languages, he was proficient in Arabic. At university he added Hebrew and Aramaic to his ancient languages, Persian

4.6
The Caetanis' fourth son, Gelasio, aged nine, in one of the terrace windows at Palazzo Caetani.

and Turkish to the modern ones. He used his vacations to travel in countries where Arabic was spoken,[22] savouring its regional differences and its evolution from classical to modern usage. The young Prince of Teano was a serious scholar, who came to know eleven languages. His friends included the Jewish fellow-Islamist Giorgio Levi della Vida, thanks to whose letters and reminiscences much personal information about Leone has survived.

Leone was also a young man who tested his physical capabilities with the same intensity that he brought to his studies. In 1891, he sailed with a friend from Liverpool to New York, then travelled by train across North America to the area around Kootenay Lake in the Canadian Rockies. The aim was to hunt grizzly bears and do some mountain climbing, and while the two young men did not accomplish everything they set out to do, they had many adventures and encountered a fair share of privations and danger.[23] Cooking and sleeping outdoors, trading his "European" clothes for the "American" ones worn by loggers and trappers (a Stetson, a coarse woollen shirt and jacket, rough pants, and hobnailed boots) produced an exhilarating sense of freedom in this twenty-two-year-old prince, so very conscious of what was expected of him as the heir to the dukedom.

This creative tension between scholarship and action was shared by two of Leone's brothers, Livio and Gelasio. Livio combined an interest in ancient civilizations with the very practical desire to join the diplomatic service. At about the time that Leone was shooting grizzlies in the Rockies, Livio entered the University of Florence to study jurisprudence. He was the least-extrovert of the Caetani brothers, a lover of nature and of long solitary walking trips that took him all over Italy, observing and making notes on everything from agricultural practices to folk songs. Around the edges of his legal studies he taught himself Chinese, in the hope that this might result in his being given a diplomatic posting to China – as, in fact, it did. In 1899 he was appointed second secretary of the Italian legation in Peking.

He was there less than a year when the Boxer Rebellion erupted, and the legation, like all foreign outposts, came under attack. When cannon fire damaged the building and his superiors were wounded, Livio took over and had the oak furniture from its offices chopped up to use for repairs. The legation staff were clerks, not soldiers (although there were some Neapolitan sailors among the defenders), but Livio organized them in such a way as to make them seem better armed and more numerous than they were. Most importantly, during what became a forty-five-day siege, he manned "a barricade exposed to very severe shell and rifle fire,"[24] with little rest or thought for his own safety, until relief arrived. Livio was eventually evacuated to Japan, then home to Italy, where he arrived in 1901, unaware that he had at one point been reported dead, or that he was now a national hero, the recipient of the Silver Medal for Military Valour.[25]

Gelasio was the Renaissance man of the family, supremely talented in so many fields that he confounds any attempt at easy classification. He was both scientist and humanist, but above all, he was practical in outlook, with much of Ada's executive ability and much too of her personal charm and ready sympathy. As the fourth son, he was also the member of his generation most determined to make his own way in the world, yet it was he who would become the family genealogist, and he who would arrange the thousands of documents recording its history into the archive that survives today. The usual career options open to younger sons – the church, the army, or the diplomatic service – did not attract Gelasio, but engineering did, and in 1896, aged nineteen, he enrolled in that field at the University of Rome. On qualifying as a civil engineer in 1901, he decided on further study in mining, first at Liège and then at Columbia University in New York. Like Leone, he was attracted by the North American wilderness, so great a contrast to urbanized Europe with its hierarchical social structures and millennia of history.

Roffredo was unique among his siblings in having a vocation for music, evident from a very young age. His godfather was Franz Liszt, who frequented Palazzo Caetani as a friend, first of Duke Michelangelo, and then of Onorato and Ada. Of the Caetani children, Leone and Giovanella also took piano lessons (and Gelasio for a time played the violin), but Roffredo's gift was of another order. His first piano teacher was Giulia de Cousandier Cerasoli,[26] but his tuition was soon entrusted to Liszt's friend and protégé, the Anglo-Italian pianist, composer, and conductor Giovanni Sgambati, who from 1877 taught piano at Rome's Liceo Municipale. Like Liszt himself, Sgambati had been a child prodigy, and Liszt may have recommended him for Roffredo on perceiving that his godson's talent too was prodigious. He urged Duke Onorato to take his son's vocation seriously by often reminding him that "My godchild Roffredo's gift for music is simply astounding."[27]

Roffredo was just eleven years old when he wrote the short piano piece called "Fogliano" that is his earliest surviving composition. As any parent of a child with an outstanding ability knows, hard choices about the use of time have to be made in order to accommodate and develop it. Perhaps this is why less is known about Roffredo's childhood than, say, about Leone's or Gelasio's; while the latter was enlisting his friends in his "Cowboys and Indians Society" or devising his plant-watering apparatus, Roffredo was deep in music theory, alone at the piano.

As an adolescent, in addition to his studies with Sgambati at the Liceo Municipale, Roffredo took classes there in harmony and counterpoint with the composer and conductor Cesare De Sanctis. Later, he studied composition with Guido Tacchinardi, possibly in Florence, and Giuseppe Martucci in Bologna and Naples. Tacchinardi and Martucci were among a group of Italian composers promoting a revival of interest in instrumental and orchestral composition, extolling German composers such as Mendelssohn, Schumann, Wagner, and Brahms, at a time when public taste in Italy favoured the operatic realism, or "*verismo*," championed by Giordano, Mascagni, Ponchielli, Leoncavallo, and others. All of Roffredo's teachers, including Liszt as his juvenile mentor, leaned towards instrumental work, and it is hardly surprising that Roffredo's own compositions, from the earliest to those of the early 1900s, were written for the piano, for orchestra, or for chamber groups.[28] Liszt died at Bayreuth in 1886 (during the festival of Wagner's music directed by his widow, Liszt's daughter Cosima), and thus did not live to see the publication of his godson's String Quartet no. 1, op. 1 in 1888 by the German house of Schott in Mainz (which would publish all Roffredo's work), or the first performances of his music in Rome that same year. Nonetheless, Liszt left Roffredo a most meaningful bequest: his own piano, the veteran Bechstein instrument that had accompanied him all over Europe. He could have chosen no better way to indicate his faith in the young man's talent.

In the 1890s, the decade that coincided with Roffredo's twenties, Rome as a capital was culturally provincial compared to London or Paris. These were cities he already knew, and, in any case, he was already drawn to the music recommended to him by his teachers, especially Wagner's *Der Ring des Nibelungen*. He spent the winter of 1893 and the spring of 1894 abroad, first in Berlin and later in Vienna. Today it is easy to overlook, after a century in which two world wars have damaged the respect for German culture in much of the West, what a high regard it previously enjoyed among educated people. Before 1914, not only the spoken language, and an acquaintance with the writings of Goethe, Schiller, and Heine, but an awareness of the German contributions to philosophy, Classical studies, and archaeology, the sciences, and art history, were part of any well-stocked mind. It seems that Roffredo's few months' residence in Berlin and Vienna was devoted to broadening his horizons in this way, since he used them to immerse himself in German music, read the German poets, and study the philosophy of Schopenhauer. Tangentially, he developed an interest in Hinduism that led him to study the ancient Indian text *The Ramayana*, with a view to making it the basis for a three-part music drama.[29] In this he may have been inspired by Wagner's use not only of the medieval *Nibelungenlied*, but also of the far earlier Norse *Eddas* and *Sagas*, in the creation of *Der Ring des Nibelungen*.

Between 1895 and 1900, Roffredo's chosen career gained momentum with the composition, publication, and first public performances of a number of instrumental and orchestral works.[30] Onorato entertained great hopes for his son's success as a composer. Since Roffredo had no specific role in the management of the family estates, and since his father encouraged him, there was nothing to counter his conviction that he would have to move abroad if he were to achieve recognition outside Italy. Composition required solitude, but a career as a composer required wider fields. As the century drew to its close, and his younger brothers set off on their chosen paths – Livio to China, Gelasio to New York – Roffredo prepared to move to Paris. Soon, only Leone, Giovanella, and ten-year-old Michelangelo remained.

In 1900 – that terrible and portentous year for Italy, in which King Umberto was assassinated – Leone reached the age of thirty-one. He stood to inherit the family title and all that it entailed, yet he still had no clear-cut function, no definite job to do. Onorato held the reins of management, his authority absolute and undiminished. Given Leone's penchant for long periods of uninterrupted reading and writing, this

4·7
The only girl: Giovanella Caetani.

may have suited him, but perhaps it was not necessarily good for him as a future duke. He had set up a study for himself at Cisterna, and now spent months at a time there, alone with his books, striving for a vision of Islamic civilization as a whole. He had also begun to collect the manuscripts that would enable him to sift fact from fiction concerning the life of the Prophet Mohammed. The outline of a multivolume work on the Islamic world was taking shape, a project to which he envisaged devoting the rest of his life.

One spring day in 1901, a party of young aristocrats from Rome arrived at Cisterna by motor car, and asked to be allowed to picnic at

Ninfa. Among them was twenty-year-old Vittoria Colonna, the elder daughter of Prince Marc'Antonio Colonna, the head of a family with which the Caetani had clashed repeatedly over the centuries. Leone joined the picnic – and his life changed forever. Vittoria was a pretty and vivacious girl, who loved to be entertained, while Leone was dedicated to his work, meditative even at his most active. It was an immediate attraction of opposites, but perhaps the more compelling for that. Leone and Vittoria were engaged within a fortnight. Amidst the splendour of the Palazzo Colonna picture gallery, they married on 20 June 1901 – the first marriage between the two families since 1560.

With a new Prince and Princess of Teano in residence at Palazzo Caetani, the place recaptured something of the gaiety it had enjoyed when Onorato and Ada were young, and such high-spirited events as "a steeplechase of ladies" over towel horses and piles of bedding were held in the vast ballroom.[31] Leone was charmed out of his austerity to become the host at parties where once again the aristocratic youth of Rome danced and dined the nights away. He kept a scrapbook during the early years of his marriage in which to record these occasions, and similar events in other grand houses. One entry from 1903 describes a roller-skating party at Palazzo Caetani, when the ballroom was cleared for skating, and a lavish banquet was held in the adjacent dining room. All the Caetani brothers had been brought up to enjoy a good party, and at Christmas time, when everyone was home, there are glimpses of Roffredo accompanying the carols on the piano, and Gelasio "leading a cotillion with great energy at three in the morning." For a time, Leone and Vittoria were Rome's gilded couple: rich and titled, handsome and glamorous.

Leone was not the first of the Caetani siblings to marry; that honour went to Giovanella, who had married Baron Albéric Grenier, at that point the Belgian ambassador to Italy, on 17 February 1900. Their son, Eric, was born in Rome on 31 August 1901 – the first grandchild for Onorato and Ada. The second was Leone and Vittoria's son, Onorato, born on 24 April 1902. Both little boys were healthy and bright,[32] and they seemed to render even more improbable the curse hurled at the Caetani by "Pio Nono" thirty years before.

When in Rome, Leone, Vittoria, and "Onoratino" lived at Palazzo Caetani, with the duke and duchess, Michelangelo and his tutor, and any other members of the family who happened to be in residence at a given moment. The Greniers were often there (though less often after the baron's posting to Madrid in 1904), and the presence of interesting guests to luncheon or dinner was still a frequent occurrence. In a memoir published half a century later, Vittoria left a vivid portrayal of life at Palazzo Caetani, which she considered a bleak and depressing residence. Some aspects of the Caetani ménage were unconventional: the generally relaxed view of time, which meant that meals were seldom taken at regular intervals, but once begun, went on for hours, and the dietary idiosyncrasies that marked each person's place at table with assorted bottles and jars. Leone was not prepared to confront his father over the fact that he and Vittoria were given bedrooms on separate floors, nor about the chill that pervaded the palace because the duke, ever conscious of expenditure, refused to heat it.[33] As Leone's studies gradually exerted their old fascination, Vittoria, an intelligent woman despite her love of the social whirl, found herself increasingly left alone. She had relatives in England, and began to find frequent excuses to visit them, taking little Onorato with her.

Volume 1 of Leone's *Annali dell'Islam* was published, to immense acclaim, in 1905. It was awarded the Royal Prize of twenty-five thousand lire by the Accademia Nazionale dei Lincei, a tremendous honour in itself, but an even greater one considering that this prize was presented only once every five years. The effect, not surprisingly, was to confirm in Leone the desire to move on to the next volume. The sense of dissatisfaction that had arisen between him and Vittoria settled into habit. But from the autumn of 1907, when five-year-old Onoratino caught measles on a visit to cousins in Scotland, the situation took a tragic turn. From this point onwards, Leone's letters to Ada and other members of the family mention the child's problems with hearing and coordination, the operations on adenoids and tonsils, suggesting that the illness may have had serious consequences. No one at that time knew how devastating measles could be, or suspected it, given that most children suffered no ill effects. For Leone and Vittoria, their son's sudden difficulties were an added source of tension in an already strained relationship. Nor was it helped by Leone's decision to enter politics. In 1908 he was elected as a member for Rome to the Camera dei Deputati, or Lower House, where his socialist views soon provoked the ire of conservative colleagues and the derision of the popular press. As his life became increasingly beset by demands he could neither fulfill nor abandon, he increasingly took refuge in his studies.

The other siblings, meanwhile, were each pursuing their respective aims in foreign parts. Livio, having survived his adventurous posting to Peking, was sent to Belgrade, an altogether quieter spot, where as secretary of the legation he was made a knight of the Crown of Italy. In 1903 he was transferred to London, a capital he knew well, where he had relatives. This was perhaps his most enjoyable posting, but it lasted only two years before he was sent to Addis Ababa, in what was then called Abyssinia, where the stirrings of Italian colonial ambition were already causing problems. While there, he financed an expedition to the little-known interior of the country, revealing that his taste for adventure was far from spent.[34]

Gelasio's love of travel and the outdoor life was well served by his move to the American West. Having graduated from Columbia as an Engineer of Mines, he joined the Bunker Hill and Sullivan mining consortium in Idaho. Increasingly he was drawn to research metallurgy, and was sent by his company to investigate the process of ore extraction and refining in Alaska, Mexico, and California. Ever observant and inventive, he improved the company's existing mining and smelting methods and created new ones, work that culminated in the construction of an entire mill for the concentration of ores, designed to his own specifications.[35]

However much he enjoyed his work, part of Gelasio's mind was always reserved for projects relating to the Caetani estates. Between 1903 and 1910, these were principally two: how to organize the thousands of documents relating to the history of his family; and what could be done to improve conditions at Ninfa and the marshlands around it. Long journeys and free evenings were employed in designing and sketching, in recording his thoughts, and in writing innumerable family letters, often illustrated with drawings. The fruits of all this would only become apparent years later, but it was essential groundwork, made possible at this stage when Gelasio was far from home, because so much thought had already gone into it. His great ally in anything concerning Ninfa was Ada, who had long since realized that she and Onorato had done all they could at Fogliano, and needed another gardening challenge.

Giovanella was also an inveterate correspondent. She wrote to both her parents and all her brothers regularly, around the edges of a busy diplomatic life, much of it lived on the move. Her daughter, Livia, was born in 1906, but whether this baby and her brother, Eric, accompanied their parents when Albéric Grenier was posted to Peking in 1907 is unknown. Giovanella had become a fine photographer; whether her children accompanied her or not, her photographic apparatus certainly did, and some of the results survive.[36]

In Rome, the idea that a member of his venerable family could also be a composer may have meant that Roffredo was taken less seriously than he deserved to be. In this respect, as he had hoped, Paris was a welcome change. He met that great musical patron, Countess Greffulhe (who already knew Ada and Onorato socially, and was a friend of Giovanella's through the Belgian court), at Bayreuth in 1902. From then on, he had the best possible entrée to the Parisian musical scene. He was soon introduced by the countess to the Princesse de Polignac, and was invited by both women to appear as composer-pianist at their recitals.[37] His work reached a larger audience when his first Symphonic Prelude was performed as part of the Lamoureux concert series in December 1902. From then on, he began to enjoy modest success. In almost every year until 1909, one or another of his compositions was performed, either in Paris, or in Brussels, London, Monte Carlo, New York, Chicago, or Boston. In 1905, for example, no less a personage than Pietro Mascagni conducted the third and fourth movements of Roffredo's Suite pour Orchestre, op. 10, again in the Lamoureux series. His work was well reviewed in *Le Figaro*, the *New York Times*, and other leading papers. Back in Rome, concert organizers also registered the fact that his reputation was growing. His Symphonic Preludes were performed on 14 April 1907 at the Teatro Comunale Argentina, only steps from Palazzo Caetani. The pride and delight of Onorato and Ada on that occasion can only be imagined.

Of course, acquiring a reputation as an up-and-coming composer automatically led to a degree of speculation about Roffredo. The year 1909 saw the arrival in Paris of Sergei Diaghilev's Ballets Russes, jointly sponsored by Countess Greffulhe and the Princesse de Polignac. The Russian impresario was a notorious gossip, and the origin of the allegation that Roffredo was not the godson, but the illegitimate son, of Franz Liszt, has been attributed to him, and to his musical collaborator, Igor Stravinsky, who apparently repeated it[38] around the salons of the French capital. Whether Roffredo himself was aware of this rumour will never be known, but what has already been said about the marriage of Onorato and Ada should be sufficient to disprove it. Further skepticism arises from the incontrovertible evidence of photographs, which reveal that not only had Roffredo inherited his father's great height; he also had his father's ears.[39]

In 1908, Roffredo began work on a music drama on a theme that had occupied his thoughts for some time: the story of Hypatia, the brilliant Neoplatonist philosopher who lived in fourth-century Egypt and was massacred by a mob for her advanced ideas. He completed the libretto in French within a year, and set to work on the Italian version. A personable, intelligent, and titled man is unlikely to be allowed by his friends to work *all* the time: what else did Roffredo do in Paris, when not composing? He frequented the theatre, the opera, and the gatherings held at the British embassy, where his uncle by marriage, James Lindsay, the 26th Earl of Crawford (married to Ada's sister Emily), was ambassador. He knew Prince Emmanuel and Prince Antoine Bibesco through Countess Greffulhe: all three attended the wedding of the Greffulhes' only daughter, Elaine, to the Duke of Guise at the church of La Madeleine in November 1904, when – according to the press the following day – the still-beautiful countess outshone the bride. Neither was Roffredo always in Paris: he travelled, visiting his

Lindsay cousins in England and Scotland, he returned often to Rome to spend time with his parents, and was welcome in the homes of friends, especially at "I Tatti," the villa belonging to art connoisseur and historian Bernard Berenson and his wife, Mary, just outside Florence.

He was also, inevitably, the veteran of several love affairs, which for one reason or another had not led to marriage. These had left him disillusioned about the prospect of meeting a woman with whom he could spend his life, but resigned to making the best of his otherwise enviable circumstances. Not until his meeting with Marguerite Chapin, following that evening at the theatre in the spring of 1911, did Roffredo's world come alive for him in the way he had longed for. By then he had celebrated his fortieth birthday, and his reputation as a composer was in the ascendant. With his engagement to Marguerite, his inner life was transformed – but there was still an obstacle to be overcome en route to matrimony.

5

A STRAINED COURTSHIP WITH A HAPPY OUTCOME

Getting married is usually a simple matter. Two people fall in love, become engaged, and as long as no legal impediment bars the way, marry as and when it suits them. For most people, this held true in 1911 too – but as Marguerite soon learned, marrying a prince was different, and there was a matter of protocol to be satisfied before she and Roffredo Caetani, Prince of Bassiano, could make their wedding plans.

Despite his having proposed to Marguerite and been accepted, Roffredo – even at the age of forty – needed his father's consent to marry. Since the Duke of Sermoneta's word was law, filial duty demanded no less, but just as compelling was Roffredo's situation, as a younger son, of complete economic dependency. The Caetani patrimony belonged entirely to Duke Onorato, and while their father lived, Roffredo and his brothers each received an allowance drawn from the rents and revenues generated by the family estates. The laws of inheritance prevailing in Italy meant that, on Duke Onorato's death, the greater part of this wealth would pass to Leone, Prince of Teano. This system derived from ancient Frankish Salic law, and aimed to keep ancestral lands and possessions intact between one generation and the next.

The political and economic changes that took place in the nineteenth century meant that, by the end of it, if not before, the estates of many noble European families were no longer as productive as they had once been – or perhaps, too, that what they produced did not go as far as it once had. Sons other than the first-born depended on allowances that permitted them a standard of living appropriate to their rank, but in social circles where a life of ease and personal fulfillment was the aim, the idea that a younger son might earn his living in one of the professions or in business was highly unusual. The stipend of a younger son carried no automatic right of increase on marriage, so that what provided a comfortable living for one had eventually to do for two, and then for three – or more. In practice, the unwritten law for younger sons intent on maintaining their standard of living after marriage was "marry money."[1]

Had Roffredo wished to "marry money," he could by now have done so on several occasions. Two known relationships – with the beautiful, brilliant, but unstable American heiress Gladys Deacon in 1904,[2] and with the music-loving Belgian Countess Adelaide Spoelberch de Louwenjoul (a friend of Giovanella's from the court in Brussels, where both were royal ladies-in-waiting) in 1908[3] – would have improved his financial position, but in neither case had Roffredo been convinced that the woman in question possessed the character he was looking for. In the person of Marguerite, his ideal was realized. Quite how Roffredo managed to combine his proposal with explaining to her that he needed his father's consent to act on it was probably not the easiest of tasks, but Marguerite, having fallen in love with him as he had with her, accepted this as the essential formality it was.

Through ancestry and inherited wealth, Marguerite's place in the American "aristocracy" was indisputable, but Roffredo knew that Onorato would want legal assurance of this, so she at once wrote to her trustees in New York for the documents needed to confirm her identity and financial standing. Confident that these would arrive quickly, Roffredo wrote to his father to pour out his feelings and request formal permission to go ahead, asking too that he be permitted to introduce Marguerite to the rest of the family. In his letter, he placed much emphasis on the similarity between her tastes and his own, "not only in art and literature, but in her way of life," and asked for his father's guidance, saying – rashly, under the circumstances – that he would do nothing without Onorato's approval.[4] The duke's reply was immediate, but cautious: Roffredo could introduce Marguerite to the family if he wished. He himself was unwilling to meet her until he knew more about her. An American! What was her background? What was her moral character? And could the documents attesting to her independent means – when they arrived – be relied upon? As to consent – he was unable to give it until he was satisfied on these three points, and certainly not before he had made her acquaintance.[5] It was a classic chicken-and-egg situation, not helped by the duke's apparent suspicion that any unmarried American woman living in Europe was likely to be hunting a title, a fortune, or both.

In the face of this, Roffredo's thought of inviting Marguerite to Rome evaporated. Besides, there were rumours of cholera in Rome, and the summer heat would be at its worst. Inviting his mother to Paris was similarly out of the question. He knew that his aunt Emily, from the unimpeachable heights of her position at the British embassy, might well try to persuade Ada of Marguerite's unsuitability, either on the grounds of being American, or because of the independent life she led.[6] Marguerite herself, alarmed by the prospect of intense scrutiny by Roffredo's parents or by the terrifying Countess Crawford, favoured a less-formal introduction. Neutral ground seemed preferable, a relaxed setting in which she could get to know Roffredo's family gradually, while she awaited the documents that would put all to rights.

Fortunately, the cholera scare had prompted Ada and Giovanella to plan some time in their favourite resort: St Moritz, in the Engadine. Marguerite knew this part of Switzerland well from her holidays at Sils Maria, a few kilometres away. Surrounded by mountains and famed for its health-giving climate and thermal baths, St Moritz was more popular in summer with the English upper classes than with the Roman aristocracy, and thus ensured a degree of discretion. Ada and Nella would be staying at the Hotel Engadiner Kulm (still operating today as the Kulm Hotel), and Roffredo helped Marguerite to reserve rooms there for herself and her lady companion. It was the oldest and best-appointed of the town's grand hotels, set in ninety-nine acres of lakeside gardens. By developing the ski slopes and the famous Cresta bobsled run, the Engadiner Kulm's owners had created a winter sporting season, so that the place now functioned all year round, attracting an international crowd of the titled and rich. The excellence of its dining room was legendary; it had a good library, and, for anyone wanting to explore the area, boat trips, excursions by carriage, and guided walks could be arranged.

While most of Europe sweltered (the summer of 1911 was one of the hottest and driest of the twentieth century), St Moritz was one of the continent's more agreeable places to pass the time. By mid-August, Ada and Nella, Marguerite and her lady companion, were all settled at the Hotel Engadiner Kulm. For propriety's sake, Roffredo stayed at the little chalet he had bought some years earlier at Pontresina, five kilometres away, proposing to make the short journey to St Moritz daily by carriage. Onorato remained in Rome with nineteen-year-old Michelangelo (the only one of his sons who did not enjoy good health), whom Ada had left "green and pale" from the stifling heat.[7] The duke had made no commitment to come to St Moritz.

The redoubtable Ada would keep up a stream of letters to her husband and sons during the next few weeks. The subject of Roffredo's new relationship was naturally a compelling theme. On 19 August she dashed off a note to Livio at his diplomatic post in St Petersburg, to convey a brief first impression of Marguerite: "Weren't you surprised to hear of Roffy's idea. I had made up my mind that he would remain a bachelor. I have seen the girl. She seems very gentle and good-tempered and intelligent. I fancy Father will like her even more than Adelaide." (This comment referred to Countess Spoelberch de Louwenjoul, with whom Roffredo had been involved a few years earlier.)

Ada was sixty-five years old in 1911, her energy only slightly diminished from the era when she had hiked, camped, and hunted all over the Caetani estates and the moors of Scotland, usually with some of her children in tow. Mountain climbing and ballooning were by now long in the past, but she still maintained her stud farm in the Pontine Marshes and rode the horses she bred. Marguerite was unlikely to have met many duchesses who shared such a robust appreciation of the outdoor life. Ada was still a handsome woman, with a forthright look that conveyed interest, but did not – at least, not yet – invite intimacy. Giovanella offered the possibility of greater closeness, partly because she and Marguerite were roughly the same age (Nella was thirty-four), and partly because she too was an avid reader with a gift for languages. The Greniers had returned from Peking and were now based in Rome, which enabled Nella to spend much of her time with her parents. At six feet tall, she towered over Marguerite, but she was sensitive to the effect of her height on others, and in conversation bent down solicitously to catch what was said.

For those who were taking cures, the daily routine in St Moritz centred on the baths, situated by the lake. Those who were there merely for a change of scene enjoyed the clear air and the views. The "Hof," or upper part of the town, provided the setting for the fashionable parade past shops and restaurants, the daily meetings and greetings that were the life of the resort, the taking of coffee and pastries and ices, the leisurely study of passersby. By early September, after a fortnight of meals together, excursions, lakeside concerts, and evening strolls in the hotel gardens, the members of Roffredo's party were getting along well. There were some unusual diversions: a guest at the hotel had brought along a Bengal tiger cub the size of a mastiff, and one evening everyone gathered in a salon to watch it play, the handler never letting go of its leather lead.[8] But as the days passed, the documents from New York did not arrive, and the silence from Rome remained absolute. Ada wrote again to Livio (by now on leave in Rome). This time it was a long letter marked "Private," which she began by confessing that "We are all three so curious to know if Father discusses with you and Miche the new idea of Roffredo & if he shows you all our letters." She then went on to describe what was becoming an awkward situation, not least for Marguerite:

> Roffredo always impetuous has gone much too far to be able to retire, so Father's delay in coming to see her is useless. She has not yet had an answer about all the details of her fortune though she wrote nearly a month ago. She is now going to telegraph to hasten her bankers who are her trustees. Roffredo is very distressed at Fathers [*sic*] not coming as he would like to be married in London, very privately ... in November or December ... We all here are in a very difficult & false position especially the girl

> herself who is getting thinner and thinner. Nella declares that when she brushed her gown the other day she could not feel anything under it!!! It seemed empty.

The discrepancy between the "jolly" and intellectually assured Miss Chapin of the lunch parties in her Paris apartment and the visibly waning, less-confident Marguerite depicted in Ada's letters can only be attributed to the fact that her situation was indeed becoming deeply unnerving. And yet, her essential character and charm shone through, and made a favourable impression. Ada went on to record the conclusions reached by herself and Nella after nearly three weeks in Marguerite's company. Sometimes their views were at variance with Roffredo's own, as when he apparently described Marguerite to his mother and sister as "a sweet-tempered girl with no will of her own." "Instead," Ada went on,

> we both think that she is unselfish, tactful, loving, & an intellectual mind, but that she has lived too long with only dependents not to have a strong will of her own ... We are trying to persuade Roffy not to think that she only wishes to obey. If he wants to change things he must do so very slowly and carefully.

Ada and Nella were initially surprised by Marguerite's simple way of dressing, which was so very different from the elaborate gowns and jewellery worn by upper-class women in Rome. Ada was somewhat puzzled by her son's attraction to the unassuming Marguerite, yet sought to be objective:

> She is very ladylike but insignificant, the last woman one would have guessed he would have chosen. She is not at all an adventuress as Father fears. She is now very modest & shy, only every now & then showing americanisms. I fancy however as Roffy's wife she might get to show herself airs. I fancy you, Father and Miche will all like her, though of course one would have liked

> him to choose somebody of more importance. She is alas! very delicate & highly nervous, very ready to laugh and to listen.[9]

Presumably Ada – born into one noble family and married into another – equated "importance" with the possession of a title. A more appreciative assessment came from Nella, in a long letter to her eldest brother, Leone, who was resting from the strain of political life by taking a cure in Lausanne. She found much to admire in her new acquaintance:

> And now I will tell you about Marguerite. She and I are becoming friends, as we have seen each other every day for nearly a month. She is the least American of all the Americans I know. She is a being possessed of an extraordinary sensitivity, very affectionate, intelligent, with a great sweetness of manner (*câline*) – but underneath her sweetness I discern a will that is firm and not easily influenced by the arguments of others. Her great passion is reading, she always has a book in her hand – and the books she has with her are always very serious, never novels or decadent authors. She loves music very much, she sings, and has a lovely contralto voice, she doesn't care much for the fast social life, but prefers to be surrounded by a group of close friends sharing intellectual interests.

It is interesting to note the contrast between Count Kessler's references to "the beautiful Miss Chapin" of only a few months earlier, and Nella's evaluation of Marguerite's appearance and manner:

> The first impression she makes in the physical sense may be a disappointment. You may find her unsophisticated, over-sensitive, insignificant – but she is one of those people that, the more you see them, the more they please you. I now actually find her pretty. Mama has had the very same impression as I. All the things I have told you about her have been gleaned bit by bit in the

> course of our numerous conversations. I believe she may be just the right person for a man like our dear Roffi, so much so that there is never a gesture, never a word that jars. There remains only her American accent which lessens when she is feeling shy but is more pronounced when she is talking one to one. I think she is a bit extravagant, something that won't suit our Roffi's spendthrift ways one bit. Let's hope that the experience of life as a couple and later of children will teach them economy.

Nella shared the condescending view of Americans typical of her class and era, and admitted to having been "at first very surprised and disappointed in the fact that Roffi had chosen an American." But after nearly a month in Marguerite's company, Nella could assure Leone that "now I am convinced that he has chosen well and I believe that if they steer their boat well, they can be happy." She then went on to the matter that was so deeply important to the family, especially to Onorato: Roffredo's career as a composer, and his current project, his opera, *Hypatia*. "I spoke to her about Roffi's great work and she has assured me that her greatest wish was to press on with it and see Papa's dream realised." This commitment on Marguerite's part set the final seal on Nella's regard for her prospective sister-in-law.[10]

On 12 September, the documents from Marguerite's trustees finally arrived, and Roffredo set out for Rome to see his father. The interview took place the following day, and (as Onorato later confided to Leone) was an emotional occasion. Roffredo was

> convinced that he will be happy with this girl: he had with him sufficient information regarding the respectability of her family, the girl's moral standing and her fortune … and he asked for my consent, which there could have been no further reason whatever to deny him, from the moment that the three conditions indicated were verified. And now if there is a personal God, one who would heed the supplication of the good and honest, may he listen to my plea, which comes from the depths of my heart, that Roffredo may be perfectly happy.[11]

Roffredo stopped long enough to send a telegram bearing the joyful news to Marguerite before dashing back to St Moritz. On 15 September, the long weeks of uncertainty over, Marguerite condensed her feelings into a brief but moving note to her future father-in-law:

> My dear Father,
> Since Roffredo has telegraphed me the words containing my happiness – that you are willing to accept me as your daughter – I think I may call you thus. With the help of my great love for him I hope to find the way to your heart and I am impatient to show you the love and gratitude that I feel in mine for you.
>
> As it was music that brought Roffredo and me together so my dearest wish is to make his music the greatest interest of my life. I hope so much to see you very soon so that you may begin to love me as quickly as possible and believe me your loving daughter,
>
> Marguerite[12]

Now the letters welcoming Marguerite into the family, and hers in acknowledgment, flew back and forth: first from Leone, then from Michelangelo and Leone's wife, Vittoria. In a humorous exchange with Leone, who confided that the Caetani often greeted one another by rubbing noses, "like Eskimos," Marguerite replied: "The habit of which you speak as prevailing in your family is highly approved of by me and I am most impatient to meet you to put it into practice at once." She also admitted that it was "a most unexpected and truly deep joy to me to become one of a family where judging from those I already know – and love [*sic*] I shall love all as if they had always been my own."[13] It was this aspect of Marguerite's happiness – the sense of having come home – that Ada mentioned to her eldest son in a letter of 17 September: "She has most intense feeling & is so happy to belong to a family she can love. That is what she has missed so much till now." Ada herself had clearly warmed to Marguerite. It was not simply that she was "always running about on little errands for me," or that it was "curious how much her and Roffy's tastes are alike"; it was, as she went on to relate, Marguerite's personality that had won her over:

"Her German dragon of a *dame de compagnie* adores her, says that everybody who knows her feels her charm."[14] Relieved that the matter was finally settled, Leone in reply expressed the view (perhaps ruefully, reflecting on his own experience) that Roffredo had made "a very good choice, much better than a silly worldly goose full of money and nonsense."[15]

Any written comment from Roffredo on the subject of his fiancée had up to now been lacking, but on 20 September, now officially engaged, he replied to Leone's letter of congratulation with a letter of his own. In the absence of any similar observation from Edouard Vuillard, during the period in which he was infatuated with Marguerite, or from Count Kessler, who clearly found her company delightful, it is notable that Roffredo stresses her shyness, mentioning the "*feroce timiditá*" that made her "a person it takes some time to get to know. Since she has always lived alone she has the tendency to be somewhat reserved and silent – like Livio." But, he went on, "when you get to know her – she possesses a most noble soul, and is full of altruism, and is such pleasant company for her great naturalness."[16]

The summer season was now almost at its end, and in St Moritz the hotels were closing; the Hotel Engadiner Kulm was the only one still open. Ada and Nella prepared to move on to Aix-les-Bains, where they would each take a cure (for rheumatism and kidney stones, respectively). Marguerite and Roffredo would stop briefly there en route to Paris, as it was at Aix-les-Bains that Onorato would finally join the party and meet Marguerite. This occasion took place on 24 September at the Regina Hotel. The immensely tall duke, with his white beard and darkened spectacles, was an imposing figure, but Marguerite saw in his height and features the origin of Roffredo's, and experienced an immediate rapport with him. For the first time she saw Roffredo's parents together, and could appreciate the closeness of their relationship, as well as the banter and jokes that were a feature of it. As for Onorato, as he assured Leone by letter the following day, "The impression Marguerite has made upon me is of the best [*ottima*]. Time will bear out the prospect that our Roffy may be happy."[17]

Once back in Paris, Marguerite and Roffredo issued the formal announcement of their engagement, which appeared on the front page of the popular daily *Gil Blas*, on 1 October. In the days that followed, they settled the date and place where they would be married: Monday, 30 October, in the Queen's Chapel of St James's Palace in London. Neither of them wanted a lavish wedding, much less the lengthy guest list that a ceremony in Paris would force upon them. The only guests on 30 October were to be family members who wished to travel to London. They had also decided to continue to live in Paris for half the year, and at Palazzo Caetani in Rome for much of the other half. Roffredo's apartment there would suit them well enough, since the simple life they planned to lead required neither a grand reception room nor servants' quarters. In Paris, they would live at Marguerite's garden apartment at 11, rue de l'Université, and Roffredo gave notice on the lease of his flat at 39, rue d'Artois.

Count Kessler was only one of the friends who were surprised by the engagement, confiding to his diary on 17 October the news passed on by José Maria Sert – prematurely, as it happened – that "the beautiful Chapin has married prince Caetani."[18] He went on to recount the reason for an otherwise puzzling event: the sale of Edouard Vuillard's painting *The Library*, which had been installed in Marguerite's apartment only six months earlier.[19] Vuillard learned of Marguerite's forthcoming marriage on returning home from holiday at the end of September. Given his feelings for her, the news came as a shock, but the note he received from her a day later, saying that the painting would shortly be sent for auction, came as an even bigger one. She gave no reason for seemingly rejecting a work which had initially pleased her, but according to Kessler, it was Roffredo who did not like it, nor the other "wall decorations" by Vuillard and Bonnard.[20] In the end, *The Library* was in fact the only work sent to the Hôtel Druout, where it was bought by two of Vuillard's friends and returned to his studio. Much to his credit, the episode did not tarnish the painter's friendship with Marguerite. She continued to commission work from him, and he would remain part of her circle until his death in 1940.

In mid-October, barely a month after Roffredo's momentous interview with his father, Marguerite and Roffredo left Paris for London. There they joined Nella at the Ritz Hotel in Piccadilly, on the edge of Green Park. The days passed in a blur of dress fittings and shopping, luncheons, teas, and dinners. Roffredo's English and Scottish relatives together formed an enormous clan, only some of whom Marguerite would meet before the wedding. One day she lunched with Leone's wife, the ultra-chic Vittoria, who was on one of her frequent visits to her Norfolk grandparents. On 26 October Leone himself appeared, tall and bearded in the fashion of King George V, and presumably greeted Marguerite in the customary Caetani manner. Onorato and Ada, accompanied by Michelangelo, arrived the following day to take up their suite at the Ritz. Only Livio, back in St Petersburg, and Gelasio, in California, were absent. The haste of the wedding arrangements made it impossible for Gelasio to attend the ceremony, but he sent his heartiest good wishes and a cheque for his share in the silver table service for twelve that Nella had organized as the siblings' collective wedding gift. Their other gift, the publication in facsimile of a document entitled *Origine dei Caetani e suoi stati*, dating from a Caetani wedding of 1642, was very likely Gelasio's idea, given his consuming interest in the family's genealogy.[21]

On Saturday, 28 October, the duke and duchess were hosts of a dinner at the Ritz in honour of their son and his bride-to-be. The guests were drawn mainly from Roffredo's extended family, the only representatives of Marguerite's family being her Chapin and Gibert uncles and their respective wives. Following the canapés and consommé, the company enjoyed a formal dinner in the hotel's best French culinary tradition, the menu of which was prettily engraved in sepia on cream card:

Suprême du Sole á la Ritz
Timbale de Poulet Régence avec Riz á la Crème
Selle de Pré-Salé aux Primeurs avec Pommes Fondants
Soufflé de Jambon Muscovite

Perdreux á la Broche avec Salade
Mousse Reine Mary avec petits-fours
Profiteroles Parmesanes

All of this was matched by fine wines: a Saarbourg Moselle and a Pontet Canat 1899, with a Mumm 1900 for the toasts, Martínez port to follow, and finally, liqueurs and brandy. Leone had some of those present sign the back of his copy of the menu: besides Marguerite's signature, large and sweeping, and Roffredo's, small and spiky, there appear those of the Caetanis, of Ada's brother Major Lionel Bootle-Wilbraham and his daughter Evelyn (who together with Nella would be a bridesmaid), and of various members of the Lindsay family.[22]

Marguerite spent her last night as an unmarried woman at the home of Robert and Adèle Chapin at 34 Kensington Square. Robert Chapin was to give her away, and so the next day he accompanied her in the carriage that took her to St James's Palace and the Queen's Chapel. This handsome little building had been designed by Inigo Jones (and later remodelled by Sir Christopher Wren) as a Roman Catholic chapel for the use of foreign diplomats accredited to the Court of St James. Queen Henrietta Maria, the wife of Charles I, is also known to have worshipped there. Since the Restoration, being married in the chapel had required a royal dispensation: in the case of Marguerite and Roffredo, the intermediary in obtaining this was likely to have been Archbishop Bourne of Westminster, who conducted the marriage ceremony and was a friend of Ada and Onorato.[23]

The report of the wedding that appeared in the *New York Times* the next day claimed that "The hour and place of the wedding was kept secret even from friends, some of whom had been wrongly informed as to the time and address." Perhaps the usual cadre of press reporters was among the misinformed, as no description of Marguerite's dress or details of the ceremony were included in the account cabled back to New York. On 30 October, Marguerite's Gibert and Chapin relatives were the only guests seated on her side of the aisle; on Roffredo's were the members of his own family, together with his Lindsay cousins, Lord and Lady Balcarres, Ada's great-nephew the 3rd Earl of Lathom and her brother Major Bootle-Wilbraham, and the Marchesa de Francavilla, the wife of the Italian ambassador.

As Marguerite entered the Queen's Chapel on the arm of Robert Chapin, shortly to emerge as the Princess di Bassiano – she vanishes from documentary view and does not reappear for another fifteen months. She and Roffredo covered their tracks well: nothing has come to light to indicate where they spent their honeymoon, nor when they returned to Paris. To hazard a guess, it might be that, after a few more days in London, they travelled northwards to the country seats of the Bootle-Wilbrahams: Lathom Park, near Ormskirk in Lancashire, and Rode Hall in Cheshire (where Marguerite would have seen the family theatre and magnificent collection of porcelain described by Ada during some lakeside stroll in St Moritz). They may even have gone on to the Crawford estate at Balcarres in Fife, taking in Edinburgh on the way. All this would have made practical, familial, geographical sense – but there is no evidence for it.

It is also reasonable to suppose that Marguerite spent her first Christmas as Roffredo's wife at Palazzo Caetani in Rome. There, the couple would have celebrated the holiday with Onorato and Ada, Nella and her children, Leone, Vittoria, and "Onoratino," and Michelangelo. A visit to Roffredo's aunt Ersilia Caetani, still a practising archaeologist in her seventies and living nearby at Palazzo Lovatelli-Caetani, initiated another friendship. Marguerite may even have had the pleasure of meeting Livio, once again home on leave. If so, yet another tall figure would have bent to kiss her hand – and perform that other, less-formal greeting – but this one had an exquisite gentleness of manner and a faintly distracted air. Perhaps it was hard for Marguerite to imagine such a diffident and studious man as the hero of the Boxer Rebellion, but his wry humour endeared him to her. Even Leone's wife, Vittoria, gregarious as she was, considered Livio her favourite brother-in-law.[24]

Has anyone ever set foot in Rome for the first time and not been overwhelmed by it? Roffredo had described to Marguerite the Eternal City's unique juxtapositions of ancient and modern, but nothing could have prepared her for her first sight of the Colosseum or the

5.1
Palazzo Caetani, Via delle Botteghe Oscure, Rome.

Forum, for the sheer architectonic audacity of the Pantheon or the view of St Peter's and the Castel Sant'Angelo from the other side of the Tiber. Rome was as close to being Roffredo's native city as any could be, given that the Caetani traditionally considered the Pontine Marshes their true home. He knew it intimately, from the Aventine to the Janiculum and Trastevere, from the splendour of Santa Maria Maggiore to Campo di Fiori and the winding alleys of the Ghetto that lay between Palazzo Caetani and the river. He must have enjoyed guiding Marguerite around it, showing her the places and monuments associated with his family. These included *Isola Tiburina*, or "Tiber Island," where the fortress-like San Bartolomeo palace loomed over the water, and the Caetani chapel, in the exquisite small church of Santa Pudenziana. Perhaps, in a lighter vein, he even showed her the ornamental pond in the gardens of the Quirinal Palace, into which, as children, he and his brothers had tossed their friend Prince Victor Emmanuel: now King Victor Emmanuel III.[25]

During the Christmas season of 1911, or on a longer visit in the summer of 1912, Marguerite was taken on a tour of the Caetani estates. These lay roughly fifty kilometres southwest of Rome, between the Lepini mountains and the sea. Reaching them involved a journey by sturdy carriage or car and made over several days, so extensive was the area to be crossed and the wealth of sights to be taken in. Driving south along the Via Appia Antica, dead straight and lined with umbrella pines, travellers were soon deep in a flat and marshy landscape, on a road elevated above the reeds. These were the famous Pontine Marshes, an area of the former Papal States measuring some eighty thousand hectares and rendered almost uninhabitable over the centuries by the prevalence of mosquito-borne malaria. Depending on the season, it was also alive with flowering plants and migratory birds not seen elsewhere.

Becoming acquainted with the region that had shaped the lives of the Caetani for generations brought Marguerite new insights into the history of the family that was now hers. The first ducal residence on the route was the palace at Cisterna, where Ada's stud farm was located. Since about 1900 it had also been Leone's country residence, where he secluded himself to work, and where he had written the *Annali dell'Islam*. Fogliano, situated on a coastal lagoon, boasted the garden created by Onorato and Ada, and the country-style house with its huge veranda, colloquially known as the "*villa inglese*," surrounded by the "Congo." The use of bamboo and ornamental grasses among the huge beeches and palms enchanted Marguerite, as did the climbing roses brought by Ada from England decades before.

If her visit to Fogliano showed Marguerite the family's creative side, the castle of Sermoneta revealed another aspect. High on a rocky crag, this was the medieval Caetani stronghold and seat of the dukedom, towering over the tiled roofs of the town strung out along a ridge, with precipitous descents on every side. The nearby hill towns of Norma, Norba, and Bassiano (from which Roffredo's title derived) were little worlds in themselves, their ways of life, based on agriculture and cattle-rearing, scarcely altered since medieval times. From the ramparts of Norma, Marguerite could look westward over the marshes, stretching away to the silver line on the horizon that was the Tyrrhenian Sea. Below, and in the middle distance, stood an area of ruins: jagged towers, broken walls shrouded in vegetation, and seven roofless churches. This was her first view of Ninfa, the ruined town that would come to play such an important part in her life. Gelasio's engineering works to drain and clear it were already in progress, but as yet the effects were barely noticeable. From afar, and even in its desolate and overgrown state, Ninfa exercised its haunting fascination.

Of all the Caetani possessions, Marguerite most enjoyed Fogliano, the family's second home, so full of childhood memories for Roffredo. Her interest in the garden stirred Ada to relive aloud its transformation from wilderness to unique retreat, while beach and dunes became another source of pleasure, offering protected swimming in the lagoon

5.2
Swimming at Fogliano, 1912: Roffredo, with Giovanella, her husband, Baron Albéric Grenier, and their son, Eric. Did Marguerite take the photograph?

5·3
The Caetani family on the terrace of Palazzo Caetani, December 1912. From left to right: Onorato, Leone, Roffredo, Livio, Giovanella, Gelasio, Michelangelo, Eric (Grenier), "Onoratino," Livia (Grenier), Ada.

and soft sand on which to sunbathe afterwards. In July 1912 Marguerite wrote to Gelasio – whom she had not yet met – describing "a wonderful month at delicious Fogliano which I adore – going in swimming every day and otherwise leading a blissfully lazy life." Meals out of doors and leisurely walks alternated with long stretches of work on *Hypatia* for Roffredo and reading for Marguerite. All the family were there, except for Gelasio, and Marguerite hastened to tell him how much he was missed. Her spontaneous, "American" side seemed to find an outlet in her relationship with this as-yet-unknown brother-in-law, who was so at home in the United States. Gelasio planned to spend the Christmas of 1912 in Rome, passing through London and Paris on the way. On 2 October, with the prospect of finally meeting him in view, Marguerite exclaimed in a letter, "What a joy that in a little over two months you will be knocking on the door of 11, rue de l'Université! – That is to say you will never have time to knock as Roffy and I will be waiting for you in the middle of the street!" The visit, however long it lasted, set in motion a friendship that would survive some rocky episodes in the years ahead.[26]

In the autumn of 1912, Marguerite's stepmother, Cornelia Chapin, and half-sister Katherine crossed the Atlantic to visit her and meet Roffredo. This was a happy experience for all concerned, with a good deal of concert- and theatre-going and a fair amount of entertaining.[27] The apartment at 11, rue de l'Université was beginning to feel a little cramped, since Marguerite and Roffredo enjoyed a full table, but could not comfortably invite more than six people at a time to a meal there. To Onorato, Marguerite described the small dinners "*chez nous*" that included, on one occasion, "the Casati" (the flamboyant Marchesa Luisa Casati and her husband), the society painter Giovanni Boldini, and (despite his earlier prediction that they would not meet again) the poet Gabriele D'Annunzio – a lively group of guests, to be sure. On another, the company consisted of the conductor and composer André Messager, a friend of Roffredo's, and the de Reszkes.[28]

Marguerite and Roffredo returned to St Moritz for part of the Christmas holiday season of 1912. On New Year's day, 1913, Marguerite wrote to Duke Onorato from the Palace Hotel, describing the pleasant time they were having with a group of friends, enjoying the snow and the calm and sunny weather. This holiday was the prelude to momentous news in mid-February, when Marguerite announced to her parents-in-law that she was pregnant. To Onorato, who was naturally delighted and sent reams of advice, she replied:

> I am following your orders absolutely and taking the most ridiculous care of myself – that is to say I only get up for lunch which I take from the sofa in the library and then shortly after I go back to bed again. This regime must apparently keep up until about the middle of March. I read a good deal, someone comes to see me nearly every afternoon, and Roffredo is a devoted angel and the time passes not too slowly ...[29]

This amount of bed rest was customary at the time, but must have been something of a trial for as active and energetic a woman as Marguerite. As a voracious reader, she probably bore it better than many. She was also fortunate in having another focus of attention in the form of Roffredo's music, which she was naturally the first to hear and discuss with him. "Roffredo is working well and happily – I have not yet heard any of the third Act but am promised it in a few days," she wrote to Onorato in February, referring to the progress of *Hypatia*, the Italian text of which had been completed and printed in April 1910. By August 1913, the score was finished, and she reported that "Roffy has finished putting his text *en propre* and is having it typewritten so now he can go back to work on the *partition d'orchestre* with a free mind."[30] Until he began work on *Hypatia* in 1908, Roffredo had written only instrumental works for orchestra, chamber groups, or the piano. His decision to write an opera had marked a change of direction. His choice of the fourth-century philosopher and mathematician as his protagonist suggests that he wanted to make explicit his high regard for the female intellect.[31] He knew many highly educated and accomplished women (his aunt Ersilia Caetani and the Countess Greffulhe being prime examples). Now he had married one – and one, moreover, who was a trained singer – and it is logical to suppose that he sought her views on the work in progress.

Marguerite's professional training made her an able collaborator and critic for her husband, but there must also have been much to discuss concerning current musical developments. The romantic and harmonic traditions in which Roffredo had been trained were being challenged by the idea of atonality devised by Arnold Schoenberg, and by a new appreciation of the primitive and the exotic. In 1909, Diaghilev's Ballets Russes had burst upon the Parisian musical scene, shaking accepted standards of performance art to their foundations. Were Marguerite and Roffredo among the audience at the Théâtre des Champs-Elysées on the evening of 29 May 1913, when – sandwiched between a performance of *Les Sylphides* danced to the music of Chopin, and *La Spectre de la Rose*, performed to Weber's *Invitation to the Dance* – Stravinsky's savage masterpiece *Le Sacre du Printemps* (*The Rite of Spring*) received its premiere? If so, they would have seen the clash between traditional music and the avant-garde personified, as conservative ballet lovers and the partisans of novelty fought one another in the aisles, drowning out the orchestra with shouts of rage and derision.

Fortunately, such periodic violence was confined to the theatres and the streets outside them, far removed from the rue de l'Université and the state of contentment in which Marguerite now found herself. This was a time of fulfillment: she loved, completely and overwhelmingly, and was loved in return. On the brief occasions when Roffredo was away, they wrote daily; to her, he was "Amore mio" or "Carissimo Amore," while she to him was "My own Beloved." Marguerite's feelings had expanded to take in the whole Caetani family. As she wrote to Gelasio, "What a wonderful family it is! Whatever affection the father and mother have for me I return it to them a hundred fold. I love them both with all my heart – What beautiful, rare personalities they are – I really feel as if my own beloved father and mother had come back to me."[32]

The freedom of expression that colours her letters to Onorato and Ada suggests that she had found genuine love and acceptance in her relationships with them. Her reserve vanished, and a childlike affection took over as she became to them "your adoring daughter" or "your most loving daughter, Margherita," who sent them "heaps and heaps and heaps of love." To Onorato she sometimes sent "lots of nose rubbings" or "nose touchings," and when writing to only one of them, referred to the other as "the delicious Mother" or "the delicious Father."[33] All of this was grounded in security, in the sense of having an essential role to play in Roffredo's creative endeavour, and the anticipation shared with him as the birth of their child drew near. As the summer approached, they abandoned Paris for the leafier surroundings of Versailles, taking a suite at the Trianon Palace Hotel while a room in their apartment was being adapted as a nursery. In late August, when the worst of the heat had passed, Marguerite advised Onorato of their return to the capital, "in spite of the fact that the apartment will be full of workmen for another week, I fear."[34]

Lelia Calixta Ada Caetani was born on 4 October 1913 (the feast of St Francis of Assisi), ten days later than expected, but, to everyone's relief, healthy and strong. As Marguerite explained in a letter to Gelasio five days after the birth, her first name was chosen for Marguerite's mother (although in fact the latter had always been known as Leila);

5·4
"It's such fun having a baby – I adore it": Marguerite with Lelia, aged about six months.

the second was Roffredo's suggestion, after his Polish grandmother, Calixta Rzewuska; while the third was an obvious choice. The baby's blue eyes were a surprise, both her parents' eyes being brown.[35] She was, as Marguerite reported, "splendid, and so sweet, smiling and cooing the whole time," and it was "such fun having a baby – I adore it."[36] Despite the construction of the nursery, it was not long before Marguerite and Roffredo began to feel the need of more space, and again looked towards Versailles. Their first tenancy of a house or an apartment there may date from the spring of 1914.[37]

Political tensions were on the rise in Europe, even before the assassination of the heir to the Hapsburg throne in Sarajevo on 28 June. In an atmosphere of increasing menace, the continental system of alliances drew one country after another into a position where conflict became inevitable. By the end of July, Austria and Serbia were at war; on 1 August, Germany declared war on Russia, and on 3 August, on France. The German invasion of Belgium on 4 August brought Britain into the war as France's ally. Despite the fact that Italy was allied with Austria-Hungary and Germany under the terms of a treaty of 1882, the country remained neutral, King Victor Emmanuel III and his government being unwilling to enter a conflict in which Italian interests were not directly involved. Like much of the Roman aristocracy, Onorato and Ada were anglophiles by blood and affinity, and considered that their country should – and eventually would – side with Britain and France, rather than with the Entente. In the meantime, London seemed a safer place to be than Paris, and they were anxious that Roffredo, Marguerite, and Lelia join them there. In September 1914, while relative calm prevailed, Roffredo and Marguerite travelled to England to present Lelia to her various relatives. At some point that autumn, Onorato and Ada returned to Rome. Roffredo and Marguerite passed through Paris to close up the apartment, then they too set out by train for Rome (guided by notes from Gelasio about what to take on what – due to troop movements and security clearances – had become a complicated journey), little knowing that they would not see the "City of Light" again for another four years.

6

A FAMILY IN WAR AND PEACE

The promise of further colonies after the war overcame any scruples on the part of the Giolitti government regarding the alliance with Austria-Hungary, and, in April 1915, Italy signed the secret Treaty of London and entered the war on the side of the Allies. Inevitably, the rhetoric of war equated expansionist nationalism with patriotism. Once the conflict was over, such sentiments were used by the rising politician Benito Mussolini to justify his more extreme doctrines concerning the role and power of the state. In this sense the popular Italian nationalism that grew up during the First World War can be said to have paved the way for fascism, though there were many nationalists who were not fascists. On a purely human scale, the polarization of politics during and after the war divided the Caetani, as it did thousands of Italian families, driving one brother into self-imposed exile and setting another on a political course that would prove deceptive.

All five Caetani brothers served in the war as volunteers, even though Leone, aged forty-six, Roffredo, forty-four, and Livio, forty-two, were over-age, and Leone, as a socialist, publicly opposed it on humanitarian grounds. Gelasio, aged thirty-seven, foreseeing the likelihood of conflict, sold his share in the mining partnership in California and returned home in the summer of 1914. For all the pleasure of his stay in Paris two years earlier, its brevity meant that Marguerite had not really had the chance to get to know him well. Now, on finding him in Rome when she and Roffredo arrived there from London with one-year-old Lelia, she had another opportunity. There was much common ground, since, although Gelasio was an engineer, many of his interests were artistic. Since boyhood he had sketched and sculpted, like his grandfather Duke Michelangelo, but he was also an expert photographer, documenting his travels in North America using the latest cameras. His restoration of the castle at Sermoneta, begun in the late 1890s and paid for by Onorato, was complete, but Gelasio's plans for Ninfa were only just taking shape, and listening to him talk about them brought them to life for Marguerite and Roffredo.

Gelasio's boundless energy kept him constantly busy. While he waited on events back in Rome, he arranged a thousand years' worth of family documents into an archive, as part of his compilation of the genealogical record *Domus Caietana*.[1] In view of the importance the Caetani patrimony held for him, it was ironic, and not a little unfortunate, that he was in love with the wife of another Roman nobleman, from whom divorce was impossible, though she had been living apart from him for several years. Making the best of this situation, Gelasio confided to Ada that he thought marriage would be a brake on his activities. Given the range and intensity of them, he was probably right.[2]

By early 1915 Marguerite was once again pregnant. On a few occasions she accompanied Nella and Vittoria on charitable visits to nearby hospitals,[3] but as the year advanced she remained quietly at Palazzo Caetani with Onorato and Ada, who suffered greatly from anxiety once Italy entered the war. By the summer of 1915, Leone and Roffredo were in charge of hospital trains run by the Order of Malta.[4] These trains conveyed food and medical supplies in one direction, carloads of wounded men in the other, between Italy's northern cities and the front lines along the Austrian border. Livio commanded a military base camp near Padua. Gelasio, a sub-lieutenant in the 8th Mountain Company, was on the front lines in Val Cordevole in the Dolomites, and Michelangelo, aged just twenty-five, was in an aeronautical regiment camped near Florence, awaiting orders. Onorato confided to Leone that Palazzo Caetani seemed cheerless and empty without his sons. Feeling old, with "sight failing and full of cares," he spent his life "making up packages and writing letters" to them all.[5] Nonetheless, the elderly duke found time to serve as president of the Italian committee for Belgian war relief, which Gelasio established early on at the request of his old acquaintance Herbert Hoover, based in London as chairman of the Commission for Relief in Belgium.[6]

As well as the worry for their sons' safety, Onorato and Ada were concerned about the personal situation of Leone. His political career was already in tatters as a result of his outspoken opposition to the invasion of Libya in 1911, and his pacifist stance on the war had damaged his reputation beyond repair. Added to this was his distress concerning thirteen-year-old "Onoratino," enrolled at Westbourne House School in Folkestone. At the end of the academic year the headmaster had written, suggesting that the boy needed more support than the school could provide. Leone, dissatisfied, sought a formal diagnosis of his son's condition from doctors at the University of Rome during the summer. He and Vittoria were devastated when the diagnosis revealed that their son suffered from "incurable motor and neurological disabilities." Far from being able to offer each other comfort, the couple were at the mercy of the incompatibility that had marked their marriage from the beginning. To Duke Onorato, Leone wrote of feeling utterly despondent, and of longing to escape what he felt was a foundering marriage and a heavy burden of responsibility. For the moment, Leone's military obligations kept him and Vittoria apart, aside from periodic visits. There was no formal, legal separation, but from the summer of 1915, they began to lead more independent lives.[7]

During July and August 1915, Marguerite experienced for the first time the debilitating effect of Rome's summer heat. Nighttime brought little relief, though the cavernous rooms of Palazzo Caetani were shrouded by day to keep out the sunlight. Mid-September saw Marguerite and Lelia settled at the Villa Granduchessa in Florence, rented so that they could await the birth of the baby in peace and seclusion. Everyone was convinced that this child would be a boy, to the extent of choosing his name – Camillo – well in advance. On 1 October Nella ended a postcard to Roffredo with "I hope Camillo will be born soon!" but it was not until 23 October that Camillo Benedetto Gelasio Caetani finally arrived, to the joy of his parents and the entire family: a healthy son, and – given the problems of the young Onorato – a probable heir to the Caetani dukedom. In November, Marguerite had him photographed and sent the result to Ada and Onorato: "*Ecco* Don Camillo, two weeks old! He is rather sweet, isn't he? You can't see his delicious big eyes which I think and hope will be like Roffy's."[8] A few weeks later, the proud grandparents came to visit "Don Camillo" and his family: a cheerful interlude for them, amidst all the worry.

All too soon, their forebodings were realized. On 6 December, Onorato wrote to Leone that "Michelangelo's letter has filled me with terror. Vittoria has found Livio confined to bed at Padua." Returning from a visit to Leone at the Front, Vittoria had stopped in Padua to see Livio and discovered that he was ill in a nearby hotel. When it appeared that he was recovering, she returned to Rome, but once there, received a telegram notifying her that he was failing. She and Nella, Onorato, and Ada travelled to Padua with all speed, while Leone hurried there from the Front. They managed to reach Livio's bedside before he died of pneumonia, there being nothing that could be done to save him.[9] The death of the gentlest of the brothers left the family grief-stricken, no one more so than Onorato, of whom it was rumoured that Livio had been his favourite son. Gelasio wrote sadly to his father that "The mystical circle of happiness that united us children and you as parents is broken; in all future hours, including those of happiness and peace, we will always feel that there is an empty place at our table … I think of you dear ones and I get a lump in my throat."[10]

In April 1916, like some glimmer of light penetrating the family's sorrow, came news of an extraordinary feat performed by Gelasio. This was the destruction of an Austrian advance position on a mountaintop known as the Col di Lana in the Val Cordevole. In appalling winter conditions, the ill-equipped and inadequately clothed Italian troops tried repeatedly to capture the battery, but were at a disadvantage, because the Austrians occupied the higher ground, from which any approach on the Italian side was immediately visible. Gelasio's mining and engineering skills enabled his sappers to tunnel into the side of the mountain and plant tons of explosives in its depths, with the result that – on the night of 17 April, and at a given signal – the top of the mountain, enemy battery and all, was literally blown into the air.

6.1
Gelasio at the Col di Lana in the Dolomites, 1917.

Of the more than 250 Austrian soldiers belonging to the 2nd Regiment of "Tiroler Kaiserjäger," who were manning the battery, 108 were killed and 146 taken prisoner. Gelasio was awarded the Cross of the Military Order of Savoy and three medals for valour for this achievement, though he felt great remorse over the loss of life involved.[11] Late in 1917 he returned to Rome to a hero's welcome, although (having lost all his possessions in action) he had to cable home for clothing in which to receive it.[12]

Remaining as physically close as possible to Roffredo was Marguerite's priority during the war. Moving about the country with two small children and a nursemaid was a challenge. In rising to it, she showed determination and organizational ability, all the more remarkable for a non-Italian in wartime, when the availability of civilian transport was governed by military necessity. Having money to draw upon of course made it easier: for part of 1916, while Roffredo was based in Milan, Marguerite stayed at the splendid Villa d'Este on Lake Como. At other times she and the children set up house in a rented apartment in Varese. Marguerite and Roffredo managed to meet regularly, but the latter found separation from his family hard to bear. Their correspondence reveals the degree to which each found refuge in the other from all the cares surrounding them. If either was the more dependent, it was Roffredo, whose expressions of love and esteem for his wife are moving to read. Late in the year he was suddenly posted to Ravenna, and sent a telegram to advise Marguerite. Distressed because she was ill with tonsillitis and had looked forward to his coming to Varese, he wrote the next day, ending wistfully with "how I wish I could protect you with my love from all the pains, all the sorrows of life."[13] He could not protect her, alas, from the inconveniences of a peripatetic existence, if they were to have any time together as a family, she replied – to which he in turn agreed, adding, "I have no words to express to you the many ways in which I love you." A photograph of Roffredo in uniform holding three-year-old Lelia dates from an occasion when they managed to meet near Padua; another, with Camillo, is from Trento. In lighter moments, Roffredo penned some thoughtful farewells: "Summum love to you loving and lovable beings" was one of the better ones.

All this moving about often meant that news from Paris or from New York did not reach Marguerite for months. In April she was saddened to learn of Audinet Gibert's death on 9 February in Paris. His body had been returned to New York for burial, and his widow, in view of the proximity of the German forces to the French capital, had departed for England. Midway through 1916, Marguerite finally received a letter from Katherine, written in January, bringing congratulations on the birth of Camillo and the concerned good wishes of Paul and the two Cornelias. For a time in the autumn, Marguerite and the children stayed at I Tatti, near Florence, the home of Roffredo's friends Bernard and

Mary Berenson, while the latter were on a visit to London. The kindly Mary provided her with introductions to the neighbours, Mrs Janet Ross at Poggio Gherardo and Lady Sybil Cutting at the Villa Medici in Fiesole. (On paying Lady Sybil a call, Marguerite very likely met her daughter, Iris. Years later, married to Marchese Antonio Origo and farming the estate of La Foce in southern Tuscany, Iris Origo would write to Marguerite for advice on gardening, and the two would become friends.) From London, the Berensons reported a city much altered by the war: it was dark and there were no taxis for long journeys, yet they noted "a tremendous outbreak of mad extravagance and gaiety in certain sets" and concluded that this was "an offset to the trenches of the men and the anxiety of the women."[14]

The only bright spot during the next few months was the entry of the United States into the war in April 1917. One of the minor, personal consequences of this was the arrival of Marguerite's half-brother, Paul Chapin, in France, as a 1st Lieutenant of Cavalry, assigned to the headquarters of the American Expeditionary Force at Chaumont. Since his graduation from Harvard Law School in 1911, Paul had been practising law in Manhattan. By letter and telephone he brought Marguerite family news. The house at 5 West Thirty-seventh Street had been sold, and Cornelia had moved to an apartment nearer to Central Park. Funds from the sale of the Rock Lawn estate had been used to commission the architect Frank Mead to design and build the Palomar Apartments on a plot of land facing Balboa Park in San Diego, California. Mead was a friend of Charlotte Osgood Mason's, and the Palomar building was novel in combining modern trends with Islamic influences derived from Mead's travels in Spain and Morocco. Cornelia kept one apartment and rented out the others, so that the family could spend the winter months in California. Katherine was studying anthropology with Franz Boas and the new science of sociology with Max Eastman (both these pioneering scholars were friends of Mason's) at Columbia University. She was engaged to Paul's friend and fellow lawyer Francis Biddle of Philadelphia; they planned to marry when the war was over.

6.2
Marguerite's half-brother, Paul Chapin, in uniform, 1918.

The younger Cornelia was learning stone carving, intending to make sculpture her life's work. Both she and Katherine were active in Mason's crusade to identify the artistic genius of Black and Native Americans. At the philanthopist's opulent Park Avenue apartment, both women helped "Godmother" host her protégés and administer the financial support she gave them.

6.3
After the sale of the third "Rock Lawn," Cornelia Garrison Chapin commissioned the Palomar Apartments, San Diego, California, retaining one apartment as a winter retreat. Wallis Simpson lived in the building in 1919, and Charles Lindbergh in 1927, during the building of "The Spirit of St. Louis."

All this, laudable and interesting though it was, seemed worlds away from Marguerite's present life and the difficulties facing the Caetani family. In June 1917, it became apparent that Duke Onorato, by now seventy-five years old and almost blind, was weakening, and Roffredo obtained leave to travel to Rome. Finding his father mentally confused and almost immobile brought on an oppressive state of mind. On 17 June, patently gripped by a sense of isolation, he wrote to Marguerite, who was staying at Forte dei Marmi to escape the heat: "You are so necessary to me that when you are far away I feel like a weight and that everything I do is useless." He sought to bridge the distance between them by writing almost daily – on 19, 21, 22, 24, 26, and 28 June, and again on 1 July. His letter of 22 June was particularly full of feeling: "O my love, with what infinite affections I embrace you, and with what infinite longings I feel your absence, and such nostalgia to be with you and the babies. O my darling, all my love is for you."

In late July, when Onorato had rallied somewhat, Roffredo and Marguerite managed to spend a few days together in Milan. However, during August, Onorato once again hovered between life and death. The ferocious heat in Rome drove Ada to rent part of the Villa Torlonia, situated on higher ground on the Via Nomentana, which she thought might be cooler than Palazzo Caetani. Roffredo left for a new posting at Mestre, but had no sooner arrived there than a telegram from his mother brought him back to Rome. Marguerite was now anxious to return to the capital, but for once Roffredo discouraged her: Palazzo Caetani was closed up, there was little space at Villa Torlonia; the heat was appalling, and in any case, there was nothing she could do.[15] Ada, Roffredo, and Nella kept vigil as the life of Onorato, 14th Duke of Sermoneta, ebbed away. He died on 2 September 1917, leaving instructions that his funeral should be the simplest possible.[16]

Some days after it, and the translation of Onorato's body to the Caetani mausoleum in Rome's Campo Verano cemetery, the duke's will was read. As anticipated, the major share of everything went to Leone: the estates at Cisterna and Fogliano (though Ada was left a life share in the latter), all the agricultural land and the greater share of the income from rights, produce, and tenancies, leaving aside the amount needed to support Ada at Palazzo Caetani. But Onorato had introduced some variations to the usual formula. At Ada's request, Ninfa and the land around it was left exclusively to Gelasio, the castle of Sermoneta was to be available for the use of all the Caetani offspring, including Giovanella. Roffredo, Gelasio, and Michelangelo were to retain their respective apartments at Palazzo Caetani.[17] Of the funds available at Onorato's death, Leone was to receive a little more than half, Roffredo (who had clearly been allotted Livio's share) just under a quarter, Gelasio and Michelangelo less than an eighth each, and Giovanella the small percentage that remained. The division of future annual income from specific possessions, such as woodlands and fishing rights, affords a further example of the family hierarchy. Leone was to receive three-fifths, Roffredo one-fifth, and Gelasio and Michelangelo a tenth each, while Giovanella did not benefit at all from this income.[18]

It would be some time before Marguerite and Roffredo could evaluate their financial position, since by the end of 1917 the Italian lira had fallen gravely against sterling and the dollar.[19] Roffredo's apartment at Palazzo Caetani was too small for four, and so Marguerite took a lease on a villa at Castel Gandolfo, awaiting the day when she and Roffredo could realize their hope of returning to Paris. The atmosphere they had known there, where they could dine out and entertain in style, where stimulating conversation was the norm, and the sole difficulty was finding time for all the concerts and theatre on offer, was worlds away. Who knew, amidst the reports of the seemingly endless stalemate on the Western Front, of revolution in Russia and the murder of its royal family, when – or whether – such times would return? The humiliating defeat and frightful loss of Italian lives in the battles of Caporetto in October and November 1917 threw a pall of despair and anger over the entire country. The course of the war through the winter of 1918 and the German offensive and Allied counterattack in the spring did nothing to lift it. When peace finally came with the Armistice of 11 November 1918, Italy was all but prostrate. Three years of war had cost more than the total of sums expended by successive governments in the previous fifty years. The toll in human terms was equally appalling: nearly two million Italian soldiers were dead, wounded, or crippled for life.

There were few Italian families psychologically unscarred by the loss of life, but the end of the war brought fresh hardships. Soldiers returning home found that there were no jobs for them, and it was soon a common sight to see the able-bodied begging in the streets alongside the maimed. Poverty, whether in the mean alleys of the industrial cities or in the agricultural south, had always been harsher and more widespread in Italy than in the rest of the Continent. In large cities such as Rome and Naples, where inflation and shortages affected the poor most acutely, Bolshevist and radical ideas inevitably gained ground. At the end of 1918 came the Spanish influenza pandemic, making terrible inroads upon a debilitated population.

Against such a backdrop it is hardly surprising that there is little information concerning Marguerite and Roffredo during the last year of the war, or in 1919. Tragedy seemed all around: the de Reszkes' only son was killed an hour after the Armistice, while Nella and Albéric Grenier's son, nineteen-year-old Eric, died – like the poet Guillaume Apollinaire and the playwright Edmund Rostand – of the Spanish influenza. No sooner had the Greniers buried their son than Albéric, suffering from cancer, also died, leaving Nella a widow at forty-five.

Roffredo's work with the Order of Malta was now over, and at some point during 1919 he and Marguerite returned to France. Initially, while they decided where to live permanently, they settled in the quiet Normandy village of Banneville, near Calvados, where Roffredo could work on *Hypatia*.[20] It is a pity that their reactions to the peace conference and the treaties signed at Versailles are nowhere recorded. The Italian representatives who attended (including Gelasio, as a military attaché) believed their country badly treated by the Allies, in that not all the promises made to Italy under the Treaty of London were kept. In the light of their acquaintance with him before the war, one would also give much to know how Marguerite and Roffredo received the news of Gabriele D'Annunzio's famous raid on Fiume on 12 September 1919.

The immediate postwar period proved challenging for each member of the Caetani family. Ada was seventy-two when the war ended, still mentally and physically energetic. Her response to the loss of Onorato, after fifty years of marriage, was initially to spend more time at Fogliano, the scene of so much family happiness. There she dedicated herself to improving the rose gardens, and to organizing help for those tenants who had returned from the war incapable of resuming their work on the land. In this she had the support of Gelasio, who left the army as a colonel as soon as the war ended. In the next few years he would oversee the provision of improved housing for the agricultural tenants on the Caetani estates and establish two schools for their children and a hospice for the elderly at Fogliano.[21] Eventually he decided not to return to the American West, but to stay in Italy and enter politics. Impressed by the power of industralization he had seen in the United States, Gelasio had become convinced that only through modernization could Italy recover from the devastation wrought by the war and regain a measure of its former greatness. It was perhaps this last aspect that gave him an affinity with the small Italian Nationalist Party founded in 1910.

He also recommenced his plans for the restoration of Ninfa. The immediate priorities, now that the marshy soil within the walls of the ruined town had been drained, were to clear centuries' worth of overgrowth, then to identify what each building had once been and evaluate its condition. As an engineer, Gelasio understood the importance of establishing a basic reference for subsequent work, and thus began by making an accurate survey of every surviving wall and every surface, noting the different materials and successive phases of construction. History, geology, archaeology, surveying, and the science of building came together in this task, even before he set about cleaning and stabilizing the outer walls, the fourteen towers, and the remains of the seven churches. He considered the condition of Ninfa a reproach to the family, and was determined to find productive uses for the place.[22]

At this stage, in 1920, Gelasio was primarily interested in what remained of Ninfa, rather than in the land around it, though he did plant a number of trees that in time would provide interest and definition, as well as shade and privacy: a black walnut, umbrella pines, giant cedars and magnolias, and the avenue of cypresses marking the course of the ancient Via Romana. His major contribution, in the first few years after the war, was to create or improve the infrastructure on which all later work depended. Working closely with him was Ada, who brought cuttings from Fogliano as the first stage in creating the gardens.

The member of the family whose life had changed most dramatically since 1915 was Leone, the scholar-prince and disgraced socialist deputy, who increasingly saw no place for himself in the Italy that emerged from the war. Sometime in 1916, afflicted by loneliness and disillusion, Leone had begun a relationship with Ofelia Fabiani, the daughter of a wealthy Roman engineer. Extramarital liaisons were on the whole well-tolerated in aristocratic circles, the singularity of this one being the disparity in the ages of those involved: Leone was forty-seven when he met Ofelia, but she was only twenty, and was still living under her parents' roof. Amidst all the consternation surrounding Duke Onorato's declining condition in August 1917, the birth of Leone's illegitimate daughter, Sveva, on 6 August went all but unnoticed. Within weeks of the birth, Onorato had died and Leone became the 15th Duke of Sermoneta. Responsibility for the administration of the Caetani estates was added to that of two families and the weight of his sense of personal and political failure. His inheritance helped to resolve some of his immediate difficulties. In March 1918, seeking to placate Vittoria and provide her and sixteen-year-old Onoratino with a permanent home, Leone bought the Orsini Palace,[23] which faced the Tiber some three hundred metres from Palazzo Caetani and incorporated that extraordinary survival from ancient Rome, the Teatro di Marcello. He also purchased a plot of land on the Janiculum, and engaged an architect to build a mansion with a tower and an enclosed garden – the Villa Miraggio – as a residence for Ofelia and Sveva.

Leone feared for the future of the Caetani possessions in an Italy which he saw as beset by anarchy and Bolshevism, though in principle, if not in practice, he had a degree of sympathy with the latter. In his current situation, he preferred to realize enough of his inheritance to leave Vittoria and Onorato secure by selling Cisterna to Gelasio in July 1919.[24] (Gelasio was not only a more capable administrator than Leone, but he also preferred to buy what his brother wished to sell rather than see it pass out of the family.) Then, in September 1919 – with the best of intentions and the worst of judgments – Leone allowed himself to be drawn into the formation of the Società Bonifiche Pontine, the initiative of a Milanese businessman called Gino Clerici, ostensibly created to manage Fogliano for a period of twelve years.[25] At Leone's instigation, Roffredo and Michelangelo also invested in the SBP, and the management of Fogliano and the area around it passed into the hands of Clerici and his associates. Only Gelasio refused to take part – and indeed, would carry on a legal dispute with Clerici for the next several years. Gelasio and Leone fell out over the latter's attitude to the family possessions, but they were also by now at opposite ends of the political spectrum: Leone as a socialist, and Gelasio as a member of the Nationalist Party. In November 1919, Gelasio confided to Ada that "Leone is rather disagreeable, but I see him seldom," and added disapprovingly, "It seems that Ofelia is spending like a queen."[26]

Michelangelo, the youngest and least-robust of the Caetani brothers, had been invalided out of the army before the end of the war, suffering from what seemed to be severe arthritis in his left knee. Even after six months' bed rest, he was sometimes barely able to walk. His great height – like his father, he was six feet six inches tall – did not help, but everyone, Michelangelo included, assumed that the knee problem would eventually ease. Fortunately, he loved to read, and had a circle of good friends in Rome with whom to pass the time. From his letters, Michelangelo emerges as a highly intelligent and observant man, with a gift for anecdote and a delightfully dry sense of humour. At some point in 1919 he became engaged to the glamorous, "willowy" Cora Maria Antinori,[27] whose mother was half-American, and whose father, Count Piero Antinori, belonged to one of the noblest families in Florence.

The first trace of Marguerite and Roffredo after the war comes in a series of letters from the beginning of 1920. At some point they must have relinquished the apartment at 11, rue de l'Université, and put its furnishings into storage. Roffredo was in Paris, looking for a suitable house to rent. Marguerite insisted that it be in an area where the air was pure, and that it have facilities for the childrens' recreation, an apartment for a live-in tutor, and servants' quarters. This was a tall order for postwar Paris, and Roffredo widened his search to the leafier suburbs. One house after another was visited and found wanting, and he sent a wistful note to say how different the experience would have been had she been with him. "My love, I cannot live happily far from you and this feeling grows with the passing of the years,"[28] he wrote at the end of another fruitless day. At last, returning to Versailles, where they had lived while awaiting Lelia's birth in 1913, he found what they were looking for: a very large villa set in extensive grounds, recently used as the headquarters for the British delegation to the Paris peace conferences. By May 1920, Marguerite, Lelia, now six, and four-year-old Camillo were settled at "Villa Romaine" on the recently renamed avenue Douglas Haig. Villa Romaine would be their home for the next twelve years. Roffredo longed for the time to resume work on *Hypatia*, but returned to Rome for Michelangelo and Cora's wedding on 31 May. Even in the wedding photographs, Michelangelo is seen favouring his left knee, a hint of trouble to come.

Marguerite and Roffredo were now engrossed in re-establishing their lives in France. Furnishing the villa and finding servants took time. So did unpacking their vast quantities of books and deciding where to hang their pictures. Since the childrens' education was a priority, Marguerite insisted that any tutor be English-speaking, so that at this early age they could become fluent in English, French, and Italian (German would be added within a few years). There is a sense, in the letters exchanged when Roffredo was on his visits to Rome, that Marguerite now favoured remaining in France for as much of the year as possible. In part, this was to give the children a calm environment in which to develop and learn, and in part because Marguerite herself found the Roman summer hard to bear. Paris was where she flourished: it was where she and Roffredo had spent the idyllic first years of their lives together, and where Roffredo could concentrate on his music.

To all these factors in favour of France was added alarm over the political tensions in Italy, confirmed by Roffredo's first-hand reports on his returns from Rome. The old middle ground of socialists, liberals, conservatives, and nationalists looked set to fragment. Both extremes – the "Bolshevism" so long feared, and the Fascists led by Mussolini – seemed equally dreadful, and Roffredo wrote of his "general conviction that everything is heading for the abyss."[29] When Gelasio offered himself as a Nationalist Party candidate in the elections for the *comune*, or municipal area of Rome, Roffredo assumed that any contribution his brother could make would be beneficial. These elections took place in November 1920, but Gelasio's fame as a war hero was outweighed by his position as a member of the aristocracy, which went against him. The elections for the Camera dei Deputati – the lower house of the Italian parliament – in May 1921 offered him a broader canvas. He was elected as the member for Rome and Lazio, representing the rural area south of Rome with which he identified himself, as well as the capital.[30]

If the year 1921 brought Gelasio public acclaim, it brought Leone's private desolation to a climax. Matters concerning Fogliano took a regrettable turn at the end of 1920. Faced with tax demands, high personal expenses, and the spectre of rampant inflation, both Roffredo and Michelangelo needed to realize their investments in the SBP. They did so by selling them to Clerici and his associates, since Leone, having by now sold off and spent so much of his inheritance, could not afford to buy them out. The realization that he was now outweighed by the Clerici consortium and doomed to lose Fogliano, the one Caetani possession he had planned to retain for himself and Onoratino, precipitated a desperate course of action. In March 1921 he left Italy with Ofelia, Sveva, his Swedish secretary, Miss Jüll, a cook, and a valet. Initially he said nothing to members of the family, leaving Ada calmly gardening at Ninfa and Roffredo in Versailles, suspecting nothing amiss. Later it emerged that he and his entourage had sailed from Liverpool to New York and made their way by train across the United States, stopping at the major cities, and into Canada. (Since Ofelia alone brought thirty trunks containing her personal belongings, this must have been a daunting undertaking.) Leone headed for the town of Vernon, British Columbia, in the area of the Rocky Mountains that he had visited and admired twenty years earlier. Once there, he bought a house with a garden, an orchard, and a nearby plot of woodland, and settled down to live the simple life he had longed for during his decade of mental anguish. He soon wrote to Ada to assure her that he was well, but the letter did not arrive until June, and it was not until July that Roffredo learned of his brother's departure. Having telephoned Michelangelo for family news, he dashed off a note to Marguerite (in Deauville with the children), in which the exclamation marks tell all: "At this very moment Leone is in Canada!!! Why?"[31]

Roffredo received another piece of news from Michelangelo, and it was considerably happier than what he was told concerning their elder brother. Cora was pregnant, and wanted the baby to be born in

6.4
Leone Caetani, Ofelia Fabiani, and Sveva Caetani, Paris, 1921, just before their departure for Canada.

Paris, where her mother lived. On 5 December 1921, Michelangelo and Cora became parents with the birth of their daughter, Topazia. Despite the sad loss of the young Eric Grenier, a total of six children now comprised the next generation of the Caetani family. At least its future seemed assured, even if great physical and psychological distances now separated some of its members.

7

VILLA ROMAINE AND THE GENESIS OF *COMMERCE*

Like Marguerite, Leone's wife, Vittoria, was born in 1880. Her memoir *Sparkle, Distant Worlds*, published in 1947, begins with the observation that the 1914–1918 war had exactly bisected her life, both chronologically and in the sense of being a watershed: the event after which nothing was ever the same again. In the golden age before the Great War, Vittoria recalled,

> Our homes and our cities seemed as safe as the ground under our feet; we could not conceive our relations with people of other nationalities being anything but polite and friendly. When we wanted to travel we just bought our tickets, made our reservations and started for any part of the globe we fancied. Passports did not exist, and we changed our money unrestrictedly into any other currency we required.[1]

Here Vittoria is describing the conditions that prevailed for the upper classes during Europe's long peace, unbroken by a major international conflict (apart from the war in the Crimea) since Waterloo a century earlier. It was a peace that stretched back generations, a peace that had fostered the rise of the nation-state, the evolution of a pan-European culture, and a capitalist economic system based on industrialization that looked set to go on forever. The traditional structure of European society remained largely in place: the wave of popular revolutions around mid-century had challenged, but not displaced, the dominance of the landed aristocracy. A stability that had lasted as long as anyone could remember was the bedrock of society, linking aristocrats like Vittoria and the Caetani to the poorest tenant farmers on their estates. On the land, generation succeeded generation, owning and working the same soil, the highest and the lowest connected by mutual ties of obligation.

Such a situation was, as Vittoria put it, "scarcely conceivable" by the time the guns fell silent in 1918. The technologies that produced the trains and motor cars that allowed her and others like her to travel at will from one European capital to another also produced the tank, the Maxim gun, the poison gas, and other terrifying weapons that devastated half of Europe and wiped out much of a generation numbering in the millions. In the aftermath of four years of carnage, the old ideals and certainties, the old reverence for institutions and authority, were as dead as the soldiers that had fought for them. Those who had seen action would bear the physical, mental, and emotional scars for the rest of their lives, while grief for the loss of loved ones became the internalized burden of those who had stayed at home. Worse still was the widely felt sense that it had all been for nothing. The long-existing, simmering tensions for which the war had been an outlet were not resolved by it. The map of Europe redrawn by the peace accords of 1919 reveals ancient nations dismembered, territories ceded and merged, new countries brought into being, and whole populations forcibly displaced. Thus were the seeds of the next international conflict sown, almost before the ink was dry on the treaties signed at Versailles.

When Marguerite and Roffredo returned to France in 1919, it was with the aim of resuming the life they had led there before the war, but between the world they now inhabited and the one they had known in 1914 lay the appalling, destructive reality of the greatest conflict in human history. If peace brought the revival of the cultural life they valued so highly, the difference was that now, added to the creative mix, like a fiery spice tipped into a hallowed recipe, was the frenetic pursuit of novelty and the angry rejection of authority that were part of the Great War's psychological legacy of despair. War had always been cruel, but no previous war had proved so annihilating to the fundamental belief that human beings have dignity and value. For many who survived it, despair seemed the only rational reaction to its absurdity and horror, and the pursuit of the moment could be justified by the nihilistic conviction that hope was an illusion and "the moment" was all there was.

This was not, of course, the position in which Marguerite and Roffredo found themselves, although, through the death of Livio and the sufferings of friends, they too had experienced grief, pain, and loss. In the art being produced after the war, they found ample reflection of such emotional wounds: depictions of material reality as shattered and fragmented, canvases imbued with the sense of randomness and chaos, an obsession with technology and speed, with violence, with absurdity and futility, that expressed the rejection of traditional meaning and context. The prevailing creative mood denied that the values of the past could serve a modern reality, but had, as yet, nothing to put in their place. New artistic movements – Futurism, Dadaism, Divisionism, Suprematism, early Surrealism, and a host of others – proclaimed the death of traditional representation, yet their extremism pointed only towards the meaninglessness of absolute subjectivity.

All of this Marguerite and Roffredo no doubt found compelling, as artistic interpretations of the times they lived in, and therefore essential to understand. Their broad cultural frame of reference, however, gave them an added perspective: the conviction that the artist's fundamental task is to search for meaning, even amidst disorder and despair. When Marguerite again began to buy works of art after the war, these tended to be works that affirmed this more comprehensive approach, and on the evidence of the collection of paintings she built up between the wars, this continued to be true.[2] She had, if it can be stated so simplistically, many personal and material reasons to be positive, but her fundamentally classical cultural background would also prove important in guiding both what she bought, and what she did in the literary sphere.

Her own and Roffredo's personal circumstances had altered since the halcyon days before August 1914, most obviously in that the well-being

7.1
Marguerite's postwar purchases of works of art included many on paper, such as a set of Edward Gordon Craig's illustrations for *Hamlet* (one of which appears here), commissioned by Count Harry Kessler and published by his Cranach Press, Weimar.

7.2
Another of Marguerite's acquisitions: theatre designer Fortunato Depero's *Ballerini*.

and education of two small children was now their most important concern. In the end they had chosen Versailles, and proximity to Paris, rather than the uneasy, edgy atmosphere of postwar Paris itself, as better able to provide the space and closeness to nature they wanted for Lelia and Camillo. In summer they rented the house where they had lived for a few months in 1919 – Mon Rêve at Banneville, near Calvados on the Normandy coast – so that the children could enjoy the sea air and the beach. Their economic situation had also changed, in that Roffredo's inheritance, added to Marguerite's own, made them exceedingly well-off, although there are no figures to suggest what annual sums they had at their disposal. It is safe to say, however, that they could live as they pleased. Their new home, Villa Romaine, was set in a walled park, with woodland and more than an acre of formal gardens. Photographs of it taken around the turn of the century show the villa as imposingly large

7·3
The "romantic" wing of Villa Romaine, Versailles.

and grand, with two wings in contrasting styles. Its name derived from a front elevation with two round towers and crenellations that hinted at "romance," or fantasy. The other wing had a severe neoclassical facade, surmounted by a balustrade and a somewhat ungainly square tower. Below the tower, a terrace gave onto an expanse of lawn. Walking paths of a forbidding straightness formed the boundaries of the parterre, at the centre of which stood a round concrete fountain.[3] From one side, then, the villa had a whimsical and romantic visual charm, while from the other, it looked more like a sanatorium or a residential school than a private residence.

Marguerite and Roffredo soon made the place their own, as a series of photographs taken during their time there show. The contrast between the decorative and the severely unadorned wings of the house may have been precisely what appealed to them. In one part of the house, neoclassical features abound (pilasters sweeping up to high ceilings, oval windows, and a glassed-in conservatory, or *orangerie*, where orange trees stood in square wooden planters). The use of white paint gave an effect of airy simplicity not unlike that achieved in Marguerite's garden apartment at 11, rue de l'Université. From a spacious ground-floor vestibule, a book-lined staircase ascended to a square gallery, where sunlight poured in through a skylight to reveal even more volumes. In the other wing, the stenciled panelling common in French country houses was allowed to remain, along with the stone fireplaces and leaded windows typical of the Gothic revival. Throughout the villa, much of the colour came from paintings and books, propped and stacked wherever they could not be hung or fitted onto shelves. The floors were of black-and-white Dutch tiles, or wooden parquet overlaid with oriental rugs. Any furniture visible in the photographs seems ageless: fat sofas that offer the prospect of a comfortable hour's reading; oak and leather chairs of a design to be found in sixteenth-century paintings and still on sale today; a wooden chest, gleaming with the patina of age; solid tables with heavy, turned legs; and sideboards of the darkest walnut. It was the kind of interior that evokes timelessness and serenity. Thanks to these photographs, we also see the personal touches – the fifteenth-century panel of a Madonna and Child on a wall

7.4 Villa Romaine interior: note the dog bowl.
7.5 Living space at Villa Romaine.

of the dining room, the vases and ornaments, the well-placed cushions, the letters and papers lying about – which prove that, for all its grandeur, Villa Romaine was a home, not just a stage set. One, for instance, shows the homely detail of a bowl set down at the corner of a carpet, presumably holding water for the Briard puppies, Moony and Beary, acquired shortly after the family settled in Versailles.[4]

In this enormous abode, Lelia and Camillo had their separate quarters – bedrooms, schoolroom, kitchen and dining room, playroom, library and sitting room. Nearby was their tutor's apartment, and a separate one for guests. Half a dozen or more domestic servants lived in, while the gardeners needed to tend the lawns and flowerbeds were recruited locally. Presumably the chauffeur also lived at Villa Romaine, since so many of those invited to lunch or dinner there mention[5] having been collected on a Sunday morning, or driven home late in the evening. Marguerite and Roffredo entertained often, both at home in Versailles and at Paris restaurants.

The life that Marguerite and Roffredo created for themselves after the war was still, as it had been before it, one that was centred on music, the visual arts, and the exchange of ideas. They were in a position to afford material comfort, even luxury, and in this sense they were privileged, and knew it. They were not, for all that, "dilettanti" – the dismissive term sometimes used to designate those who possess the means to dedicate themselves to the arts, not as practitioners but as patrons. Marguerite and Roffredo each possessed a wide-ranging and profound knowledge of music, art, and literature, deliberately built up through years of discerning reading, listening, and viewing. For them, these were not merely ways of passing the time, but serious considerations of how the arts addressed the problem of living in a fully human way. Their commitment to providing a forum for the exchange of views was their way of contributing to the pool of ideas that their creative friends might draw upon.

Roffredo's life was shaped by his vocation as a composer. In retrospect, the war can be seen to have marked a watershed for him too: in serious composition, atonality was in the ascendant, just as jazz was in the popular scene. The kind of music Roffredo had written before

1914 was by now part of the past that a new generation of composers was busy rejecting. His opera *Hypatia* still required revision before it could be performed. The long period after 1918 during which Roffredo wrote no new music has perplexed modern scholars, but the reasons for this hiatus will gradually become clear.[6] For Marguerite, the intellectual life she wanted meant keeping up with what was being written across the broad sweep of the four languages in which she was now fluent. Very likely, she regularly read the *Nouvelle Revue Française*, founded by André Gide, Jean Schlumberger, Gaston Gallimard, and Jacques Rivière in 1909, and still indisputably France's leading intellectual review. The bookshops of the Left Bank, and the recently established American Library on the Right, were easily accessible. There were also the readings, the presentations of new works, and the literary salons that took place, as they had before 1914. Marguerite could attend these when she wished, thanks to having a car and driver to take her where she wished to go. Drawing upon acquaintances from before the war and those more recent, she began to extend her circle of literary friends.

There were two important additions to the Parisian literary scene since 1914. The first was the bookshop La Maison des Amis des Livres, set up in 1915 by a twenty-three-year-old Frenchwoman called Adrienne Monnier. Her aim was not only to sell books, but to encourage people to read by inviting those who visited the shop to borrow the merchandise. Her bookshop at 7, rue de l'Odéon on the Left Bank was the first free lending library in France, an atmospheric place furnished with worn armchairs and a refectory table, where books lined the walls and were stacked knee-high all around them. In 1917 she began holding regular *séances de lecture*, or readings of work by their authors, to an audience of as many people as could cram themselves into the shop. Monnier specialized in contemporary French literature, and La Maison des Amis des Livres soon acquired a following among young avant-garde writers, as well as those of an earlier generation, such as Marguerite's friend Paul Valéry, the poet and essayist held to be "the last of the Symbolists," who as a young man had been part of the group surrounding Stéphane Mallarmé.

In that same year, 1917, Sylvia Beach, an American studying modern French literature in Paris, sought out Monnier's shop and was inspired by conversation with its proprietor to set up her own bookstore, specializing in English and American books. The legendary Shakespeare and Company opened a few streets away from La Maison in 1919, but in 1921 it moved to 12, rue de l'Odéon, facing it on the other side of the street. Shakespeare and Company became a home away from home for the many American writers, including Ernest Hemingway, E.E. Cummings, F. Scott Fitzgerald, John Dos Passos, Ezra Pound, and Archibald MacLeish, who flocked to Paris after the war. In the words of Gertrude Stein, who had lived in the city since 1906, these young American writers belonged to "The Lost Generation," out of whose shattered world view a radically new one was being forged. As she put it, "Paris was where the twentieth century was," and residence there, at least for a time, was an essential experience for any serious modern writer or painter.

One member of that generation was Janet Flanner, the Paris correspondent for the *New Yorker*, who arrived in 1922 and rapidly became acquainted with Monnier, Beach, and the literary circles that mattered. She left a vivid impression of the bookshop at 7, rue de l'Odéon:

> A French literary centre not only for the most superior contemporary French writing but for its authors as well, such writers as André Gide, Jean Schlumberger, the poets Paul Valéry and Léon-Paul Fargue, and the novelists Valery Larbaud and Jules Romain. At all hours they frequented the Monnier shop and on special days held reverent sessions there, attended by Sylvia and occasionally by a few of us American writers as well, in which they read aloud from their unpublished manuscripts.[7]

Was Marguerite in the habit of attending these readings? Given that, of the authors named as "regulars" by Flanner, only one would not later be associated with her, the odds are high that she did. She had met Paul Valéry before 1914, but did she come to know Monnier, Fargue, and Larbaud through meeting them at these events? It is possible, even probable, but hard to pin down with any certainty.[8] However they met and became friends, they were soon part of a new literary venture in which she assumed the leading role – but to move straight on to that is to pass over another set of circumstances weighing upon the Caetanis in their first few years in Versailles.

The term "annus horribilis," used by Britain's Queen Elizabeth II to describe 1992 (the year that included the fire at Windsor Castle and the Princess Royal's divorce) has become a catch-phrase of our time, but it might equally be applied to the year 1922 for Marguerite and Roffredo. This was a year when all manner of tensions became entwined, demanding of Roffredo in particular great patience and forbearance. For some time Gelasio had been urging him to return to live in Italy, suggesting that Roffredo's interests there were at risk should he live abroad too long. He was already the owner of a large plot of land in Rome's Valle Giulia, near the Villa Borghese, bought in 1919, complete with sitting tenants and sub-tenants. By 1922 he was seeking the official permissions necessary to renovate an existing villa on the site as a family home for the winter months. But the increasing polarization of the political situation in Italy was alarming, as communists and anarchists on one hand, fascists on the other, claimed more of the middle ground with every passing month. Gelasio, as a Nationalist member of parliament for Rome and the Lazio, had drawn up plans for the draining of the Pontine Marshes, and while Roffredo approved of this project, he and Marguerite were dismayed at Gelasio's positive view of Mussolini, the Fascist Party leader, whose claims for the all-embracing nature and power of the state they found menacing and distasteful.[9]

Where their interests coincided was in the matter of Ninfa, where Gelasio was continuing his work of restoration. By now he had turned the former *municipio*, or town hall, into a comfortable country retreat, and Ada's multitude of climbing roses were beginning to soften what was still a somewhat harsh and forbidding scene. Unfortunately, Ada's health was in decline, and Nella, whose obligations at the Belgian court often required her presence in Brussels, was increasingly uneasy about leaving her alone.

By the summer of 1922, Leone had been settled in Vernon, British Columbia, for just over a year. Although he would return to Europe several times during the 1920s, in practical terms he had abdicated his position and responsibilities as 15th Duke of Sermoneta without legally renouncing them. Roffredo thus inherited the responsibilities, but not the title or the income that might have made them easier to bear. At least Leone had found peace of mind and a sense of well-being in Vernon (or so he wrote to his mother), as he set about clearing his woodland acres and selling the timber: "You may like to know that I am living most happily and peacefully on the verge of civilization ... I live the life of a peasant, a very simple life, and enjoy it ... You can have no idea all the good, moral and physical which this life has given me, and I hope I may also make money with patience, prudence, and hard work."[10]

Once settled in British Columbia, Leone had resumed contact with the Accademia Nazionale dei Lincei with a view to establishing a foundation for Islamic studies there and endowing it with his priceless collection of books and manuscripts. How to make his collection available to scholars had been on his mind for years, and in finding a solution, he shed another burden of responsibility.[11]

Ada was by now seventy-five, an age when most people have ceased to worry about their children, and have accepted that what will be, will be. No such relaxation was possible in her case, with her eldest son living "the life of a peasant" in the wilds of Canada, and her youngest by this time all but immobilized by the unrelenting pain in his legs and back. In August, Roffredo left Marguerite and the children at Mon Rêve to accompany Michelangelo to Biarritz, in the hope that the sea air and the sun treatment available at a specialist clinic there would do him good. On arrival, he wrote to Marguerite that "The journey went off as well as it could go, Miche hardly complaining of his pains,"[12] and on the following day, he entrusted his brother to the care of the clinic's Dr Fauret.

The cause of Michelangelo's suffering was finally identified after an analysis of his synovial fluid revealed the presence of the Koch bacillus. Michelangelo had tuberculosis of the joints and spine, at that time an incurable and crippling condition. Recalling that the youngest of the Caetani had only just turned thirty-two, had been married barely two years, and had an eight-month-old child, Dr Fauret's summary of his situation in a letter to Roffredo makes particularly poignant reading. The only treatment was "x-rays and sunlight, with the aim of getting the organism into a state of defence" (what today would be called "remission," one imagines). The doctor went on to note "the difficulty of treating an intelligent man who knows a considerable amount about medicine and is fairly contemptuous of doctors," without letting on to him the truth about his condition.[13]

After a few weeks, Roffredo left Michelangelo in Biarritz and returned to Versailles. The news from Rome was alarming: Italy seemed to be slipping into political chaos. In late October, before going again to Biarritz to escort his brother home, he visited Rome. (Did he break the news of Michelangelo's illness to Ada, or did he keep it, for the moment, to himself?) He arrived just in time to witness the March on Rome on 22 October: the collective manifestation of right-wing political interests that brought Mussolini and his Fascist Party to power. Gelasio participated in the march as a Nationalist; soon after it (the ten Nationalist deputies having been offered places in the new government by Mussolini), he was appointed Italian ambassador to the United States and prepared to leave for Washington.

This meant that for the next three years – the usual length of a diplomatic posting – Roffredo was on his own as nominal head of the family. The concerns of its various members – Ada and Michelangelo, his aunt Ersilia, now in her eighties, the widowed Giovanella and her daughter, even Vittoria and her problematical son, Onoratino, now twenty – would, at the very least, require frequent absences from Versailles. His letters to Marguerite are reminiscent of those written when they were forced to be apart during the war: "So sorry to be again away from you, my incomparable darling, and when I left you at the station I felt such a grief! I believe it will always be more and more painful for me to separate myself from you!"[14] The circumstances giving rise to such feelings should be kept in mind when considering Roffredo's seeming

7.6
Gelasio Caetani in ambassadorial splendour, just before leaving for Washington, 1922.

lack of musical inspiration after the war. As it was, he managed to polish *Hypatia* and send it off to Schott, the German music publisher, which published it in 1924.

When Roffredo was at home in Villa Romaine, family life and gatherings of friends provided a counterweight to the worries in Rome. Marguerite was in her element in the company of friends, while Roffredo was a superb and attentive host. There were sometimes thirty people around the table for Sunday lunches, and the conversation ranged widely over the latest books, films, and theatre. Afterwards

Roffredo sometimes settled at the piano for an impromptu recital, or Marguerite might guide first-time visitors around the gardens and the house. Those invited included some of the best minds and outstanding talents of the era: André Gide, the Abbé Mugnier, Edith Wharton, Walter Berry, the Berensons when they were in Paris, old friends like Reynaldo Hahn, Edouard Vuillard, André Derain, and Aristide Maillol, newer ones like Erik Satie and André Dunoyer de Segonzac, and, above all, the writers that Marguerite had come to know: the novelist Valery Larbaud; Léon-Paul Fargue, the "poet of Paris"; Paul Valéry (who after a long creative drought, had published three volumes of poetry since 1917); Jean Paulhan, the deputy editor of the *Nouvelle Revue Française*, and his wife, Germaine; and the diplomat and poet Alexis Saint-Léger Léger. With the latter, Marguerite shared a faint but interesting connection, in that he was a native of Guadaloupe, the French *département* in the Caribbean that had been the birthplace of her maternal great-grandmother, Catherine Audinet.

The year 1922 ended with the sorrowful news of the death of Marcel Proust on 18 November, but it also saw the completion of Rainer Maria Rilke's *Duino Elegies* and *Sonnets to Orpheus*, the publication of T.S. Eliot's *The Waste Land*, and that of James Joyce's *Ulysses*. Sections from *Ulysses* had already been published by Harriet Weaver and Jane Heap in the *Little Review* in the United States, but the book was banned there in 1920 after the *Little Review* was tried for obscenity. Among English speakers in Paris, Joyce's masterpiece was received with particular fascination, partly because it was "forbidden" in America (it was banned in the British Isles, too), and partly because its author, wearing his distinctive dark spectacles, was often to be seen in the vicinity of the rue de l'Odéon. As Janet Flanner put it, "The publication *in toto* of *Ulysses* in 1922 was indubitably the most exciting, important, historic single literary event of the early Paris expatriate literary colony … it burst over us, young in Paris, like an explosion in print whose words and phrases fell upon us like a gift of tongues, like a less than holy Pentecostal experience."[15]

The inspiring story of Sylvia Beach's role in bringing Joyce's great work to fruition, then in publishing and distributing it, is too well known to need repetition here.[16] It should be remembered, however, that even though *Ulysses* was published and available in France, it was inaccessible to most French readers, since the published text was in English. Auguste Morel's French translation of the whole work did not appear until 1929.

At one of the many Sunday gatherings at Villa Romaine during 1923 or early in 1924, there arose the idea of founding a review dedicated to literature per se: poetry, prose, and drama.[17] There were plenty of publications already offering other kinds of reading, such as criticism, commentary on the current literary scene, or the polemics of writers actively linked to some faction or other. The idea put forward in the salon at Villa Romaine was something different: writing drawn from any historical period and any language, whose only claim on the reader's attention would be its literary quality. According to Marguerite, when asked years later how the review came into being, it happened in the following way:

> One day, Valéry said out of the blue: "Why don't we continue our conversations, our dialogues, in published form? As a title, I suggest 'Commerce,' exchange of ideas." Everyone present was delighted by the idea. The directors (Larbaud, Valéry, Fargue) were appointed straightaway. Adrienne Monnier and I were put in charge of getting it going and we began at once. What the result was, remains for you to judge. I was helped immensely by Paulhan who allowed me to search among the manuscripts that he received for the NRF as well as by Alexis Léger who chose the poems that we published.[18]

It has also been suggested that the title "Commerce" owed something to a line from one of Léger's poems that referred to "le pur commerce de mon âme" ("the pure commerce of my soul"), but claims could as well be made for the "commerce" of Walt Whitman, where the meaning seems to be "communication," or for Ezra Pound's "pact" with his great predecessor ("let there be commerce between us"), or, if a more venerable and strictly French antecedent is wanted, the "commerce of ideas" proposed by Madame de Staël. The concept of "commerce" as an exchange of elements surely originates with Heraclitus: while reality can be described in all its endless variety, the underlying unity of all things can only be represented symbolically. Perhaps Valéry, with his Symbolist past, did not feel that he had to explain this to people as well-read as those present when he made his suggestion.

The participation of Adrienne Monnier in the project lasted only a short time. She withdrew from it after a few months, for what were ostensibly personal reasons stemming from a disagreement with Léon-Paul Fargue. (It is interesting to note that in 1925 she launched her own literary review, *Le Navire d'Argent*; perhaps she felt that if she were going to administer a review, it might as well be her own.) *Commerce*'s debt to Jean Paulhan and Alexis Léger, on the other hand, was lasting. Each of them had a motive for not wishing to be identified publicly with the new initiative, but supported it unofficially and behind the scenes. Paulhan, as deputy editor of France's leading intellectual journal, could not assume at the same time the direction or editorship of a rival publication. Léger was a member of the French diplomatic service, and felt that he could neither take an active role in directing *Commerce* nor publish anything in it under his own name. When he did contribute to it, he used the pseudonym "Saint-John Perse." An even more shadowy figure in relation to *Commerce* was Marguerite's third cousin T.S. Eliot, whose own review, *The Criterion*, had been launched in London a year earlier. Eliot and Marguerite had always been on good terms, but not particularly close (though when Eliot spent nearly a year in Paris in 1910, he chose to live for part of that time only a few doors away from her in the rue de l'Université). After the war, their mutual literary interests strengthened their relationship, and now, as friends, they often traded ideas and recommended writers to each other. In time, four of Eliot's poems would appear in translation in the pages of *Commerce*.[19]

Early on, some guidelines for the kind of material *Commerce* would publish must have been agreed on by the small group – Marguerite, the three "official" directors (Valéry, Fargue, and Larbaud), and the "unofficial" ones, Paulhan and Léger – committed to taking the project forward. No copy of these guidelines survives; they can only be deduced from the evidence of what *Commerce* eventually published. First of all, since the review sought to offer a selection of writing new to its readers, the pieces chosen for it could not have been previously published elsewhere. Secondly, although the review was to be published in French, it was to have an international focus. The aim of making French readers aware of writing in other languages through the medium of translation was very likely Marguerite's contribution, given her cosmopolitan outlook and the fact that all of the review's directors, both official and unofficial, were French. Thirdly, readers were to be exposed to the juxtaposition of work by young, contemporary writers, and texts by medieval or classical authors. A further idea, that a poet's work could be best translated by another poet, was one that was put into effect from the beginning, and would underlie the breadth of the contacts made by Marguerite in seeking translators as the review gathered momentum. Lastly, but perhaps the defining feature of *Commerce*, would be the absence and avoidance of an editorial presence, or any sense that the review occupied a particular position on the literary or political spectrum.[20] The content of its successive numbers would affirm the commitment to literature itself, rather than to any identifiable tendency.

Fortunately, a document does survive that reveals the pivotal role played by Marguerite in the essential matter of funding and administering the review. Working through the Paris branch of the Morgan Harjes bank, she set up the so-called "Société Anonyme 'Commerce,'" with six hundred shares and a share capital of sixty thousand francs. Each of the three directors was allocated a hundred shares worth a hundred francs each, as an acknowledgment of the value to the review of his association with it. The remaining share capital would pay for running costs – printing, binding, paying translators, and so on – and be recouped by the sale of copies of the review. The report of the society's *commissaire*, or "chief organizer," the painter André Dunoyer de Segonzac (a friend, whose work hung on the walls of Villa Romaine), dated 28 November 1924, makes clear the benefits to *Commerce* of the participation of the three directors. It describes Marguerite as *administratrice statutaire*, or "legal administrator," but her most essential role is not mentioned.[21]

Marguerite took on the financial responsibility for *Commerce* by drawing upon her personal fortune, assuming the role of literary patron in a way reminiscent of the days when, as Miss Chapin, she had commissioned and bought paintings. She could not have realized how much more complex her involvement would become as *Commerce* developed. Her position at the centre of a network of intellectual and artistic friends was initially that of an intermediary, who brought them together for their mutual interest and benefit. Nonetheless, once the review came into being under her guidance, she found the pursuit of excellence deeply satisfying. Directing *Commerce* fanned her instinct for recognizing good writing into a vocation to find and promote it. This would come to fruition years later, in another place and another venture, but her experience in creating and guiding *Commerce* would one day be seen as a fundamental part of that achievement.

The review's first issue was published in August 1924 (a few months later than intended), the initial number in a series of "three-monthly journals published under the auspices of Paul Valéry, Léon-Paul Fargue, and Valery Larbaud,"[22] names so eminent in French and European intellectual circles that *Commerce* was virtually guaranteed serious attention. Its 158 pages contained a contribution by each of the three directors, a section of a longer poem entitled *Amitié du prince* by Léger writing as "Saint-John Perse," and several fragments of James Joyce's *Ulysses*, translated into French by Larbaud and fellow-writer Auguste Morel. Since Joyce's novel had already been published in English by Sylvia Beach, the appearance of parts of it in French was an exception to the first of the guidelines above, but the importance of the work and the desire to offer some parts of it to French readers while it was still topical clearly outweighed a policy decision taken months earlier. Did it also outweigh concern over the propriety of publishing excerpts from a book that had become notorious in such a short time? It must have, since Marguerite held a lunch to celebrate *Commerce* and the publication of the first extracts to be translated into French, at which Joyce's presence was, as Sylvia Beach put it, "counted on."[23]

It comes as a surprise, to anyone knowing of Marguerite's connection with it, to find that her name appears neither in the first number of *Commerce*, nor in any of the twenty-eight issues that succeeded it over the next eight years. This was a matter of temperament and personal preference. She was no longer shy or retiring; rather the contrary, as the guests around her table discovered, as the deftly guided conversation sparkled, and each and every one of them was drawn in by their vivacious hostess. It was simply that she did not like the limelight, and perhaps even felt that the appearance of her name as Princess di Bassiano would be likely to attract it. Perhaps, in this too, she may have deferred to Roffredo, who may have had reservations about the appearance of his title in print. These attitudes would change with the times, but for the moment, it meant that her essential role in *Commerce* remained discreetly unacknowledged, at least publicly.

As 1924 drew to a close, Gelasio sent greetings from the Italian embassy in Washington, and Leone, relieved that his Islamic scholarly foundation was now a reality, from Vernon, British Columbia. Marguerite sent the second number of the review off to the printer in November and was pulling together the items to appear in the third, while Roffredo was in Bologna, discussing the possibility of producing *Hypatia* at La Scala in Milan. If the Italian political scene continued to alarm them, the year had at least had been creatively satisfying. Even the children had been inspired. Together they were writing and illustrating a story in Italian called *Piski, Poska e Pisca* as a Christmas gift for Roffredo. Its protagonists, driven by the desire to escape a bad dog called Beri (Beary) and see the world, set out to explore it by horse and train, camel, elephant, ship, and airplane. Along the way, they survive pirate attack, an encounter with alligators, and other perils to return safely home to Versailles … via Goa, the Gobi desert, and Tibet! The range of vocabulary and the imagination evident in this little book were remarkable, even for two children growing up in an atmosphere as stimulating as that of Villa Romaine.[24] This was probably the conclusion of their parents, too, and with Roffredo's plans for the villa in Rome temporarily stalled (the sub-tenants had acquired the right to renew their tenancy) and *Commerce* now heading into its third issue, the quality of the childrens' education provided a further reason for remaining in France.

8

A UNIQUE VOCATION: FOSTERING THE *COMMERCE* OF IDEAS

On 7 January 1925, the Austrian poet Rainer Marie Rilke returned to Paris for the first time in five years. He had recently emerged from a Swiss clinic, where treatment for a mysteriously recurring, debilitating illness had seemingly restored him to health, and was eager to reconnect with literary friends in the French capital. Paul Valéry was the first of these to seek him out at his lodgings at the Hôtel Foyot, near the Luxembourg Gardens. A few months earlier, Valéry had asked Rilke for prose or poetry that might be suitable for *Commerce*, and a poem entitled "La Dormeuse" was one of those Rilke had sent him. When Valéry visited him in Paris, he brought along copies of the second number of *Commerce* (autumn 1924), in which the poem appeared. Rilke was impressed by the review, and on 5 February he was invited to lunch to meet its moving spirits. He already knew fellow poet Léon-Paul Fargue, and was especially glad to find himself seated next to the diplomat Alexis Léger, whose work he admired. It was Marguerite's conversation, however, that captivated him, and led him to write appreciatively to her on the following day: "Yesterday's lunch was charming, with its spontaneous closeness ... and I admired your stroke of genius in suggesting to us all those topics for activities and intellectual pastimes whose importance surpassed the delights of the moment."[1]

Marguerite responded by sending him a German translation of a satirical work by Denis Diderot,[2] and Rilke, when invited to Villa Romaine ten days later, presented her with a copy of his novel, *The Notebooks of Malte Laurids Brigge*, and of the recently completed *Sonnets to Orpheus* and *Duino Elegies* (inscribed with a dedication to her as "animatrice de nos meilleurs efforts et protectrice des afinitées"). Rilke was proud of his ability to produce poetry in French as well as German, and into the copy of the *Duino Elegies* he slipped such a poem, written especially for Marguerite.[3]

This gracious touch sealed a friendship that lasted the remaining twenty months of the poet's life, though neither he nor his friends had any idea that the time remaining to him would be so short. He and Marguerite corresponded often, always in French, to discuss what they were reading, or some matter related to *Commerce*. She for him was "Ma chère Princesse," while she, in the large, dashing handwriting that often lacked the necessary accents, was soon addressing him as "Très cher Ami," or "Très cher Ami et Grand Poête." While he remained in Paris, he was frequently the guest of the Caetanis for lunch, whether in town or in the more intimate setting of Villa Romaine, but it was never a one-sided friendship. When, for instance, Léon-Paul Fargue let Marguerite down by not producing a piece he had promised for *Commerce*, it was Rilke who supplied a text at short notice. He provided Marguerite with tickets to what he considered an outstanding marionette show, to which, one imagines, he thought she should take the children.[4] He also did Roffredo the favour of looking over the German translation of the libretto of *Hypatia*, an invaluable service in light of the probability that the opera would be produced first in that language.[5] This was a true friendship, too, in that Marguerite respected Rilke's well-known resistance to any kind of commitment. When she invited him to become an official correspondent for *Commerce*, it was with no sense that he should feel obliged, for friendship's sake, to accept. He in turn declined, freely expressing his reservations about the responsibilities such a position might require of him.[6]

Still, it was not only her hospitality, but also Marguerite's sensitivity and gift for friendship that would be recalled by many writers. Her relationship with Rilke, so short in chronological terms, was no exception in being rich in thoughtful gestures. In April 1925, for example, when the poet was confined to bed with influenza, Marguerite sent a nurse who had just spent a few weeks at Villa Romaine to look after him at the Hôtel Foyot, and to report to her anything he needed. While such attention to his physical well-being was appreciated, Rilke was even more deeply touched by her generosity where his poetic imagination was concerned. One Sunday at Villa Romaine, he and Jean Paulhan leafed through a folio edition of William Blake's drawings and engravings – Blake being an author and artist greatly esteemed by Marguerite and Roffredo. When Rilke wrote a day or so later to ask, hesitantly, if he might borrow "the precious volume ... almost a piece of furniture ... that immense volume (immense for its content too)" for a few days, Marguerite replied by packing it up and sending it, via Paulhan, to Rilke's hotel. In the note accompanying it, she wrote, "I am happy that you asked me for it. Blake will be even more precious and dear to me, crowned with your praise."

Later, with the vast tome open before him, Rilke confided to Marguerite his conviction that it was not mere chance that had led to this auspicious re-encounter with Blake's illustrations, some of which had for him "the force of revelation." They were consummate works of the imagination that stirred his own:

> I have always measured the success of a work of art by its ability to embody not only certain objects and figures from the inside, but by its ability to render at the same time the reality of this imaginary space that contains them inside us, this space being infinitely and subtly different from the other external space. From this point of view: what an unrivalled world of the soul, what distances of the spirit there are in these outpourings that make use of drawing to arrive directly at a pure, simultaneous, and perceptible music.[7]

Through Rilke, Marguerite and Roffredo met his companion, the artist Baladine Klossowska, whose younger son, Balthasar, grew up to become the enigmatic painter Balthus, and a friend of the Caetanis in his own right.[8] Rilke very likely also introduced Marguerite to the Austrian novelist and poet Hugo von Hofmannsthal,[9] who arrived in Paris in January 1925 to visit his daughter, Christiane. Like Rilke, Christiane was staying at the Hôtel Foyot, and on 25 February Marguerite and Roffredo invited Rilke and the Hofmannsthals to lunch in the hotel's restaurant.

Marguerite exchanged letters with Hofmannsthal until his death in 1929, and two pieces by him appeared in *Commerce*.[10] While Marguerite's friendship with him was intensely literary, it came to include his whole family. It was also helpful to Roffredo, since Hofmannsthal had written the libretti for no less than six of the operas of Richard Strauss,[11] and with Strauss and the playwright Max Reinhardt, had founded the Salzburg Music Festival in 1920. Roffredo sent him the German text of *Hypatia*, and in early May 1925, while on a trip to further the production of the opera the following year, visited him at his home near Vienna. Later he wrote an account of the visit to Marguerite:

> I lunched with the Hofmannsthals in their small country house in Rodaun. – They were most sympathetic – so simple and sincere. He has read very carefully the libretto of Hypatia and told me things which gave me a great pleasure ... The Hofmannsthals are very poor having been ruined by the war. – The daughter is living on nothing, we'll have to help her.

Marguerite and Roffredo duly befriended Christiane, inviting her to stay at Villa Romaine on several occasions, and Marguerite sent her books and articles of clothing. The Hofmannsthals, father and daughter, returned to Paris to attend a special event organized by Marguerite at Villa Romaine on Saturday, 23 May: a performance of excerpts from *Hypatia*, given by five soloists, before a select audience of twenty that included Rilke, Valéry, Larbaud, Fargue, and Paulhan, and patrons of the Parisian musical scene such as Count Boni de Castellane and the Princesse de Polignac. After this occasion, Hofmannsthal wrote to his wife, Gerty, concerning Marguerite, that "she is such a delightful woman, it's so easy to have fun with her. She can't be much younger than you (with Americans it's hard to tell) but she gives the impression of being young."[12] Hofmannsthal's efforts to promote the production of *Hypatia* were appreciated, and while they lived in Versailles, Marguerite and Roffredo supported their friend's involvement with the Salzburg Festival by attending it and inviting friends to join them every August. Marguerite also made a point of introducing Hofmannsthal to writers he wanted to meet, such as Paul Claudel (even if he did not, as in that instance, end up liking them very much).

In contrast, to Marguerite herself Hofmannsthal penned the following tribute, in a letter of 2 July 1925:

> It is an exquisite pleasure to think of you. You surround yourself with poets and artists, and the air around you remains very pure and very clear, with no shadow of snobbishness. You talk to dogs as one should talk to dogs, you talk to plants as it is fitting to talk to plants, you talk to poets as one should talk to poets – and you remain yourself, of an unfailing grace. You are admirable.[13]

As the opening paragraph of a letter to a friend this can hardly be surpassed, but it is also a revealing evocation of Marguerite at the point when *Commerce* had added a new dimension to her life. This dimension was secondary, to be sure, to that nucleus consisting of herself and Roffredo, Lelia, and Camillo, around which all else moved, but it was important, nonetheless, in that it mobilized her intellect, her very considerable energy, and her gifts of character to a new and unexpected degree. As will become apparent, the beneficial repercussions eventually rippled outwards from her family and social circles to the wider cultural milieu.

For the moment, however, she needed all of that "unfailing grace" to keep the aspects of an increasingly demanding life in some kind of balance. Ronald Davies, an English writer resident in Paris, had replaced Adrienne Monnier as administrator for *Commerce*, so that, as yet, Marguerite was still at one remove from the actual production of the review. By the early spring of 1925, three numbers had been produced, bringing to a discerning French readership an array of writing, in superb translations, by such internationally recognized figures as T.S. Eliot, James Joyce, Rainer Maria Rilke, Max Jacob, André Breton, and Georg Büchner (the author of *Wozzeck*), as well as essays and poems by Fargue, Larbaud, Valéry, Paulhan, and Saint-John Perse. In

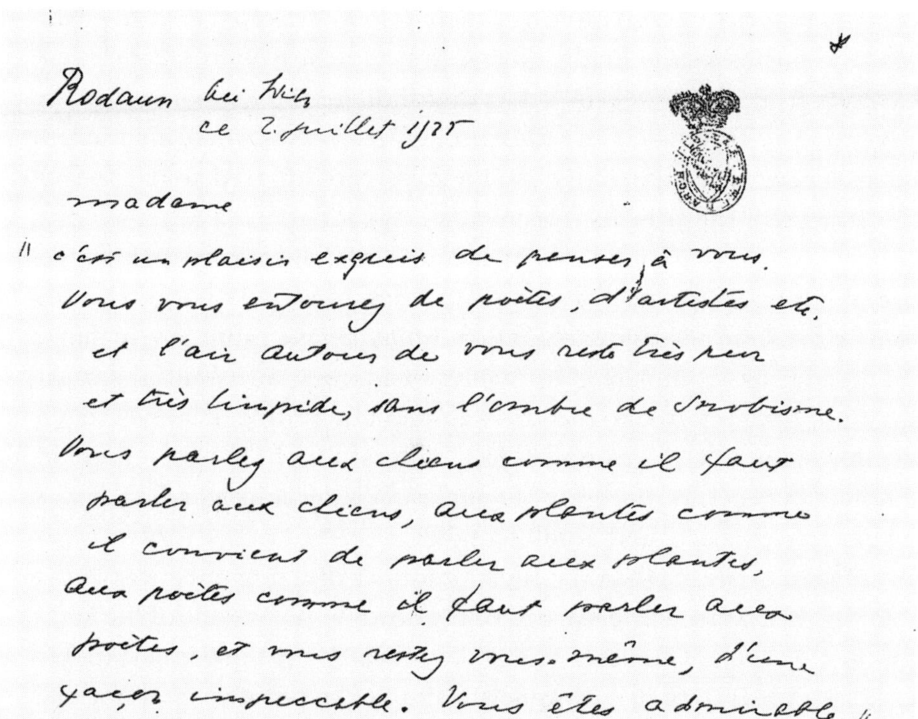

Rodaun bei Wien
ce 2. juillet 1925

Madame

// c'est un plaisir exquis de penser à vous.
Vous vous entourez de poètes, d'artistes etc.
et l'air autour de vous reste très pur
et très limpide, sans l'ombre de snobisme.
Vous parlez aux chiens comme il faut
parler aux chiens, aux plantes comme
il convient de parler aux plantes,
aux poètes comme il faut parler aux
poètes, et vous restez vous-même, d'une
façon impeccable. Vous êtes admirable //

// Vous m'avez fait connaître Claudel, et je
vous en reste infiniment reconnaissant.
Tout dans ce souvenir, m'émeut étrangement,
même ce qui semble embarassant:
sa lourdeur, l'apparence bourgeoise,
l'absence de goût, de finesse et de
toutes leurs qualités qu'ils estiment trop.
Il ne s'agit pas de tout ceci; il ne

8.1
A page from Hugo von Hofmannsthal's letter to Marguerite of 2 July 1925, a delightful word portrait of her, from an appreciative friend.

contrast to these modern offerings, there were two from the seventeenth century: poems by the English metaphysical poet Robert Herrick and excerpts from the travels to Persia and India of the French nobleman Jean-Baptiste Tavernier. The appearance of *Commerce* would alter somewhat during the course of its life: the different-coloured covers meant to distinguish the seasons, for instance, would give way to a simple, cream cover. Speculation has arisen concerning the meaning of the figure of a Roman (or steelyard) balance that appeared on the cover of every issue. One possible explanation is that it was a rebus, a visual pun on the idea of "commerce," of which weighing is an essential part. It may also have referred to the idea that modern writing, however much greater in quantity, is grounded in the literature of the past – finite in amount, but equally "weighty" in quality. Whatever its meaning, it was an attractive device, and a talking point.

In March 1925, when the fourth number of *Commerce* was being put together, Marguerite learned of the death in New York of her stepmother, Cornelia Garrison Van Auken Chapin, at the comparatively early age of sixty-two.[14] Marguerite and her stepmother had not met since the latter's long trip to France with Katherine in 1912, and no correspondence between them survives. In the aftermath of the death, the younger Cornelia, now aged thirty-two, came on a five-month tour of Europe, staying with Marguerite and Roffredo at Villa Romaine from 18 May to 18 June. At that time of year, the grounds surrounding the house were at their best, and as Cornelia recorded in her travel journal, Marguerite's home seemed to her "a Villa in fairyland. My large room looks on to the garden – main floor off the childrens' salon – such books, paintings – all is Beauty!"[15] Moony, the female Briard, had produced four pups a few weeks earlier ("What on earth are we going to do with such a large family?" queried Roffredo by letter, on learning of the event), and this added to the general gaiety of the reunion after so many years.

As Marguerite discovered, her younger half-sister was determined to achieve her goals in life, and was already an accomplished sculptor. She and Katherine were products of the first wave of "progressive" women's education in the United States. Cornelia began to draw and

COMMERCE

CAHIERS TRIMESTRIELS PUBLIÉS PAR LES SOINS DE PAUL VALÉRY, LÉON-PAUL FARGUE, VALERY LARBAUD.

RÉDACTION ET ADMINISTRATION
160, RUE DU FAUBOURG SAINT-HONORÉ
PARIS-VIIIe

AUTOMNE 1925 CAHIER V

IL A ÉTÉ TIRÉ DE CE CAHIER 2.850 EXEMPLAIRES DONT 100 EXEMPLAIRES SUR HOLLANDE VAN GELDER NUMÉROTÉS DE 1 A 100, 250 EXEMPLAIRES SUR PUR FIL LAFUMA NUMÉROTÉS DE 101 A 350, ET 2.500 EXEMPLAIRES SUR ALFA NUMÉROTÉS DE 351 A 2.850.

EXEMPLAIRE IMPRIMÉ POUR

LE PRINCE ROFREDO CAETANI DI BASSIANO.

N° 2

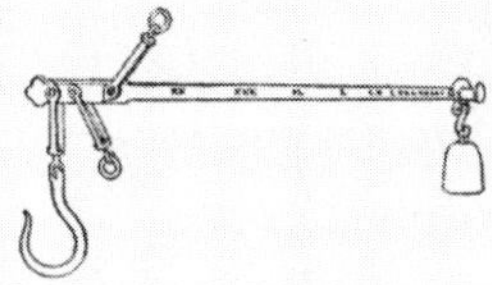

SOMMAIRE

PAUL VALÉRY
A B C
LÉON-PAUL FARGUE
TUMULTE
JEAN PAULHAN
L'EXPÉRIENCE DU PROVERBE
* * *
RA-CHRYSALIDE
* * *
NUKARPIARTEKAK
RUDOLF KASSNER
LE LÉPREUX
FRANCIS PONGE
POÈMES
ARCHIBALD MACLEISH
POÈMES
JEAN PRÉVOST
L'HOMME A LA MONTRE
ANDRÉ BEUCLER
ENTREPRISES DE FÉERIES
HŒLDERLIN
POÈMES
suivis d'une documentation sur la folie de Hœlderlin réunie par B. Groethuysen.
MAURICE SCÈVE
Fragments de MICROCOSME
suivis de Notes sur Maurice Scève par Valery Larbaud.

8.2 *Clockwise from top left Commerce*, autumn 1925: a) cover, b) inside cover (with the device of the Roman balance), and c) table of contents.

paint, model and carve in her teens, spending much of her time at the Metropolitan Museum and New York's many art galleries. She studied first with the painter and sculptor Gail Sherman Corbett, only settling on sculpture as her medium, and animals as her subjects, in her mid-twenties. In 1925 she had not yet settled on the technique of carving from the live model that would later distinguish her, and the pieces she created, compared with later ones, were still on a small scale.[16] In addition to sculpture, she had other interests. She was one of the first women in America to gain a pilot's licence, and for a time kept her own airplane. Like Katherine, she was a talented actress, belonging for a time to a good amateur theatre company. She shared Marguerite's passion for book collecting, and had a particular interest in typography and design – subjects on which the shelves of Villa Romaine had much to offer. The walls of the villa, too, repaid leisurely study. Marguerite's collection of modern paintings now included works by De Chirico, Balla, Picasso, Braque, Derain, Segantini, De Segonzac, and Roualt, Masson, and Breton, as well as the smaller works by Bonnard and Vuillard from before her marriage. Since the war she had also acquired numerous prints, woodcuts, and other works on paper.[17]

This visit was, in fact, the first time that Cornelia had met Lelia and Camillo, soon to turn twelve and ten. Through the photographs brought by her, they in turn "met" their cousins: Katherine's sons, Randolph and Garrison, now five and two, and Paul's three sons, Paul, John, and Schuyler, the last-named also just two. Marguerite had not yet met Katherine's husband, Francis Biddle, nor her brother Paul's wife, Leila (née Burden). Cornelia had also brought papers regarding a further bequest to Marguerite from their father's estate, of which his widow had enjoyed the use during her lifetime. (The bequest, as Cornelia confided to her diary, came as "a surprise to her. Will she use it for the children or *Commerce*?") Given Cornelia's job as Charlotte Osgood Mason's secretary, she was eager to tell Marguerite about her employer's financial support of struggling Black writers, but did not receive the response from her sister she had hoped for. As Cornelia explained, Mason's sponsorship, though generous, was conditional on her protégés' acknowledgment of her as "Godmother" (although they were not to speak of her as such to others), and she claimed ultimate control over the work they produced. To Marguerite, for whom the imagination and artistic freedom were virtually sacred, this demand for subservience was deeply distasteful. She was genuinely interested in the new writing Mason fostered, but talk of Mason herself was received with perceived coolness.[18]

Cornelia's visit passed in a blur of social and cultural events, including the recital at Villa Romaine of excerpts from *Hypatia* on 23 May. As she recalled many years later, Marguerite and Roffredo were a handsome couple, and it was "thrilling to go about with them" when they all went into Paris to dine or attend the theatre. She met Paul Valéry, Valery Larbaud, and the others who worked so closely with Marguerite on *Commerce*, and writer-friends who had been drawn into it by one or another of them. Among these was the German-born philosopher Bernard Groethuysen, a long-standing friend of Jean Paulhan's. Groethuysen is little known in the English-speaking world today, but between the wars he was one of the Continent's leading academics and intellectuals, holding degrees from four German universities, but equally at home in France.[19] He wrote mainly on the philosophers of the Enlightenment; he had translated works by Goethe into French, and would later perform the same service for Kafka. In May 1925 he and the Caetanis had only recently met, but they were becoming friends. His enthusiasm for finding suitable "ancient texts" for *Commerce* greatly pleased Marguerite. The Tavernier piece in Cahier II and the *Fragments mystiques* by the fifteenth-century German religious writer Meister Eckhart in Cahier IV were the first pieces he suggested and translated for her. His sensitivity to the nuances of meaning in several languages made him invaluable to Roffredo as well.

Villa Romaine in the mid-1920s brought together under one roof – or within the same garden, depending on the season – an international group of people, and provided them with relaxing surroundings in which to carry on their exchange of ideas. Given the times, it is hard to imagine that political discussion had no place in this, but anything heated or divisive is unlikely to have found much favour with Marguerite. This placed Villa Romaine in the direct line of succession of the classical

Paris salons of the nineteenth century.[20] At the same time, it was resolutely modern in its openness to new ideas and modes of expression. Above all, the atmosphere was truly civilized in being stimulating and inclusive, a hospitable, unpretentious, American-style open house, where people ate well and abundantly, and laughed a lot. If Valery Larbaud characterized *Commerce* to Marguerite as "cette belle maison où vous recevriez qui vous voudriez bien honorer de votre confiance,"[21] the Italian poet, Guiseppe Ungaretti, considered that Villa Romaine reflected the same direct, cosmopolitan outlook as the review, "a true Italian home on French soil, open to anyone regardless of nationality."[22] Ungaretti, temporarily living in Paris in 1925, was another friend of Paulhan's, initially drawn into *Commerce* as an expert translator, and then invited to recommend pieces by Italian authors. Georges Limbour, who contributed numerous translations to the review and years later produced an index to it, was another who characterized *Commerce* as having set itself "above rivalries, clans and parties, exclusivism and fanaticism … as a place of reconciliation."[23]

On the whole, those who were invited to Villa Romaine prized the experience, but inevitably, it did not please everyone. One disgruntled visitor was the English art critic Roger Fry, the organizer of the first great London exhibitions of Post-Impressionist French painting in 1910 and 1912, and the founder of the Omega Workshops. His account reveals more about his own outlook than it does about the occasion:

> Yesterday Groethuysen, that extraordinary pig-eyed Russian, Dutch, German, Frenchman, came to fetch me to the Princess Bassiano's … The Princess, who is a nice innocent little American with all an American's passion for poetry, came and took us off in her car to her splendid villa at Versailles. A big grand house and horribly cold – a very good dinner; she's celebrated for her *entremets*, but alas! Only champagne (tho' good of its beastly kind), two exquisitely pretty children. The Prince is Italian and a caricature *en beau* of the English Lord. A family of enormous Sussex sheep dogs, which had to be continually shepherded back into the corner where they were supposed to lie. Groethuysen

> waving his hands in the air as he speculated in the abstract. After dinner Groethuysen and the Prince retired to work at the German translation of an opera which he has written in Italian and composed the music of – can so pretty a prince really be a musician and a poet? – and I was left to talk poetry and painting, Waley, Eliot, Ezra Pound, Virginia Woolf, etc., with the Princess – and to go round a picture gallery, Derain, Marchand and a fine screen by Vuillard and her latest addition, that beastly young Surrealist Masson on which she had my opinion *sans réserves*. To see people who've got Vuillard and Derain and Segonzac, now buying out of sheer docile snobbism this foul art nouveau muck made me let fly quite impolitely and impoliticly. The time began to drag heavily, and at last Groethuysen and the Prince appeared and we were motored back to Paris.[24]

The condescending tone of this missive does little credit to Fry, and since the work of André Masson now hangs in most of the major art collections of Europe and America, it would seem that, in the long run, Marguerite's judgment trumped the critic's. Whatever it was that he said about her pictures on the evening he came to dinner, she was glad to include a story by him, "Moustiques," translated by Charles Mauron, in Cahier VII (Spring 1926) of *Commerce*, alongside "Poème" by Edith Sitwell, translated by Valery Larbaud.

As the review gained momentum, and as the circle of friends and collaborators involved with it grew, it inevitably anchored Marguerite and Roffredo yet more firmly to France. More important, even, than *Commerce*, or than her own inability, because of low blood pressure, to bear Rome's summer heat, was Marguerite's conviction that Lelia and Camillo were receiving a better cultural formation in Versailles than they would in Rome. A new factor now added weight to this belief. Lelia's interest in painting is usually dated to around the time when she was twelve. Had Cornelia Chapin, whose lengthy stay at Villa Romaine that year must surely have included some sketching sessions, offered her niece some guidance and encouragement? Given that Lelia was growing up in a house filled with works of art, a house in which artists of every kind were frequent guests, it is perhaps not surprising that she began to paint. Marguerite, with years of experience of looking at other painters' work, soon discerned that her daughter had an artistic bent. Helping her to develop it became a priority for Marguerite, and in the mid-1920s this tended to reduce still further the time that she and the children spent away from Versailles.

All the same, Roffredo's commitments in Italy remained pressing. He continued to travel back and forth about once a month to see Ada and Michelangelo (and Nella too, if she happened to be in Rome). His distinguished aunt Ersilia Caetani Lovatelli died, aged eighty-five, on 22 December 1925, but Roffredo kept up with his cousin Filippo, a sculptor, and helped him to resume his career after an illness.[25] In the autumn and spring he journeyed by way of Nice or Monte Carlo, so as to be able to escort Michelangelo, and sometimes Ada as well, to or from some villa or apartment rented for the winter months. Even if the sunshine prescribed by Michelangelo's doctors did little to alleviate his physical discomfort, the change of surroundings seemed to do him good. Witnessing his struggle to retain mobility as his joints stiffened was hard for Ada: Roffredo and Giovanella were all too aware of this, but even Leone, reading between the lines of his mother's letters in far-off British Columbia, perceived that it must be "a most painful and trying experience ... especially at your age, when one would wish and hope for a little more rest in life."[26]

There is no doubt that Roffredo found these absences from Marguerite and "the babies," as he called them, hard to bear. One letter, written the day after he had sent Marguerite a less-personal, more matter-of-fact account of his doings, reveals a surprising degree of insecurity:

> My beloved Darling,
> I am in much need of writing to you as it seems to me that this brings me nearer to you – I sometimes am taken by fear that you are so far away from me, and then my life seems to fade away into nothing. – I believe the "fool" we see on the stage is nothing but the living expression of that uncertainty that creeps in our

> lives; that mixture of drama, absurdities and pain. For some people life is a song, for others a blunder; for me it is an incessant effort to attain that perfection in my inner life that leads to a certain form of happiness, a form that since I've met you centers [*sic*] round your dear self. But let me say with Goethe "Lass das Vergangen vergangen sein!"[27]

The last line, from Goethe´s *Faust*, means, roughly, "Let bygones be bygones," though quite what the bygones referred to might have been is anybody's guess.

When he was compelled to be away, Roffredo made the best use of his time by presenting *Hypatia* to anyone he believed could assist it into production: prolific operatic composers such as Umberto Giordano, who lived in Rome and whom he knew personally, and music directors such as Arturo Toscanini at La Scala in Milan and Franz Schalk at the Vienna State Opera House. In other free moments he visited artists' studios, in search of "anything worthy of the Villa Romaine." "I went to see De Chirico," he reported to Marguerite. "Very few pictures in his private house arranged with awful, banal, sous-Borsch taste. Nothing I saw was tempting in any way."[28] He also made the rounds of the antiquarian book dealers, looking for fine editions of travel narratives for Marguerite's collection of this kind of literature, and sent her details of the condition and price of anything he thought worth her attention.[29] At any social gatherings, he sought people's views on possible authors for *Commerce*.

One positive development was that, early in 1925, Gelasio returned to Italy. Before leaving America he persuaded the Rockefeller Foundation to fund a program for controlling the malarial mosquito in the Pontine Marshes, and to set up a research station to monitor the effect of this on the health of the workers living there. In his two and a half years in Washington he was considered to have accomplished a great deal.[30] As the spokesman for the Mussolini regime, he was charged with increasing support for it among Italian-Americans (many of whom were strongly anti-fascist), and in American commercial and banking circles. The regime's drive for modernization and greater efficiency, at a time when the dread of Bolshevism dominated much public debate, was seen positively by American financiers, especially by men such as Thomas Lamont of J.P. Morgan and Company, whose endorsement was being sought for loans and investment.[31]

Other tasks undertaken by Gelasio included negotiating more favourable terms for the war reparations payments being made to Italy. Astonishingly, he found time to initiate the reform of the consular service, to establish an exchange program for young Italian and American engineers, and to put in train the design and building of a new Italian embassy in Washington. These were projects dear to his heart, in which he could invest his own expertise. The land he purchased for the new embassy was located at Sixteenth and Fuller streets, on what became known as "the Avenue of the Presidents." The design for the building was executed by the architects Warren and Wetmore, but Gelasio is said to have contributed the graceful loggia that is one of its most attractive features.[32] Around the edges of all this activity, he produced scientific articles for the engineering and metallurgical press, popular ones for *National Geographic* and *Time* magazines, political tracts, and dispatches. His duties were nothing if not varied: when the great Italian actress Eleanora Duse died suddenly in Pittsburgh while on tour, at Mussolini's request Gelasio even organized her four-day lying-in-state in New York, and the transport of her body to Italy at the regime's expense.[33]

Gelasio returned to Rome in triumph, the recipient of three honorary doctorates (from Columbia, Yale, and the University of Idaho), and was promptly made Honorary Royal Ambassador and appointed to Italy's Office of External Affairs. He was also appointed vice-president of the newly formed AGIP (Azienda Generale Italiana Petroli, or Italian General Oil Company) oil consortium. His engineering qualifications and knowledge of the Pontine region made him even more useful in Rome than in Washington, and he was made a technical consultant to the Mussolini regime's three-phase marshland drainage scheme, which began in 1926.[34] In between trips abroad on behalf of the AGIP, he spent time at Ninfa. His ever-fertile mind was usually juggling several projects at once, and being on the other side of the Atlantic had meant only a temporary hiatus in carrying out those he had left behind. The internal economy of the Caetani estates was a matter of urgency, as taxes had gone up by 50 per cent and the value of the lira had fallen by the same proportion in the previous five years. At Ninfa, Gelasio set about increasing revenue by extending the cultivation of pears, melons, peaches, walnuts, hazelnuts, and almonds, and by introducing tobacco. The sale of these crops generated enough to offset the taxes by the summer of 1927. Somehow he found time to see three immense genealogical works through the press in the first few years after his return: the *Regesta Chartarum*, in volumes issued between 1925 and 1932, the *Epistolarium Honorati Caietani, Signori di Sermoneta*, in 1926, and the second and third volumes of *Domus Caietana* in 1927.[35]

In Gelasio's absence, the administration of the family estates had fallen to Roffredo, and this allayed any suspicion that might have arisen on the part of the regime on account of his living abroad. When Gelasio returned, however, he again emphasized to his brother the importance of being resident in Italy to protect his interests, which would one day become Camillo's. The Villa delle Tre Madonne on Roffredo's plot of land in the Valle Giulia was by this time free of encumbrances, and the idea of rebuilding it as a home for the winter months was revived. It needed extensive renovation, but it bore similarities to Villa Romaine, and had an enormous garden that Roffredo thought would please Marguerite: "I see in that property a delightful house and a garden that is *yours* in which you can enjoy yourself during the three months of winter,"[36] he wrote in 1924, but by 1926 the eloquence of events suggests that Marguerite did not see the prospect of uprooting the children and producing *Commerce* from Rome in quite the positive light that Roffredo did. Between the urgings of his brother and his concern for Ada and Michelangelo on one hand, and Marguerite's preference for life in Versailles on the other, Roffredo found himself in an uneasy middle ground. Since in any case he had to travel often to Rome, he pressed ahead with his project, despite the political outlook that so alarmed Marguerite.[37]

In contrast, his dream – and Marguerite's, too – of seeing *Hypatia* produced looked set to be realized early in 1926. Through the mediation of Count Harry Kessler, Roffredo received a firm proposal to stage the opera in German from Ernst Praetorius, the director of the Vereinigte Stadtische Theater (National Theatre) in Weimar. The date set for the premiere was 23 May of that same year. In the months before it, Marguerite organized invitations to the major music critics in France, England, Germany, Austria, and Switzerland. Having reserved most of the hotel rooms in Weimar, she wrote to members of the family and close friends, inviting them to be Roffredo's guests at the premiere. The news was circulated to acquaintances and professional contacts all over Europe well in advance. Roffredo himself was in Weimar for a month before the event, and Marguerite for a week, to greet those who came, some from halfway across Europe. The occasion brought together the Crawford cousins, Vittoria, Cora, and Topazia, Gelasio and his companion, Countess Piccolomini, old friends like Count Kessler, newer ones like the Hofmannsthals and the Paulhans, and supporters such as the cultural philosopher and translator Rudolf Kassner, of whom Marguerite had heard much, but had not actually met.

The opera was staged during a two-week period, during which it was well attended and reviewed. As Marguerite later wrote to Rilke, who was back in the Val-Mont sanatorium and thus unable to attend, it was a splendid and celebratory launch: "Roffredo has had a great triumph and everything has gone better than anyone could have imagined. All the big critics came and there were marvelous articles about *Hypatia* in all the papers."[38] Of Kassner, whose friendship she would enjoy for the next three decades, she wrote, "What a charming and extraordinary being. I find him totally delightful."[39]

Back in Versailles in June 1926, Marguerite set to work on the summer issue (Cahier VIII) of *Commerce*, and Roffredo once again departed for Rome. In his absence there took place one of the most memorable musical events of the 1920s – or indeed, of the entire twentieth century. On 19 June, the *Ballet Mécanique*, by the twenty-three-year-old American composer George Antheil, was given its premiere at the Théâtre des Champs-Elysées. As Sylvia Beach observed, the venue was

8.3
Roffredo (centre), with Ernst Praetorius, conductor (left), and Ludwig Roffmann, tenor, looking over the score of *Hypatia*, Weimar, May 1926.

packed. Antheil's supporters were led by Ezra Pound, but there was a large contingent of troublemakers among a crowd of the merely curious. Those attending – presumably in support – included other literary figures: "There were the Joyces in a box. There was our rarely seen T.S. Eliot, so handsome and so elegantly dressed, and with him was Princess Bassiano."[40] Written for pianola, three grand pianos, a xylophone, bass drums, and a collection of sound-producing objects including electric buzzers, airplane propellers, a gong, and a siren, the performance left no one unmoved. Insults flew and fights broke out in the aisles. In the resulting pandemonium, Pound is said to have leapt to his feet and bellowed, "Vouz êtes tous des imbéciles!" Antheil was elated to have provoked "the biggest riot since the première of Stravinsky's *Rite of Spring* eleven years earlier" (or, as composer Aaron Copeland put it, to have "outsacked the Sacre").[41] One would give much to have overheard the homeward-bound conversation of Marguerite and "Tom"

Eliot after this event. To attend *Hypatia*, the *Ballet Mécanique*, and Wagner's Ring cycle (to which she took the children) within the same five-week period must surely qualify Marguerite as a heroic music lover, as well as one who possessed a catholic taste.

Simply because she was always there, Marguerite spent more time with Lelia and Camillo than did Roffredo. The three read and conversed, they listened to music, they had guests to lunch and went to Paris for exhibitions, the theatre, and concerts. Marguerite and Lelia played a great deal of tennis on the court at Villa Romaine, and, of course, Lelia sketched and painted. Marguerite also had a greater share in the children's education than their father did, though Roffredo kept in close touch by letter when he was away. In a New Year's letter to Gelasio, she related how she was "reading Herodotus to the babies and they love it, occasionally I find myself plunged in the middle of some rather impossible passage but after a little floundering about I get out again somehow" (a comment that suggests that she might have been translating aloud from the original Greek!)[42] It was Marguerite who engaged her old friend and admirer Edouard Vuillard as Lelia's painting tutor, and arranged for him to accompany them both on outings to the Louvre. It was she who decided to employ the former journalist Andrea Caffi (a friend of Giuseppe Ungaretti, who recommended him) as Camillo's tutor in 1927.[43] Unlike Lelia, who was a studious child, but who, like Marguerite at the same age, was extremely shy, Camillo was not by nature particularly bookish, but was outgoing and affectionate. He loved animals and the natural world, and enjoyed photography as a hobby. As time went on, art and archaeology would capture his imagination, which gave him even more in common with his mother. Marguerite supervised her children's development closely, ensuring that they got sufficient practice in Italian, French, and English to be trilingual, though it is not known whether they ever achieved that standard in German. This mix of languages sometimes had amusing results, as when Camillo, aged eleven, addressed his mother in a letter as "Dear Suite."[44]

It was by now apparent that Camillo would have to supplant Leone's son, Onorato, as heir to the dukedom.[45] Despite suffering from a degree of intellectual impairment, Onorato was able to drive a motor car – and,

8.4
Onorato Caetani ("Onoratino") (1902–1946), Prince of Teano and, from 1935, 16th Duke of Sermoneta.

in August 1927, aged twenty-five, sustained a broken leg through doing so at breakneck speed. But Leone's letters to Ada reveal his son's limitations, and how disappointing his own relationship with him had become. The young man lived in Vittoria's apartment in the Orsini Palace, but as she was often elsewhere, and since there was little contact between his parents, his father could truthfully comment to Ada: "Of Onorato I know very little. He hardly ever writes to me anymore … I found it very trying to be alone with him in Rome. No conversation at all, but only absorbed in his own thoughts. How sad and tragic!" A few months later, Leone reverted to the same theme: "Our correspondence has all but ceased. I cannot find anything to tell him in my letters, and his too, poor boy, don't say much."[46]

In contrast, of his daughter, Sveva, now on the cusp of adolescence, Leone wrote proudly that she was tall, like all the Caetani, and that since she spent so much time out of doors, she was sturdy and tanned.

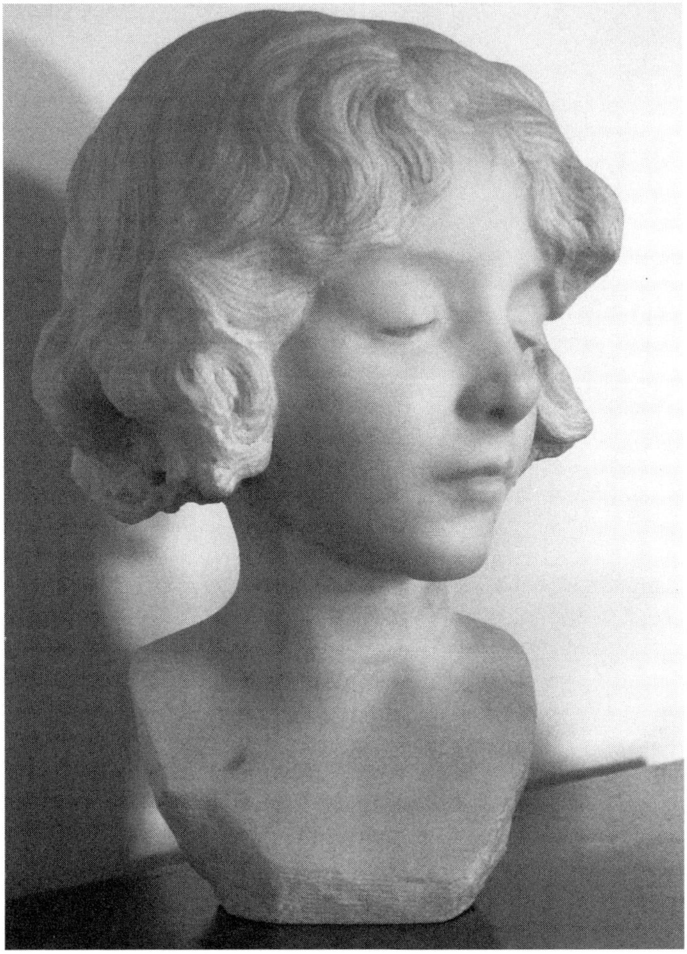

8.5
Sveva Caetani, aged eight, by her cousin Filippo Lovatelli Caetani.

"She is ever so intelligent and turns out successfully in whatever things she tries her hand: music, drawing, writing stories also. She has a passion for reading, and prefers books of adventure."[47] It was Marguerite, in fact, who kept Sveva supplied with regular shipments of books as she grew up, and was the member of the family who, apart from Ada, wrote most regularly to Leone. His letters to Ada also make it clear that he did not intend to stay in Canada for good.[48] Although he never mentioned

Ofelia, there is an underlying sense that she had not adapted to life in Vernon. Leone had also come to believe that Sveva deserved a more intellectually stimulating life. In 1927 he began the process of legitimizing her under Canadian law, since the Italian legal system would have denied her even a part of his estate because of her illegitimacy. Leone had finally sold his share in Fogliano in 1925, because he believed the fascist regime would eventually take it from him,[49] but he still had some investments, and there were other places than Italy – the south of France, for instance – where he felt at home.

On his periodic visits to Europe, Leone (and sometimes Ofelia and Sveva too) stayed with Roffredo and Marguerite at Versailles. To Ada, he wrote that he was "convinced that Marguerite's intellectual influence on the children is a very good one," but that Lelia, though an attractive girl, was "so reserved and self-contained that one cannot make out what she feels and thinks." Camillo was "splendid and a darling," but Leone wondered whether he might be "too gentle to make his way with sufficient force in life."[50] Perhaps it was this sense that Camillo's character needed firming up if he were to administer his inheritance effectively that led Roffredo to insist on his spending more time in Rome once he entered his teens. It would not do for the boy to be virtually a foreigner by the time he came of age. Leone and Gelasio no doubt encouraged this idea, and certainly Ada felt that Camillo, though hardly lacking in social graces, should acquire "the education in good manners" appropriate to his class. At one point she sought an English tutor for the periods when he was in Rome,[51] much to Marguerite's irritation, as the influence of Caffi was expressly intended to keep such pretensions at a distance.

It is easy to forget that, alongside her family and social life, Marguerite was determining the content of *Commerce* and carrying out much of the editorial work involved in producing it – an immense task, the motive for which was, very simply, her love of literature, and the wish to introduce a selection of the best of it, ancient and modern, to a discerning French readership. All of this implied hours each day spent reading texts and writing letters. Having servants and a tutor for the children made it possible to find those hours, but a woman with less physical and mental energy than Marguerite might have used her time in other ways, or been less efficient at organizing it. She had support, of course, especially from Jean Paulhan (now the director of the *Nouvelle Revue Française*, following the death of Jacques Rivière in 1925), who received hundreds more manuscripts in the course of a year than he could use, and allowed Marguerite to sift through the surplus for pieces suitable for *Commerce*.

The readership for poetry in translation has never been large, in any country or at any time, nor is there usually much of a market for translated works of prose, however eminent the authors. That *Commerce* greatly increased its print run, from the 1,600 copies of Cahier I (Summer 1924) to the 2,850 copies of Cahier V (Autumn 1925), is remarkable, although it increased only marginally thereafter, to 2,900 copies, for Cahier IX (Autumn 1926), and remained at that level until the last number in 1932.[52] *Commerce* was at its height between 1926 and 1930 – the years when four numbers a year were published, as had been the founders' intention. In the course of producing the first half-dozen *cahiers*, Marguerite created the network of contributors that from then on provided the kind of material she wanted in sufficient quantity. Printing was now carried out on a regular timetable. There were no such things as formal editorial meetings, though she saw each of her "official" and "unofficial" colleagues fairly often socially. She carried on a lively correspondence with each of them concerning suitable texts; she commissioned translations into French where necessary; she coordinated the material she received, attempting to maintain a balance between prose and poetry, and to keep the length of each number to a manageable two hundred pages. Most importantly, although she sought and welcomed suggestions, she had an absolute veto over what went into the review, so that it is fair to say that the appearance of a text in *Commerce* reflected not only its unwritten ethos, but also her belief in its literary worth.

Valery Larbaud's familiarity with other literatures made him an invaluable source of recommendations and translations. He had lived in Spain for several years and knew Spanish and Portuguese literature well. Thanks to him, pieces by José Ortega y Gasset, Federico García Lorca, the Mexican writer Alfonso Reyes, and the Argentinian Ricardo Güiraldes were drawn to Marguerite's attention, and subsequently appeared in *Commerce*. Italy and its literature was another of Larbaud's passions, but his real strength was his knowledge of British, Irish, and American authors. He particularly admired James Joyce, and recommended to Marguerite the publication of the excerpts from *Ulysses* that appeared in the first number of *Commerce*, sharing with Auguste Morel the task of translating them into French.[53] Sometimes, instead of translating the pieces he suggested, he wrote long articles on their authors, as in the cases of Sir Thomas Wyatt, Robert Herrick, and Nathaniel Hawthorne. Larbaud's health was delicate; Marguerite sent him tonics, books, and the welcome opportunities for distraction afforded by trawling through his fifteen-thousand-volume library in search of suitable texts. He, Fargue, and Valéry contributed most frequently to *Commerce* throughout its life, as had been expected from the start. Apart from the odd occasion when circumstances made it impossible to do so, the three fulfilled their commitments, being paid for the pieces they wrote – twenty in the case of Larbaud, nineteen in that of Fargue, and eighteen in that of Valéry[54] – in addition to the annual honorarium each received.[55]

Marguerite paid her contributors and translators generously, as letters of thanks from many of them attest, but she also considered them friends, and treated them as such. She included them in social occasions, invited them to join her, Roffredo, and the children at the beach in Normandy or in the mountains of Switzerland; she inquired after their health, their wives and children, their work in progress; she sent them books; she sent other gifts when she knew that a particular thing would please. Paul Valéry, writing to thank her for one such item, advised her that "I shall become extremely prudent and when I see you I shall beware of admiring anything in your house, for fear of receiving it the next day."[56] Rudolf Kassner, revisiting Paris after many years, later wrote to her: "All Paris is for me still a *brouillard*; there is only one luminous point in it, it is you and your kindness."[57] The confidence of friendship worked both ways. When a forthcoming *cahier* was in need of something to make up the pages, she had no hesitation in appealing for help. There were numerous occasions when she urged one

8.6
A soberly dressed Paul Valéry with Lelia, Camillo, and Beary (the dog that terrified James Joyce, see note 23), on the beach at "Mon Rêve," Normandy, summer 1924.

or the other of her associates to "be an angel" – a favourite phrase – by producing something to fill a gap, even at the last minute. Here is Paul Valéry again:

> You are kind and terrible, an affectionate friend and a cruel tigress, and one feels that however hard one may try to hide oneself in the infernal regions, to transform oneself into a swallow, to grow a beard and wear green spectacles, it is all in vain. One cannot escape from your charm or your arrows. But truly, my dear friend, how do you expect me to write anything whatever (even very bad) for this autumn which is already here?[58]

By the very fact that her associates were all French, many of the texts they brought her – besides the pieces they wrote themselves – were naturally by French authors. A sampling yields such names as Louis

Aragon, Paul Claudel, André Gide, Jean Giono, Max Jacob, Francis Jammes, Marcel Jouhandeau, Georges Limbour, André Malraux, Louis Massignon, Henri Michaux, Francis Ponge, Jacques Prévert, Jules Supervielle, and Roger Vitrac. These represented a fair cross-section of writing since the turn of the century, and included writers associated with the postwar Surrealist movement, such as Antonin Artaud and André Breton, whose presence in the review was welcomed precisely because it aimed to be inclusive, and not because it advocated Surrealism.

The international character that Marguerite insisted on for *Commerce* was achieved, in part, through the aid of writer friends abroad whose work she admired and whose judgment she trusted, and who were well placed to identify emerging writers or unpublished work by established ones. They sometimes translated pieces for her, and supplied pieces of their own for others to translate. First among these allies was her cousin and friend "Tom" Eliot, who was now (having left the Bank of England) a senior editor at the publishing house of Faber and Faber in London, and editor of *The Criterion*. For the German-speaking world, she had Bernard Groethuysen, and Rilke until shortly before his death (from what turned out to be leukemia) in December 1926. Thereafter Marguerite enlisted the help of Hugo von Hofmannsthal, and following his death in 1929, that of Rudolf Kassner. Giuseppe Ungaretti recommended Italian writers, and Valery Larbaud those from the Americas, the British Isles, Spain, and Portugal. D.S. Mirsky, an exiled prince teaching at London University and author of *A History of Russian Literature to 1900*, still used as a textbook today, suggested compatriot writers and translated them from Russian into French.

Each of these writers kept an eye open for essays or poems from past centuries that could be set alongside contemporary writing. This kind of juxtaposition was another of the review's aims, and the result was an astonishing array of literature that spanned the centuries and the cultural gulfs dividing East and West. The poems of Wyatt and Herrick, those of Giacomo Leopardi, the fragments from the mystical writings of Meister Eckhart, and the travel narratives that appeared in the early *cahiers*, were joined in later ones by excerpts from Sir Thomas

Browne's *Hydriotaphia*, reports written by the Jesuit missionaries in China, scenes from medieval drama, folksongs from Madagascar, Sufi texts, a description of Zen Buddhism, classical Chinese poetry, and extracts from the Byzantine historian Michael Psellos. In the translation into French of this cultural treasure trove, Valery Larbaud, Georges Limbour, Bernard Groethuysen, Jean Paulhan, and Paul Valéry were notably active, but there were a dozen others who contributed to a more modest degree.

Marguerite evidently enjoyed placing historic texts, such as those cited above, in the company of work by more recent authors, not only, one might speculate, because she found the incongruities of time, place, and subject matter satisfying, but also because she wished to highlight the freshness of perception and expression that characterized great writing, old and new alike. Joyce and Eliot have already been mentioned, but other writers in English whose work appeared in *Commerce* in excellent French translations included Thomas Hardy, George Meredith, T.F. Powys, Edith Sitwell, Virginia Woolf (an important excerpt from the penultimate reworking of *To the Lighthouse*), Richard Aldington, and Liam O'Flaherty; among the Americans were venerable figures such as Nathaniel Hawthorne, Edgar Allan Poe, and William Faulkner, and younger poets like Archibald MacLeish and Roy Campbell. Writing translated from German included pieces by Rilke, Hofmannsthal, Büchner, Kassner, Nietzsche, Kafka, and Hölderlin, and from Danish, by Kierkegaard. The Russian authors included Pasternak, Mandelstam, Rosanov, and Pushkin, and the Italians, Leopardi, Ungaretti, Cecchi, Barilli, and Bacchelli.

It is hard to exaggerate the importance of *Commerce* in introducing to French readers – even though the *côterie* that subscribed to it was relatively small – this astonishing variety of translated material, ancient and modern. Marguerite sought translations of the highest accuracy and literary quality, being convinced, rather as were the compilers of the King James version of the Bible, that "Translation it is that openeth the windows to let in the light; that breaketh the shell, that we may eat the kernel." From personal experience, she understood the revelatory effect that removing, as far as possible, the barriers of language can have upon an individual's view of the world, but she was after something more. In principle, the best translation does more than just erode provincialism and enrich the common store of understanding; it clarifies both the experience conveyed, *and the reader's own*, and so bestows upon him, or her, an unexpected gift. This was perhaps one reason why Marguerite placed so much emphasis upon the translation of one poet's work by another poet: she believed that only a fellow poet could bring into being, in a second language, the gift inherent in a piece written in the poet's own. What she was seeking to do through translation was consistent with the original conception of *Commerce* as a review aimed at an intellectual elite, yet it brought to that elite the daring invitation to sample a range of literature not available elsewhere, rife with new ideas or with perennial ideas writ new.

And here, running through *Commerce* like a coloured thread through a tapestry, is Marguerite's other aim: her determination to set the literature of her own time in the context of the universal mainstream of human concerns. She loved what was new and fresh and stated with wit and style, in literature as in painting, yet she read, incessantly, the literatures of the past as well as the present. That Joyce's *Ulysses*, informed by Freud's theories of the subconscious and sexuality, marked a revolution in fiction, no one could deny, but its themes – love, the nature of fatherhood, identification with place – were as old as humanity itself, and as true of some rural village in medieval China as of Joyce's Dublin. The restatement in novel and modern terms of the perpetual themes of human existence was what interested Marguerite. This consideration may perhaps clarify the otherwise enigmatic comment that is her only known formal declaration of intent. It was made in a letter to Elisabeth Förster-Nietzsche, the elder sister of the German philosopher, to whom she was writing to ask permission to translate for *Commerce* two as-yet-unpublished pieces by him:

> *Commerce* has as its aim to give voice not only to those who can be said to be young today, but precisely and above all to those

> who will remain so … It is precisely in the union of that which has remained young, and will remain so always, with that which our own age contributes to the new, that I see the vocation of a review like *Commerce*.[59]

Whatever Marguerite meant by "young," it clearly did not refer merely to the chronological age of the writer, although in a given case, it might include that. Perhaps she had in mind something as simple as "whatever has stood the test of time," or, at a more sophisticated level, the Blakean celebration of the heightened consciousness, in and of the present moment, that distinguishes the poetic vision. She wanted whatever appeared in *Commerce*, ancient or modern, to possess an immediacy and authenticity of perception that transcended the centuries and the cultural barriers between writer and reader. This was the pleasure she herself derived from her wide reading, and through *Commerce*, she sought to share it.

Late-twentieth-century cultural theory has identified the technological, scientific, and psychiatric discoveries of the early part of the century, and the widespread traumatic effects of the First World War, as the origins of "modernism," and the art and literature produced after 1918 as "modernist" in having been influenced by them. Naturally, such terminology did not exist in Marguerite's day, though the conditions giving rise to it would have been all too familiar. Recently, the criteria for literary modernism generally agreed upon since the term arose in the 1970s have been applied to *Commerce*, and indeed (and perhaps not surprisingly), an analysis of the review has shown that it fulfills them. *Commerce* was "modernist" in that it provided a space for unpublished work by contemporary authors, both known and unknown; in that it set such pieces alongside texts from other eras and cultures; in that it avoided literary partisanship, and eschewed any kind of editorial intervention; in that it featured writing inspired by recent discoveries in psychology (such as the excerpt from Virginia Woolf's *To the Lighthouse*, translated by Charles Mauron, that appeared in Cahier X); and in that, by example, it proclaimed the cross-fertilization of ideas that translation could provide. In all these areas, Marguerite was a pioneer, though whether she would have conceived of herself as such we shall never know.

Where it is impossible to overstate her importance is in the matter of getting work that she believed in, even when she could not publish it, translated into other languages, and so made available to a vastly enlarged audience. One such instance (there would be others) was that of the epic poem *Anabase*, written by Alexis Léger during his term as a secretary of the French legation in Beijing, between 1916 and 1920. It first appeared in the *Nouvelle Revue Française* in 1923 under the author's pseudonym of "Saint-John Perse." The title was taken from Anabasis, the best-known work of Xenophon, the great military historian of the ancient world. The Greek word means, roughly, "a trek inland." The subject of the poem is enlightened kingship, but the underlying theme is that of human evolution, against a background of partnership with nature and the endurance of spiritual values through adversity and change.

On reading *Anabase*, Marguerite became convinced that her esteemed friend Léger had written one of the great poems of recent times, and that it should be translated as well and as rapidly as possible into the major European languages. Early in her friendship with Rilke, knowing that he had already translated poems by Paul Valéry into German, she invited him to undertake the task of translating *Anabase*. When he gently refused, she encouraged Hofmannsthal to do so. In the end, though each of these poets offered insights, it was Walter Benjamin who produced the first German translation, and Hofmannsthal and Bernard Groethuysen who improved on Benjamin's work. The German translation of *Anabase* was published in 1929 by Count Harry Kessler's Cranach Press, based in Weimar. Marguerite also brought *Anabase* to the attention of "Tom" Eliot, who agreed with her estimation of it to the point of undertaking the translation himself, and publishing it through Faber and Faber as *Anabasis* in 1930. Giuseppe Ungaretti undertook the poem's Italian translation, which was published in 1931. Interestingly, Marguerite did not have to seek translators for a Russian version, since two young Russian poets living in Paris, Georgii Adamovich and Georgii Ivanov, had independently published one in 1926. The point, however, is that, with that sole exception, the first translators of *Anabase* were literary colleagues and friends of Marguerite's, mustered by her in what amounted to a personal crusade to obtain for the poem and its author the recognition she believed they merited. In this, she acted as catalyst and promoter, yet typically sought no thanks, adulation, or recompense for doing so. It remains for writers of a later age to seek these for her.

9

THE MOVE TO ROME, AND NINFA

By the beginning of 1929, Marguerite had come to view more positively the prospect of spending the winter months in Rome. The renovation of the Villa Tre Madonne was in its final stages, after several years in which the project was plagued by bureaucratic delays and rising costs.[1] Roffredo had taken on a heavy mortgage to complete it, and was looking forward to seeing in the New Year 1930 under his own roof.

These hopes were shattered by the Wall Street Crash of October 1929, the greatest financial cataclysm of the twentieth century. All the signs that the market was unstable were there, but investors large and small had assumed that the speculative bonanza of "the Roaring Twenties" would go on indefinitely. When the bubble burst, industrial and financial systems collapsed, first in the United States, and then across the developed world. The great American corporations saw the value of their shares decimated, and in those countries dependent upon American investment and loans, such as Germany, the contagion of financial ruin and unemployment quickly spread.

The immediate effect of the Crash for Marguerite was dramatic, since part of her fortune was made up of American stocks and shares that plunged in value. The rest of it consisted of property: solid assets, in the form of apartments in Manhattan and commercial premises on Long Island and in the Chapin family seat of Springfield that produced rental income. This lulled her into thinking that the situation was not as serious as it first appeared, but as the American economy slid into depression, these properties ceased to generate income and became a massive tax burden. To add to this altered situation came the news that a friend to whom she had made a sizable loan could not now afford to repay her.

Neither were Roffredo's finances left unscathed. Following the introduction of the Dawes Plan in 1924, he had subscribed for shares in German government loans that were now suddenly all but worthless. Much of his capital was tied up, either in Villa Romaine or in the new villa in Rome, on which the mortgage became more onerous just at the point when renting it out – always Roffredo's fallback position – became most difficult. Compounding this situation was the hefty rise in the taxes payable on the Caetani estates in Italy, imposed by a fascist regime bent on increasing its revenues by any possible means.

Like his brothers, Roffredo was liable for a share of these taxes, but as it soon transpired, Michelangelo too had suffered substantial losses through having invested in Chilean loans. Neither brother was in as dire a position as Leone, who had no assets left in Italy except Villa Miraggio on the Janiculum, but who was heavily exposed in markets elsewhere. Having succeeded in legitimizing Sveva under Canadian law, Leone was in fact house-hunting in the south of France when the Crash occurred, and the value of his investments plummeted. His dream of living close to Italy and resuming his studies, of giving Sveva the education she deserved and Ofelia the sophisticated life she missed, were reduced to the all-too-familiar sense of bitter disillusionment. He made a quick visit to Rome to see Ada and Michelangelo before departing once again for Canada, where the house in Vernon offered sanctuary. In his haste – and possibly constrained by shipping costs – Leone abandoned a trunk filled with personal belongings in the left-luggage facility at Rome's Termini Station. It would come to light only decades later.

For a time, Marguerite viewed the change in her circumstances as something from which she would suddenly awaken to find everything restored to normality. She inevitably felt the suffering of those ruined by the Crash: "Auspitz tried to throw himself in the Danube and Octave Homberg is completely ruined,"[2] she wrote to Roffredo of two acquaintances, one the head of a private bank, the other a railway magnate. Some American members of the Paris-based expatriate community were forced to return home, while others clung on in reduced circumstances. There were family worries, too, quite apart from the plight of Leone, Ofelia, and Sveva. She shared the helpless indignation of Roffredo, her

9.1
Gelasio's terracotta bust of poet Giuseppe Ungaretti, 1929.

brothers-in-law, and Nella on the publication of *Times Past*, Vittoria's sometimes fantastical account of her marriage, with its unflattering portrait of life at Palazzo Caetani and allegations of discord over Onorato's will. Worse still was the news of the death, on 22 November 1930, of her seven-year-old nephew Garrison, the younger son of her sister Katherine and brother-in-law Francis Biddle.

And then there was Gelasio, whom she loved dearly, but whose support for the Mussolini regime she privately deplored. He often passed through Paris on his travels for the AGIP, but in the autumn of 1929 he arrived depressed and weary. Years of overwork were taking their toll in the form of back trouble, skin ailments, and general malaise. Leone had speculated in a letter to Ada a year earlier that his brother was finally disillusioned with politics, but Gelasio's idea of taking "time out" in Paris to work seriously at sculpture came as a surprise to everyone. In a rented house in the avenue Victor Hugo in the sixteenth arrondissement, he set about rebuilding his health with the aid of a homeopathic doctor and plenty of rest. In sculpture, as in any of his activities, Gelasio turned out to be extraordinarily talented. He began by modelling small clay figures, and moved on to gesso busts of Nella, Ada, and Onorato, working from memory or photographs. Only after mastering clay, terracotta, and gesso did he try to capture the likenesses of other friends in marble and stone. A number of these busts, such as one of Giuseppe Ungaretti, reveal astonishing skill and powers of observation.

An additional weight on Gelasio's mind and heart at this point was the illness of Annina Piccolomini, his companion of many years. As early as the summer of 1927, when, by chance, she and Ada were both taking cures in Berne, Gelasio became aware that Annina was not well. He later wrote to his mother about her, and in so doing, provided one of the few references to her in any of the Caetani correspondence:

> She has *so much* appreciated your attention towards her. Annina is such a responsive soul and so sensible to the good that other people bestow upon her that she would give everything she possesses in the world for the good of others. In this she resembles you to a great extent. It is a pity that circumstances have not permitted [*sic*] to have her as my companion in life.[3]

Annina had been estranged from her husband, Enea Silvio Piccolomini, the 15th Count of Triana, since shortly after their marriage in 1905.[4] Little is known of her apart from her patronage of the arts – and if her name survives today, it is perhaps because, in 1917, the composer Ottorino Respighi dedicated his *Deità Silvane* to her.[5] It would seem, reading between the lines, that Annina's illness may have been some form of cancer. Leone, writing to Ada in May 1928, asked her to "Let me know something of Annina Piccolomini's operation" and added: "Poor thing! It will have been the death blow to her looks. Is Gelasio also as faithful and devoted to her?"[6]

Whether Annina was with Gelasio during his time in Paris is never mentioned. To Ada, he reported visiting Marguerite and Roffredo, and that "Everybody is very nice and Margh. is taking interest in my efforts."[7] He also sent his impression of Lelia's development as an artist: "Lelia is doing remarkably well; she studies now with Vuillard ... who has put her to enjoying great drawings and her work is A.1. Really remarkable for the correctness and especially for the life and character she gives to her drawings. At times the copies are better than the originals."[8]

But Lelia was still very shy. In the autumn of 1930, by which time Gelasio had moved to a house with a larger studio at 96, avenue des Termes, he described to Ada how "Lelia came yesterday to lunch at my studio quite alone and tried hard to become talkative: her eyes speak but timidity bottles up the words in her throat."[9] On another occasion, she stood for more than an hour in a corner of the studio watching him work, and when he looked up, she had slipped silently away.

By the time Gelasio recorded these impressions, Marguerite and Roffredo had faced the cold reality of having to economize. The life they led at Villa Romaine – the number of servants and groundsmen, the spontaneous purchases of books and works of art, the Sunday gatherings, the entertaining of friends in Paris restaurants, the annual week at the Salzburg Festival, and the summer vacations in Switzerland and Normandy – had been drastically reduced. In a letter to Roffredo, probably written when he was visiting Michelangelo and Ada in Monte Carlo, Marguerite suggested renting out the Villa Tre Madonne when it was completed, rather than occupying it themselves, and spending the winter in Rome "in Osborne's flat" at Palazzo Caetani (the former tenant being Michelangelo's friend Sir Francis D'Arcy Osborne, a diplomat attached to the British embassy to the Holy See). She was also prepared to let Villa Romaine for the winter months.

But Roffredo was gloomy about the future, feeling overwhelmed by his expenses and tax obligations, and the fear of being compelled to let both his villas. Marguerite made a determined effort to shake him out of this mood: "*Please* don't be depressed – it spoils all life for me and the years are passing so quickly and there are other things so much more important than our money affairs. I am doing all I can to economise … when I speak of bills you must remember my income was cut of [*sic*] short without warning." Given her American citizenship, she could even suggest the option of spending time in the United States, which might possibly have had advantages for Camillo. She then went on to declare, with singular optimism, "I am not a bit afraid of the future as long as we all have good health and the children are happy … there are many worse things that can happen than [*sic*] even if we all have to work for our living. Please don't be so pessimistic."[10]

This was a refreshing assertion of values from someone who had never in her life had to worry about money! A few days later, Marguerite reiterated that "the only thing for us to do is live on the first floor of the Palazzo this next winter – that would certainly be the cheapest thing we could do." She even ventured to suggest that "We could make a lovely living room out of the ballroom." But she did not wish to leave Paris for good, so as "not to take Lelia away from the life she should have – the contact she should have with life. Any amount of sacrifice is worth that."[11]

Marguerite was referring here mainly to Lelia's artistic development, though she may have been thinking ahead to her matrimonial prospects too. There was, quite literally, no price she could put on being able to call upon a painter-friend like Edouard Vuillard to tutor Lelia. As she and Roffredo discussed what to do, other concerns surfaced. Economizing was one thing; putting all their financial eggs in a single basket by leaving Villa Romaine was another, especially when the "basket" was fascist Italy. By now all political opposition to Mussolini had been eliminated. The situation of dissidents and left-wing intellectuals was fraught with danger, though Roffredo, once again in sunny Monte Carlo, seemed to need persuading of it. In Paris, Marguerite met Italians who had been arrested without warning, and heard of others who had been beaten up by blackshirt thugs or whose homes had been ransacked. One of her few sharp exchanges with Roffredo was on the subject of bringing Camillo's tutor, Andrea Caffi, well-known in Italy as a socialist journalist, to Rome with them:

> It is evident from your telegram that you know nothing of what has been happening lately in Italy from one end to the other. Anyone suspected of anti-f. sympathies or of being friends with those already arrested can be at any moment arrested. There has never been a moment so dangerous for anyone like Caffi. This is the truth if you don't like it *tant pis*.[12]

Caffi did not in the end accompany the family to Rome for the winter of 1930–31, and in fact remained at Villa Romaine for only a few months after Marguerite and Roffredo returned to Versailles in March 1931 to begin the process of dismantling their life there. Their priorities by then were to find tenants for Villa Romaine, and then to get themselves and their possessions to Rome.

Marguerite had a priority of her own: finding a Paris apartment, to be paid for and maintained out of her own funds. Quite apart from her ambitions for Lelia and Camillo, she was unwilling to leave behind her many friends, or to trade the cosmopolitan ambience of the City of Light for Rome's relative provincialism. To spend part of each year in Paris was something for which she was prepared to make hard choices, one of which was to sell a number of her paintings.[13] With the proceeds, she bought an apartment at 4, rue du Cirque – a short street running between the Champs-Elysées and the rue St Honoré in the eighth arrondissement. This was an investment that was likely to appreciate, and a means of keeping some funds outside Italy. The apartment would remain Marguerite's Paris address until her move to 67, rue Madame in 1960.

Her most obvious economy was, of course, ceasing to fund *Commerce*. To Valery Larbaud, in a note written on New Year's Day 1931, she had already admitted that the review had become a heavy financial burden.[14] She apologized for the need to reduce the honoraria and payments to her collaborators, due to the fact that subscriptions and sales of the review in 1930 had recouped less than half the cost of producing it. Only two *cahiers* were produced in 1931: XXVII (Spring) and XXVIII (Summer), though the presence of pieces by Valéry, Claudel,

Kassner, and others, as well as the first French translation of Georg Büchner's *Woyzeck*, ensured that their quality was up to standard. The final issue of *Commerce* was Cahier XXIX (prepared in the autumn of 1931, as the family's belongings were being packed up for shipping), and issued as the winter number for 1932. It contained such varied offerings as T.S. Eliot's "Difficulties of a Statesman," translated by Georges Limbour, the *Récits de missionaires Jésuites* in China, edited and introduced by Bernard Groethuysen, and William Faulkner's chilling story, "A Rose for Emily," translated into French by Maurice-Edgar Coindreau. There were also shorter pieces by Henri Michaux, Georges Garampon, Georges Roditi, and the faithful contributors and friends, Paul Valéry and Valery Larbaud.

With Villa Romaine let, the move to Rome became the focus of everyone's attention. The question still hanging in the air was whether the state of Roffredo's finances would permit him to reside for long in the Villa Tre Madonne, now completed. His financial plight was aired by Michelangelo in a revealing series of letters to Gelasio in August 1931. Despite his affliction, the youngest of the Caetani was generously offering to vacate his own rooms and move to Palazzo Orsini nearby (and, he confided, to risk running into Vittoria), but only if Roffredo was serious about taking up *permanent* residence with Ada at Palazzo Caetani. Roffredo was apparently renowned in the family for indecision. Conversation with him left Michelangelo with two things clearly understood: first, "that Roffredo is still terribly vague about his future plans, especially when these consist of painful and inconvenient economies" and, secondly, that "his eventual arrival will be of a purely experimental character." Their brother's distress at his calamitous financial situation restrained his siblings from probing further, but for the moment, Michelangelo stayed where he was.

The furnishings from Versailles arrived at the Villa Tre Madonne late in December 1931, and Roffredo, Marguerite, and the children moved into their palatial new residence in the New Year. It was a short-lived idyll. In August 1932, in an effort to consolidate his debts, Roffredo took out a mortgage of six hundred thousand lire on the villa, but even this was not enough to stave off the need for further retrenchment.

Midway through 1933, the Villa Tre Madonne was let, then sold in May 1934.

So it was that Roffredo, Marguerite, Lelia, and Camillo took up residence at Palazzo Caetani, sometime in 1933, for a period intended to provide a financial breathing space. Since 1920, parts of it had been turned into apartments and let to tenants (mainly foreign embassies or their staff) to provide income, while, between them, Gelasio and Michelangelo covered the general expenses. Since Gelasio's return from Paris, he had lived a peripatetic existence among his apartments at Palazzo Caetani, Ninfa, Cisterna, and the castle at Sermoneta. Michelangelo thus felt able to devise an arrangement that converted some seldom-used parts of the palace into bedrooms to accommodate the new arrivals – the trade-off for Gelasio's loss of a private bathroom being that expenses would now be divided three ways, not two.[15]

It was one thing to have spent Christmas and other holidays at Palazzo Caetani over the years, and quite another for Marguerite to view it as home for the foreseeable future. If the new arrangement was to some extent makeshift, she was as good as her word, and made – as she had suggested – "a lovely sitting room out of the ballroom." That great salon had been the scene of so many lively gatherings through the generations that it seemed to hold the sounds and memories of past times. Always an excellent raconteur, eighty-five-year-old Ada grew animated in telling Lelia and Camillo of her early years at Palazzo Caetani, when the ballroom witnessed gatherings of the best minds in Europe around Duke Michelangelo. She described the pranks played on their delighted guests by the old duke and his brother "Don Pippo," the costume balls that went on until dawn, and how conversation gave way to silence as Liszt wrought his magic at the pianoforte. The parties given by Leone and Vittoria as newlyweds had left another set of echoes: laughter, and the chink of crystal as wine and punch were poured; the musicians tuning up, not for the next waltz or polka, but for the new, syncopated dances derived from ragtime.

And of course Ada evoked for her grandchildren the most singular feature of their heritage: the landscapes of the Pontine Marshes as she had known them as a young mother, the herds of wild horses and buffalo that roamed freely, the almost feudal conditions prevailing on the estates, and the way of life of the tenants. She summoned up the semi-tropical wilderness of Fogliano as it had been when she and Onorato created their first garden there at the edge of the lagoon. Lelia and Camillo had spent summers at Fogliano as children, before it was ceded to the Bonifacio, and they remembered the dunes, the swimming parties in the lagoon, and their grandmother's garden. In her old age, Ada's mind often turned to Fogliano, the beloved place whose drifts of daffodils recalled her English childhood at Lathom House and Rode Hall. Ninfa, where the task to be done in clearing, restoration, and planting was still so enormous, even after twenty years of her own and Gelasio's best efforts, was still for Ada "the new garden."

The transition to Rome in straitened circumstances was hard for Roffredo, but even harder for Marguerite. Rome was Roffredo's city and the palace his home, and if he was inwardly pained by his personal situation as well as the political one, pride and family considerations disposed him to find ways of tolerating them. For Marguerite, matters were more complex. Dictatorship was to her inherently wrong and hateful. She adapted without a qualm to the huge, chilly rooms and centuries-old furnishings of Palazzo Caetani, and even to the relative loss of independence that living there involved, but she was used to a social milieu in which people spoke their minds and discussed ideas – as indeed, until the advent of fascism, they had done in Rome. As someone who thrived on dialogue, she deplored the restrictions on freedom of expression that now prevailed in Italy, and the day-to-day violence used to enforce them. Above all, she found it hard to be open and sincere in the circles she was expected to frequent, since much of the Roman aristocracy and intelligentsia tacitly supported the regime. It would take her some time to find kindred spirits.

If the atmosphere of Rome was tense, that of Ninfa always restored a sense of proportion and well-being. Taking Ada and Michelangelo on excursions there provided a beneficial change of surroundings. Gelasio's improvements to walls, bridges, and waterways were by this time largely complete. Trees he had planted a decade earlier were becoming stately, especially the cypresses, which now formed an avenue framing a view

9.2
The villa at Ninfa, made habitable again by Gelasio Caetani in the 1920s.

of Sermoneta on its distant hilltop. Since inheriting Ninfa, Gelasio had sought ways of financing its restoration. To that end, the *hortus conclusus*, or "enclosed garden," now yielded artichokes and asparagus, tomatoes and other vegetables, that were regularly sent to market. The orchards of apple, plum, and Californian peach trees outside the walls were also commercially viable, the peaches being wrapped for shipment in the leaves of the small Concord grape known as *uva fragola*, cultivated at Ninfa more for the usefulness of the leaves than for the grapes themselves. Gelasio had thought of everything: to enhance the pollination and yield of the orchards, he had instituted beekeeping on a large scale.[16]

Countess Piccolomini had died in 1932, and, in his sorrow, Gelasio buried himself in his projects. Among these were the last two of the six volumes of the *Regesta Chartarum*, consisting of charters dating from 954 to the eighteenth century. Now that the family archives were arranged and listed, he approached the Biblioteca Apostolica and the Archivo Segreto del Vaticano concerning their transfer to one or the other: the Biblioteca Apostolica accepted the donation gratefully.[17] Sculpture continued to occupy him, to the point of exhibiting at the Venice Biennale and the Quadriennale in Rome. He also continued to attract appointments to the boards of industrial companies, though how much participation these demanded of him is unclear.

The drainage project in the marshes was by this time in full operation. Since 1926, some 14,000 labourers had been digging channels to carry to the sea the water pumped out of the salt flats. The result was the transformation of a vast area measuring 70,000 hectares (about 172,000 acres) of uninhabitable malarial swamp into fertile agricultural land. Of that area the Caetani owned just over 1,000 hectares (about 2,500 acres), but the success of the project spelled the end of private ownership of the area reclaimed.[18] The expropriation was a bitter blow to Gelasio, a man for whom ownership was stewardship, and his family's patrimony almost a sacred trust. The reclaimed land of what became known as the Agro Pontino was allocated to fascist families from northern Italy willing to relocate. Each was given a house, livestock, and implements with which to begin farming, and trained to help in the task of keeping the area free of malaria.[19] Within a few years the region had become one of the most productive agricultural areas in Europe.

If Fascism was firmly entrenched in Italy, matters were even more alarming in Germany. Adolf Hitler was appointed chancellor on 30 January 1933, and within weeks the Enabling Act gave him the powers to turn the country into a dictatorship. The Weimar period was over, and the great exodus of intellectuals and artists began. Among them was Count Harry Kessler, who left Weimar in March 1933, never to return. On 1 April the Nazi boycott of Jewish-owned businesses and Jewish professionals came into force. As Kessler wrote in his diary, "This criminal piece of lunacy has destroyed everything that during the past 14 years had been achieved to restore faith in, and respect for, Germany." Many of the exiles were drawn to Paris, enriching still further that city's store of creativity.

Through the 1930s, Marguerite and Lelia continued to spend the summer months in the apartment in the rue du Cirque, leaving Rome in May or June and returning in September when the heat had passed. *Commerce* had absorbed a great deal of Marguerite's time and energy, and freedom from the task of producing it helped to offset the loss of the many satisfactions it had given her. At this point it was refreshing to have time to read, meet with friends, and renew her interest in modern art.

She was soon invited to take an active role in Les Amis de l'Art Contemporain, an initiative set up by her friend Alice Warder Garrett, the wife of John Work Garrett, the American ambassador to Italy.[20] Alice Garrett was a serious art collector, and a champion of new work by young artists. Having assembled a committee that included leading experts and conservators from some of the Paris museums, with herself and Marguerite as joint vice-presidents, she rented a townhouse at 20, avenue Georges V, just off the Champs-Elysées, to serve as a gallery. The idea was to offer to artists, especially the young and impecunious, a means of exhibiting and possibly selling their work without incurring the usual costs involved in doing so. All the expenses were to be born by the Amis (which really meant Marguerite and the Garretts), the price paid for any work sold going directly to the artist, without commission. During the summer of 1933, Alice Garrett and Marguerite planned a series of exhibitions for the following spring, contacting artists, collectors, and other galleries to arrange loans and transport to the gallery premises. Not all the works were for sale; some of what was exhibited came from Marguerite's own collection, and was there to add context and interest.

She was back in Paris in April 1934 to prepare for the opening of the first exhibition on 4 May, and to Roffredo reported that

> Truly great things have been accomplished at the Gallery – 9 big *panneaux* of Vuillard have been put in place and look as if they had been made for that salon also the big *panneau* with me which looks beautiful ... everything will be in order by Monday evening when we give a cocktail party for the press French Italian English

> American [*sic*]. I am hanging the drawings of Fazzini on the stairs out of reach 3 on each side. They will look splendid *en attendant* the sculpture. The house looks marvelous with the stuff on the walls and Alice's furniture. I have been working like a dog at *everything* but now we will have a little more peace I hope. The next show will be on May 25th.[21]

The "big panneau with me" to which Marguerite refers must have been *The Library*, making a reappearance after twenty years in Vuillard's studio, and listed at the exhibition as *Panneau Decoratif pour une Bibliothèque*. Besides the large-scale works by him, this first exhibition showed the work of French painters Pierre Bonnard, André Dunoyer de Segonzac, André Masson, and Charles Despiau, together with the Italians Pericle Fazzini and Corrado Cagli and books edited by the art dealer and publisher Ambroise Vollard. It was well attended, and by the time the second exhibition opened, Marguerite was "getting quite hardened at interviewing the Press – what I have always avoided as the pest [*sic*] but it is really quite easy when it isn't for *oneself* – and then I realize how it can help Lelia all the friends I am making in the journalistic world – for all the American papers we have spoken of her and her work in detail."[22]

The second show brought together works by André Derain, Lawrence Binford, Aristide Maillol, Raoul Dufy, Roger Chastel, and a dozen other artists and sculptors, while the third, which ran from 14 June until 1 July, was more international, and included decorative pieces as well as paintings by Georges Rouault, and works by Walter Sickert and Giorgio Morandi. While the exhibitions were on, Marguerite confessed to Roffredo that she had so little free time that she had taken to asking friends to meet her at the gallery, but being involved to this degree was evidently something she found exhilarating. Sizing up the current scene, deciding which artists to invite to exhibit, discussing their work with them, then hanging the pieces offered to best effect, were challenges to which she brought discernment and experience. Just as she had acted as a catalyst, bringing together writers that she thought really *should* know one another, so now she did the same for the painters,

9.3
Gino Severini's portrait of Lelia, commissioned by Marguerite.

sculptors, engravers, and printers whose work was shown together under the auspices of Les Amis de l'Art Contemporain.

It is not surprising to find her the prime mover behind the formation of a similar initiative in Rome a few months later. The Società l'Arte d'Oggi, with its headquarters at Palazzo Caetani, had the Princess of Piedmont as honorary president, Roffredo, Giuseppe Ungaretti, and the painter Gino Severini among its committee members, and Marguerite as secretary-general. It aimed to "encourage and provide a forum for

9.4
Portrait of Cornelia Chapin by her teacher, the Spanish sculptor Mateo Hernández, 1936.

young artists and contact with other societies with similar aims elsewhere,"[23] rather as the French Amis did. Its first (and, as it turned out, only) initiative was to co-sponsor, with the Société de l'Art Présent in Paris, "The Franco-Italian Exhibition" at the Wertheim Gallery in London in June and July 1935, which brought together the work of twenty-six French and twenty-three Italian artists, to considerable acclaim by reviewers.[24]

The spring of 1934 was memorable for two further events that brought joy to Marguerite: her half-sister Cornelia Chapin arrived in Paris, intending to pursue her career as a sculptor there, and Lelia had her first formal exhibition. Cornelia had seen the work of the Spanish animal sculptor Mateo Hernández in New York, and came to Europe with the aim of persuading him to accept her as a pupil. His specialty was working from live models – usually zoo animals, since for the modest price of zoo admission he could study them closely all day long – without any preliminary drawings or models. The temperamental Hernández, then living in Paris, had always refused to take on pupils, but, on meeting Cornelia and seeing her work, changed his mind. She became the only pupil he is ever known to have accepted, and she was soon a well-known sight in the zoos of Paris, Sèvres, Vincennes, and other towns, pushing a cart holding her tools and her block of wood or stone.[25] She soon had the attention of the art critics, too, one of whom wrote of her:

> Cornelia Chapin, indifferent to the false amenities of worldly life, who passes her hours, her days, her life, chiseling in the block of stone, roughing out with her sensitive and vigorous hands the unruly resisting substance – follower of those early Roman sculptors of capitals – of the medieval imagists; as of Mateo Hernández, who has communicated to her his fervour and his faith.[26]

For Lelia, still timid enough at twenty-one to find meeting the press an ordeal, the first exposure of her paintings to public gaze resulted in a new measure of confidence. Marguerite secured the venue at 7, quai Voltaire, and the presence at the opening on 15 June of officials from the Musées Nationaux, while Vuillard wrote a preface to the list of the works. A review of the show in a Paris newspaper (preserved by Gelasio in a private file), reported that "A few minutes after the opening a painting was bought by the *Société des Amis du Luxembourg*." It also observed that Lelia was equally adept in oils and watercolours, and that

> Fortunately for her personality, she has developed her craft along strictly individual lines and her acute sincerity has always preserved her from the dangerous pitfalls of slavish imitation. She is at her best in landscapes, views of Italian hills and buildings, sketches of the Seine at Paris, or popular crowds at Montparnasse. Her smallest watercolours are brilliant and powerful.[27]

For some reason – possibly the garden party given by Gelasio at Ninfa to mark his appointment as a senator – Roffredo was unable to be in Paris for Lelia's show. From Rome, he reported that he was reading Marguerite's "dear letters" aloud to Ada, Michelangelo, and Camillo. He regarded Lelia's exhibition as "a triumph for both of you," and declared, "I believe that really Lelia will develop into a true artist, and so much the greater the more she will master that form of indolence that rather holds her back. She must now be very satisfied with the reception she has found among the artists; and you, my dear, how happy you must feel![28] Perhaps by "indolence," Roffredo meant the passivity and tendency to give way that others noted about Lelia, especially in her relationship with her mother, to whom she was very close, but whose stronger personality overshadowed her own.[29]

It must have been at about this time, in the spring or summer of 1934, that the renowned sculptor in wax, Catherine Barjansky, and her husband, Alexandre, a virtuoso cellist, were invited to lunch at Palazzo Caetani. She later wrote a memorable account of the occasion. Roffredo was in residence, and was described as "a tall man with black eyes and white hair and extremely handsome," while Gelasio's clay sculptures were "Like himself … in extremely good taste and beautiful in line." But it was her meeting with Michelangelo that left her astonished. After lunch, Gelasio asked whether she would like to meet his brother, and conducted her to the room in another part of the palace where, day after day, the youngest of the Caetani "hung from the ceiling in a kind of hammock," as thin as "a skeleton with twisted limbs." Catherine was dumbfounded at seeing him suspended there, "his body motionless, useless, dead except for its pain." Michelangelo could no longer move, not even to drink a glass of water, but coming near him Catherine saw that "He had a beautiful head, and his eyes when I met them were black, and so full of life and joy and enjoyment that for a moment I could not breathe." The three then talked at length about wax sculpture, which Michelangelo had read about, thanks to an invention of his own:

> His eyes looked towards the ceiling, for that was the only position in which he could be comfortable. Affixed above his head was a mirror of which he was very proud, because he had worked it out in his head. A book was hung over him, not touching him. He could not move, he could not turn the pages, but he could read in the mirror over his head.

It seemed to Catherine that Michelangelo's determination to live as fully as he could constituted some kind of motive force that gave light to the cavernous palace. It was, she wrote, "the most complete victory I have ever seen of the mind over the body" on the part of someone "whose lot had seemed too tragic to be bearable."[30] This impression has been confirmed by those who remember Michelangelo as a man of immense courage, intelligence, and sensitivity. He was particularly close to Gelasio, the brother nearest to himself in age (the former military hero and ambassador still addressed Miche tenderly as "my little one," as he had when they were children). His relationships with Camillo and Lelia were another source of moral support. He was sometimes able to attend meals, using a wheelchair and accompanied by a male nurse. Sad to relate, even some of these small consolations were shortly to be taken from him.

In July 1934, it became apparent that Ada was failing. She had just celebrated her eighty-eighth birthday, though she conceded nothing to age beyond agreeing to make the journey to her favourite spa in Berne in the ambulance car of the train. Nella and Gelasio, on joining her at the spa, found her unwell, and moved her back to Italy, first to a chalet in the cooler climate of Ostia, and then, as she grew weaker, to Rome. She died at Palazzo Caetani on 16 August.[31] Ada had such strong and unique relationships with her children that they each, in his or her own way, were left desolate at her death. Those who had married into the family found that she was the axis around which all revolved, and so, for Marguerite, the death of her mother-in-law (whom she had always addressed as "Mother") marked the end of an era. Ada's approach to life was practical rather than cerebral, but in their physical energy, interest in people, and sense of fun, she and Marguerite were alike and had got on well. In addition, their shared love of gardening had always given them something about which they could converse.

It was Gelasio, Ada's favourite, who took her death most stoically. He suspected his own serious illness even as his mother's hold on life was slackening and, as if determined to spare her grief, refused to give in to his own suffering until she was gone. In mid-September, a month after her death, Gelasio entered a private clinic near Palazzo Caetani, where he was given various X-ray treatments that suggest cancer,[32] though his final illness has always been attributed to a "malignant meningitis" contracted from the bite of a malaria-bearing mosquito in the marshes around Ninfa. After a month in which his condition steadily worsened and he became blind, he died on 23 October, aged just fifty-seven. Camillo – on whose nineteenth birthday this terrible event took place – was with him when he died, and left an account of it in a letter to a friend. In his opinion, his uncle's demise "was due more to the very bad general condition he was in through long overwork and an unhealthy life than to the illness itself,"[33] which raises the question of whether such a degree of overwork, and whatever was meant by "an unhealthy life," may have been Gelasio's way of dealing with the loss of Annina. Whatever the underlying factors, the death of this most dynamic member of the family fell heavily upon the others, although, as Camillo confided to his friend, "it was better that he did not live" in the condition in which his illness would have left him if he had.

Much about Gelasio's last years, including a possible shift in his political stance, must remain unresolved, but there is no doubt whatever about the reaction to his death, not only within the Caetani family, but in Rome and far beyond it. He had been the foundation stone of his generation of Caetani, the one to whom each member of it, with the exception of Leone, was closest. He was also the one whose awareness of his family's past greatness, together with a personal sense of noblesse oblige, supplied the motive power for all he did, from meticulous scholarship to the restoration of Ninfa, from serving as ambassador to draining the Pontine Marshes. He exemplified that ancient ideal of *praxis*: the man of action who turned good ideas into realities for the benefit of others – and the ranks of those "others" ran into the thousands. Cited in a biographical memoir of him is a letter describing how

> The day after Don Gelasio's death there was a constant stream of people towards the church where his body was lying – high and low, rich and poor, his old companions in the War, mutilated soldiers who had fought under him, peasants from all over the countryside, unknown people he had been kind to. It was an extraordinary tribute to a splendid man.[34]

Crowds watched silently on 25 October as the horse-drawn catafalque and a long procession of carriages passed by on their way to Rome's Campo Verano cemetery, men removing their hats and women tossing flowers onto the flag-draped coffin. From the gates of the cemetery to the Caetani mausoleum, the mourners were led by Roffredo, Marguerite and Lelia, Camillo pushing Michelangelo in his wheelchair, Leone's son, Onorato, and Nella with her daughter, Livia, and the latter's husband, Count Francesco Durazzo. Among the dignitaries were representatives of most of the political, mercantile, and cultural entities with headquarters in Rome.

Tributes to Gelasio poured in from all over Europe and from across the Atlantic. The one he might have liked best came from the United States – the country in which, apart from Italy, he had felt most at home. Robert and Mildred Bliss, the American philanthropists who had often entertained him at their home, Dumbarton Oaks, during his time in Washington, shared with him a love of Dante's *Divine Comedy*. In a wisteria arbour in the garden, still to be seen today, is a stone plaque dedicated "*all'amico Gelasio*," inlaid with lead lettering that reproduces the typeface of the *Codex Caetani*, and quotes lines 139 to 141 of Canto XXVIII of the *Purgatorio*:

Quelli chanticamente poetaro
Leta dell'oro / e suo stato felice
Forse en parnaso esto loco sognaro

(Those who in olden times sang of the Golden Age,
and of its happy state, perchance upon Parnassus
dreamed of this place).[35]

Gelasio had made a point of trading or buying parcels of land and buildings from his brothers over the years, in an attempt to keep the family possessions intact.[36] This immense patrimony now passed to Camillo as his heir: Palazzo Caetani, and the Caetani possessions at Cisterna, Sermoneta, Bassiano, Norma, and Ninfa, although Roffredo was designated "administrator" until his son came of age. Camillo was authorized to choose three items from among Gelasio's personal effects, after which all else was to be divided equally between him and Livia. Gelasio's four sets of rooms were stuffed with possessions that took Roffredo, Livia, and the notary weeks to list, and Livia readily accepted Roffredo's offer to buy, on Camillo's behalf, much of the furniture, carpets, plate, pictures, and books for which she would otherwise have had to find house room. (For that reason, the properties belonging to the Caetani foundations today – apart from the palace in Cisterna, which was partially destroyed by bombing in 1944 – still reflect Gelasio's catholic taste and passion for collecting.)[37]

All of the events mentioned so far – the move to Rome, Marguerite's involvement in the Paris art scene, the deaths of Ada and Gelasio – took place against a background of European affairs that was growing ever more sombre. By 1935 Italy was once again embroiled in conflict, this time in Abyssinia, impelled by Mussolini's colonial ambitions. In far-off British Columbia, Leone read the newspaper reports of the latest land-grab in the Horn of Africa, no doubt recalling, somewhat ruefully, his own stand against the Italian incursion into Libya in 1911. With Gelasio dead, the Mussolini regime now used Leone's opposition to the earlier colonial adventure as the pretext for stripping him of his Italian citizenship. Equally contemptibly, it also exerted pressure on the

Accademia Nazionale dei Lincei to expel him. In his self-imposed exile, and at such a dark hour of Italian history, the thought that in some future time his reputation would be restored and his memory honoured probably did not occur to him. In Canada he claimed to have found "that priceless asset of a great spiritual, purely contemplative, serenity, free from ambition or regret, ready to accept all the vicissitudes of fate calmly." Soon after writing this, sixty-six-year-old Leone found that he was suffering from cancer of the throat. He did not wish his family in Rome to know of his illness, though an Italian consular official wrote in the strictest confidence to Roffredo once it was clear that his brother had not long to live. One of the greatest Islamic scholars of his own or any age, the donor to the Italian State of a priceless library, died alone in a Vancouver hospital ward on Christmas day, 1935, believing himself to be a failure and forgotten by the world.[38]

Leone's death left eighteen-year-old Sveva devastated. Her life was the one her father had created for her, and she was utterly disoriented by her loss. The fragile Ofelia had never adapted to life in Vernon, nor learned English. Obsessed by anxiety in the aftermath of Leone's death, she refused to allow her daughter to leave the house. Sveva's memories of the glamorous life she had led with her parents in Europe, of Rome and Palazzo Caetani, of her grandmother Ada and other relatives, including Marguerite and Roffredo and her cousins Lelia and Camillo, helped to sustain her during the twenty-five years that followed, when she had no contact with anyone other than Miss Jüll, her old governess, who kept the household going. Ofelia, increasingly beset by paranoia and hypochondria, intercepted the occasional letters from Rome, and Sveva found herself forcibly cut off from the rest of the family.[39]

The death of Leone also created a somewhat awkward situation for Roffredo and Marguerite. Leone's son, Onoratino, was to some degree mentally afflicted, but he was now, at least in name, the 16th Duke of Sermoneta. He lived alone at Palazzo Orsini – a solitary man of thirty-three who had never learned to use his time productively or make friends – while Vittoria, whether in Europe or the United States, continued to style herself as Duchess of Sermoneta. Following the deaths of Gelasio and Leone, the entire responsibility for the Caetani patrimony fell upon Roffredo – there was no other member of the family who was of age, or well enough, to share it. This was a full-time occupation: getting to grips with its economy, setting priorities in consultation with the foremen of the various estates – in effect, trying to "be Gelasio," in ensuring that it survived and prospered in increasingly adverse conditions.

It was only after Gelasio's death that Marguerite and Roffredo began to spend more time at Ninfa, and when Marguerite and Lelia were in Paris in the summer, Roffredo continued this pattern. What began as the need to oversee the estates and the commercial projects established by Gelasio soon became something rewarding in itself. Ninfa is, of course, unique in Italy and possibly in all of Europe for its microclimate and the striking feature of the icy, spring-fed river that flows through what is left of the ancient town. Gelasio and Ada had shared a vision for the garden they had established amidst the ruins. They sought to create an integrated whole that was more than the sum of its parts, yet within which diversity flourished. The challenge for Roffredo and Marguerite, as the next generation of custodians, was to build on these foundations while conserving a precious equilibrium.

Marguerite's love of gardening stretched back to the Chapin estate at Waterford and her apartment in the rue de l'Université, but whether Roffredo had shared his parents' enthusiasm for "growing things," as Gelasio had, is not at all clear. It seems that Marguerite was actively involved in planting at Ninfa from the mid-1920s, lending a hand whenever she was there, as Ada's energy declined. The priority back then had been to cover and consolidate the ruins once Gelasio had removed the brambles and ivy that shrouded them. Ada's climbing roses – some apparently offshoots of the venerable English ones at Fogliano – had done this admirably, adding both beauty and support to the ancient walls.

What Marguerite and Roffredo planted at Ninfa before the Second World War can today only be guessed at, since records of plants purchased, and therefore of decisions made, were kept only from 1949. Gardening experts and their research have attributed to Roffredo the creation of streams, weirs, and sluices designed to carry water to distant parts of the garden, but also intended to produce the pleasing sounds that were his particular contribution to it as a composer and musician.[40] Marguerite is credited with having planted the two avocado trees that today are a feature of the *hortus conclusus*, as well as having introduced many citrus trees. She planted weeping willows along a stretch of the river, and is thought to have introduced jasmine and clematis to vary the climbing theme established by Ada's roses. She is also known to have bought many climbing and rambling roses herself, mainly classics such as Zéphirine Drouhin, Mutabilis, François Juranville, Albertine, Mermaid, and Rosa Mundi. She had a particular love for spring-flowering shrubs and trees – lilacs, magnolias, dogwoods, camellias, mimosas, crab apples, and Japanese flowering cherry trees – which she planted in great abundance. (Photographs of her taken in the mid-1950s show these cherry trees as mature, which

9.5
One of Roffredo's "musical streams" at Ninfa, flowing from the lake into the river.

suggests that they date from the 1930s rather than the postwar period.) Apart from roses, her favourite flowers seem to have been irises, carnations, and lupins.[41]

During the periods spent at Ninfa, Lelia began to know the garden in detail, to walk and explore its twenty acres, and to study it with the close attention of an artist. It was here that she discovered her second vocation, as a gardener – or, more accurately, as what English professional gardeners call a "plantswoman": someone who not only knows what to plant where, and how to care for it, but whose interest has led her to a knowledge of the particular characteristics and habits of each plant, of how each is affected by conditions, and how each will develop in relation to what else is around it. Lelia acquired just such a sensitivity, and brought it, not only to the garden, but to her paintings of it. In the closeness to nature that she experienced at Ninfa, Sermoneta, and the surrounding countryside, she perhaps found solace after the recent deaths of people close to her, and from the tensions of living in Mussolini's Italy. Certainly Marguerite and Roffredo did so, and began to invite like-minded friends to join them for lunch at Ninfa, as once they had at Villa Romaine.

In the autumn of 1935, the Biddles made a lengthy visit to Europe. Cornelia was exhibiting her sculptures alongside those of Mateo Hernández at the Salon d'Automne in Paris, and the occasion brought the Chapins, the Caetanis, and numerous mutual friends together in the French capital. The critical acclaim that greeted Cornelia's work was the prelude to her election – the only woman to have been so honoured – to the Sociétaire Salon d'Automne in 1936, and the award of the Second Grand Prize at the Paris International Exposition in 1937.

From the travel diary in which she recorded this visit to France, Katherine emerges as a thoughtful and compassionate woman, the "hinge" between Marguerite, who seldom revealed her emotions, and the frank, outspoken Cornelia. The days in Paris were filled with meetings with people Katherine had heard much of from Marguerite. One was Jean Paulhan, whom she characterized as "gentle of tone, but what a penetrating critic," while Sylvia Beach and Adrienne Monnier, still providing a literary refuge to writers from abroad, charmed her. Katherine

9.6
Marguerite in Mateo Hernández's studio with some of his sculptures, Paris, 1936.

9.7
Marguerite relaxes in the garden of Mateo Hernandez's Paris studio, 1936.

was now a published poet, fluent in French, as Marguerite was, and, in the time the two spent together, they discussed "Eliot, Joyce, G. Stein … Americans," but when Katherine asked for the names of "young French poets of talent" she received the somewhat surprising reply that "there are none." Since Garrison's death, Francis Biddle had channelled his grief into work, but Katherine's found its way into her poetry, which she assumed would strengthen her bond with Marguerite. "Bright Mariner," Katherine's poetic tribute to her little boy, drew from Marguerite a positive, but not an enthusiastic, response, that left its author somewhat disappointed: "About Mgte I feel I have failed – not to break down that personal reserve. Once I was the only person who did it. I feel C. is nearer to her now … Evidently she will slide over every emotion." Katherine elsewhere alludes to the "adolescent shyness" she sometimes felt with Marguerite, and perhaps the latter, too, found it impossible to abandon the role of "elder sister" and be as spontaneous with Katherine as she was with others.

Camillo, meanwhile, had grown into a good-looking young man with his parents' dark eyes and hair, less tall than the family norm, but still a respectable height at just under six feet. He took after Marguerite in being somewhat extravagant, and in enjoying the performing arts as a spectator rather than as someone with any artistic pretensions. In 1934 he entered the University of Florence to study law, the idea being that, following his graduation in June 1937, he would spend a year at Harvard Law School studying business administration to prepare him for the time when he would inherit the family estates. His time in the United States, during which he visited his Chapin relatives, including his uncle Paul Chapin and family in New York and Katherine and Francis Biddle in Philadelphia, lasted from the summer of 1937 to late October 1938.

Camillo was not an especially dedicated student, and admitted in his letters home that he maintained a precarious balance, "like an acrobat on a tightrope," between the demands of his studies in Boston and the attractions and temptations of New York City. (To the latter he attributed "a 'brutal' or 'ugly' or 'formless' vitality that makes European cities seem tame.") Despite the diversity of backgrounds among

9.8
Camillo, just off to Harvard, 1937.

his fellow students, he found that Harvard induced a great similarity in their ways of regarding the world, and a level of conformity that surprised him. The impressions of American social life with which he regaled Marguerite, Roffredo, and Michelangelo included the following: "for a popular girl the height of delight is to be cut in on by as many partners as possible while dancing, and one simply says 'thank you' to the offgoing or the incoming male, and they to her, so there's no conversation to speak of," and "When one goes into a bar the barman calls you boy, young fellow, buddy or sir with equal facility, and without any intention of being insolent."[42]

A number of people, including his slightly younger cousin Schuyler Chapin, recalled Camillo as seeming "infinitely more sophisticated" than American boys of his age. He was the possessor of "a car as handsome as he was" and an engaging manner that won the hearts of pretty

9.9
Three of Cornelia's sculptures: frog, elephant, bear.

girls at nearby Sarah Lawrence College.[43] It seems that Camillo was somewhat forgetful (one of Michelangelo's letters to him – dictated, of course, to an amanuensis – let him know that "the cat was out of the bag" concerning the family party in New York, at which the only person missing had been ... the guest of honour), but as he also had his mother's charm, no lasting damage was done. In the summer of 1938, he went travelling in Mexico and Central America with a friend called Henry Head, the son of neighbours in Versailles. He was already interested in pre-Columbian art, having visited the American museums with notable collections. The Mayan ruins in Mexico impressed him greatly, while Lake Atitlan in Guatamala was "a wonderful place, like nothing I have ever seen ... with perfectly unspoiled indian [*sic*] villages all around."[44]

Earlier that summer, Marguerite had finally crossed the Atlantic, fulfilling a long-held wish to revisit the relatives and places she had known as a girl. Lelia went along, the presence of Camillo in Boston and New York being a pretext for the voyage, but it may also have been motivated by the ominous turn of events in Europe. Cornelia Chapin had returned home in April, convinced by Hitler's annexation of Austria a month earlier that war was on its way.[45] As it happened, she was exhibiting at a gallery in New York when Marguerite and Lelia arrived. With Camillo, Katherine and Francis Biddle and their son, Randolph, Paul and Leila Chapin and their sons, Paul, John, and Schuyler, the family group made a pilgrimage to the former Chapin home at 5 West Thirty-seventh Street, then walked to Times Square, which Marguerite had not seen since 1908. The Metropolitan Opera House, where she had first heard Jean de Reszke perform, still occupied the same site nearby. Late in life Schuyler Chapin recalled how Marguerite was "enraptured" by the neon lights and the modernity of it all, but quite sure she could no longer live in a place where everything moved so fast.

10

WAR AND TRAGEDY

By September 1938, Marguerite and Lelia were back in Italy, in time to join Roffredo in overseeing the grape harvest and the planting of spring bulbs at Ninfa. In the area around the ancient site, the landscape had altered. Now, wheat fields and market gardens stretched away into the distance, proclaiming the gains made – although at tremendous human cost[1] – by the *bonifica integrale*, the three-part government plan, consisting of drainage, agriculture, and settlement, that had reclaimed the marshes and rid them of malaria.[2] Four new towns – Littoria (the capital of a province of the same name, both of which would be renamed "Latina" in 1946), Sabaudia, Pontinia, and Aprilia – housed a growing population of settlers, and a fifth town, Pomezia, was on the verge of completion. Thanks to Italy's colonial adventures, there were thriving markets for Littoria's agricultural produce, conveyed to the markets of Rome and the shipping terminals of Naples by rail.

The tranquility of Ninfa was worlds away from all this activity, and from the palpable tension in Rome as the European political scene grew steadily more menacing. With Hitler's implacable demands for control of the "Sudetenland" area of Czechoslovakia, the spectre of war again loomed over the continent. The Munich conference at the end of September (which Marguerite's old friend, the poet-diplomat Alexis Léger attended as an aide to the French President, Deladier), temporarily defused the crisis. Even the betrayal of Czechoslovakia, as the Allies scrambled to appease the German dictator, could not mar the collective relief of a Europe still haunted by the 1914–18 war. In November came the promulgation in Italy of the "racial laws" that robbed Jewish citizens of jobs and property.

During Marguerite's absence, Roffredo learned to his surprise that he had "made his lands available for the building of a new airport"[3] near Cisterna, and spent considerable time negotiating compensation for the terrain being expropriated. Shortly thereafter, the Littoria branch of the Partito Nazionale Fascista announced the requisition of a villa on the Caetani estate at Tor Tre Ponti as a headquarters. In response to the insolent demand that Roffredo continue to pay for its upkeep, he adopted what would become his standard method for dealing with the regime's representatives: courteous prevarication, answering one letter by another, so as to avoid confrontation, and spinning out the matter in question as long as possible. It is worth recalling that many of the local *fascisti* were men known to Roffredo, and he to them. As a large landowner, he was viewed with both deference and a degree of resentment, and in his communications with these officials he chose his words carefully. In the instance of the villa at Tor Tre Ponti, for instance, he "regretted having to report that it was already let to a tenant with a large family, fully engaged in agriculture for the *Patria*." His method seems to have worked: in 1942 the Commune of Littoria wrote politely to ask for the use of land for an access road to a new factory, and even offered a moderate rent.[4]

The outbreak of war between the Allies and Germany in September 1939 did not formally involve Italy, but Italian troops were ordered to Libya and Albania in the spring of the following year, in operations approved by Hitler for their psychological effect on the local populations.[5] Although Italy signed the so-called "Pact of Steel" with Germany on 22 May 1940, Mussolini cynically waited until 10 June before declaring war on the Allies, convinced that Dunkirk and the fall of France heralded a German victory from which Italy could profit.

Camillo was the member of the Caetani family most directly affected by Italy's declaration of war, but, like his parents, he was repelled by fascism and had no wish to fight on the side of the dictators. Besides, having finished his studies and come of age, he was living life to the full, thanks to the inheritance left to him by Gelasio. In the winter of 1939–40, as the little notebook in which he kept his personal accounts reveals, he kept a horse and an Alfa Romeo sports car, and bought himself a serious camera – a Leica III with a Summitar lens. The meticulously-kept accounts show that, although he could afford luxuries, he was far from frivolous: month by month, every purchase is recorded and described, every expenditure added up, including, now, a share in the expenses of Palazzo Caetani.[6] Camillo at twenty-four was a sociable young man with a pensive, serious side. Peter Tompkins, an American brought up largely in Italy, had made friends with him at Harvard and admired his "other-worldly poise and at times monk-like detachment." He later recalled how he and Camillo "spent much of the summer of the *drôle de guerre* in 1940 pondering about the meaning of life and the roles we should play."[7]

Stories survive of how, despite his detestation of fascism, Camillo eventually came to join the Italian army. One account relates how, after a round at Rome's prestigious Acqua Santa Golf Club, he overheard Count Galeazzo Ciano – Italy's foreign minister, and Mussolini's son-in-law – say in a loud voice to a companion, "There goes the young Roman aristocracy, playing golf instead of going to war," whereupon Camillo swore he would enlist the following day. Cora Caetani, Michelangelo's wife, who knew Ciano, is said to have telephoned him to beg him not to permit Camillo to volunteer, as he was an only son and the heir to the dukedom.[8] The story told by Marguerite to author Nicholas Tucci years later seems to follow on from this. "Someone from the Ministry" had telephoned her, and offered, given the circumstances, to find Camillo a desk job – to which she replied that "no Caetani will ever accept a favour from a fascist," and replaced the receiver.[9]

The American journalist John Thompson Whitaker, who considered "Camillo of the laughing eyes and quick wit" his closest Italian friend, later recalled the conversation that took place over drinks at his flat the night before Camillo left to join an artillery battalion at a training camp near Modena. When Whitaker asked, "Hating fascism and your German ally, how can you go off to fight?" Camillo replied: "It's a purely personal matter with me. I have come to hate fascism, yes. These fascists have made me ashamed of every drop of Italian blood in my veins. But I have got to go ... I have got to prove to myself that under fire I will behave like a Caetani."[10]

Implicit in this is Camillo's desire to emulate Gelasio in valour, if not in political outlook. From his training camp, he sent military post-cards to his parents to assure them that there was no need to worry about him. Marguerite, visiting Milan for a few days, reported thinking constantly of Camillo, especially on seeing planes passing over the city. Roffredo channelled his feelings, as usual, into music. Some time after Camillo joined up, he set the Te Deum, that Latin hymn of joyous praise and thanksgiving, to music for choir and organ as *In te Domine speravi*, as if in the expectation of welcoming his son home again. As of 4 November 1940, Camillo still did not know where he was to be sent,[11] but in early December his battalion embarked for Albania. Then there was silence. Not until 2 January did a military telegram arrive to inform his family that he was missing. Four days later came the dreaded and worst possible news: Camillo had died of wounds received in a skirmish with Greek forces on a remote Albanian mountainside on 15 December.

Grief now engulfed Marguerite, Roffredo, and Lelia like an unquenchable fire. A death certificate arrived from the military authorities, but there could be no formal burial while Camillo's body lay where he had fallen. On 15 January, nine days after the news of his death reached his family, a Requiem Mass was celebrated for him in the Caetani chapel at the church of Santa Pudenziana in Rome. Following it, *In te Domine speravi* was sung. The Te Deum is not often sung at requiems, and when it is, it is offered in the faith and hope that the soul of the one who has died is already enveloped in the merciful love of God. Faith, hope, and love are, of course, the theological virtues: the virtues that, according to Catholic doctrine, give life to the soul. The performance of Roffredo's composition on this occasion was thus not just a final gift to his son, but the statement of a personal credo, hurled in the face of desolation.

Three weeks after learning of Camillo's death, Marguerite poured out her feelings to Katherine, who had also passed through the appalling experience of losing a son:

> I am sure you understand fully the despair and anguish of my poor heart. The atrocious sorrow that seems unbearable. I must think of Lelia all the time who is pathetic to see – she feels it terribly and poor Roffredo ... On January 2nd we were told he was missing and we lived four days of anguish, I never leaving the telephone, hoping against hope that we would hear that he was prisoner [*sic*]. Then January 6th we were told the truth. I can't tell you how I longed for you and Cornelia. It seemed to me as if I couldn't bear it unless I were with you both. To you I could tell all the depth of my sorrow, with you I could cry all my tears – and I have so many bitter feelings in my heart about it all ... We are in the country for a few days but it is even worse here where I did everything to please him. Oh sister, darling, how can I bear it.[12]

In the weeks that followed, as the news of Camillo's death became known to friends near and far, many sent letters of condolence. One of the most incisive of these came from Marguerite's cousin "Tom" Eliot, who wrote:

> You have been much in my thoughts, and I knew that your loss would not become easier. I do not pretend that such a loss ever does; only in time it is perhaps simply like learning to live without one's eyesight, or crippled. One just makes do and carries on the rest of life. I don't even maintain that faith makes loss easier; it just, if I may say so, improves the quality of the suffering and makes it sometimes fruitful instead of useless.[13]

Neither before nor after Camillo's death did Marguerite ever divulge her personal religious beliefs, but perhaps one can infer, from the sharing of this intimate reflection on Eliot's part, his awareness that she had some. To some observers, what showed was anger and despair. Harold Tittmann, appointed by Franklin D. Roosevelt as America's chargé d'affaires to the Holy See, confided in a letter to his wife, Eleanor, that "Marguerite is so desperate that she would willingly go out and start a revolution,"[14] while Sir D'Arcy Osborne, the British Minister Plenipotentiary to the Holy See, recorded in his diary an entry for 30 January 1941 that read: "Marguerite Bassiano came ... She was very sad and said 'There is nothing they can do to me now.' There was no way of comforting her."[15]

Roffredo too received his share of commiseration, notably from Michelangelo, for whom his nephew's daily visit had been one of the few cheering experiences left to him:

> With the passing of the years, Camillo had little by little occupied in my heart that great emptiness left by the death of poor Gelasio. He not only honoured me with his sincere and warm affection, but he put his confidence in me for advice about everyday life. The idea that never, never again, will I have that dear godchild near me, to chat together like two brothers, fills my soul with such torment that I dare not tell myself that it is true.[16]

Michelangelo, more than anyone, understood the additional, unspoken aspect of his brother's grief: with the death of Camillo, the Caetani family line had very possibly come to an end. Leone's son, Onorato, was physically and mentally compromised, Sveva illegitimate under Italian law, Lelia and Topazia unmarried, and Livia Durazzo as yet childless. Now that Michelangelo, Roffredo, and poor Onorato were the only male survivors of the Caetani dynasty, it must have seemed that the curse laid upon the old Duke Michelangelo by the infuriated "Pio Nono" had come true. The letter of condolence written by Paul Chapin, the eldest son of Marguerite's half-brother Paul, drew from the heartbroken Roffredo the reply that "Indeed our misfortune has ruined our life as all our hopes were centred on our dear and only boy. Thank God we have Lelia left to us and she will henceforth be our only consolation."[17]

Written in a shaky hand on black-edged notepaper and signed "Your old uncle," Roffredo's reply to Paul is a reminder that he was only a few months short of his seventieth birthday. Seeking an explanation of the tragedy, he wrote to the Ministry of War asking to be allowed to visit the hillside in Albania where his son had died. On 21 January, he learned that, since the Greeks now occupied the area, this was impossible – as was the recovery of Camillo's body – for the foreseeable future. It was not in fact until May 1941 that the land was retaken and the body found, formally identified, and moved to a plot in a military cemetery in Velona, near the Albanian capital, Tirana. Meanwhile, in March, Roffredo received written statements from the men serving with Camillo when he fell, who described the fateful advance into the line of mortar and gunfire and their last sight of Camillo. Other soldiers in their battalion had been wounded and killed, which would seem to temper the allegation that arose after the war to the effect that Camillo had been deliberately sent forward as an act of revenge upon his anti-fascist parents, that he was killed by "friendly fire," or was assassinated on the orders of Mussolini.[18]

With Camillo's death, life for all those who had known and loved him changed forever, as though the door to a sunny room had been closed and locked. Photographs of him were put away, and apart from relating to Nicholas Tucci the incident cited above, Marguerite was never known to mention her son again. A pall of sorrow fell over Palazzo Caetani, Sermoneta, Ninfa, and everyone in them, family and servants alike. Marguerite took refuge in her room, and Lelia in a remote part of the garden at Ninfa. Roffredo could not bear to touch his beloved piano, and although he would in time take up playing once again, his composing genius seldom sought an outlet in the years to come. For Michelangelo, the death of his nephew was the final addition to a physical and emotional burden that had become unbearable. He died four months later, aged fifty-one, on 10 May 1941. His burial vault at Campo Verano bears the phrase, "E venne del martirio a questa pace" ("And he came from martyrdom into this peace"), derived from lines 128 and 129 from Canto X of Dante's *Paradiso*. They allude to the beatitude, after earthly torments, attained by Boethius,[19] the author of *The Consolation of Philosophy*, which had been a favourite book of Michelangelo's.

Through this dark period, friends such as William Phillips, the American ambassador to Italy, and Myron Taylor, the American ambassador to the Holy See, supported Marguerite as best they could, as did Harold Tittmann.[20] Through them Marguerite could keep in touch with Katherine and Francis Biddle in Washington without having to risk using the regular postal service, which was known to be riddled with spies and corruption. Sir D'Arcy Osborne, whom she knew from the days when he lived at Palazzo Caetani, proved to be another good friend.[21] Osborne's detached manner disguised immense courage and resilience. Between June 1940 and June 1944 he was a prisoner in the Vatican, yet remained an important figure in the undercover operations that supported the anti-fascist resistance. With the German occupation of Rome in September 1943, he became a link in the Rome Escape Organization created by Monsignor Hugh O'Flaherty, which hid some sixty-five hundred Allied POWs, Jews, and anti-fascists in church properties, palaces, safe houses, and private homes all over Rome.[22]

So far, Marguerite had been in no actual danger, but with the Japanese attack on Pearl Harbor, and America's entry into the war, that suddenly altered. Italy's declaration of war on the United States, on 11 December 1941, meant that she was now an enemy alien, and could be arrested and imprisoned. Unlike some other Americans who remained in Italy, such as Bernard Berenson and Iris Origo, she left no diary documenting the events going on around her. Traces of her movements between January 1942 and March 1944 are minimal and sometimes unclear, but there are occasional glimpses of her in the correspondence of others. With the declaration of war, Harold Tittmann was forced to leave the hotel where he had been living and move into the Vatican precincts. During Christmas 1941 and the New Year season of 1942, Marguerite helped him to furnish an empty apartment in the Santa Marta annex. Tittmann's letters to his wife, living with their two sons in Geneva, refer to Marguerite's generosity in providing him with furniture from Palazzo Caetani, and include the delightful comment that "the Bassiano bed is so very comfortable and the room so dark in the morning that I do nothing but sleep late."[23]

In a letter to his wife of 17 January 1942, Tittmann reported that "Marguerite Bassiano left last night for Switzerland," and asked Eleanor to "Be sure to be especially nice to her," since "She has been wonderful to me in furnishing my flat." Marguerite was probably in Geneva, staying somewhere near Eleanor, at the end of January, since Tittmann asked his wife to "Tell Marguerite Bassiano that those beautiful white lamps with shades have arrived."[24] In March, a note from the composer Samuel Barber to Katherine Biddle in Washington seems to corroborate Tittmann's comment, and even to suggest that the family was together ("I was delighted to hear that the Caetanis are out of Italy and have already written them"), but Barber does not say how he received this news, nor indicate the address to which he had written.[25] Now that Italy and the United States were at war, the affairs of American citizens were being handled through Swiss diplomatic channels. Marguerite very likely had an Italian passport, or even a Swiss one, since Roffredo still owned the little chalet at Pontresina; she certainly could not have used an American one after 11 December 1941. The likely purpose of her journey to Geneva was to establish some reliable means of receiving funds from the United States, since her bankers in New York could not now have sent payments to Rome.[26] At some point, presumably, she must have returned to Rome – but how, and when?

There is no mention anywhere of Roffredo and Lelia until September 1942, when together they submitted a request to the Commune of Littoria for permission – which they needed because the wartime demand for troops meant that hands were scarce – to rebuild a *vaccheria*, or "cattle barn," at Ninfa. Roffredo's opera *L'Isola del Sole* was performed in Rome on 30 January 1943, though why it came to be performed at such a time is puzzling. Even more perplexing is Harold Tittmann's comment in a letter to Eleanor of 12 February 1943: "I gather that Marguerite thought that the moment was not propitious to leave Roffredo. I think she could have gone all right if she had wanted to."[27] Had Marguerite indeed returned to Italy – or had she ever really left? The suggestion is that Roffredo was unwell or frail, and that Marguerite felt that she could neither move him nor leave him. And where was Lelia? In the tumultuous state of affairs prevailing in Italy, it is impossible to say.

Even before the Allied landings in Sicily in July 1943, popular feeling against the Mussolini regime was on the rise, after Italian military reversals in the Balkans and North Africa. Following the dictator's removal from office on 25 July, King Victor Emmanuel III appointed a new government headed by Marshal Pietro Badoglio. A negotiated surrender to the Allies on 3 September heralded one of the most dramatic events of the war for Italy, when the country changed sides and declared war on Germany on 13 October. As the Germans sought to block the advance of British and American troops up the Italian peninsula, they embarked on a campaign of reprisals against the local population. The deliberate destruction of historic monuments included the burning of the university library at Naples and the looting of dozens of churches and properties. The suffering in the countryside, as harvested crops and livestock were pillaged to provision the German armies, has become legendary. People living on the land survived on whatever they managed to hide, but in the winter to come, many succumbed to starvation.

The Germans occupied Rome on 10 September 1943. From then on, the city's once-thriving markets were empty and the streets unlit. The residents of Rome risked being shot for violating any of the dozens of petty regulations enforced on civilian life in the city, but particularly the curfew that ran from five o'clock in the afternoon to eight in the morning. On 16 October came the round-up of Jews living in Rome's ancient Ghetto. Of Rome's 12,000 Jews, 1,260 were deported on this occasion, while nearly all the rest, despite the harshness of the racial laws, survived the German occupation with the help of fellow citizens, Roman Catholic clergy and the religious orders, and the foreign embassies. Some are said to have found shelter at Ninfa, at Palazzo Caetani, Palazzo Lovatelli-Caetani in the Ghetto, and the convent of the Filippini Sisters, a known safe-house, on the other side of the Via delle Botteghe Oscure. Camillo's friend Peter Tompkins, who spoke impeccable Italian, had joined William ("Wild Bill") Donovan's recently formed Office of

Strategic Services, or OSS, and was put ashore by night on an isolated coast north of Rome. Having made his way into the city, he assumed the identity of a non-existent "brother" of Camillo's in order to make contact with people who could help him. As an intelligence agent, he eventually operated from a secret office with a radio transmitter in Palazzo Lovatelli-Caetani. At tremendous risk, on receiving a given signal, he would take a circuitous route through the back streets to the Vatican precincts for a clandestine meeting with Sir D'Arcy Osborne.[28]

The first sign of Marguerite's presence at Ninfa, with Lelia, comes in letters to Roffredo, undated and guarded in tone, but clearly written while the Germans were occupying Rome and holding off the Allied forces in the *Agro Pontino*. For Marguerite to be in Italy at all was dangerous, but to have been in Rome was particularly so, while it would have been imprudent, to say the least, to leave Palazzo Caetani unattended, which was one reason why Roffredo had returned there. (Another was the presence of his two Rzewuska cousins, Lela and Toutou, who had fled occupied Poland and were being hidden in one of the apartments.) These letters were carried between Ninfa and Palazzo Caetani by trusted household staff, who travelled by train between Rome and Littoria. There are mentions of sending Roffredo food the same way, hidden under someone's jacket or skirt, although, as Marguerite pointed out in one missive, "nobody searches on the trains," and the security checkpoints at Termini and Littoria were lax. She also mentioned "children" to be cared for: were these the tenants' children, Jewish children, dispossessed or orphaned children? Marguerite and Lelia were sometimes at Sermoneta, and in one letter, Marguerite suggested "hiding" some of Ninfa's Rhode Island Red hens and best cows there, no doubt to preserve them from the German soldiery. In one panicky letter she related how her nightmares materialized one morning, when a contingent of Germans banged on the door at Ninfa and wanted to camp in the garden. She managed to dissuade them – in German – by pointing out a better spot for their camp nearby, but begged Roffredo to come in case the soldiers returned.[29] He did.

The Allied landings at Anzio in January 1944, though welcome, brought new peril to the local population. Through the winter months,

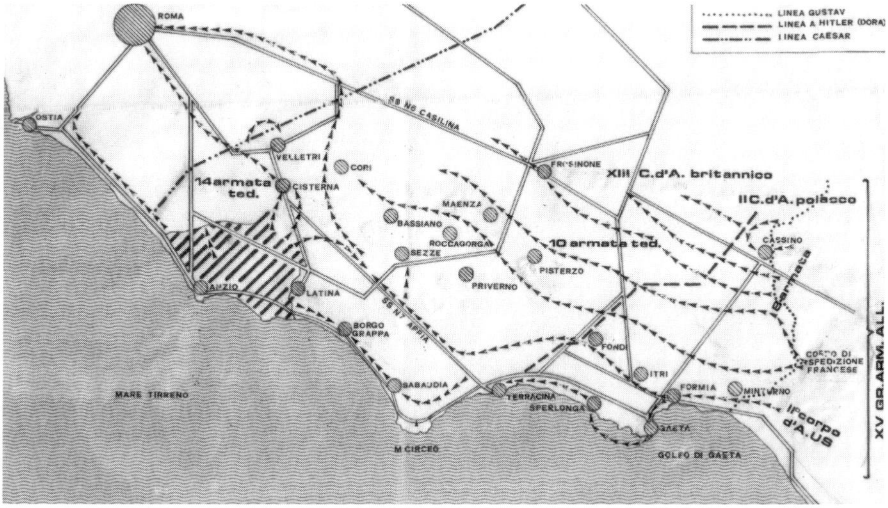

10.1
Map showing the breakout from Anzio. Ninfa and Sermoneta were on the route of the Allied advance to Cisterna.

while the American Fifth Army was held down by the Germans, sporadic fire sometimes overshot the intended target and landed kilometres away – on at least one occasion, in the gardens at Ninfa. Incessant noise and columns of smoke rising into the air reminded everyone of how close the battle was. When a bomb destroyed an outbuilding and blew out all the glass in the *municipio*, the time had come to retreat to Sermoneta. Roffredo later recorded how he hastily burned papers relating to Marguerite's American investments to prevent them falling into the hands of German troops, who within a day had occupied the house.[30] Roffredo, Marguerite, and Lelia, the house staff, the gardeners and their families from Ninfa, and the tenants from the surrounding estates moved up the hill to the castle, bringing with them any livestock and provisions they still possessed. Members of the Resistance were also sheltered in the castle, and given food, clothing, and money.[31] Cold and hunger prevailed, though Marguerite apparently organized the castle kitchen so as to provide a daily hot meal for everyone. Years later, an American journalist would describe how Lelia set up her easel in the

10.2
Attorney General Francis Biddle. The telephone on the left was his encrypted hotline to President Franklin D. Roosevelt.

midst of the chaos of refugees and animals and sketched the views of the countryside that she feared would shortly be destroyed.[32]

Back in Rome, in the aftermath of the destruction of Monte Cassino, Harold Tittmann noted the many appeals he received (or was asked to pass on to the Pope) from Italian bishops, pleading that historic towns and churches be spared Allied bombardment. The damage and loss of life resulting from Allied bombing in and around Rome a year earlier was still deeply felt, and the Vatican used diplomatic channels to convey these requests to the American and British military authorities. In the Commune of Sermoneta, such monuments included the twelfth-century monastery of Valvisciolo and the town of Sonnino. The latter, alas, was bombed on 22 April, with the loss of forty-five lives.[33] Whether anyone pleaded for Sermoneta is not known – but oral history in the area relates that a huge American flag was fashioned out of bedsheets by Marguerite and Lelia, then painted and spread out on the

10.3
Cisterna in the aftermath of Allied bombing, 1944.

castle roof, so that low-flying aircraft would register Sermoneta as "friendly territory." Given the Biddles' visits to Ninfa and Sermoneta in happier times, requests to spare both places may well have been made at the highest level: Francis Biddle was now Attorney General of the United States, appointed by President Roosevelt in August 1941.

In late May 1944 came the breakout from Anzio, as the American Fifth Army pushed the retreating Germans inland and back towards Rome. Ninfa was directly on the path of the Allied advance to Cisterna and Cori. The battle for Cisterna resulted in the destruction of most of the town, including severe damage to the Caetani palace and the deaths of a number of people sheltering there. Months earlier, General Mark Clark had secretly visited Ninfa and met Marguerite, but even so, damage was inevitably done, if not by the bombardment of the advancing

10.4
The restored tower and keep of the castle of Sermoneta. From January to March 1944 it sheltered the local populace (including Marguerite, Roffredo, and Lelia) as Allied and German forces clashed nearby.

Americans, then by the retreating Germans in their determination to leave nothing of value intact. Wanton destruction and plunder by the Germans even provoked an Official Report on the part of the British government. This would be read to the House of Commons on 1 August 1944, and included the not-altogether-accurate claim that "The Castello Caetani at Sermoneta and the Caetani villa at Ninfa were despoiled of their furnishings" by vengeful troops.[34]

The worst atrocity, which leading authorities have since qualified as an act of biological warfare, was the deliberate recreation of the saline conditions in which the sole variety of mosquito able to breed in them could thrive. This was done by stopping the pumps that carried brackish water to the sea, then reversing them to reflood the *Agro Pontino* with salt water. The year 1944 saw an epidemic of malaria on an unprecedented scale, with some 55,000 cases (up from 1,217 in 1943) and many deaths.[35] In addition, the resalination of the soil rendered it unfit for cultivation. Luckily, Ninfa's independent irrigation system and the pure water of the Ninfa spring itself prevented the poisoning of the soil.

By mid-March Marguerite, Roffredo, and Lelia had, in fact, left Sermoneta for Rome (though no information survives about how they made the journey), confident that the Allied victory could not be long in coming. The appalling massacre of Italian civilians at the Ardeatine Caves was the worst, but not the only, atrocity committed by the Germans in this last, desperate phase of the Occupation. Marguerite later described this period of living "half-hidden, as all our friends" as exceedingly stressful: "It has been a real reign of terror."[36] Not until 4 June did the first American troops enter Rome, to be followed the next day by the men of the Fifth Army and the British Eighth Army. By then the German Tenth and Fourteenth armies were in full retreat, and the

10.5
The *Agro Pontino* after sabotage activity by the retreating German armies, 1944.

people of Rome spilled onto the streets, hysterical with joy, to welcome their liberators. One Fifth Army soldier later wrote, in a history of the battle for Rome, that "what the Germans had never been able to do, the solid masses of the Roman throngs had accomplished: they stopped our tanks."[37] Peter Tompkins, who had slipped out of Palazzo Lovatelli-Caetani the previous evening and seen American Jeeps parked in Piazza Venezia (he even cadged a cigarette from one of the drivers), knew that liberation was imminent. The next morning, he made his way to the Capitoline Hill to mingle with the crowds and watch the generals arrive.[38] Marguerite viewed the passage of the armoured traffic and marching men from the roof of Palazzo Caetani, laughing with relief and pride.[39]

In a letter to Katherine, written two weeks later, Marguerite assured her sister that "We are all well, but *exhausted.* I suppose it is now that we are feeling the constant nervous strain of the past months ... Now a miracle has happened and the past seems like a bad dream." She signed off with the touching postscript, "I have forgotten how to write."[40] She had been fortunate: Vittoria, half-English and outspoken in her approval of Italy's *volte-face* in 1943, had been hunted through the labyrinthine cellars of Palazzo Orsini by the Gestapo. Cora (part American) had even been arrested. She spent Christmas 1943 in a German detention centre, then took shelter with Topazia and Vittoria at Palazzo Orsini until the three women were able to reach Palazzo Caetani.[41]

While the worst, in a sense, was over, there now began the long struggle to rebuild what had been destroyed. On what remained of the Caetani estates, the first priority was to restore the drainage system, and so, on 29 July 1944, Roffredo and Lelia jointly applied to the Allied Control Commission for the sum of 820,000 lire to be used for "cleaning ditches, repairing culverts and draining mosquito breeding places on the Caetani properties near Cisterna," and were granted their request in the ACC's reply on 21 August.[42] There were few able-bodied men available to carry out this or any other work, so that any project took twice as long as it once might have. The Ministry of Public Works also contributed to the drainage repairs, but in February 1945, when Roffredo and Lelia sought compensation from the ministry for damage done in and around Sermoneta and Ninfa by serial bombardment, they were less successful. They listed the damage to roofs, walls, and windows, the destruction of equipment and tools, and the wreckage of interiors, but were told by the ministry's lawyer more than a year later that they must supply documentary proof of the previous good state of everything on the list; the limit of compensation was in any case only three hundred thousand lire: a fraction of the value of what had been destroyed.[43] Getting things done and moving again was essential, and rather than wait any longer, Lelia and Roffredo sold off some small plots of land around Cisterna and Littoria to pay for repairs.

Marguerite had recovered a measure of her former energy and will to live. She had somehow assimilated, if not overcome, the loss of Camillo, and helped those closest to her to bear it. (It is interesting to observe how frequently she would continue to write to Katherine, whose chalice of grief she herself had been forced to drain to the very dregs.) Privation, fear, and the suffering of others had perhaps put her own feelings into perspective – she seldom expressed them, but the sight of so much human misery in the area around Sermoneta and Ninfa stirred the conviction that she must do what she could. Her first concern was to ensure that any local children orphaned or left homeless were fed and cared for until relatives could be located or homes otherwise found for them. This emergency help evolved into what Marguerite and Lelia called their *colonie di bambini*, or childrens' summer camps, in the castle in Sermoneta, which provided the children of the area with milk, healthy meals, and remedial education in the post-war period. Local women were employed to cook and sew clothes for the children, and young people to play with them and teach them sport. All this was a help to the area's devastated economy, as well as to the children themselves.

Before and during the war Marguerite had made a number of friends, three of whom now proposed that, by working together, much could be accomplished. These were Giuliana Benzoni, a courageous Milanese aristocrat who had acted as a courier for the Resistance during the war; the exceedingly capable and well-read Elsa Dallolio, the daughter of a former mayor of Bologna, who worked for the Italian Red Cross; and

10.6
One of Marguerite's postwar childrens' summer camps, or *colonie di bambini*, held at the castle of Sermoneta.

Elena Croce, whose father was the famous Neapolitan philosopher Benedetto Croce. Elsa Dallolio's close friend Iris Origo, whom Marguerite had met some thirty years earlier in Florence, was another who became part of the Caetani circle. During the Occupation, Iris and her Italian husband, Marchese Antonio Origo, had sustained the local partisans, hidden numerous Allied airmen, and sheltered hundreds of orphans at their farm, La Foce, near Siena. They were now about to buy an apartment in Palazzo Orsini, steps from Palazzo Caetani.

In August 1945, Marguerite wrote to Katherine describing a new initiative begun with these women, which had been given the name *Il Ritrovo* – "the meeting place," or "gathering":

> I am starting a club with a group of friends – an Italian initiative encouraged by the Government and as soon as we are well estab-

> lished the allies will form up with us ... The idea is to have the best gathering of Italians possible to meet the different allies and the allies to meet among themselves which happens rather rarely – what marvelous news! It's too thrilling.[44]

This was Marguerite, aged sixty-five: an age at which many women are beginning to slow down, but at which she seems to have received a fresh injection of energy and purpose. Elena Croce observed that her friend had two distinct personalities. One of them was "Marguerite," the "impatient detester of any dusty old-fashioned worldliness" and "daringly adventurous expert on modern art." The other was "Princess Caetani," or more accurately, "di Bassiano," "the descendant of an old New England family," in whose disdain for anything vulgar or mean was combined the attitudes of the patrician European and the American puritan. Il Ritrovo provided ample scope for the exercise of both these aspects of her personality. Her connections included people on every level of the social scale, but more importantly, these connections were inevitably people of good will and considerable creativity, glad to assist in recovering Italy's sense of national pride in the aftermath of the disastrous fascist interval.

Il Ritrovo began with some small art exhibitions, of the kind that Marguerite was by this time adept at putting together, and for which she could supply the paintings. It went on to organize talks on subjects of cultural interest, followed by modest receptions and simple lunches at which one of the guests was invited to speak on some current topic, with the aim of encouraging more general discussion. These occasions brought together members of the Allied armed forces, diplomatic representatives from across the spectrum of countries represented in Rome, and Italian politicians, writers, artists, and journalists. If the setting was imposing ("an enormous apartment in a princely palace," as Elena Croce put it), the atmosphere was informal. There was no receiving line, and the usual protocol that governed social events in Rome was abandoned. Those invited could arrive when they could, circulate freely, chat to whomever they wished, and leave when they liked. Sometimes the animated discussions went on well into the afternoon. The aim was the furtherance of mutual acquaintance, understanding, and respect. Much of the cost was underwritten by Marguerite, but she was also good at enlisting contributions from others well-disposed to the venture. Both she and Lelia acted as translators, making sure that American, British, French, and Italian guests met one another and felt at ease.

Il Ritrovo was one of the dozens of small initiatives that arose in postwar Italy in an attempt to rehabilitate public life and recover national dignity in the wake of fascism. Popular opinion was deeply divided about how recovery could and should take place. Italy had always been a predominantly Catholic country, but in great swathes of it, where the ruin of local economies provided the conditions favourable to the spread of ideology, communism had made enormous gains, with the consequent polarization of political debate. War-weariness, mistrust, and the need to attribute blame pervaded social relations. The widespread disruption of education during the war had left thousands of young people without training or prospects, while the loss of so much agricultural and manufacturing capacity soon set in motion the mass emigration of working people that came to characterize the postwar period. As for the propertied interests that had once occupied the top of the economic pyramid, they had long since been forced into a defensive posture, and in the aftermath of the war tended to focus on retaining what they could of ancient lands and privileges. None of this was conducive to restoring a sense of solidarity, or in formulating any collaborative forward-looking solutions to Italy's problems. In its modest way, Il Ritrovo fostered the connections between people that could lead to such solutions. Her participation in it placed Marguerite once again at the centre of a circle of intellectually audacious people, as in the days of *Commerce* and the French and Italian societies devoted to modern art. She had missed such stimulation, and all but forgotten how good she was at animating others. It would not be long before an even more ambitious idea would draw these abilities together in a new and yet more challenging initiative.

11

NEW BEGINNINGS: *BOTTEGHE OSCURE*

On 21 December 1946 – the winter solstice – Leone's son, Onorato, aged forty-four, died at Palazzo Orsini. The life of "Onoratino," as he was known within the family, left few traces beyond a handful of references to him in his father's letters and his mother's books. His disabilities, whatever they were, had always kept him on the sidelines of family and public life, although between 25 December 1935 and 21 December 1946, he was, de facto, the 16th Duke of Sermoneta. With his nephew's death, Roffredo, who had carried the responsibilities of the dukedom since Leone's departure for Canada twenty-five years earlier, finally inherited the title that corresponded to them. Marguerite awoke on the morning of 22 December to find herself Duchess of Sermoneta, although most people would continue to call her "Principessa."

For two or three years after the liberation of Rome, Il Ritrovo filled a vital role in bringing together Allied leaders with Italian writers, artists, and public figures. Then, as postwar recovery got under way, it quietly faded out of existence. Much as Marguerite enjoyed its gatherings (especially the luncheons, where Lelia's gentle sense of humour sometimes produced "interesting" seating plans[1]), another project had taken shape in her mind, and she was impatient to move it forward.

Through the war, the recollection of *Commerce* had served Marguerite as a kind of talisman, a memory that held out the hope of an eventual return to civilized life. It was a distraction from scarcity and cold and boredom, and even an antidote to fear, as on the nights at Sermoneta when bombardments lit up the sky and shook the castle, producing hysteria among the country people sheltering there. Perhaps, too, it even served as a counterweight to grief. There was plenty of time to think about what would be needed after the war. Once the tide had turned and an Allied victory was certain, Marguerite began to consider how to put her experience with *Commerce* to use in the radically different circumstances of postwar Italy.

Among those who got in touch with her after the liberation was her cousin "Tom" Eliot, eager for news: "I was a good deal concerned about you from the time the invasion of Italy began ... I do hope you are all well, and that you have enough to *eat*, and whether there is anything you would like sent, and whether I could send it, and whether it would reach you [*sic*]."[2]

Whether Marguerite reassured him on these points or not, she lost no time in broaching the subject on which she wanted his unique perspective: the idea of a new "international," multilingual review. Eliot replied on 22 May 1945. He was just back from a conference in Paris, where he had met some of the old circle connected with *Commerce*: Paul Valéry, Jean Paulhan, and Bernard Groethuysen. The literary scene they described to him was confusing (not very different from that of postwar London, he concluded), and he found it hard to discern "what is needed and what there would be a public for." One point upon which he and the others agreed, however, was that "a magazine that was polyglot – in which contributions were published in their original languages, English, French, and Italian – could probably not have more than an artificial existence." Eliot thought that "what people prefer is a review published in one place and in one language; and that the best course would be to have everything translated, *but* to give the original texts of *poems* as well as translations."[3] Prompted by what Eliot told him about Marguerite's idea, Jean Paulhan wrote to her too: "People are still asking about *Commerce*," he said, but "*Commerce* in three languages frightens me a little. And without translations, more."[4] It was clear that neither Eliot nor Paulhan saw much future for a review along the lines Marguerite was proposing.

Cautious opinions from two such experienced friends might have discouraged anyone else, but they were so at variance with her own instinct that Marguerite simply set them aside and kept thinking. In a letter to Katherine of 12 April 1947, she confessed that "I am terribly tempted to try a sort of Commerce Prose and Poetry – French Italian and English no translations [*sic*]. One is suffocated here by the quantity of publications political, critical, historical dry as dust. One longs for some light and air and a bit of phantasy [*sic*]. Perhaps it is only a dream and impossible to accomplish now."[5] As she saw it, the international focus of *Commerce* was precisely what had made it unique. Within its pages, quality writing from a dozen countries had found a place, and it was this, she considered, that had broadened its appeal in a way never imagined – or intended – by its founders. That international outlook seemed even more necessary in a postwar world divided by ideologies, and a Europe whose cultural and moral foundations were as devastated as its cities.

In any case, restoring civilization must surely imply more than rebuilding economies and infrastructure? It must also mean the reassertion of human values, in which literature and the imagination that inspired it had a vital role. This seemed to Marguerite particularly important with regard to Italy, whose national identity and image abroad were tarnished by its quarter-century as a fascist power. Italy's writers, particularly the new generation of writers that had lived through the repression of the fascist years and the war, had things to say worth saying, but fascism had destroyed their means of participating in the international literary scene. Marguerite believed that, if they could do so, the recognition they deserved would be forthcoming – and that the intellectual respectability largely lost under fascism would again begin to accrue. In her view, a place for new writing was therefore not a luxury, but a necessity, and one that Marguerite was convinced she had the experience and financial means to provide.

This was a daring proposition, but in fact Marguerite's idea went farther still. She recognized that Italian society under fascism had become narrow and provincial, that what was needed was a steady current of intellectual fresh air. Her review would begin with Italian writers, but it would go on to present them in the company of their peers from other countries, writing in different languages. Occasionally, but by no means always, she envisaged that a poem or story might be translated into one of the other major languages represented in the review, where no such translation already existed, but in general work written in a given language would be published as written, without the benefit of translation. This seemed to turn Marguerite's former emphasis on the importance of translation on its head, but there was method in it. In *Commerce*, the translation into French of writing in other languages had provided a literary experience in its own right. The new review would provide much less translation, but it would be more truly international, with a readership whose common ground was a dedication to good writing for its own sake, in whatever language it was written. The assumption here was that most members of that readership – academics and students, diplomats, people in the arts and publishing, expatriates, those working abroad, and writers themselves – were at least bilingual, and likely to be intrigued by the review's multilingual content.

Elena Croce passed on as much advice as she could, as Marguerite worked out the practicalities of producing her new review. If not a veteran publisher, Elena at least had the experience of one literary journal (the short-lived *Arethusa*, which ran from April 1944 to January 1946). In 1947, she and her husband, the journalist Raimondo Craveri, were preparing to launch *Lo Spettatore Italiano*, a cultural and political monthly that aimed to bring together diverse strands of opinion in a kind of open forum. As a lawyer, journalist, editor, and translator, Elena had professional contacts that she offered to Marguerite. The one that would prove most valuable was a thirty-one-year-old poet named Giorgio Bassani, whom she recommended as an editorial assistant.

Marguerite liked Bassani's poetry, and was impressed by his background. He had studied art history at the University of Bologna with Roberto Longhi (a renowned expert on Caravaggio, and the translator into Italian of Bernard Berenson's *Italian Painters of the Renaissance*), and had considered a career as a concert pianist until his anti-fascist activities landed him in prison in 1943. Since his release after the fall of Mussolini, writing and editing had kept him afloat. Besides the editorial virtues claimed for him by Elena, he impressed Marguerite as just the kind of young, thoughtful, and provocative writer she wanted to publish.

Through friends abroad, Marguerite was well-informed of what was being written, and by whom, in French, German, and English, and of course knew the pre-war Italian literary scene well. Where she recognized a weakness was in her personal contact with the new generation of Italian writers. Because of the country's regional and linguistic variety, much of its literary life was centred in the major cities, and much of the work being produced was in dialect. Postwar Rome seethed with pent-up creativity, but young writers tended to congregate in the city's bars and cafés, not an ambience that Marguerite and Roffredo had ever frequented. The backlash against fascism meant that intellectual circles were divided by passionate convictions: communist on one hand and pro-Western libertarian on the other. Even literary discussions inevitably reverted to politics. Since Marguerite had no intention of turning her review into an ideological arena, she needed guidance in finding a varied selection of writers for the first few issues. Giorgio Bassani proved invaluable in providing such contacts. He and Marguerite began to work together in the summer of 1947, aiming to bring out the first *quaderno*[6] of the new review in the spring of 1948. Bassani would edit its Italian section, and assume much of the responsibility for producing the review overall, but the decision to publish his work was made by Marguerite.[7]

The world has Elena Croce to thank for suggesting the title Marguerite gave her review,[8] though the origin of it is clear enough. *Botteghe Oscure* took its name from the street in Rome in which Palazzo Caetani is located: the Via delle Botteghe Oscure, or "Street of the Dark Shops," so-named because it had once been bordered by a row of small shops set into the arches of the ancient Circus Flaminius. No doubt the shops *were* dark, thanks to the shadowy passage that separated them from the road, which at night would have given pause to even the most intrepid stroller. In the 1930s the street was widened as part of Mussolini's plan to improve Rome's traffic circulation, and acquired a more open, modern look, as well as a good six metres of pedestrian space. Palazzo Caetani was not the only well-known building in the Via delle Botteghe Oscure. A little farther along stood the headquarters of the Italian Communist Party (a building whose garish cream and maroon paintwork was its only notable feature), for which the street's name often served as an epithet. A few steps away, the mother house of the Society of Jesus – the Jesuits – was also sometimes referred to by the name of the street. In years to come, Marguerite would occasionally be asked why she had given her review so ambiguous a title. This inevitably produced a radiant smile and the claim that "the Caetani were there a thousand years before" their neighbours.[9]

Another of Elena Croce's contacts, Riccardo Ricciardi, was a publisher whose high reputation rested on his fidelity to traditional printing methods and attention to detail. Marguerite entrusted the production of *Botteghe Oscure* to him, and together they agreed on the various aspects of its design. Marguerite wanted the review to have the simple elegance of *Commerce*, yet intended the look of it to be specifically "Roman." The cover was plain ivory card, with the title and volume number in red in antique Roman lettering (the "u" made more classical-looking by being printed as "v") and, initially, the same image of the Roman balance that had appeared on the cover of *Commerce*. The typeface chosen was Bodoni, a late-eighteenth-century serif font known for being easy to read.[10] Marguerite insisted that the paper used must be worthy of what was to be printed on it: easy on the eye, of satisfying weight, and durable (unlike the paper so often used for "little" reviews, that was thin enough to see through and apt to become brittle with age). Ricciardi took an almost fatherly interest in the layout, ensuring that each page was visually pleasing by surrounding the text with ample space.[11]

Botteghe Oscure made its debut, somewhat later than expected, on 7 July 1948. Quaderno I was devoted entirely to poetry and prose by Italian authors, most of them friends or contacts of Giorgio Bassani's. Eugenio Montale, whose poem "L'Anguilla" ("The Eel") opened the volume, was one of the great figures of Italian letters, but others, like Guglielmo Petroni, whose novella *Il Mondo e una Prigione* ("*The World Is a Prison*") came next, were little known outside their own provincial circles – in Petroni's case, Florence. Bassani himself contributed "Storia d'Amore" ("Love Story"), while a third piece of fiction was written by Manlio Cancogni, who later went on to produce more than twenty novels and story collections. The rest of the 226-page volume was dedicated to poetry by, among others, Attilio Bertolucci, soon to be acknowledged as one of Italy's leading modern poets,[12] Augusto Guidi, who became a noted translator of English poetry into Italian, and Sandro Penna, one of the first modern Italian poets to deal openly with homosexuality.

The outstanding piece in this issue was undoubtedly Petroni's eighty-three-page novella, which took up a third of the volume and recounted the experience of a former prisoner during the Occupation trying to adapt to life after the war. Of all the writers included in Quaderno I, Petroni had the most surprising personal history. Born in Lucca to a poor family, he began working alongside his father as a shoemaker at the age of ten, and was all but illiterate until adolescence. Self-taught, he published his first book of poems, *Versi e Memoria* (*Verses and Memory*), to great acclaim in 1935. His account of Nazi brutality at the Via Tasso prison was based on his own imprisonment and torture there as a member of the Resistance. He owed his life to the liberation of Rome by the Allies the day before he was due to be shot.

The acclaim with which *Botteghe Oscure* was greeted by Marguerite's friends was general, but not universal. Elena Croce wrote to say that "Everyone who has seen it has found it most beautiful,"[13] but, predictably, some felt that Giorgio Bassani's hand in it was all too apparent. In a letter to Jean Paulhan, Giuseppe Ungaretti railed against the influence of the "Croce-Craveri group."[14] For him, the first number of *Botteghe Oscure* fell short of the standard set by *Commerce*, and he vowed that he would never send Marguerite anything for it (and he never did). Paulhan candidly told Marguerite, when she asked for his views, that the overall quality of Quaderno I made it "a handsome Anthology," but that it lacked her personal imprint, her taste for adventure and new departures, that he saw as having characterized *Commerce*.[15] Perhaps Marguerite expected her friends to understand her altruistic aims, and in the light of them, to overlook any shortcomings in the actual achievement. Paulhan clearly considered his frank answer the reply a friend should give, but Marguerite took offence, and for a time there was coolness between them. They made it up, of course: the number of Marguerite's old friends in France had diminished with the deaths of Edouard Vuillard in 1940, Paul Valéry in 1945, and Bernard Groethuysen and Pierre Bonnard in 1946. Of those remaining, Jean and Germaine Paulhan were among the closest. This minor spat was nonetheless a foretaste of a worse one that would derail their friendship a few years later.

Pressed for time due to the delay in publishing Quaderno I, Marguerite and Bassani were already pulling together Quaderno II, ostensibly for the autumn of 1948. Marguerite had resumed the pattern of life that enabled her to escape the summer heat. Once the spring flowering at Ninfa had passed and the nightingales had flown, she and Lelia left for Paris, stopping in Switzerland in one or both directions. Being away from Rome made it essential that Marguerite be able to rely on Bassani's judgment. This she felt able to do, and writing to Elena Croce Craveri in July 1948, she was fulsome in her praise: "I can never thank you enough for introducing me to Bassani. He's a young man so exceptional from every point of view and then so financially sound that for sure without him I could never have done the review."[16] From wherever she was, Marguerite fired off frequent letters to Bassani in her large, dashing hand, to which he responded at length in his meticulously even script. He never hesitated to express his own views, but deferred to her, not just as proprietor and employer, but as someone who knew foreign literatures far better than he did, although he had the greater knowledge of Italian. Marguerite might agree with him, or not, but she always wanted his opinion. Even when they cordially agreed to disagree and she had the last word, she inevitably thanked him. In a matter of months, he went from being "Caro Bassani" to "Caro Giorgio," then "Caro Amico." To Bassani, on the other hand, she was always (with one sole exception) "Principessa," even when she signed herself "Marguerite C."

In the run-up to the production of Quaderno II, Marguerite had a difficult decision to make. Riccardo Ricciardi was a perfectionist who took on boys orphaned by the war as apprentices and trained them to set type by hand and develop his own discerning eye for detail. His publications were superb, but bringing them to birth was a slow process. If *Botteghe Oscure* were to fulfill its promise to subscribers to appear twice yearly, in spring and autumn, it would have to be produced less expensively, and on a schedule. For this reason, Marguerite left the Ricciardi firm for the Istituto Grafico Tiburino, run by Luigi De Luca, located in Tivoli, just outside Rome. De Luca was an art lover, like Marguerite, and had already published several journals of art and ideas. Their harmonious working relationship grew into a valued friendship, and lasted, like that between Marguerite and Giorgio Bassani, as long as the review itself.[17]

Beginning on 2 September, De Luca had to work quickly to bring out Quaderno II before the end of 1948 – it was in fact dated 30 December. It was worth the effort: a volume that nine Italian authors shared with some older, well-known British and American poets (Edith Sitwell and Walter de la Mare, Conrad Aiken, Marianne Moore, and William Carlos Williams), and an array of modernists from both sides of the Atlantic (among others, W.H. Auden, Cecil Day-Lewis, Kathleen Raine, E.E. Cummings, Richard Eberhart, Karl Shapiro, and Theodore Roethke). There was also work by some dynamic younger poets whose recognition came later: Richard Wilbur, William Jay Smith, and Hayden Carruth. In the Italian section, established poets Libero de Libero and Giacomo Noventa rubbed shoulders with the youthful Rocco Scotellaro.[18] Giorgio Bassani contributed a long poem, and Mario Soldati, who went on to become a major film director, a story entitled "La Giacca Verde" ("The Green Jacket") that he later turned into a musical. There was also a translation into Italian of a portion of Plato's *Meno* by Marguerite's friend, the Austrian philosopher and cultural essayist Rudolf Kassner.

It was a rich selection, on this occasion chosen with the aim of gaining English-speaking subscribers for *Botteghe Oscure*, especially in the United States, as much as for the aim of promoting lesser-known authors. It is worth mentioning, since Giorgio Bassani was so helpful in generating Italian submissions, that Marguerite relied with equal confidence on others to do the same elsewhere. In London, these included T.S. Eliot at Faber and Faber and John Lehmann, the publisher of the literary review *New Writing* (and later of the Penguin volumes of the same title). She kept up to date with what was being written in the United States through subscriptions to the *New York Herald Tribune* and the best-known reviews of poetry and new writing, as well as the "annuals" of new work produced by publisher James Laughlin's New Directions. Publishers' catalogues were another source of information, but Marguerite's best personal contact was probably her sister Katherine. She was by now the author of a number of books of poetry, an avid reader and literary scholar, who was constantly recommending works that she considered ground-breaking.[19] Katherine and Francis Biddle befriended many poets, including Alexis Léger, who moved to the United States in 1940 after the Vichy government stripped him of his French citizenship. Another old friend whose judgment Marguerite valued was Archibald MacLeish, by this time Assistant Secretary of State with responsibility for culture, having won a Pulitzer Prize for Poetry in 1933 and served a six-year term as Librarian of Congress.[20]

Jean Paulhan, as editor of the *Nouvelle Revue Française* and of a review called *Cahiers du Pleïade*, assisted Marguerite in bringing together the French section of *Botteghe Oscure*, beginning with Quaderno III in the spring of 1949. It opened with poems by Paul Valéry, as a tribute to him, and included work by, among others, Paulhan himself, Georges Limbour, Francis Ponge, and René Char – a poet whose work immediately appealed to Marguerite. The advent of a third language made *Botteghe Oscure* genuinely international, although in this particular quaderno, as if to redress the imbalance created in the previous one, there were only four offerings in English, one of them Katherine Biddle's "Legend (Ninfa)."

This title in the third number of *Botteghe Oscure* is a reminder that Ninfa had resumed its place in the lives of the Caetani as a retreat from Rome. Damage to the house had been put right, drainage channels repaired, crops planted in the surrounding fields, and the old seasonal round of activity in the garden resumed. The anti-malaria unit from the

11.1.a
A 1940s view from the terrace of Ninfa's villa, formerly the town hall.

11.1.b
Ninfa's spring feeds the icy river that glides through the garden, nourishing abundant vegetation and contemplative thought.

11.2.a *Opposite*
Marguerite and Lelia gardening at Ninfa, spring 1947.

11.2.b
The same spot today, near the restored church of Santa Maria Maggiore.

Rockefeller Foundation was back carrying on the work of Dr Lewis Hackett, who had lived at Sermoneta during the early 1930s at Gelasio's invitation.[21] From shortly after the war, Marguerite, Roffredo, and Lelia began to spend four or five days at Ninfa every other week. Spring was Marguerite's favourite season there: in March 1947 she described to Katherine how "Ninfa is a dream of beauty with everything flowering all over the place," and how she and Lelia were spending Easter week "digging and sowing and transplanting and having a wonderful time."[22] Mother and daughter were never happier than when gardening together, though each had her alternative, absorbing activity: Marguerite her reading and voluminous correspondence, and Lelia her painting.

Roffredo, who over half a century had seen Ninfa evolve from an abandoned wilderness to a uniquely enchanting garden, found particular solace there. He could date every tree, recall the occasion when this or that channel was dug or bridge repaired, remember when a certain rose was planted or the year of the bumper crop of figs. His "alternative, absorbing activity" was still, of course, music, in that he often sat for a time at Liszt's piano and played snatches of melody, but he had ceased to compose seriously.[23] He claimed to begin his day by reading a page from the Caetani manuscript of *The Divine Comedy*, complete with annotations by Marsilio Ficino,[24] but his greatest pleasure now came from the garden:

> To take an old abandoned garden in hand and give it life again, uncover paths of worn stone, free plants surviving as the result of those unexplainable mysteries of nature from brambles and ivy, can be one of the most exciting experiences a gardener can ever know. And as the old ruins come to light bit by bit, new ideas take shape and the creative imagination which will give

11.3.a
Beauty amidst the ruins: Ninfa provided Marguerite and her family with solace and a sense of continuity after the war.

11.3.b
Lelia painting in the *salone* at Ninfa.

> life to the new garden bursts forth: the new garden springs and rises from the deep roots of one of the gardener's ancestors. Then the fancies, needs and tastes of the new owner are inserted into the new garden which keeps memories of the past deep in its underground veins.[25]

Everything at Ninfa reminded Roffredo of members of his family, lost to him through death, but, in what some of them had created in that astonishing place, ever present. Part of his enjoyment no doubt came from observing how Lelia incorporated the garden into her paintings, and brought her paintings to life in the garden. Her creative gift was a dual one, where each part nourished the other. Now a tall, fair woman in her mid-thirties, Lelia's inwardness, the adult version of her adolescent shyness, could be understood as a reflection of her extreme sensitivity to her surroundings, rather than an awkwardness to be overcome. She is recalled as sweet-natured and calm, if somewhat detached: pleasant company, but not at all intellectually audacious, as Marguerite was. Lelia was most herself at Ninfa, where she could potter silently for hours among her flowers. Then, at her easel in the salon, she would lovingly depict them, in the same recollected spirit. She painted a great deal in the first few years after the war, and exhibited on several occasions: once at the Galleria André Weil in Paris in 1948, and again at the Lefevre Gallery in London in 1949, as well as in the annual *Exposizione* held at the Quirinal Palace in Rome.

For Marguerite, as for Roffredo and Lelia, Ninfa was an earthly paradise, a retreat from the artificiality of urban life, but with some additional dimensions. It was, of course, one place where she could be alone to commune with Camillo. He was never spoken of, but those who knew her understood that certain secluded corners of the garden evoked his presence for her. Secondly, her ambitious planting schemes suggest that she saw Ninfa as a garden still in the making. If Roffredo looked back through the decades, appreciating the continuity inherent in what lay all around him, Marguerite looked forward, her imagination prompting her to see what could be done to enhance what was already there. She began ordering plants in quantity in October 1949,

11.4
Inspired by her surroundings: Lelia's paintings of a) a view from Ninfa, looking towards the Lepini mountains; b) summer flowers from the garden; and c) a panoramic view from the castle, showing the tiled roofs of Sermoneta and the surrounding mountains.

when she and Lelia made a tour of England following the latter's London exhibition, and visited the nurseries of Hilliard & Sons of Winchester for the first time. On that occasion she ordered 128 different varieties of rose and 35 different species of rhododendron, together with "fifteen species of viburnum ... four species of Pyracantha, many types of clematis ... nine of magnolia" and many more, to a total of five hundred plants in all.[26] Conveying all these to Ninfa was no easy feat. This first order was dispatched by rail, but the next, a similarly large one in 1950, "was sent by ship via Amsterdam, needing about five days: the more delicate plants were sent by air."[27]

Finally, Ninfa after the war became even more a place in which Marguerite loved to entertain and spend time with friends, much as Villa Romaine had been. The first entry in the Visitors' Book dates from August 1944, when the house at Ninfa was still almost uninhabitable. If the entries were at first sporadic, subsequent ones soon took on a regular pattern as repairs were made. At first the guests were old friends, mainly Italian, British, and American. There were the twin daughters of Count Pasolini Dall'Onda, Desideria and Ginevra, who had known Camillo; Nina Ruffini, Giuliana Benzoni, and others from Il Ritrovo; the Craveris and their children; Myron and Annabel Taylor; Harold and Eleanor Tittmann; Sir D'Arcy Osborne; Bill Phillips, the American ambassador to Italy, and Mason Hammond, an eminent classicist at the American Academy in Rome, with their respective families; Bernard Berenson, Nicky Mariano, and Count Umberto Morra di Lavriano; Iris and Antonio Origo and their daughters, Benedetta and Donata. Ninfa was a paradise for children: after lunch on the terrace, the young Craveris, Tittmanns, Hammonds, and Origos "ran wild" in the garden, swam in the icy, fast-flowing stream, and played hide-and-seek, while their parents talked the afternoons away.[28] What they later recalled of Marguerite was her vitality: dark eyes sparkling with curiosity and fun, and the sense that here was someone who was interested in them and in how they viewed the world. Despite her white hair, "la Principessa" did not strike them as "old." As a later generation would say, she was "on their wavelength."

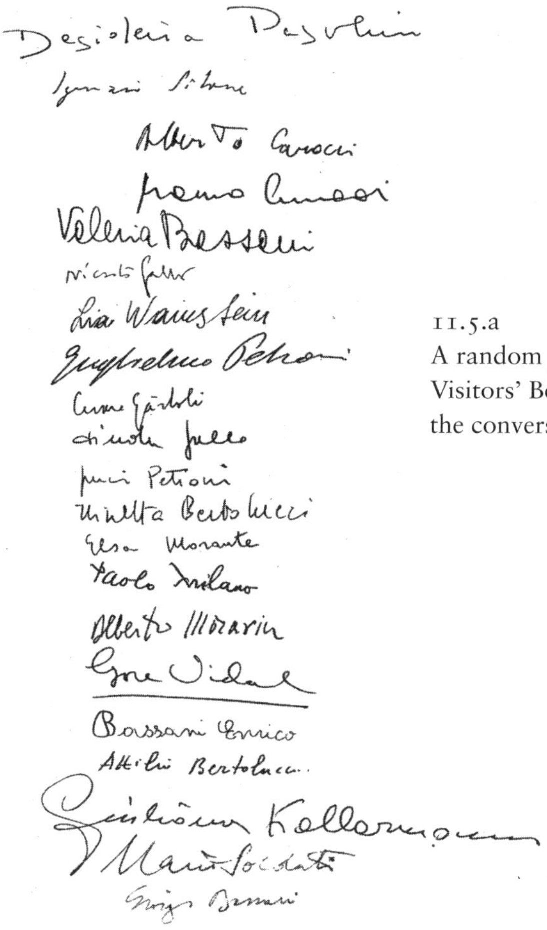

11.5.a
A random page from the Ninfa Visitors' Book: can you imagine the conversations?

Even before the founding of *Botteghe Oscure*, there were a fair number of writers among the guests at Ninfa: John Wyndham, Edmund Wilson, Madeleine de Waal, Carlo Levi, David and Tamara Talbot Rice, Raleigh Trevelyan, Fitzroy Maclean, Alberto Moravia and Elsa Morante, Agatha Christie, John Lehmann, and many others. As the review involved more contributors, they too were included in gatherings at Ninfa, and it is hard to find a name from *Botteghe Oscure* that is not paralleled by a signature in the Ninfa Visitors' Book. That is not to say that such gatherings were exclusively or even predominantly literary.

11.5.b
Not the best of photographs, but this was the smile that welcomed visitors to Ninfa: Marguerite in her element.

From the world of music and performance came Gioconda de Vito (to whom Roffredo had dedicated his *Festa campestre per violino e pianoforte* in 1936[29]), the composer Jacques Ibert, the great Russian pianist Nikita Magaloff, conductor Igor Markevitch, and composers Gian Carlo Menotti and Samuel Barber. Other guests were drawn from the foreign cultural institutions and the various archaeological schools in Rome. Princess Maria of Piedmont, who had known Roffredo since childhood, was another frequent visitor. Members of the Caetani and Chapin families had standing invitations. Katherine and Francis Biddle came to stay in May 1946 and again for Christmas in 1948, while during the Nuremburg trials, at which he was a judge, Francis was occasionally able to escape to Ninfa for a restorative few days.[30] George Biddle, Francis's younger brother, a former war artist and a leading social-realist painter, visited with his wife, the sculptress Hélène

Sardeau. Giovanella and Vittoria came very occasionally, but now that Cora was living in Paris, managing the showroom of Jensen, the design firm, Roffredo made a point of including his niece Topazia.[31] Then there were the people passing through Rome, whom Marguerite and Roffredo might not know personally, but for whom there was always a welcome: friends of friends, journalists on assignment, academic and diplomatic contacts, promising doctoral candidates. Any of these, invited to Ninfa, might find themselves lunching or dining on the terrace with a dozen others, for a memorable combination of traditional Italian fare and stimulating conversation. Those lucky enough to be invited to dinner between mid-May and mid-June were treated to one of the glories of Ninfa. As dusk fell, Marguerite would call for silence and lead them across the grass to a spot near Gelasio's thatched *capanna*, as from the shrubbery came the liquid trills of a male nightingale, filling the twilight with the song that inspired the poets of ancient Rome.

Among the earliest names in Ninfa's visitor's book is that of Hubert Howard, the third son of Esme, first Baron Howard of Penrith (1863–1939), a former British ambassador to the United States, and his wife, Princess Isabella Giustiniani Bandini, who had known the Caetanis since childhood. The Howards became friends with Duke Onorato and Ada through embassy circles, during a diplomatic posting in Rome in the 1880s. On occasion they had toured the Pontine Marshes and been guests at the bleak Palazzo Caetani in Cisterna. From 1938, when their youngest son, Henry, married Adèle Le Bourgeois Alsop, a cousin of Marguerite's, the connection became a familial one. Henry and his brother Hubert subsequently served in Italy during the Italian campaign, and it was Henry who introduced Hubert to Lelia as soon as the war was over.[32]

Hubert and Lelia began as acquaintances: each was more at ease politely conversing with others than talking about themselves, but since their backgrounds were similar and they shared a number of interests, they soon became friends. Hubert's mother was Italian, Lelia's American; both their lives had been spent moving from place to place, each had been educated in several languages and brought up with a distinct

11.6
Lelia and Hubert Howard on their wedding day, 17 September 1951.

sense of noblesse oblige. Lelia's spiritual response to nature had a counterpart in Hubert's devout Roman Catholicism. His idea of entering the priesthood had been set aside when duty called in 1939, but he remained a deeply religious man, who emerged from the war still uncertain of quite what it was that he was called to do in life.

When he was demobbed, Hubert bought a small estate called Lyulph's Tower, on Lake Ullswater, close to Greystoke Castle, the Howard estate where his father was born. His aim was to set up a dairy farm. In August 1947, Marguerite and Lelia made a tour of the British Isles by car, following an itinerary that included "a place in Cumberland near Hubert Howard for 5 days, then Ireland,"[33] which suggests at the very least a pleasant exchange of hospitality. Lelia seemed to blossom in Hubert's company, while for his part, the barriers of doubt and uncertainty gradually dissolved. The leisurely pace of what Marguerite and Roffredo hoped was courtship gave time for everyone to become better acquainted. Other members of the Howard family were drawn into the Caetani circle, notably Hubert's brother Edmund, an attaché at the British embassy in Rome from 1948 to 1951, to whom Roffredo kindly offered an apartment in Palazzo Caetani. "Mondi" and his wife, Cécile (née Geoffroy-Dechaume), and their children – Esme, John, Anthony, and Katherine – became frequent visitors to Ninfa.[34]

Hubert proposed to Lelia, and was accepted, in January 1949. Even then, they did not rush things, but settled into a comfortable engagement that lasted until their marriage on 17 September 1951. The wedding took place in England, at St George's Roman Catholic church in Taunton in Somerset, and was celebrated by Monsignor Ronald Knox – biblical scholar and translator of the Vulgate, academic, and wit – who was at that time chaplain to the Asquith family at their nearby estate at Mells. The reception afterwards was held at Tetton House, home of the Howards' cousins the Herberts.[35] Marguerite and Roffredo, Katherine and Francis Biddle, and a host of Howard, Lindsay, Herbert, and Bootle-Wilbraham relations were there to celebrate the occasion. A week later, from Ireland, Katherine looked back on it, aware that, despite Marguerite's happiness for her daughter, it was hard for her to relinquish the intense closeness they had always shared:

> It really was very lovely. I think the simplicity and dignity of Lelia were the things I remember most. And your courage my dear. It is hard to be much comfort to someone who is as brave and stoical as you but I hope you know how close I felt to you, and how understanding. And I did like Hubert very much & felt he was appreciative of Lelia.[36]

Lelia was thirty-eight when she married, and while Marguerite and Roffredo still hoped for an heir to the Caetani dukedom, they were simply glad to see her settled. (Katherine had summed up the situation a few months earlier, when she wrote that "you and Roffredo will be able to feel that someone will always be there to look out for her and be tender of her as she grows older."[37]) Everyone sensed that Hubert would be a capable co-administrator of the estates while Roffredo was alive, and a support to Lelia in carrying on that task after he was gone. Roffredo was eighty in 1951, still hale and well, but naturally concerned to leave everything in good hands. For her part, Marguerite knew how important this was to his peace of mind, and how essential it was, too, for Lelia to step out from her mother's shadow. Her exhibitions had done much to facilitate this, but marriage and a life of her own would do much more. Just as Marguerite divided her time among Rome, Ninfa, and Paris, the Howards from now on divided theirs among Rome (where they took over the sunny top-floor apartment at Palazzo Caetani, with its enormous terrace), Ninfa, and Cumbria, reached via Switzerland, Paris, or wherever their fancies took them. For their part, from their daughter's marriage onwards, Marguerite and Roffredo tacitly – but with relief and gratitude – relinquished the determining role in administrative matters to Lelia and Hubert.

Lelia's new-found independence freed Marguerite to concentrate yet more intensely on *Botteghe Oscure*. By the end of 1951, eight *quadernos* had appeared, averaging around 450 pages in length, handsome to look at and satisfying to handle. The standard of the material that appeared in it, and the freedom with which it was presented, ensured that the review now enjoyed a certain prestige. There was no advertising, no editorial comment, no criticism, literary theory, news, or analysis: *Botteghe Oscure* contained new writing, and nothing but, apart from the odd translational "first," such as a translation into Italian of Keats's "Ode on a Grecian Urn" that appeared in Quaderno IV, and that of Bertolt Brecht's play, known in English as *The Good Woman of Szechuan*, into French in Quaderno VI. This last item, which ran to 112 pages, was an example of Marguerite's generous editorial policy: she imposed no limit on length, and the fact that a single story might occupy sixty, eighty, or even a hundred pages was her quiet tribute to the author as the best judge of the space that he or she required. Neither did she compel an author to fit in with some perceived standard of public taste. When she bought Niccolò Tucci's story "Those Long Shadows," deemed unacceptable by the *New Yorker* unless he altered certain passages, he wrote gratefully that "You instead are giving me a chance to express myself, to live and BE, without 'corrections,' *as I happen to be*. What could be greater, more satisfying,

INDICE

Attilio Bertolucci	*A Giuseppe, in ottobre*	9
Ignazio Silone	*Una manciata di more*	10
Aldo Capitini	*La festa*	45
Pier Paolo Pasolini	*Versi friulani*	54
Anna Banti	*Le donne muoiono*	60
Romeo Giovannini	*Poesie*	82
Giorgio Caproni	*Poesie*	86
Desideria Pasolini	*Mita*	89
Luciano Erba	*Poesie*	96
Giuseppe Dessí	*La frana*	100
Giorgio Bassani	*I fiori dei campi*	161
Roger Bernard	*Ma faim noire déjà*	162
Georges Bataille	*Lettre à René Char sur les incompatibilités de l'écrivain*	172
Réne Ménard	*Le chant des serviteurs*	188
	Le retour	
Jacques Charpier	*Journée d'une mésange*	191
	Le jour s'ouvre...	
André Ravaute	*Deux poèmes pour la captive*	193
Bernard Courtin	*Poèmes*	195
Bertolt Brecht	*Le bonne Ame de Sé-Tchouan*	199
David Gascoyne	*After Twenty Springs*	313
	A Little Zodiak	
Thomas Good	*Aix-en-Provence*	320
John Heath-Stubbs	*Ibycus*	323
Louis MacNeice	*Areopagus*	325
Edwin Muir	*From a Roman Bas-relief*	330
	The Mediterranean Island	
Charles Tomlinson	*Poem*	333
	The Light and Dark	
Dylan Thomas	*In the White Giant's Thigh*	335
James Agee	*The Morning Watch*	339
Elliott Coleman	*Darkened Image Sonnets*	410
	Confetti Sonnets	
Truman Capote	*The House of Flowers*	414
Howard Griffin	*The Sleeper in the Hotel*	430
	For Alvin	
Weldon Kees	*Speeches for a Play*	433
Marcia Nardi	*And I knew the Body a Sea*	435
Julia Randall	*An Entertainment of the Imagination*	441
	As There are Tongues, are Hands, are Accidents	
Theodore Roethke	*Give Way ye Gates*	443
Karl Shapiro	*The Figurehead*	450
Robert Wooster Stallman	*The Falling out*	452
Peter Viereck	*Stanzas in Love with Life and August*	453
Robert Flottemesch	*Bingo Mountain*	457

7

11.7.a and b
Botteghe Oscure, Quaderno VI, 1950: even at this early stage, Marguerite's review offered a discerning and distinguished selection of international writing.

more valuable? ... Brava, buona Principessa ... You don't know what it means to me to have this very story published without changes."[38]

If considerations of space preclude a close examination of who and what was appearing in all three language sections of successive numbers of *Botteghe Oscure*, it is at least possible to offer an overview. Scanning the index of any *quaderno* provides some interesting name-spotting, but, taken together, they comprise a roll-call of writers who today are numbered among the best-known of the mid-to-late-twentieth century. The English section of Quaderno IV, for example, included work by Babette Deutsch, Wallace Stevens, Tennessee Williams, Roy Fuller, Hugh MacDiarmid, Louis MacNiece, Stephen Spender, Dylan Thomas, and Angus Wilson, while Quaderno VI added John Heath-Stubbs,

Charles Tomlinson, Truman Capote, and James Agee, and Quaderno VII, George Barker, Michael Hamburger, Arthur Waley, Randall Jarrell, and William Weaver – who began as a poet, but achieved his best accolades as a translator. Among the Italian sections, in addition to Bassani's, the names of Carlo Levi, Vasco Pratolini, Ignazio Silone, Pier Paolo Pasolini, Italo Calvino, Umberto Saba, and Giuseppe Dessì stand out as writers who would soon forge international literary careers. The French contingent included Pierre Reverdy, Georges Limbour, René Char, Yves Bonnefoy, Henri Michaux, Albert Camus, Bernard Courtin, René Ménard, Phillippe Jaccottet, André Dhôtel, and Georges Bataille.

The poetry of René Char, whose debut in Quaderno III was followed by further appearances in Quadernos V and VII, made much the same forceful impact upon Marguerite as Alexis Léger's *Anabase* had a quarter of a century earlier. She soon came to consider Char the finest modern French poet: high praise indeed, especially from someone who knew French literature as thoroughly as she did, and even after the dearth of French poetical talent she had reported to Katherine in 1935. Rather as she had done by facilitating translations of *Anabase*, she was impelled by admiration for Char's work to seek even greater recognition for him through translation than she could give him in the pages of *Botteghe Oscure*. More will be said about how she went about achieving this. Unfortunately, the strength of her conviction meant that any comment that ran counter to it, even from an old friend, was taken personally. In December 1951, Jean Paulhan, who had just contributed a short piece to Quaderno VIII, was rash enough to suggest that she was giving too much space in the French sections to the work of Char's "sons," or "disciples." Paulhan's letter has disappeared (though his account of what he said survives in his letters to Giuseppe Ungaretti and Francis Ponge), but Marguerite's angry reply, in which she used her very sure grasp of the French poetry scene to reduce his allegation to tatters, took the high ground in ending with "I am sad to lose your old and (until now) faithful friendship for reasons I don't understand." She and Paulhan remained in touch, mainly through Paulhan's wife, Germaine, but the correspondence between them from this point was infrequent and shows little of their earlier affection and confidence.[39] Not surprisingly, she and Paulhan also came to a parting of the ways regarding the French section of *Botteghe Oscure*, and within a year or so, René Char had replaced Paulhan as Marguerite's advisor.

One indication of how much social change had taken place in the twenty years that separated *Commerce* from *Botteghe Oscure* was the openness by which Marguerite's ownership of the latter was acknowledged. Giorgio Bassani's name appeared as editor in Quaderno IV, and in Quaderno V, the information that *Botteghe Oscure* was funded by its editor-in-chief, "Princess Marguerite di Bassiano," was finally provided. A notice inside the back cover requested that submissions be sent to 32, Via delle Botteghe Oscure (Palazzo Caetani, where the review was administered from an office on the first floor), and made clear that work accepted for publication would be paid for. It did not take long for it to become known via "the writers' grapevine" that Marguerite paid, not just well, but often extremely well, at rates that were often twice or more those paid by other reviews.

Marguerite was an ambassador for the review wherever she happened to be: Rome, Paris, London, Lausanne. She sent copies to the book editors and literary critics of the major newspapers in the United States and the European capitals. She also produced a flyer that set *Botteghe Oscure* in the context of postwar literary periodicals. Assuming that she wrote the text for it herself, the last paragraph of this flyer offered a rare statement of her objectives:

> To set the literature of all countries on an equal footing; to discover the best fruits which each literature is able to yield; to collect the younger and less known writers beside those who have already won a wide recognition, thus gauging the spiritual vitality of the different countries; to convey, as reflected in art, the most interesting problems of the various peoples; to harmonize many and different ways of life into the supreme way of being of poetical creation, so that knowledge and information may be obtained by making known first-rate work of varying tendencies – these are the aims of this new periodical, the only of its kind [*sic*] at present in Italy.[40]

The publication of the early *quadernos* prompted a few brief press notices, but as the review became better known, it became the subject of longer and more serious pieces on both sides of the Atlantic. By the time Quaderno VIII appeared, *Botteghe Oscure* had been reviewed by the "quality" press in Italy, France, Switzerland, and Germany; in Britain, by the *Times Literary Supplement*, the *Observer*, *Time and Tide*, *Statesman and Nation*, the *Yorkshire Post*, and other provincial papers, and in the United States, by the *New York Times*, the *Washington Post*, the *New Yorker*, and numerous others from coast to coast. Building up a following was nonetheless an uphill battle, since getting reviewers to write about foreign authors was difficult at the best of times. According to James Laughlin of New Directions, who was also struggling to introduce European authors to the American public, reviewers resisted writing about them, partly through postwar prejudice, and partly through a lack of confidence at being unfamiliar with literatures not written in English.[41] Initially, Marguerite did everything through personal contact, writing hundreds of letters by hand to friends and contributors abroad, asking them to spread the word, encourage subscriptions, and identify possible local points of sale. If anyone responded with the name of a likely bookshop, she immediately forwarded the information to Bassani and had a flyer sent. In the United States, the Biddles mined their academic contacts to get university libraries to subscribe. Katherine persuaded bookshops in Washington, DC, New York, and the Ivy League towns to stock the review,[42] but she also put Marguerite in touch with contacts in other parts of the country.[43] Poet-friends giving readings took their copies along. Richard Eberhart took his to the Yaddo residential writers' workshop and passed it around, while Mary Britton Miller, Marguerite's cousin, canvassed the bookshops of Greenwich Village. The sum total of such small initiatives was that *Botteghe Oscure* steadily gained a following in the United States, especially among aspiring writers.

For Quadernos II and III, Marguerite provided a set of translations into Italian (printed separately as a brochure slipped into each copy) for the work by the Anglo-American writers. In the same way, to bring *Botteghe Oscure*'s Italian authors to the attention of American and British

11.8
Three of *Botteghe Oscure*'s most active promotors in the United States: Katherine and Francis Biddle with their friend, the poet Allen Tate (left).

readers, Marguerite commissioned translations into English of poems and stories drawn from the first six *quadernos*, and edited them as *An Anthology of New Italian Writers*. Published in the United States by New Directions in November 1950, and in Britain by John Lehmann in 1951, the *Anthology* marked a turning point in the appreciation of postwar Italian writing. Both its publishers promoted the book strongly, and as a result, it received serious and positive reviews. Vitality was the characteristic most often mentioned: Edwin Muir, in a piece entitled "The Italian Spirit" written for the *Observer*, noted that:

> Princess Caetani has chosen the younger, lesser-known Italian writers for her anthology, and a remarkable set they are to be introduced for the first time to the English public. They are mostly in their thirties; in promise and performance they are equal to any group of the same age in any European country … The stories are remarkable for their insight into life, their seriousness of spirit, their luminous clarity, and their mastery of form. They are quite individual; each expresses an original and responsible vision of life, yet they have something in common which belongs to Italy itself, a soundness and sweetness which is not lost even when they deal with the morbid and the painful.

Edwin Muir, like a number of those who wrote about *Botteghe Oscure*, had also appeared in its pages, but observations such as the following must have pleased Marguerite all the same:

> Perhaps Italy's main contribution to civilization has been an open interest in human life, an interest co-operative, not destructive, constructive, not analytical. That we should still find it in the work of these young Italian writers is profoundly reassuring in a damaged world.[44]

Similarly, Margaret Bottrall – who translated Giorgio Bassani's "Storia d'Amore" for the *Anthology*, and whose husband, the poet Ronald Bottrall, was a contributor to *Botteghe Oscure* – credited both publications with transcending the "vigorous literary life" of the Italian provincial cities, which so often absorbed the local talent but at the same time restricted an author's public to his or her own region:

> This is a great point in favour of the anthology, and of the review from which it is taken. Its contributors come from all over Italy … It is unusual in Italy to find this juxtaposition of writers from various regions … It is also unusual to find a review published in Italy which is not tied to any party or school.[45]

The *Anthology* not only opened a window on the Italian literary scene for English-speaking readers; it also achieved Marguerite's aim of boosting interest in *Botteghe Oscure*. So far, the dispatch of copies to outlets abroad had been piecemeal – fifty to one bookshop, ten to another – with subscriptions being handled individually from Rome. By 1950, the number of subscribers in Italy, Britain, France, and the United States had increased to the point at which Marguerite sought booksellers and publishers who could promote the review in their respective countries. In Britain, Jamie Hamilton, of Hamish Hamilton Ltd, who admired *Botteghe Oscure* and what Marguerite was trying to do, agreed to handle it, as did publishers Gallimard in France and Mondadori in Italy. The United States was obviously a key market, and in 1950 Marguerite began to correspond with Frances Steloff of the Gotham Book Mart of West Forty-seventh Street in New York, one of the city's largest booksellers.[46] Steloff was ahead of her time in mailing out book news to a lengthy list of patrons, and in using the GBM's premises for evening events such as authors' readings, launches, and receptions. She proved an enthusiastic collaborator, despite the shipping and customs difficulties attendant on bringing a foreign review into the United States.[47] In April 1951, she set up a standing order for twenty-five copies of each *quaderno* as it appeared. Within a year this rose to a hundred copies, and there was soon a lively demand for back issues. From June 1952, Marguerite and Steloff began to work with Farrar, Straus, a prominent New York publisher, which took on the wholesale promotion and distribution of *Botteghe Oscure* to the book trade across the United States, leaving the GBM to handle American subscriptions and the New York retail trade. By June 1953, Farrar, Straus needed 1,100 copies and the GBM 400: welcome news indeed to Marguerite, who admitted to Steloff that the cost of producing the review was beginning to worry her.

Marguerite's prodigious energy was an essential factor in driving *Botteghe Oscure* forward. As she told Frances Steloff at the beginning of their correspondence in 1950, "I seem to do nothing but write from morning till night," but it should not be thought that she did all she did, editorially and promotionally, in isolation. As her correspondence with him shows, Giorgio Bassani was not only the editor of the Italian section, but also her main consultant overall.[48] Marguerite had the determining voice in deciding what to publish, but agreeing on what to include in each *quaderno* and what could wait until the next was something that she and Bassani worked out together, as was arriving at a balance between prose and poetry, and ensuring a variety of tone and level. Then there was the question of the weight to be given to the different languages within each *quaderno*, which depended on what work was already in hand (or promised but not yet received, in which case, it had to be chased, usually by Bassani). A balance among the three language sections was not really achieved until Quaderno VIII, when each language was given roughly the same number of pages. From then onwards, Marguerite chose, for some reason (which cannot have pleased Bassani), to alter the usual order of the sections, putting the French authors first, leaving the writers in English in second position, and placing the Italian section last. Finally, the highly important task of reading and correcting the proofs (there were always two, and very occasionally, three sets of them) was carried out by Marguerite, Bassani, and Elsa Dallolio. Bassani then coordinated the corrections and sent the proofs back to De Luca for resetting. The smoothness with which this process unfolded, when Marguerite was in Paris or in some Swiss resort and everything had to be sent by post, determined whether the production schedule was adhered to and the review shipped on time.

Elsa Dallolio was unofficially involved in the editorial process, and although her name never appeared in the review, her help was invaluable. Like Marguerite, she was a discerning reader of modern literature in the review's three main languages. According to Iris Origo, Marguerite relied on Elsa "for the selection of young and possibly unknown authors, trusting her ability to distinguish that which was really a new talent from that which was spurious."[49] Elsa's health was unstable (she suffered from a severe form of asthma), and since she lived with her elderly father, she worked from home. During the run-up to Lèlia's wedding, she relieved Marguerite of much of the editorial work for Quaderno VIII, including the correspondence with the various contributors. Her assistance was mainly concerned with what today would be called "continuity" and copy-editing: consistency in the use of typefaces and font sizes, and making sure that no errors found their way into the final proofs. This involved working closely with Bassani and De Luca after hours of painstaking effort behind the scenes. When Marguerite was away from Rome, she and Elsa were in constant touch; in September 1951 each penned eight letters to the other, and in October, nine.[50]

Elsa also helped to keep *Botteghe Oscure* from becoming too unwieldy. Several of the early numbers fell just short of five hundred pages, and one of her tasks came to be ensuring that the weight of the review did not carry it into a higher postage category. The task of actually packing, addressing, labelling, and posting copies of the review for European destinations, and of wrapping and crating them for shipping elsewhere (ensuring that forms and customs declarations were correctly filled in), then conveying crates and paperwork to the dockside warehouses of the shippers in Ostia or even Naples, fell to the patient administrator of Palazzo Caetani, Federico Bracco. The voluminous correspondence between Marguerite and Bracco illustrates the range of tasks the latter carried out. For him, as for Bassani, Dallolio, and De Luca, Marguerite's absence from Rome for long periods involved being on call to deal with the requests that came thick and fast in the unmistakable blue envelopes.

For Marguerite, the most rewarding aspect of *Botteghe Oscure* was of course her contact with writers and her exposure to new writing. Writers whose work she admired but whom she had never met, such as Theodore Roethke, delighted her by turning up at Palazzo Caetani. Her drawing room there was not a salon, but a meeting place where people were constantly coming and going, with or without letters of introduction. According to William Weaver, then a young and impecunious American living in Rome, "if anybody came to town they fetched up at Marguerite's for tea or for lunch or for a party or whatever." This kind of informal entertaining took time, as did reading the hundreds of submissions that arrived every month. At Ninfa, Marguerite took to carrying around a selection of manuscripts in a trug, settling on a bench in some quiet corner of the garden to pore over them. Naturally many were dross, but nuggets of pure gold turned up often enough to bring the thrill of discovery to the winnowing process. Marguerite's sensitive "inner ear" was attuned to the reworking of tradition as well as to novelty, but of both she expected an authentic and serious attempt to convey an imaginative reality on the part of the writer. William Weaver recalled how Marguerite "could look at a sheaf of poems and almost smell the right ones." He was surprised to be asked his opinion: "She would hand me some poems and say, 'What do you think of these?' ... I would say, 'Well, I like this and that one.' And she would say, 'Yes, I like those, but I like *this* one!' I would reread it. Of course, she was right."[51]

Elena Croce speculated that the rush of exhilaration Marguerite experienced on discovering "an imaginative reality" in the work of a new author gave her a sense of empowerment, to which her emotional response was a profound sense of gratitude.[52] This was one reason, perhaps, for her generosity in the matter of payment: she believed that whatever she or anyone else did to support an artist could never remove the obligation to do so, since the artist was always the greater giver. Such gratitude implies humility. Marguerite knew that she herself was not an artist; her role was to make it possible for the creative gift in others to flourish, and had its own satisfactions and celebrations. At the same time, she recognized the suffering to which that gift could subject those who possess it, and the infinite patience that is sometimes required to keep it alive. Whatever its origin, Marguerite's empathy with contributors to *Botteghe Oscure* who were known to be in dire economic or personal straits was discreet, and might come in the form of a request for a translation, paid for in advance, or a cheque for more than the sum agreed on for a particular poem or story. Giorgio Bassani sometimes received pleas for financial help that he passed on to her. She never alluded to the help she gave, partly out of respect for the recipients, but partly, too, because she viewed it as an honour from which both she and society benefited in unquantifiable terms.

Marguerite's relationship with Dylan Thomas affords an example of the lengths to which she would go to support an artist she believed in.

Vernon Watkins, whose poems appeared in Quaderno II, put Marguerite in touch with his friend Thomas in the spring of 1949. When the man generally considered to be the greatest living Welsh poet finally replied to her letter, it was August. Among the poems he sent her, together with a letter filled with typically self-castigating remarks, was "Over Sir John's Hill," for which she found last-minute space in Quaderno IV as it was on its way to De Luca. A year later, in October 1950, "In the White Giant's Thigh" appeared in Quaderno VI, and in November 1951, "Do Not Go Gentle into That Good Night" in Quaderno VIII. *Llareggub: a piece for radio perhaps* – the first half of what Dylan had described to Marguerite as "an impression for voices" that later became *Under Milk Wood* – was published in Quaderno IX in the spring of 1952.

Thomas struggled to support his family on what he could earn from reviewing and the sporadic sales of individual poems, but debt, illness, and alcoholism repeatedly sabotaged his writing commitments. During the four and a half years of their acquaintance, he and Marguerite rarely met. Dylan's account of the first occasion, in October 1949, is worth quoting, as it captures his mode of expression so well:

> I wanted to talk to you about your magazine, and to hear you talk about it … And instead of this, all I could do was to talk, disconnectedly, about myself, scatter you with ash, gollup [*sic*] your whisky-&-soda, make an inexact arrangement with you about a short story of my own, and rush off into the London night I loathe.[53]

The "inexact arrangement" was for a story for which Marguerite offered Dylan a hundred pounds. She pressed a cheque for half of this sum into his hand at once, but in the letter cited above, written on 2 November, he begged in desperation for the rest, with the story not even yet begun. She duly sent it, with something extra, which Dylan acknowledged in a letter beginning "Dear Madame de Sermoneta – is that what I should call you? You have so many names." From this point in their correspondence, Dylan opened up about the distractions of family life lived in poverty (a leaking roof, sick children, threatening letters from the bank), his endless struggles with procrastination, the anxiety that reading his poems caused him ("it reminds me that I should be writing new ones"), and even his drinking. Marguerite responded with encouragement, and, invariably, a cheque: "Thank you, from my heart, for the cheque you sent me ... We can pay some bills, and eat," Dylan replied to one such missive, while in response to another, he wrote: "All, all my thanks for your last letter and the cheque out of the great blue that made our life here temporarily bearable, and made me, once more, so deeply grateful to you. I should never, however long I live, be able to say how much."[54]

Alas, Dylan's drinking was out of control in this last stage of his life, and events did seem to conspire against him, despite the strenuous efforts and tolerance of friends for whom a poem like "Do Not Go Gentle into That Good Night" made up for any amount of outrageous behaviour. Marguerite did more than supply the hard-pressed poet with funds. For his reading tours of the United States, she created a network of contacts, and got friends to arrange social occasions for him and invite him to their homes, notwithstanding the probability of alcohol-fuelled antics. Katherine and Francis Biddle put him up in Washington; he repaid their hospitality by helping himself to Francis's shirts.[55] And yet ... despite the endless delays, the piteous appeals for money, and the broken promises to send poems, the story, the completed script of *Llareggub* (for which she had already paid), Marguerite continued to provide financial and moral support. She even sent money to Dylan's wife, Caitlin, while he was on tour in America, to tide her over until he got back.

Llareggub was not actually finished until May 1953, and by the time it was, Dylan had either forgotten, or decided to ignore, his obligation to Marguerite. In October, he sold it to the BBC, and then to the American magazine *Mademoiselle*: shabby dealing about which Marguerite learned only after Dylan's death in New York on 9 November. She was too good a businesswoman to simply write off any claim to the work, and approached David Higham, Dylan's literary agent and trustee of his estate, to see whether anything could be done to secure

11.9
Marguerite and Guglielmo Petroni on the terrace at Palazzo Caetani.

her right to publish. As it emerged, there was not, and having made her inquiry, she let the matter go, magnanimous in her hope that Dylan's family would benefit from his sales of the work to others.[56] She published three of Thomas's letters in Quaderno VIII (Spring 1954).

Marguerite's friendship with Guglielmo Petroni was more typical of her relationships with contributors to *Botteghe Oscure* whose work she particularly admired. Like so many writers after the war, Petroni eked out a precarious living by reviewing and teaching, on which he supported his wife and baby, then two babies. From the beginning Marguerite proved a generous patron: she paid well for the stories she published, sometimes sending him payment in advance when she knew he was hard up. She sought to gain recognition for him in the English-speaking world by including his story "La Casa si muove" ("The House Is Moving") in the *Anthology of New Italian Writers*, commissioning Peter Tompkins, Camillo's old friend, to do the translation.[57] She looked out for his interests concerning foreign royalties, used her influence to generate speaking engagements for him, made overtures to the American publisher Blanche Knopf on his behalf, and occasionally tucked a cheque in with a letter, with instructions to "buy something for the children." Petroni's wife, Puci, later recalled the enjoyable times the family spent at Ninfa.[58]

Had Marguerite not been so self-effacing in all she did, she might have attracted the criticism of being a kind of "Lady Bountiful," but there is simply too much testimony to the contrary to allow much room for cynicism. A trawl through her correspondence with authors, held by the Fondazione Camillo Caetani in Rome, is highly revealing in this respect. Marguerite's graciousness made the authors and their families so treated feel honoured rather than beholden, and so made clear her esteem and confidence. As *Botteghe Oscure* gained momentum in the early 1950s, Marguerite herself naturally became better known, and even revered, as its creator. She never sought such acclaim, but those whose work she published would certainly have agreed that she deserved it. Here again is Niccolò Tucci (echoed by his wife), a long way from home and depressed at the demands of American magazine editors for "happy endings" and sanitized love scenes:

> let me explain in a few words why I said you were an angel: the tone of your letter was kind, smiling, and encouraging. And Laura, who read it, too, was deeply touched by your phrase: "Sorry you are depressed. It must be terrible for your wife." She will thank you herself as soon as she has a spare moment to sit down and write, in the meantime she wants me to tell you that she is grateful to you for thinking of her plight. That's all.[59]

12

THE FULLNESS OF TIME

While family ties made Rome and Ninfa "home" to Marguerite, the other pole of her life was, of course, Paris. For a few weeks in late spring, and again in early autumn, she returned to the stimulating cultural milieu of the French capital. It was less a question now of reconnecting with old friends, since most of them were gone, as of making new ones, preferably people who could offer a view on what was being written by whom, with an eye to the French section of *Botteghe Oscure*. The apartment at 4, rue du Cirque near the church of the Madeleine served as a base for bringing such people together, rather as Palazzo Caetani did in Rome. During the greater part of the year, when she was not in Paris, Marguerite generously allowed friends and relatives to stay in the apartment – her nephew Paul Chapin, the editor (and later on, cookery writer) Judith Jones, the painter Balthus, the writer Georges Bataille, and poet René Char being only a few of those who did so.[1]

Only a few years after the war, Paris was again attracting droves of young people, many of them Americans, much as it had in the 1920s. Once again, painters and writers haunted the cafés of the Left Bank, and "little magazines" of poetry and ideas were produced on shoestring budgets. One venture that began that way but went on to become a literary institution on both sides of the Atlantic was the *Paris Review*, co-founded by the American writers Peter Matthiessen, Harold ("Doc") Humes, Donald Hall, and George Plimpton, the latter as editor from the review's first issue in the spring of 1953 until his death in 2003. Between Marguerite and the team working on the *Paris Review* (then based in the rue du Tournon alongside the Luxembourg Gardens) there was mutual respect. Both *Botteghe Oscure* and the *Paris Review* were engaged in finding and publishing new poetry and fiction, and they shared the commitment to present it free of advertising, reviews, criticism, and political slant. Not surprisingly, in time there grew up a degree of cross-fertilization between the two publications that led to a number of authors appearing in both.

Some of the Americans arriving in Paris were not so young: they were former servicemen taking advantage of the GI Bill to experience living and studying abroad. One of these was Eugene Walter, a Southerner from Mobile, Alabama, with ambitions as a writer. Quite by chance he saw a copy of *Botteghe Oscure* before leaving New York, and, on his arrival in Paris in May 1951, typed out six of his poems and sent them to Marguerite. She wrote back accepting them all, and invited him to lunch at 4, rue du Cirque.

Walter, whose delight in anything offbeat or unexpected gave him an immediate rapport with Marguerite, recalled his first meeting with her. His idea of how a Roman aristocrat would look (imposingly tall, with "a bony nose, sharp black eyes ... clanking gold jewelry and heavy eye makeup") was shattered when the door to her apartment opened, and

> glunk, my head fell, because it was this tiny little thing with hair pulled back to a knot on the back of her neck. A very beautiful, obviously French suit and a silk blouse with some kind of frou-frou at the neck and no jewelry at all except a very beautiful old Roman quartz set in gold, obviously antique, obviously either ancient or Renaissance. The Chanel suit was rust and grey and white wool with jaggy lines of those colors all mingled. Silk stockings. And good American Keds. I don't mean the latest model. I mean white, 1930s, tennis-shoe Keds. Imagine a Chanel suit with Keds.[2]

As Walter related in his memoir *Milking the Moon*, "We just got on and had things to talk about," mainly the differences between Europe and America, and the various writers each liked. Walter was a master of whimsy and droll observation, an inveterate gossip, and a creator of occasion wherever he went. If the memoir he dictated in old age is not an altogether reliable source, it is – as he was – invariably entertaining. Marguerite liked him, and began to include him in the lunches she organized for "young writers and newcomers and unknown quantities," at which she served orange juice until Walter suggested to her that "writers really do absorb stronger beverages." Later, the two would go through the manuscripts stacked on Marguerite's tea table:

> She would say, "I'm just reading this. Do you know who this is? What do you think of this one? I just love it." And so on. Everybody was always flattered to be asked advice by her. It was part of her act. But she published what she damn well pleased and didn't listen to anybody. And she would say, "Oh, Lord, I've got this pile of stuff. I've got it all mixed up. Will you just have a look at it and sort it out? Anything that's the least bit good, put it in one pile. If it's impossible, put it in another pile." She asked if I could come several times a week and help her.[3]

Walter gradually took on work for Marguerite until he was acting as her unpaid assistant. Some things he did, such as delivering a letter or manuscript by hand, were simple favours, but Marguerite soon realized that a wealth of useful talents lay just beneath the surface of his slightly camp manner. She observed that he put people at ease, and was good at solving problems and getting things done. He enjoyed bringing people together – as did she. He was quick to grasp the kind of writing she was looking for, introducing her to a number of new contributors, as well as to an expert translator when one was urgently needed. Soon Marguerite was asking him to read submissions by American authors, and later, to incorporate the changes they wanted made, since he proved to be an eagle-eyed copy editor.[4] Best of all, he made her laugh. For his part, he enjoyed the incongruities inherent in her position: one minute she was telling him about meeting the tattooed and piratically ear-ringed Thom Gunn (and liking him very much), and the next, relating some snippet from a conversation with the Dutch ambassador.

She asked Eugene to list his expenses, but he seldom did. It was enough that the literary scene of the French capital was open to him, since "In Paris, the world of literature was small and rather closed. You had to know somebody to be introduced into it. I had the highest introduction on earth: I was the editorial assistant to Princess Caetani. You can't do better than that."[5] Through her, he met Carson McCullers, William Faulkner, Archibald MacLeish, and other American writers staying in Paris, as well as permanent residents such as Alice B. Toklas and Natalie Barney, who had become legends in their own lifetimes. Marguerite passed him on to George Plimpton, who included Eugene's short story "Troubadour" in the first number (Spring 1953) of the *Paris Review*.[6] He joined Plimpton's team as an interviewer, but since all the writers connected with the *Paris Review* took part in producing it, there too he ended up doing everything from copy-editing to putting up posters.[7]

Contact with the young writers that Marguerite met in Paris allowed her to include a number of them in *Botteghe Oscure*. Besides Eugene Walter, these included James Broughton, Alfred Chester, Jean Garrigue, Julia Randall, Peter Matthiessen, Pati Hill, and Wallace Fowlie. When one of them sent her a poem or story she liked, she often bought it, not knowing when, or if, she would use it – but she paid for it at once (and well), knowing that the encouragement of earning something from writing would act as a spur to further endeavour.[8] She sometimes found, having impetuously bought a piece, that she *couldn't* use it, as in the case of a story by Alexander Trocchi that closer reading revealed to be "much too obscene and blasphemous (two things I abhor and especially together)."[9] Marguerite's sensibilities were not easily offended; indeed, for her time, she was remarkably broad-minded. Divorce, "irregular" living arrangements, alcoholism, drug use, and homosexuality had always, as it were, "gone with the territory" occupied by many of the artists she came to know and counted among her friends. But she was now in her seventies, and as the 1950s advanced, she sometimes revealed a primness that had been absent in her younger self. Gratuitous foul language and explicit sex scenes, when they turned up in submissions to *Botteghe Oscure*, were seen less as attempts to stretch the boundaries of self-expression than as failures of the imagination. Even a writer as eminent as Alberto Moravia had a story refused on these grounds.

One writer who needed particular encouragement was the twenty-five-year-old New Yorker, Alfred Chester, with whom Marguerite adopted a motherly-but-bracing tone. Chester had suffered an illness in childhood that left him completely hairless (though he wore an auburn wig). Overcoming his resulting self-consciousness was easier with the aid of alcohol, he was still finding his way as a gay man, and his health was far from robust. Marguerite was convinced of his talent: her letters to him were signed "love, Marguerite," but she never failed to stress how important it was for him to work, and she was not prepared to indulge him. She published his stories "Silence in Heaven" in Quaderno IX in 1952 and "Rapunzel, Rapunzel" in Quaderno XII in 1953, but fired his next submission back at him with "I don't like at all that story you sent me where everyone is drunk *all* the time – How could you really think I would like it? Now, Alfred!" Chester spent the next several months reworking this and other stories, one of which he sent to Marguerite. What it meant to the young man then to receive a letter beginning "Dearest Alfred, You are a wonder and your story is good, good, good! I am delighted"[10] – and a cheque for a hundred dollars – can only be imagined. The story in question, "The Head of a Sad Angel," appeared in Quaderno XIV in the autumn of 1954.[11]

Botteghe Oscure now rivalled Rome's summer heat in imposing a timetable on Marguerite's departure for Paris: no sooner did she get the Spring number out than she began work on the Autumn one, since Luigi De Luca's firm closed for the entire month of August, and the issue had to be in the United States in September to make sure of hitting the run-up to Christmas.[12] When Eugene Walter sent her a copy of one of his books, she replied a few weeks later, apologizing for not having thanked him – "but you know better than anyone what my life becomes when a number of B.O. is about to appear. Just simply chaos and no peace for me." But with the American section in good hands in Paris and the Italian one in Bassani's reliable ones back in Rome, Marguerite could return to the cause that was becoming for her a kind of crusade:

gaining an international audience for the French poet René Char. She had already commissioned translations of some of his poems from the diplomat and poet Denis Devlin, and from Jackson Mathews, an American academic specializing in French literature, whom she met through her old friend, the poet Allen Tate. These translations had appeared in Quaderno X of *Botteghe Oscure* in the autumn of 1952, together with a separate brochure containing the original French texts of the poems, some press comment about them, and advance publicity for a proposed selection of Char's work translated by Mathews. In initiating the latter project, Marguerite was surely buoyed up by the American reaction to *An Anthology of New Italian Writers*, and confident that Char's work in translation would find a similarly positive response.

By the time Marguerite met René Char after the war, he was already greatly esteemed in France, both as a poet and for his role in the Resistance, though he was actually earning his living as a brickmaker. Born in 1907 in the Provençal village of L'Isle sur la Sorgue, near Avignon, he published his first book of poems in 1928, and moved to Paris to ally himself briefly with the Surrealist movement that included Paul Éluard, André Breton, and Antonin Artaud. As he matured, he moved on, achieving a philosophically complex world view, in which the poet's "religion of independence" and self-abnegating vision was essential. During the war he left off writing his usual "prose poems" in favour of short, intense considerations that he could jot down quickly while keeping watch as a Resistance fighter. His style became condensed to the point where all superfluity had been excised and every word carried multiple meanings. His wartime notebook was published in 1946 as *Feuillets d'Hypnos* (*Leaves of Hypnos*), a collection of 237 fragments that Char dedicated to the novelist and philosopher Albert Camus, a Resistance comrade.[13]

The claims Marguerite made for Char indicate that his poetry affected her profoundly, yet nowhere did she record or divulge the reasons why. Others have remarked that she and Char were "kindred spirits," but in the absence of personal testimony, what that may have meant is uncertain. She would certainly have shared the inspiration he found in painting, such as his reference to Georges de La Tour's luminous study of patient suffering, *Job and his Wife*, in fragment 178 of *Feuillets d'Hypnos*. Char numbered as friends artists such as Braque, Miró, Picasso, and Kandinsky, who illustrated his books, suggesting that bringing words and images together appealed to him, as it did to Marguerite.[14] Then there was the intensity with which he evoked the natural world and human love, the contradictions he posed and then resolved in an almost philosophical way, and his vision of poetry as the poet's defiance in proclaiming life – a conviction rooted in the truth of simple things (a flower, a rock, the fecund earth) – and his refusal to deflect his gaze in the face of pain and violence. Through Camillo's death and her experience of the war, Marguerite was all too well acquainted with these aspects of human existence, and Char's affirmative and courageous vision may have had a particular resonance for her.

Whatever her reasons, she was sufficiently taken with Char's work to promote him, even before she commissioned Mathews and Devlin to translate his poems. Writing to Frances Steloff of the Gotham Book Mart on 20 February 1951, she expressed surprise at not finding Char's books in the GBM catalogue of foreign authors, and enclosed a copy of a new book on him ("a great friend of mine, and surely the most important French poet today") as a first step to remedying this. She then asked whether she might have "the honour and the pleasure" of personally sending copies of Char's books to Steloff. Having done so, she wrote again on 3 August for Steloff's reaction, claiming that Char "has now the greatest position of *any writer* in Paris, or France one can say ... He has had the most extraordinary success this winter with his latest book *A Une Serenité Crispée* which is one of the most beautiful, profound, and poetic works ever written."[15]

This high opinion of a work whose title in English is *To a Tensed Serenity* was shared by Jackson Mathews, and together he and Marguerite set about finding an American publisher for his translations of Char's poems. In 1953, approaches were made, first to Harcourt Brace, in part through the good offices of fellow-poet Robert Lowell, whom Marguerite also knew, and subsequently, to Random House. The latter publisher expressed firm interest, though the unhurried manner in which it conducted negotiations seemed to an impatient Marguerite to

12.1
Marguerite and René Char at Ninfa.

belie this. While she waited, she collected anything to do with Char that appeared in the press, and forwarded copies to those she knew in the United States who might eventually have an interest in the book, or be in a position to order copies.

Then it emerged that Gallimard, Char's publisher in France, was planning a complete edition of the poet's work, and, under the terms of his contract, would agree to the appearance in translation of only some of the poems, and disputed the rights being suggested by Random House. The project seemed suddenly to have run aground – or at least to be becalmed in the shallows. Marguerite was naturally irritated by the delay, and frustrated by the slowness with which the two publishers dealt with the impasse.[16] The fact that Gallimard was the distributor of *Botteghe Oscure* in France and Gaston Gallimard an old friend did nothing to help matters. Marguerite was inclined to blame Random House – but surely the fault lay with Char himself, who had allowed Marguerite and Mathews to go ahead on his behalf while neglecting to inform them of Gallimard's plans, of which he could hardly have been unaware. That Marguerite seems never to have attributed a soupçon of blame to Char suggests that, once she had taken up his cause, "the greatest living French poet" could do no wrong – an attitude that was bound to lead to difficulties with those who did not share it, however laudable her intention. Once Marguerite's friendship with Jean Paulhan had cooled (on that very point), and Char had become the consultant for the French section of *Botteghe Oscure*, no doubt she did confer with him, but his new position was also a means by which she could discreetly assist Char financially.[17]

Negotiations over the proposed Char book ground slowly on through 1954. Alongside that particular venture and the demands of *Botteghe Oscure*, family matters required Marguerite's attention. Lelia underwent a worrisome surgical operation late in 1953. Once she recovered, she and Hubert sailed to New York, a journey centred on two exhibitions of her paintings in the United States, organized with help from the Biddles and Cornelia Chapin. In the weeks preceding the first, in Washington in mid-March 1954, Katherine Biddle outdid herself in winkling out relatives and friends to attend the opening, while she and Francis hosted a number of social gatherings. The guests ranged from Hubert's mother, Lady Isabella Howard, to the debonair Schuyler Chapin, manager of the violinist Jascha Heifetz. "Great Aunt Sue" (Susan Revere Chapin, the widow of Lindley Hoffman Chapin's brother Henry), aged eighty-eight, had known Marguerite since the days of Rock Lawn, and insisted on coming down from Boston by train. Writing to Katherine in advance, Great Aunt Sue observed that Lelia "must enjoy the freedom of a husband after so many years of being a 'Mother's child' only," and added the revealing comment: "I saw Marguerite's picture in a magazine and could not believe it possible – to see such a *settled* person."[18]

The opening of the exhibition, held at a gallery near the Biddles' home in Georgetown, was, as Katherine described it later to Marguerite, "a delightful gathering of people, and I think everyone was enthusiastic about the freshness – charm – light & aspect of the work ... I got a lovely impression of both strength and light." Once the Howards had moved on to New York, where Cornelia Chapin had prepared a further welcome, Katherine wrote again to let Marguerite know that several of Lelia's paintings had been sold in advance of the opening at the Hugo Gallery there, despite the prevailing vogue for abstraction. Recalling her niece's former shyness and recent illness, she also commented on how at ease Lelia had been with people, "friends and strangers alike," during her time in Washington.[19]

Shortly after the Howards' return to Rome, eighty-four-year-old Roffredo obligingly lent a hand to new tenants attempting to move a heavy chest up some stairs at Palazzo Caetani, the object in question being too large to go in the lift. That he undertook this kindly act says much about Roffredo, but it initiated disaster. The chest slipped, and Roffredo sustained a severe blow on the head that was subsequently diagnosed as concussion. Writing to Marguerite a week later, he pronounced himself perfectly recovered (touchingly signing himself "Your old Roffredo"), but from this point onwards, he began to show signs of the decline into old age that he had managed so far to keep at bay. He spent some weeks in a Swiss clinic in the summer of 1955, while Lelia and Hubert holidayed nearby, and then accompanied them to Cumberland while Marguerite was in Paris. This set a precedent for the years that followed, as he could no longer be left on his own for long.

With time on his hands at the clinic, Roffredo finally sought to resolve the question of what should happen to the Caetani patrimony if, as seemed ever more probable, Lelia and Hubert should remain childless. At the end of the war, he had petitioned King Vittorio Emmanuele III, his childhood friend, to permit the family inheritance to pass through the female line, since with the deaths of Camillo and Onorato, Lelia was the only heir remaining. This petition was granted, and, for a time, Lelia's marriage had offered hope that the inheritance question would resolve itself. As time passed and it did not, the responsibility Roffredo bore as very likely the last duke of Sermoneta began to weigh heavily upon him. Fortunately, Lelia and Hubert were thinking along similar lines, and Hubert, when asked by his father-in-law what he thought, offered a novel suggestion.

Hubert was well acquainted with Britain's National Trust, founded in 1895 "to look after Places of Historic Interest or Natural Beauty permanently for the benefit of the nation." He and Lelia were already working with a group of concerned Italian conservationists to establish a similar entity in Italy. The result was Italia Nostra, of which Hubert was a founding member, which came into being on 26 October 1955. Through his knowledge of Italian law, gained in the course of creating Italia Nostra, Hubert saw the vesting of the Caetani patrimony in a foundation as a possible solution to Roffredo's worry, but the possessions were so immense and varied that it seemed prudent to begin with one discrete area before attempting to deal with the whole. Roffredo, Lelia, and Hubert agreed that the archive brought together by Gelasio at Palazzo Caetani should be the first candidate. It documented the history of the Caetani dynasty back to the early Middle Ages, but it also contained a wealth of documents relevant to the history of medieval Italy, the Papal States, and Rome itself. There was no doubt in the minds of its three creators about the name this first foundation should be given. The Fondazione Camillo Caetani came into being on 10 May 1956, with a remit to conserve the archive and the space in Palazzo Caetani that housed it, and to make its thousands of documents available to scholars. Publishing, holding conferences and exhibitions, and otherwise making known the fruits of research, were all included in aims that sought to benefit Italian culture.[20]

By the time the Fondazione Camillo Caetani was created, the French publisher Gallimard and the American one, Random House, had reached an agreement that allowed the latter to publish a selection of René Char's poems, translated by Jackson Mathews. The anthology, entitled *Hypnos Waking: Prose and Poems*, was published in the summer of 1956. In the long run up to it, Marguerite had continued to feature the work of Char in *Botteghe Oscure*, with extracts from *Feuillets d'Hypnos / Leaves of Hypnos* and *Lettera Amorosa* appearing in both their original French and in Mathews's English translation in Quaderno XIV in the autumn of 1954. In this interval she also produced three publications in English dedicated to Char: two small booklets (one, a translation by Robert Fitzgerald of René Menard's *Interpretive*

Essays on Two Poems by René Char, and the other a reprint of Jackson Mathews's translations from Quaderno XIV) and a longer one containing a number of essays on Char, entitled *René Char's Poetry: Studies*. These were sent to Marguerite's contacts in the United States, to academic journals, book reviewers, and the retail outlets that handled *Botteghe Oscure*, to prepare the ground for the eventual appearance of the Random House volume.

All this was an extraordinary and concerted effort on Marguerite's part, and in creating a receptive audience for Char, it paid off. *Hypnos Waking* received a number of significant reviews and sold nearly a thousand copies in the six months following its publication – a triumph for any book of poetry, but an exceptional showing for the translated work of a poet hitherto all but unknown in the English-speaking world. Mathews's translation justified Marguerite's faith in that medium, not only sparking academic interest in Char – as the number of studies, theses, and publications dedicated to him during the next thirty years would show – but revealing to a new readership the illuminating quality of his ideas and the poetic gift that Marguerite herself so deeply believed in.

By the time the goal of introducing Char in America had been realized, *Botteghe Oscure* had become even more international. The first German section appeared in 1954, and the first Spanish one a year later. Among the early contributors in Spanish were Octavio Paz, Carlos Fuentes, Maria Zambrano, and five young poets from the Philippines. Thereafter, sections devoted to German authors – among them, Paul Celan, Heinrich Böll, Rudolf Kassner, and the young Ingeborg Bachmann, as well as giants such as Hölderlin, von Hofmannsthal, and Rilke – appeared in alternate years to Spanish ones. There were also novelties, such as the Ainu epic *Kutune Shirka*, a selection of modern poems from Korea, and a group of Dutch poems, that reaffirmed Marguerite's conviction that translation broadened horizons. If, during these few years, the space given to American, British, and French writers shifted to outweigh the space allocated to Italians (in fact, for a time the Italian section became the shortest of those represented), it may have been because fully half the demand for the review now came from the United States. There

12.2
Giorgio Bassani, Marguerite's right hand, 1948 to 1960.

may also have been another factor at work. By 1956 Marguerite had published many of Italy's best postwar writers, some not just once, but several times. That said, there were still some surprising omissions, such as that of poet Andrea Zanzotto, that suggest that Giorgio Bassani had become too busy to keep the close watch on the Italian literary scene that he once had. These were the years when he was acting also as an editor for the new publishing house Feltrinelli, and for *Paragone*, a journal produced by his old mentor, the art historian Roberto Longhi. Bassani's career as a writer of fiction was in the ascendant: *Cinque storie Ferrarese* (*Five Ferrarese Stories*) won the Strega Prize in 1956. Marguerite, having encouraged him, was of course delighted,[21] but she was also feeling the need for another pair of hands and eyes.

Even with the aid of the small team comprising Bassani, Elsa Dallolio, Federico Bracco, and occasional temporary help, the production of *Botteghe Oscure* was exceedingly demanding. Each *quaderno* now ran to nearly five hundred pages – the size of a book, rather than a review – and in future, some volumes would be longer still. Truman Capote, whose pieces "The House of Flowers" and "The Grass Harp" Marguerite had published back in 1950, commented even then that "you are attempting to do too much single-handedly ... it is not possible to read, accept, reject, proofread, *ad infinitum* ... moreover, I'm perfectly certain that you have no accurate record of your correspondence." He was right on both counts, and especially about the correspondence, the pressure of which had increased a dozen-fold in half as many years. The review had a proper office only from the autumn of 1955, set up and furnished by Bracco and described by Bassani to Marguerite as "*magnifico*!" A sign outside bore the words *Botteghe Oscure Rivista Letteraria*, and inside, attractive shelving and tables and chairs made the space "ideal for intimidating any visitor, but also reassuring, in a certain sense." Still to come were a telephone, a typewriter, a low table (on which could be displayed copies of the review, one imagines), and an armchair.[22] What was missing was the person to run it. Marguerite had often wished out loud to Eugene Walter that he would come to Rome as her assistant, and in November 1955 (the GI Bill funds that supported him in Paris having come to an end), he agreed to do so.

He arrived at the beginning of 1956, staying for a few weeks with William Weaver before finding himself a cottage in a secluded corner of Trastevere, on the slopes of the Janiculum. At Palazzo Caetani, he was given a room near the office, on the first floor. Marguerite had her own salon nearby: an airy, white-walled modernist haven at the top of a flight of stairs, lined with her books and hung with her favourite paintings. It was a complete contrast to the ornate rooms below, with their coffered and gilded ceilings, curtains of jacquard velvet, oriental carpets, and walls covered with darkened oil portraits. It was there, in her own space, that Marguerite presented her new assistant to Giorgio Bassani. According to Walter, their acquaintance got off to a poor start: he found Bassani frostily formal and suspected him of flattering Marguerite. Bassani left no impression of the newcomer; as his daughter Paola recalled, he was a European to his fingertips, a man imbued with tradition, despite his modernist literary stance, and it is hard to imagine that Walter's irreverent sense of humour and casual ways did not eventually grate on his sensibilities. Walter, for his part, accused Bassani of having used *Botteghe Oscure* to further his career.[23]

The aspects of producing *Botteghe Oscure* that Eugene Walter was to help with were those that had simply outgrown the time that Marguerite and Giorgio Bassani had in which to deal with them. Marguerite still insisted on reading everything sent to her, and by this stage in her life habitually spent much of the morning in bed, skimming manuscripts. This was a task she immensely enjoyed, but Eugene was horrified to discover that her solution to a stack of "hopeless" submissions was often simply to jam them between her bed and the wall: "out of sight, out of mind," from whence a maid would eventually sweep them away. Eugene took on the task of returning each rejected script with a covering note that invited further submissions, while scripts that Marguerite considered "possibles" were acknowledged and filed. These two jobs alone saved her dozens of handwritten notes each day, and made a more professional impression. He also tackled the mode of paying the authors whose work was accepted. (Marguerite decided how much to pay, but up to now, she, Bassani, or Bracco wrote the cheques, and there was no system for keeping track of who had been paid, for what, and by whom.) Another organizational nightmare was sorting out the contact details for Marguerite's hundreds, if not thousands, of friends and literary acquaintances.[24]

In addition to establishing some routine procedures, Eugene Walter did much the same processing of manuscripts for the non-Italian sections of the review as Giorgio Bassani did for the Italian one. He also wrote the publicity copy that told the readers of dozens of learned journals about *Botteghe Oscure*, and redesigned the jacket wrappers – broad paper bands that announced the contents of the review at a glance, so that there was no need to open the volume.[25] He and Marguerite took working lunches together when there were no guests. When there were, as in Paris, Marguerite often asked him to join them. This might include being summoned at short notice to Ninfa, taking

12.3
Marguerite and Eugene Walter working at Ninfa, summer 1956.

a train bound for Naples from Rome's Termini station, and alighting at Latina. For anyone less adventurous, the first such occasion might well have been the last: ("waiting for you will be a big fat youngish man called Beppe who will bring you here on a scooter"),[26] but Eugene was in his element.

One of his more enjoyable responsibilities was looking after English-speaking authors passing through Rome. He had already met Archibald MacLeish, Carson McCullers, and Theodore Roethke, but Richard Wilbur, Cynthia Ozick, and Allen Ginsberg (in grubby shorts, after a month of hitchhiking around Europe) were among the many who visited Palazzo Caetani during his first few months there. Another was Muriel Spark, who rented an apartment in a former cardinal's palace. Invited to drinks, Walter was treated to the sight of Spark running through the vast rooms, dragging a Persian carpet, giving her cats their "evening drive." When Marguerite asked him to accompany T.S. Eliot and his wife, Valerie, to the airport, the great poet mentioned en route that he had never visited the graves of Keats and Shelley. Eugene's response was to order the chauffeur to make a lightning detour to the Protestant cemetery. He would do anything to please: when Isak

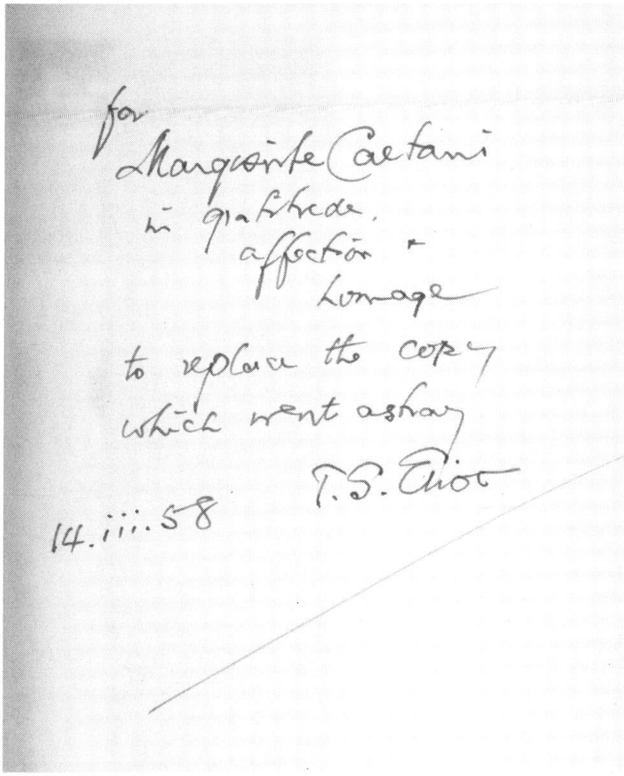

12.4
T.S. Eliot replaces Marguerite's copy of his *On Poetry and Poets* (1957).

Dinesen visited Rome (a copy of her *Seven Gothic Tales* had accompanied Eugene through the war), he organized three lively parties for the Danish writer in as many evenings.[27] At Ninfa, the somewhat wary meeting between Marguerite, in a tweed suit, as usual, and the extravagantly costumed Baroness Blixen, for whom personal attire was theatre, greatly amused him. Both, he observed, were happier in the company of men. As her guest departed, Marguerite murmured to him, "It was nice to meet such an original, but why does she wear all that black around her eyes?"

Walter and others recalled memorable vignettes of Roffredo – tall, courtly, with straight shining silver hair, and able, with an astonishingly rapid flick of his long forefinger, to dispatch any fly that dared to settle on the Ninfa lunch table. Roffredo now had days when he was clear and days when time telescoped for him and the whole of his life

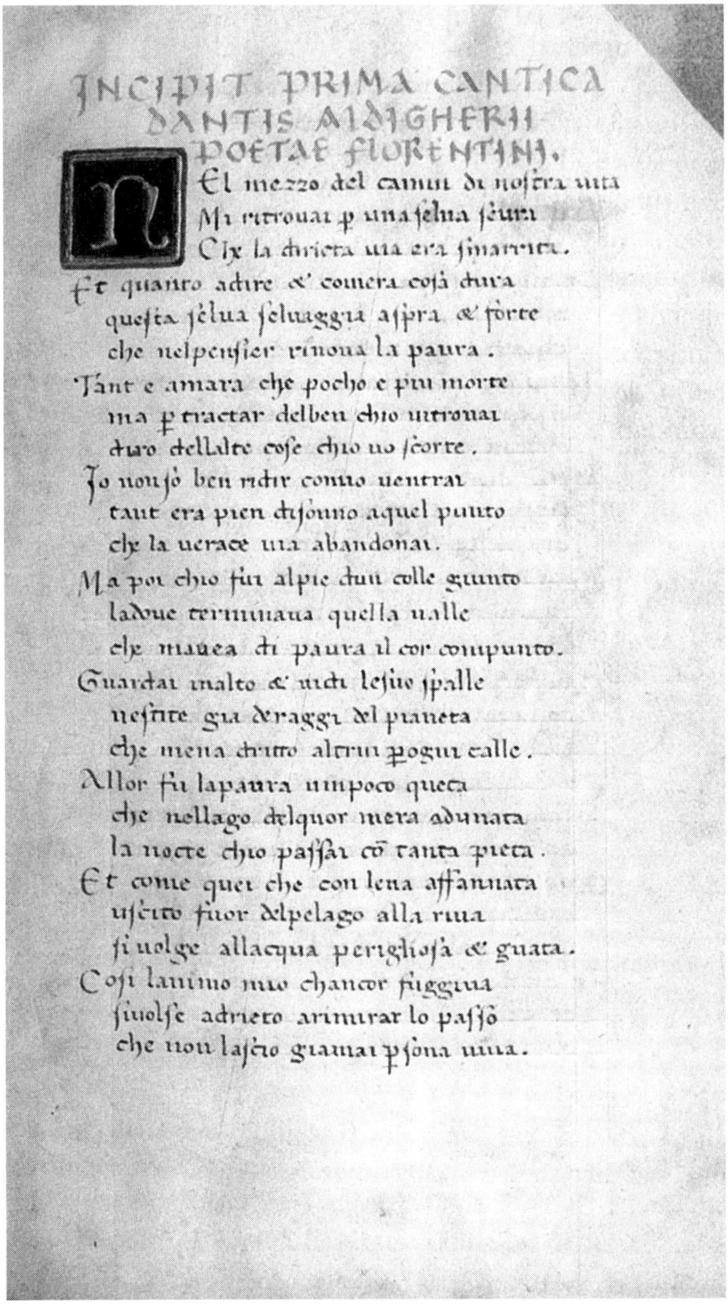

12.5

In later life, Roffredo began the day by reading a page from Dante's *The Divine Comedy*, from the volume inherited from his grandfather Michelangelo: the *Codex Caetani*, with annotations by Marcilio Ficino.

seemed all in the present. On good days, he could keep a table entertained for hours as he summoned up the notable figures that had passed through Palazzo Caetani in his boyhood. Operatic performances at Bayreuth, La Scala, Covent Garden, and Vienna were another fund of reminiscences. He still relished improvising on the piano, the agility of his fingers belying his age. Very occasionally, he could persuade Marguerite to sing to his accompaniment: Schubert lieder or songs by Fauré, Debussy, and Hahn. Eugene sometimes engaged Roffredo in conversation about music. On one such occasion, mention of a performance of Brahms he had heard on the radio the previous evening drew from Roffredo the exclamation: "Brahms! What a funny little man he is! Offered me a cigar before breakfast!"[28]

These were the lighter moments in a relentless schedule – and in what was becoming an economic quandary. With Quaderno XIX, *Botteghe Oscure* completed ten years of publication. The anniversary volume was the largest yet, at just over six hundred pages. Reviewing it for the *New York Times*, Paul Engle praised the "astonishing" range of writing offered by the review as proof that "there actually is a unity of the creative imagination," and highlighted, in this particular issue, the "life, light and variety" that brought together "newly found letters of Henry James ... fragments from the painter Delacroix and from von Hofmannsthal, a translated play by Char, a visionary poem by Theodore Roethke, new poems from Germany and Italy and France." He went on to make the important point that, although readers could find the best of European writing in *Botteghe Oscure*,

> more original work by Americans is to be found in these pages than in any publication edited in this country. Each issue wanders not only across Europe but across the U.S.A. The young American writer appears in the company not only of French and German names he has come to venerate, but also of American names whose work he has read for years: Robert Lowell in Boston, Archibald MacLeish in Cambridge, Randall Jarrell in Washington, Karl Shapiro in Nebraska, E.E. Cummings in New York, Marguerite Young in Iowa City, Herbert Gold in Detroit,

> Marianne Moore in Brooklyn, Roger Shattuck in Texas. It is amusing and heartening that the writers of America receive a fuller hearing in those Dark Shops of Rome than in the fluorescent-lit magazine offices of Madison Avenue.

Both this issue and Quaderno XX, which rounded off the anniversary year, contained numerous contributions by authors whose names were appearing in print for the first time, alongside the work of established writers such as Italo Calvino, Robert Penn Warren, Henri Michaux, Jon Silkin, Isak Dinesen, and Heinrich Böll. Quaderno XX featured an introductory essay by Archibald MacLeish entitled "Reader to Reader: A Parenthesis" that cited the astonishing statistic that, in ten years, the work of 568 writers from more than twenty nations, writing in five languages, had appeared in *Botteghe Oscure*. The point was less to celebrate the review's catholicity than to highlight two realities. The first was its "invaluable and unique role as … a means of communication between writers as writers in the Western world" in an age of ideological conflict, and the second, the admission that it needed greater support if it were to survive:

> No one who has so much as opened the magazine will be surprised to learn that the publication of such a review, with its generous policy as to space, payment and the inclusion of unknown writers, can be extremely costly, and that its survival must ultimately depend on a wide and varied support from individual readers, libraries and institutions of all kinds … It is far easier to help a publication to continue than to revive it after it has died or to start another to take its place.[29]

This was as close as Marguerite ever came to revealing publicly what she had been saying to a handful of people close to the review for some months: that it was now costing more to produce than it was bringing in. It was not just that *Botteghe Oscure* was awash with submissions, that more and more of them were worth publishing, and that each *quaderno* was therefore destined to be bigger than the last. The real problem was cash flow, in particular, from the United States. In 1956, Marguerite had changed distributors, leaving Farrar, Straus for The Noonday Press. For some reason, the latter did not remit to Marguerite more than a small proportion of the funds owing to her. To Eugene she commented that, had she remained with Farrar, Straus, she would have received $6,000 for consignments of the previous three *quadernos*, whereas Noonday had sent her only $150 for the past four, and she had already asked Stanley Young in New York to find out whether his firm would have her back.[30] From this period come the verbal accounts of how Marguerite sold two cows to pay for an extra set of proofs (of Quaderno XIX, in which one long poem was inadvertently printed with a page missing), and her letters sometimes alluded to the need to control expenditure. If it is surprising to think of Marguerite having to worry in this way, at least her concern serves as a reminder that she was still funding *Botteghe Oscure* with her own money, as she always had.[31]

The tenth anniversary of *Botteghe Oscure* prompted a degree of looking back over its past as well as a certain amount of speculation about its future. An index to the first twenty *quadernos* was already in preparation, but from France, where the memory of *Commerce* was still revered, came the idea that an index to its twenty-nine *cahiers* should be prepared as well.[32] The French ambassador to Italy, Gaston Palewski, had known Marguerite since the days of Villa Romaine, and recognized the benefits to French culture stemming from her two reviews. Whether the idea of making her a member of the Légion d'Honneur – France's highest decoration – was his, or whether it originated back in Paris, is uncertain. Neither is it known whether he broached the idea to her before the commemorative exhibition that served as the setting for the event, or whether, knowing Marguerite's reluctance to shine in public, he let it come as a surprise "on the day." The catalogue to the exhibition, entitled *Hommage à Commerce: Lettres et Arts à Paris, 1920–1935*, provides a record of the two occasions.[33] The exhibition was held at Rome's Palazzo Primoli, a palace near the Tiber once occupied by the Bonapartes, and ran from 5 December 1957 to 30 January 1958. Locating and obtaining loans of the exhibits took

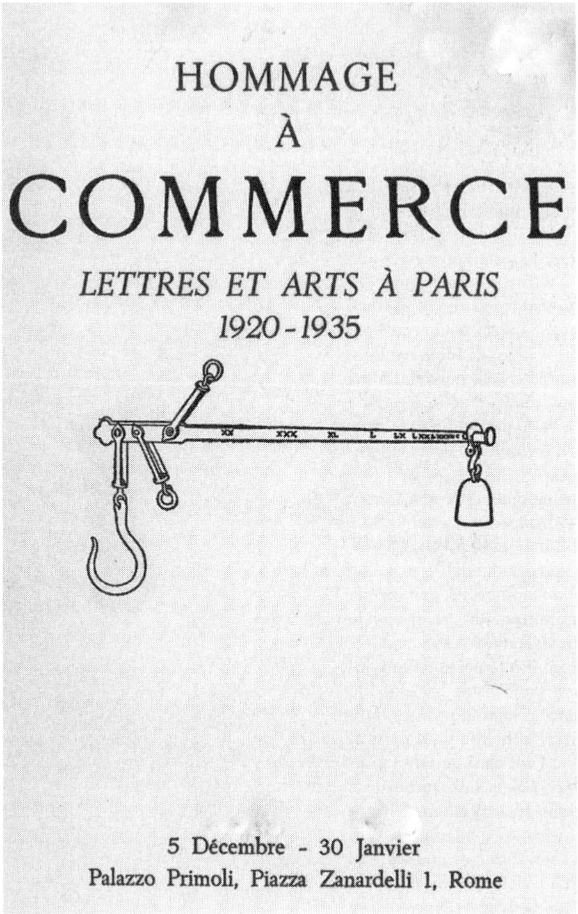

12.6
The program for the exhibition *Hommage à Commerce*, showing the review's characteristic illustration of a Roman, or steelyard, balance.

months of work on the part of two curators from Paris, the positive aspect being the renewal of contact among those who had been involved with *Commerce*. On view were manuscripts, letters, photographs, and artifacts associated with each individual issue of the review, as well as with each of its three "official" and two "unofficial" directors: Valery Larbaud, for example, sent part of his beloved collection of lead soldiers. Marguerite lent many of the paintings that had once hung at Villa Romaine, and precious photographs taken before her marriage and during her years in Versailles. Eugene Walter evoked her way of working by recreating a corner of the salon at Ninfa, incorporating her gardening

12.7
A delighted Marguerite receiving the medal of the *Légion d'Honneur* from Gaston Palewski, France's ambassador to Italy, at the opening of *Hommage à Commerce*, Palazzo Primoli, Rome, 5 December 1957.

basket, stuffed with manuscripts, into a montage of objects that included one of Roffredo's scores and Giorgio Bassani's pipe.

There was much to look at and to read on the part of some two hundred guests that crowded their way into the display space on the day of the opening. At an opportune moment, Ambassador Palewski called for silence, and, in a very simple ceremony, expressed the thanks of the French government for all that Marguerite had done to celebrate and extol the nation's literature, painting, and way of life, then pinned the medal and ribbon of a *Chevalier*, or Knight, of the Légion d'Honneur to her left lapel. There is no record of what she said in response. If it is permissible to hazard a guess, perhaps it was that celebrating the culture that she had learned to love at her mother's knee was a privilege that had turned her into a grateful debtor: that same sentiment she claimed to feel regarding the artistic gift that illuminates the realm of the imagination. Nothing she had done for France could ever equal, or even approach, what she felt that France had done for her. Friends who knew something of her remarkable effort, however, felt it was an honour entirely merited: Rudolf Kassner spoke for many in assuring her, heartily if not grammatically, that "if it depended on me, you would have got la grand croix since long having done so much for french literature."[34]

Roffredo too received an honour, equally overdue, at almost the same time: on 19 January 1958, *Hypatia* was given its first Italian concert performance by the symphony orchestra and choir of Milan's RAI, or National Radio. Marguerite and Roffredo, the Howards, and a number of friends travelled to Milan for the occasion. Fortunately, Roffredo was in good conversational form, and cut a romantic figure in a cape. This kind of public recognition was for him, as the exhibition and her incorporation into the Légion d'Honneur was for Marguerite, a complete contrast to the usual tenor of life, whether in Rome or at Ninfa. The balance of where they spent their time was gently shifting towards the latter as they grew older. Friends of the same age similarly valued the opportunity to flee the hectic life of the capital to spend a day with them in the garden.

Arriving there from Rome a few weeks after the broadcast, Marguerite, Roffredo, and the Howards learned that estate manager Sante Marchetti's youngest child, Lauro, aged eight, had been struck by a car and taken to hospital with a broken leg. Visiting him at home a few days later, Marguerite thought the fractured limb looked misaligned, and asked the Marchettis to permit her own doctor to look at it. Lauro was at once conveyed to Rome, where Dr Marino Zuco reset the leg, thereby saving the boy from permanent disability. His convalescence was pleasantly aided by visits from Marguerite and Lelia. They noticed that he liked to draw, and encouraged him to look more closely at the plants and birds he chose as subjects. Once he was well again, they took to collecting him from school two or three times a week, and he would spend time with them at Ninfa. The boy absorbed their love of the garden and the living things that made their homes there. In inclement weather, Lauro's favourite spot was under the table in the salon, while the members of the family read or painted or wrote, each working silently in his or her own corner of the room. As he got older, he took to accompanying Hubert on the long Sunday walks he took after Mass.[35] The boy became a focus for the Howards' interest and affection, and, as the years passed, they began to see in him a potential future administrator for Ninfa, who could carry on their own conservationist ideals.

The publicity surrounding *Botteghe Oscure*'s tenth anniversary inevitably prompted many aspiring writers to send in material for Marguerite's consideration. One such piece came, not directly, but anonymously, via Elena Croce – and it was not from a young and hopeful writer, but from an ill and elderly one, wearied by the experience of having his manuscript rejected by major Italian publishers such as Enaudi and Mondadori. It was the first chapter of a novel set in Sicily called *Il Gattopardo* (usually translated in English as "The Leopard"), in which the aging Prince of Salina confronts the tumultuous changes taking place during the *Risorgimento*. Marguerite was captivated by it, and published the chapter, "Una giornata del Principe Fabrizio" ("Prince Fabrizio's Day") in Quaderno XXI of *Botteghe Oscure* in the spring of 1958. Elena Croce's inquiries revealed that the mystery author was Prince Giuseppe Tomasi di Lampedusa, who had died in July 1957, shortly after sending her the manuscript. His adopted heir was happy for Giorgio Bassani to take the manuscript of the novel to Feltrinelli, where it became the Italian publishing sensation of the year, and subsequently, one of Italy's best-loved novels. It gained a posthumous Strega Prize for Tomasi di Lampedusa in 1959, with translations into other languages and the famous film directed by Luchino Visconti (starring Burt Lancaster, Alain Delon, and Claudia Cardinale) following soon after. Marguerite's initial, pivotal role in all this is seldom mentioned, though Elena Croce's and Giorgio Bassani's usually are.

Triumphs of such magnitude were, of course, rare, but the successes of writers she had championed, such as René Char, Giorgio Bassani, Alfred Chester, Guglielmo Petroni, and a host of others, brought Marguerite the satisfaction of a vocation – hers as well as their – complied with and fulfilled. And yet ... her belief in a writer could be so intense and her dislike of contradiction so apparent that friendships sometimes suffered. Such was sadly the private aftermath of the publication of René Char's poems in translation in the United States. Allen Tate was one of several friends whom Marguerite asked to review the Random House volume. Having read it, Tate found himself unable to write a favourable review ("I doubt that he's a poet – an aphorist, rather"[36]), and delayed writing to Marguerite for months, knowing that his explanation would offend her. Worse still, he had been in Paris and heard rumours that Char was weary of all the publicity, and simply wanted to return to his quiet life in the Vaucluse. Writing to Katherine on 5 February 1957, he confided,

> there is no pretending. Char *is* tired of the support he is getting, and yet (so I heard) he can't detach himself. None of us can know whether this is the result of consideration for M., or cupidity; perhaps both, and perhaps, too, he himself doesn't know. What I fear, as you seem to fear, is the "revelation" to Marguerite of a complication of motive that she couldn't at present be aware of.[37]

Whether such a "revelation" ever took place no one knows. Had Marguerite been too magnanimous to foresee that in helping to gain recognition for Char, she had unwittingly created a feeling of obligation to her that he might, in time, find onerous? Since the two remained close friends, it seems likely that their "kinship of souls" enabled them to sort it out without any damaged feelings. Other friends were not so fortunate. By chance, Allen Tate discovered that he was not the only one with reservations. On 2 April 1957 he reported to Katherine that he had met Robert Fitzgerald, the translator of some essays on Char, who had "declined to let Marguerite sign his name to them, on the grounds that Char represented a French spiritual illness!" and went on "I am sorry he wrote her this, but I think it is probably true."[38] And finally, nearly a year later, he sent news of a letter from Jackson Mathews, who apparently claimed that he had

> "broken" with Marguerite and Char, that his position as middleman had become intolerable. I can't even guess the rights and wrongs of it, but I can see that Jack's situation must have meant something like complete loss of identity, in which his sole end was to further the apotheosis of Char. Even in my detached situation I began to find several years ago that I could communicate with Marguerite only through the exigencies of the Char campaign.[39]

Tate did all he could to reassure Marguerite of his friendship, despite his inability to serve as an ally in "the Char campaign," but the damage was done. As with Jean Paulhan so many years before, she simply withdrew. Relations were maintained, but the warmth and spontaneity had gone out of them.

By the end of 1958, there were in any case other things for her to worry about.

Like the little cloud as big as a man's hand that heralds a far-off storm, the intimations that all was not well in the outer office of *Botteghe Oscure* began as trifles. Someone blamed Eugene Walter for typographical errors, someone else blamed him for a banking slip-up. A file of personal and family photographs that Marguerite had loaned to the exhibition *Hommage à Commerce* disappeared in the course of dismantling the exhibition, much to her distress. Then there were the reports that reached her ears from those who had seen Walter carousing at nightclubs in the small hours. He himself was aware that

> there were a lot of people who really objected to my closeness with the princess. And with my American impudence. They didn't understand my friendship with the princess, and they thought I was too full of levity. There was this lady who was a friend of the princess's, and she thought I was too American and too flibbertigibbet. Which was what the princess wanted. Because she didn't

> have any of that quality. She liked a gossipy account of who was at what literary gathering the night before that she wouldn't dream of going to. You see, I was an American imp for her. That's why we were friends.[40]

Years earlier, in the course of a disagreement, Marguerite had remarked in a letter upon the number of times she defended Walter against people whose feathers he had ruffled.[41] Apart from recognizing that being "an American imp" was the source of some of the resentment, he may simply have failed to see that the sense he gave of having become complacent also caused offense. Late nights meant late mornings, and being somewhat the worse for wear was not the best state in which to be reading sets of proofs. There was little in all this rumbling that he could not have put right, either by a change in behaviour or by discussing matters openly with Marguerite, but as he admitted in his memoir, he felt he shouldn't have to bother, and that the time for a change had come.

When it did, in the spring of 1959, and Marguerite let him know that she was firing him and would pay his passage back to America, he was not surprised; he claimed to have witnessed other instances where Marguerite had impatiently "turned off the faucet" with people for reasons he had not understood. In any event, he did not want to go back to America, and he was not long out of work. The Rome film industry was in its heyday. Through a friend he met Federico Fellini's casting director, and was soon given a part in *8 ½*. In all, Walter worked on some hundred films over the next several years – usually as an extra or a script translator, but, memorably, as the Mother Superior in *Juliet of the Spirits*, and as a props and sets assistant on *The Satyricon*.

With his departure, the letters and packages, invoices, bills, and manuscripts began to pile up, so that every surface in the outer office was covered. The sight of such chaos aroused in Marguerite the panicky feeling that everything was out of control. A temporary solution was to take on one or two secretaries. Recalling the daughter of her old friend Mason Hammond, Marguerite wrote to Florence ("Flossie") Hammond in New York to ask whether she knew anyone who could help. Flossie was, as she herself put it, "fresh out of college" and looking for work, and so she returned to Rome, the city where she had spent much of her childhood, as quickly as she could. Sean O'Criadain, an Irish poet living in Rome, was also taken on, and the two of them soon restored order. From Flossie Hammond comes another version of the events surrounding Walter's dismissal: "in the Palace it was whispered that he had been squirreling away manuscripts and other things with the aim of selling them in what was becoming a lucrative American market for literary papers."[42] The late Gore Vidal, who knew Eugene during his last year at *Botteghe Oscure* and liked him personally, agreed, and thought he might have been put up to this by authors he met through the review who had already taken advantage of this new source of income.[43]

If true, such a betrayal of trust would surely have caused Marguerite considerable pain. Eugene Walter had been a friend as well as an employee, but in addition, the reports of him made to her by "others," for whatever motives, shook her confidence in her own judgment. This was an unsettling period, although, as usual, she put the best possible face on it. The strain of watching Roffredo gradually succumb to dementia cannot have been easy to bear, especially when *Botteghe Oscure* demanded so much of her. Flossie Hammond was surprised at the amount of responsibility that she and Sean O'Criadain were given, only later coming to understand some of the background. Marguerite, when she appeared in the office, was inevitably direct and lively. She never alluded to problems, but was curious to know how they were getting on and what they thought of the manuscripts passing through their hands. Both she and Giorgio Bassani made them feel that their work was essential in maintaining the review's high standard.

Like most people who remain free of chronic health problems until well past middle life, seventy-eight-year-old Marguerite was taken unawares by the onset of age-related conditions for which there were as yet no remedies. Her energy was undiminished, but the satisfaction gained from working on *Botteghe Oscure* came at a higher price. She had spent as many as nine hours a day on it for years, poring over scripts and dashing off dozens of letters even on Christmas Day or from the train. Increasingly, she noticed that her vision was blurred, and that a change of spectacles had no effect. The excitement she always felt when the morning's bundle of manuscripts fell with a thump on the mat outside her bedroom door had gradually given way to apprehension, lest the submissions be too numerous to get through before her sight tired. Then there were her lapses of memory, which were frightening, but they passed soon enough to allow the illusion of normality to prevail. The deterioration in her vision was far more alarming. What in fact was the matter? Since she was not diabetic, it may have been macular degeneration (the destruction of the macula, the central area of the retina), or glaucoma, in which pressure within the eyeball damages the optic nerve. Either condition, over time, led to blindness in the era before the discovery of palliative treatments. Whether the doctors Marguerite consulted told her the terrible truth, or – on account of her age – refrained from doing so in favour of what today would be called "watchful waiting," remains unknown. Photographs taken in the late 1950s sometimes show her wearing dark glasses, but on sunny days, it would be natural to do so.

Others gradually became aware of her difficulties as months went by and they did not hear from her. In a letter to Katherine on 15 July 1959, T.S. Eliot expressed his concern at the lack of communication from Marguerite, to which Katherine replied that her sister had "severe eye problems about which she doesn't really like to speak."[44] She also alluded to the upsetting dismissal of Eugene Walter. Marguerite's failing sight was news to Eliot, but in his reply he admitted that "I did know something about the case of Eugene Walter, and indeed the account which I heard of Walter's behaviour was very severe indeed," although he did not divulge the source or nature of his information.[45] Alexis Léger, at his villa at Giens in Provence, was told by René Char that he thought Marguerite, then in Paris at her recently acquired and smaller apartment in the rue Madame in the sixth arrondissment, should not be left alone or allowed to travel by herself,[46] and wrote hastily to the Biddles to pass this on. The Biddles were even then on the Normandy coast, and Char on call to drive Marguerite wherever she needed to go.[47] Allen Tate, convinced that his lack of enthusiasm for "the Char campaign" had ruined his friendship with Marguerite, wrote to her at once on learning from Katherine the real reason for her silence. To the latter he expressed his sorrow at the news: "Poor Marguerite. I wrote her a short letter I think back in December, and of course she can't answer letters. I wish I could think of something that would please her. I will send her my essays, which of course she won't be able to read, but it will be a token of affection."[48]

Then came a further devastating blow. One evening in February 1960, when Iris and Antonio Origo were dining at Palazzo Caetani, Marguerite received a telephone call informing her of the sudden death of Luigi De Luca in a traffic accident as he returned to Rome from the printworks at Tivoli. Writing to Katherine from Ninfa on 1 March, she confessed that: "I have been going through a very sad time for me and many others. The sudden death of my editor since the beginning of B.O. and a dear devoted friend. He was killed instantaneously when a great truck ran into his auto when he was alone. He was 53 years old and a wonderful man. It is a terrible loss to Rome."[49] Her own and Roffredo's limitations had already persuaded her that she must soon bring *Botteghe Oscure* to an end, but De Luca's death was the final straw: "I forget if I told you that this past [*sic*] Spring issue of B.O. will be the last – I had more or less decided this even before this great loss."

The issue in question, Quaderno XXV, was ready, except for a brief essay by Giorgio Bassani, suitably entitled "Congedo" ("Farewell"), that was added once Marguerite made her final decision. After working so closely with her for thirteen years, there was no one better placed than Bassani to pay tribute to her, or to Luigi De Luca, and this he did, at the beginning and the end of the piece. For the most part, however, he concentrated on the ethos that had made the review unique. From the first *quaderno* to the last, *Botteghe Oscure* had maintained a coherent approach, never wavering in its commitment to writing itself, rather than to literary criticism, politics, or the cult of personality. The editorial intention had been to provide a space for writers who were still relatively unknown, especially young writers who showed maturity and

BOTTEGHE OSCVRE

XXV

CONTENTS

René Char	*Prompte*	11
	L'avenir non prédit	12
Henri Michaux	*Portes donnant sur feu*	13
Jean Beaufret	*Héraclite et Parménide*	15
René Menard	*Montagne*	31
André Frénaud	*La lumière de l'amour*	33
Guy Levis Mano	*Le dedans et le dehors*	38
Gaston Puel	*Poèmes*	42
P. A. Benoit	*Première lumière*	45
	En amont	46
Huguette Champroux	*Divorce des prés*	47
Jacques Borel	*Mort des images*	50
Frédéric Duriau	*La bataille du Jutland*	55
Paul Février	*Poèmes*	57
Jacinto-Luis Guereña	*Pour la tombe D'Antonio Machado*	60
M. Pleynet	*Paysage en deux*	61
Wallace Fowlie	*Exercices*	65

Vernon Watkins	*Poems*	68
Patrick Creagh	*Poems*	71
James Russell Grant	*Poems*	77
Krishna Balde Vaid	*Silence*	80
Sean O'Criadain	*Poems*	93
Gillian Stoneham	*Poems*	97
Theo Lang	*The watcher*	100
Noel Woodin	*The daydream of the capital « I »*	112
John Press	*Poems*	114
Midu Brock	*Poems*	116
Desmond O'Grady	*Poems*	121
Robert Musil	*The temptation of quiet Veronica*	124
William Arrowsmith	*Villanelle*	164
	Translation of two episodes from Aristophanes' The Birds	165
James Wright	*Poems*	186
Robert Bly	*Poems*	191
Claire McAllister	*Mystery*	194
	Song for a respite	196
Richard O'Connell	*Poems*	198
Jonathan Levy	*Schwartz*	208
Jack Shoemaker	*Return of the rondo from K. 614*	211
Kenneth A. Lohf	*Poems*	213
Lynne Lawner	*Poems*	216
	Proof	220

Hans Magnus Enzensberger	*Gedichte*	232
Nelly Sachs	*Gedichte*	235
Ruth Landshoff Yorck	*Georgenlegende*	238
Rainer Brambach	*Gedichte*	244
Max Bense	*Attribute Epikurs*	248
Rudolf Peyer	*Gedichte*	253
Hilde Domin	*Gedichte*	257
Manfred Günzel	*Deutsche Märchen*	260
Kuno Raeber	*Gedichte*	266
Helmut Heissenbüttel	*Vier Parabeln*	269
Werner Reinert	*Gedichte*	275
Uwe Johnson	*Besonders die kleinen Propheten*	281
Franco Giovanelli	*Poesie*	284
Beatrice Solinas Donghi	*L'aiuto ai parenti*	286
Renato Pedío	*Yorik*	359
	Albero nel giardino Zevi	360
Romeo Lucchese	*Poesie*	361
Lia Wainstein	*Il Granfrugnese*	368
Cecilia Maggioni	*Poesie*	386
Miriam Cento	*Poesie*	391
Giuseppe Mazzaglia	*La gebbia*	397
	Un fuoco di notte	414
Margherita Dalmàti e Nelo Risi	*Traduzioni da Cavafis*	428
Giorgio Bassani	*Congedo*	434

freshness of outlook, rather than those caught up in "experimental" projects or self-consciously avant-garde attempts to gain notoriety. This belief in their ability had been Marguerite's overriding commitment, vindicated when so many of the writers whose early work appeared in *Botteghe Oscure* went on to become internationally recognized.

Giorgio Bassani was of course summarizing a period he had lived through, a period that had been formative for him, as for so many of Italy's postwar poets and novelists. With the benefit of a longer and broader view, *Botteghe Oscure* can be seen as even more singular than those closest to it realized. There is, first of all, the sheer bravado of having published the work of some 650 writers from more than thirty countries in its thirteen-year lifespan. Archibald MacLeish summarized the statistics in his "Requiem for a Literary Haven," which appeared in the *Saturday Review* shortly after *Botteghe Oscure* ceased publication. Some 362 writers in English (British, Americans, Canadians, South Africans, Australians, New Zealanders, and writers from the Caribbean) had shared its pages with twenty-eight colleagues writing in Spanish (not only from Spain, but from Mexico, Cuba, and the South American countries), thirty-nine writing in German (Germans, Austrians, Swiss), ninety-eight writing in French (French, Belgian, Swiss), and a handful from countries such as the Philippines, Korea, Japan, Portugal, Holland, and India.

Then there is the curious effect that such a polyglot offering as *Botteghe Oscure* had upon its readers, lacking as it did any editorial presence that might have explained or attempted to interpret the work published:

12.8.a
Botteghe Oscure: the last *quaderno*, 1960.

12.8.b, c and d
The contents of *Botteghe Oscure*, Quaderno XXV (1960), compared to that of Quaderno VI (1950, illustrated on page 267) indicates something of the review's development in just a decade.

> the impact of the multilingual volumes was more a sense of coherence than of any kind of confusion. What was, in fact, separated by language and further by a set of national boundaries and a consequent diversity of experiences and traditions, was here joined together into a real spirit of unity, a community which would have been rare enough at any time, but was and remains all the more remarkable for happening in the grim postwar years and the decade of the Cold War.[50]

That Marguerite managed to keep politics out of *Botteghe Oscure* (especially during the 1950s), while still liking and being respected by writers of every political persuasion, was indeed exceptional. Such independence flowed naturally from her belief that the imagination is not subject to political considerations. *Botteghe Oscure* had much to say to the world, but that kind of polemic did not form part of it.

The concept of the "global village" created by technological advance is today such a commonplace that ignorance of that ideologically divided Cold War period is widespread among people too young to have experienced it. Some may find it hard to believe that there was a time, not so long ago, when in half the countries of Europe, writing or saying the wrong thing could land a writer in prison or a mental asylum. The resulting sufferings contributed to the sense of an international community of writers referred to above, fostered initially by translation, then by greater ease of travel, by organizations such as PEN and Amnesty International, and latterly, by the new media of communication. It would be an overstatement to claim that *Botteghe Oscure* had a major part in this, but it is surely no less than just to suggest that "from the first issue onward," it was "early and tangible evidence, and, as such, against the apparent grain of the times, of the evolving communal artistic spirit of the future."[51]

13

A LEGACY FOR THE FUTURE

With Quaderno XXV of *Botteghe Oscure*, Marguerite relinquished her participation in literary life, though not, of course, her consuming interest in it. As her sight failed and she became unable to read, she was read to, mainly from the books sent as gifts by authors she knew. Unable to write, she dictated what she wanted to say in response to the letters that continued to pour in. Visits remained a pleasure, though now that Roffredo's "clear days" were few, she had to hold the social fort alone. In April 1960, Francis Biddle's brother George and his wife, Hélène Sardeau, stopped in Rome en route to Taormina. To Katherine, Hélène described their brief visit:

> We were so glad to be able to see Marguerite for tea. She was very affectionate and she seemed sad and tired. Is it because Botteghe Oscure is singing its swan song? It upset me much when I first heard about it. Roffredo lank, vacant, bent (led by that sturdy peasant maid we all know) twice staggered by silently, never turning his head, with no sign of recognition or curiosity. We stayed barely an hour as there was much else to do.[1]

With the end of the review that for so many years had been her greatest interest, a vital aspect of Marguerite's life also began to fade: the contact, not only with literature, but also with young authors, that had helped to keep her outlook youthful, too. Her memory grew worse, to the point that friends who had always marvelled at her abilities of recall and description were saddened by the change in her. Conrad Aitken and Harold Steiner were only two of many who wrote to Lelia or

Katherine to express the hope that her memory might improve. Allen Tate was closer to the truth in supposing that, with loss of memory, "her life will be more and more circumscribed, with her failing eyesight and the cessation of Botteghe," and echoed the thoughts of those who had known her longest in wishing that "she could find some outlet for her energy, which must still be very great."[2]

Roffredo died peacefully on 11 April 1961, aged ninety – the last duke of Sermoneta and the last of the Caetani brothers, though not the last of his generation, since Giovanella was still in good health at eighty-six. Sorrow at his passing fell most heavily upon Lelia, who in the months preceding her father's death had succeeded in having Camillo's mortal remains repatriated from the military cemetery in Albania to the Caetani mausoleum at Campo Verano. Roffredo was laid to rest in the family vault, close to his son, as he had wished.[3] By the time Roffredo died, Marguerite's memory was so erratic that she "forgets who is talking to her," as one London friend put it, and so perhaps she was less cruelly aware of events than some feared she might be.[4] In his Christmas greeting to the Biddles that year, Hubert described her as "much better and quieter; only her memory confuses her. However, this fact does not trouble her so much now, as it did before. But it is difficult at times to fill her days."[5]

The Howards, fulfilled in each others' company and in the quiet life of the country, spent most of their time at Ninfa, where together they dealt with the myriad problems and responsibilities involved in administering the Caetani estates. There Lelia continued to garden and paint, usually while Marguerite sat quietly nearby. Esme Howard, Hubert's nephew, recalls seeing her, silent but seemingly contented, being pushed in a wheelchair to her favourite spots in the garden. One regular visitor was Giorgio Bassani, who missed Marguerite and the heady days of the review. (He also drew inspiration from Ninfa, his model for the setting of *The Garden of the Finzi-Continis*, and spent hours ensconced in "Gelasio's study," a small building near the Ponte del Macello, in the course of writing it.) The poet Kathleen Raine, a friend of the Howards, came to know Marguerite in this last phase of her life, and described how, on visits to Ninfa, "I often sat with her to give

13.1
Marguerite in a quiet corner of the garden, 1962.

Lelia a respite, and I used to read her poems. What was extraordinary was how *sure* her judgment was, and how deep her delight in poetry when all else seemed to have gone. That remained – the deepest thing, it outlasted all the rest.[6]

Would Marguerite have remembered, as her memory faded, Leone's daughter, Sveva, to whom she had once sent crates of books and drawing materials? After so many years without contact, she was not to know that, at about the same time as Roffredo died, the death of Ofelia Fabiani in far-off Vernon, British Colombia, had finally released Sveva from the virtual prison in which she had been confined since 1935. Left all but destitute, forty-three-year-old Sveva set about surviving, gaining her driver's licence and embarking on a two-year course of teacher training

13.2
The Ponte del Macello, Ninfa.

13.3
On the left, Gelasio's secluded study overlooking the river at Ninfa.
Here, Giorgio Bassani wrote parts of *The Garden of the Finzi-Continis*.

13.4
Sveva Caetani at her home in Vernon, British Columbia, now the Caetani Cultural Centre.

in Vancouver, sponsored by friends. Once qualified, she returned to Vernon and obtained a position as an art teacher there. After the isolated life she had led, these achievements alone would have made her father's family proud of her, but an even greater one was to come. In the silence of the house on Pleasant Valley Road (the faithful Miss Jüll also having died), Sveva conceived and executed the cycle of fifty-six paintings that she called *Recapitulation*: the story of her life, evoked through references to *The Divine Comedy* – which, thanks to Leone, she had been brought up to love. It was an extraordinary act of creation: everything that had kept her identity alive through a quarter-century in the company of the mentally ill Ofelia – her family history, her memories, her powers of observation and knowledge of the natural world, philosophy, and literature – was drawn together and given coherence within the imaginative framework of her own pilgrimage through life. One must only regret that Marguerite never saw it.[7]

In October 1963, Katherine and Francis Biddle made a two-week visit to Rome and Ninfa on their way home from a tour of the Mediterranean. Whether Katherine had a premonition that this would be her last opportunity to spend time with Marguerite, there is no way of telling – perhaps the fact of the visit indicates as much as anything could. Lelia later wrote "How thankful I am that you were able to come this year and see her, and it made her so happy to have you and Francis there and she enjoyed it so much."

Marguerite died, aged eighty-three, on the afternoon of 17 December 1963, after a short illness.[8] Lelia's letter to Katherine, written three days later, described her mother's last days:

> She was so well the whole autumn with the lovely weather we had … and then suddenly on December 8th, just the day after we had decided to return to Rome, she started a sore throat but with no fever. The next day the Doctor came and gave her antibiotics as a precaution but in the afternoon her temperature went soaring and two Doctors came from Rome and said she had a form of pneumonia. They gave her stronger antibiotics which brought the fever down and the next day she was so much better that the Doctors said the worst was over and that it was better to keep her in [*sic*] Ninfa till she was stronger and then bring her to Rome – Then during the remainder of the week she seemed to get slowly better, but on Sunday the fever returned and then the antibiotics had no more effect and there was nothing one could do. During most of the week she was ill she was very quiet and peaceful with no pain and fairly cheerful. Yesterday morning we had the funeral service in the country and then brought her to the cemetery in Rome where my Father and Camillo are.[9]

13.5
Katherine and Francis Biddle, on their last visit to Ninfa, October 1963.

Lelia and Hubert spent a sad Christmas and New Year, dealing with a flood of written condolences. In February they travelled to Paris to list the contents of Marguerite's apartment at 67, rue Madame. Sorting papers, deciding what to keep and what to leave, took time, and was for Lelia a heart-rending task. After several more trips, the apartment was put on the market. Writing to Katherine from Paris a year later, Lelia reported that it had been sold, and that she and Hubert were even then engaged in the "exhausting and extremely dusty" job of packing up the last of Marguerite's belongings to have them shipped to Rome.[10] Fortunately, they had found a list of items that Marguerite kept for safe-keeping at the Banque Nationale, among them a pair of silver serving spoons, each adorned with a scallop-shell and the initials "A.G.": those of Marguerite's much-loved, francophile uncle, Audinet Gibert.[11]

Testimonials from those who had been closest to Marguerite were few, since they had no need to make them. An exception was Cornelia Chapin's reply to a letter from her friend Marguerite Young (whose story "The Opium Lady" had appeared in *Botteghe Oscure*), which she copied to Katherine. Thanks to that, the following evocation of the vanished world of Villa Romaine survives:

> She meant much to me in my early days abroad, after my Mother died and I had the long visit with them at Versailles.
>
> That was when I knew her best and remember her most vividly. Her French friends were so amazed at her calm managing of affairs – musical literary – artistic [*sic*].
>
> They were such a handsome pair – she and Roffredo – it was thrilling to go about with them, and they made me feel wanted and helpful. I was shy – but not allowed to be when put on the sofa with Valéry to help him with his translation of E.A. Poe!
>
> It was a wonderful bit of the best of European life and I shall always be grateful to her for it.[12]

Reflections from friends, on the other hand, were many, sent to the Howards and the Biddles on receiving the news of Marguerite's death. Guglielmo Petroni described the experience of many when he wrote that "The letters I received from her, whenever she was far from Rome, were all marked by a tone of incomparable thoughtfulness. A poet or artist was for her a messenger of something that had to be respected, loved and helped."[13] Of the pieces written for publication, Iris Origo's "Portrait of Marguerite" was the fullest and most perceptive. It appeared simultaneously on both sides of the Atlantic (in Britain's *The Cornhill* and America's *Atlantic Monthly)* in February 1965, and was quickly translated into Italian by Nina Ruffini.[14]

> I see her still sitting under the trees at Ninfa on a sunny day in spring surrounded by the friends who helped her, with piles and piles of manuscripts stacked on the table and chairs or spread over the grass (until three great grey dogs came and started jumping all over them and we had to chase them away). Marguerite handed out pages and when any doubts were raised she always pleaded for their inclusion. "He's so very nice," she used to say about the author, or: "He's going through a difficult moment," or "He made us laugh so much last Sunday." This, at that time, was the most direct way to her heart. When she spoke her clear gaze seemed turned not so much towards the person she was speaking to as towards the beauty of the scene around her, to the new clematis flowering on the walls and, beyond, to the far-off, ideal world of the poetic imagination. And so, under the flowering trees at Ninfa, the numbers of the magazine grew ever thicker.

Action would have pleased Marguerite far more than words, and so, on the suggestion of Archibald MacLeish, an *Index to Botteghe Oscure, 1948–1960* was prepared and published within months of her death. The renowned poet and former Librarian of Congress, who had known Marguerite and Roffredo since his five-year stay in Paris in the 1920s, was one of the few people who had watched both *Commerce* and *Botteghe Oscure* come into being, evolve, and end. While the exhibition *Hommage à Commerce* celebrated the cultural contribution of the first, the second was too recent to have received the attention it deserved. "It is difficult," he confessed, "to speak of Marguerite Caetani as a person now that she is dead: her memory is too living in too many minds – her delighted spirit." To refer to *Botteghe Oscure*, in which her presence was so evident, was not only easier; it was what she would have wanted. MacLeish had reason to highlight the international significance of Marguerite's achievement: he was a lifelong liberal, who had spoken out against McCarthyism and the scaremongering that marred American political life in the 1950s:

> In an ignorant and fanatical time, paralysed by public hatreds, she kept a small flow of international literature alive and gave hundreds of young writers, in the loneliness of their defeated work, the hope that they too might become a generation – perhaps the first of all the literary generations to inherit the wholeness of the world.[15]

"The wholeness of the world" would have to wait some decades yet to come into being, and would owe more to technological advances than to governments when it finally did – but again, *Botteghe Oscure* was a harbinger of such a time, created by someone able to imagine it, who did her best, always, to help it into being.

Katherine Biddle was another who was moved to action rather than to eulogy, since she was Marguerite's literary executor. Shortly after her sister's death, she began planning a volume of writing drawn from *Botteghe Oscure*, a project that she knew had always been in the back of Marguerite's mind. Sifting through the *quadernos* and arriving at a final choice of what to include was a monumental task, complicated in its later stages by the stroke Katherine suffered in 1972 following the death of her other sister, Cornelia Chapin. (According to Kathleen Raine, Hubert Howard's "great family feeling" led him to be concerned that an anthology of work from *Botteghe Oscure* might include pieces written by "the wrong people – who had exploited the Duchessa in her last years, shown ingratitude, and so on," though there is no hint as to who was meant.[16]) The *Botteghe Oscure Reader*, edited by George Garrett of Wesleyan University, assisted by Katherine, did not appear until 1974, but when it did, it resembled in size as well as content a volume of *Botteghe Oscure* itself. The texts chosen made up a hefty tome of nearly five hundred pages, and were arranged by language, as in the review, and by chronological order of publication, rather than by author. The criterion for inclusion was not the fame of the writer, nor the singularity of the subject matter, but quality – and perhaps a touch of that "immeasurable and unspent energy, a restless and lively spirit, which persists, simply refusing to lie down, lie still and play dead" that had animated the review throughout its twelve years.[17]

With the death of Marguerite, her personal story of course came to an end, though for Lelia, and perhaps for some who had known her at Ninfa, the sense of her abiding presence remained. After a period of mourning, Lelia wisely decided that she should introduce some changes at Ninfa. She had the weeping willows that overhung the river cut down, as she considered that they fostered a sense of melancholy, and moved stridently coloured plants to less prominent positions. She also set about filling the areas within the walls as yet unplanted, ordering hundreds of new specimens in a delicate range of colours from the specialist catalogues. Life at Ninfa ceased to revolve around entertaining, literary events, and lively conversation. The Howards' interests lay in other fields and they had their own friends, although of course they retained the friendship of those who had known Marguerite and Roffredo, including Giorgio Bassani, their close collaborator in Italia Nostra. Their time at Ninfa was altogether quieter and less social: they walked, they listened to music, they attended Mass at the abbey of Valvisciolo. When they were in Rome, they entertained modestly in their apartment on the top floor of Palazzo Caetani.

The Howards' guiding principle, with regard to the Caetani lands and properties inherited by Lelia, was stewardship. In the first instance, this meant preserving and protecting them, but as the 1960s advanced, they came to see that the real challenge, in a rapidly changing social climate, was to find ways of providing public benefit that were compatible with these aims. Maintaining a building like the castle of Sermoneta, for instance, implied an immense financial responsibility, for which there was no state subsidy. Regarding it as a resource, on the other hand, by inviting the public to share the enjoyment of its history and artistic features, could help to offset the financial burden, while at the same time benefiting the visitors. The same could be said of Ninfa, the upkeep of which was prodigious, but whose variety of plants, including many rare species, began to attract the interest of gardening enthusiasts.[18] Lelia and Hubert were dedicated to keeping Ninfa's singular ecosystem as free as possible from human interference and from artificial substances. To witness organic gardening on such a scale was in itself an attraction for those with similar aims. A first small and intrepid step was occasionally to open Ninfa to guided groups. Then, in 1963, the Howards founded a chamber music festival, based at Sermoneta, in which the castle played host to a series of concerts that counted Yehudi Menuhin, Nikita Magaloff, Alberto Lysy, and Jacqueline du Pré among the early participants. As this event grew, the local government of Latina and the regional government of the Lazio began to take an interest. In 1972 this event was taken over by the Campus Internazionale di Musica di Latina and evolved as a musical celebration for mature students and professors, and eventually into the six-week-long Pontine Music Festival of today. Similarly, in 1968, the Howards began to make the castle available to the International Study Centre for the Conservation and Restoration of Works of Art, affiliated to UNESCO. Soon, experts and students from all over the world began coming to study the traditional techniques and materials used in restoration. The frescoes that adorn the walls of the castle and a number of the ruined churches at Ninfa have greatly benefited from their attention.

While doing their best to ensure the survival of the Caetani inheritance, the Howards did not lose sight of a more distant future. On 14 July 1972, Lelia created the Roffredo Caetani Foundation, named after her father, "to conserve and restore, from an historical, artistic, and environmental perspective, the Castle of Sermoneta and the Garden of Ninfa and its historic ruins; to preserve and develop Ninfa and adjoining lands as a wildlife protection area; and to permit public access to both properties without prejudice to their conservation." The foundation's other raison d'être is the diffusion of knowledge concerning the history of the Caetani family and the contributions made to culture and the arts – for example Roffredo's music, Marguerite's literary activities, and Lelia's painting.

Lelia and Hubert were generous collaborators in a multitude of causes related to the protection of nature and Italy's heritage. On various occasions they fought hard, and successfully, in the face of vested interests, to ensure that Ninfa's unique microclimate should not be damaged. Having been a founder member of Italia Nostra, Hubert had begun working closely in 1962 with Europa Nostra, which owed much to its Italian predecessor, while Lelia was invited to become the honorary president of the Italian branch of the World Wildlife Fund. Together she and Hubert procured changes in the hunting laws in the Lazio so as to make possible, in 1973, the designation of some 1,852 hectares, extending from the borders of Sermoneta to Cori, and including Ninfa, as a wildlife protection zone.

Such activities demanded forthright opinions, and sometimes attracted a degree of publicity that neither Lelia nor Hubert found easy to manage. Lauro Marchetti recalls them as tranquil beings who disliked conflict of any kind. Lelia had "the sweetest nature" he had ever

13.6
"*Il colletto*," the rock garden at Ninfa, created by Lelia in the late 1950s.

13.7.a
Lelia at Lyulph's Tower, Cumbria, 1973.

come across: she loved her plants as though they were children, particularly the delicate alpines that grew in her rockery, known as the *colletto*, and could not bear to see any growing thing suffer through being deprived of the light or space it needed. (When the branch of a large magnolia began to overhang a path and she was asked whether she wished to have the branch trimmed, she replied, "No, move the path a little.") Hubert, who administered the estates with a firm but sensitive hand, had the advantage of speaking excellent Italian. He was unassuming and approachable, knew all the gardeners, the tenants, and their families by name (no mean feat, when the total number of these was well over a hundred people), and was welcome in every home. He and Lelia were happiest when working silently together in the salon at Ninfa: Lelia at her easel next to the windows, and Hubert reading or writing on the other side of the room.

This idyll was tragically short. Lelia was diagnosed with cancer in 1976, and having spent her last few weeks in England undergoing treat-

13.7.b
Hubert at Ninfa, 1985.

ment, died at Castle Hedingham in Essex on 11 January 1977. Her tomb in the Caetani mausoleum bears the simple phrase "Painter and Gardener," which she apparently chose. Hubert was heartbroken by his wife's death, unable to imagine what joy or even pleasure the world might still hold for him without her. His letters make clear how much he relied on his Roman Catholic faith. The Caetani Foundations became the focus of the ten years left to him, during which he redoubled his efforts on behalf of the local environment, and set about learning all he could about plants, now that he was largely responsible for Ninfa. He also began to prepare seriously for the eventual transition to Lauro Marchetti as curator of the garden. When Hubert died on 17 February 1987, the Rome-based *Il Messaggero* announced that "The Oasis of Ninfa has lost its Father."

With Hubert's passing, the Roffredo Caetani Foundation assumed the role envisaged for it. While a degree of vigilance is still required to protect Ninfa from urban encroachment and environmental pollution, the foundation has so far succeeded in doing so. Public openings, specialist international tours, and the foundation's commitment to the education of young people in conservation principles have aroused increasing local and national interest in Ninfa's protection. Committed also to that protection is an international association of "Friends of Ninfa," established in the UK in 2005, and which, with other conservation bodies, is an associate of the foundation itself. Today, the garden receives sixty thousand visitors a year – a figure that would once have been unimaginable – including many parties of schoolchildren. Adding to the attraction of Ninfa itself is a new hundred-hectare wetland park called "Pantanello," officially opened in 2009. Situated adjacent to the garden, it represents an extraordinary rolling back of history to the time of the Pontine Marshes, and is once more a thriving habitat for migrating wildfowl and rare amphibians.

Similarly, the foundation ensures that the Caetani castle of Sermoneta is prominent in the cultural life of the Lazio. Visitors are offered a variety of displays and multi-media presentations on the history of the region, including the dominant role of the Caetani through the centuries and the transformation of the Pontine Marshes into the *Agro Pontino*. The castle is used throughout the year as an atmospheric venue for conferences, seminars, courses, book launches, and other events. Mutually fruitful relationships have been developed with provincial and local government, and some of these events, such as the Pontine Music Festival, are organized or sponsored by them. At the foundation's administrative headquarters at nearby Tor Tre Ponti, some three hundred of Lelia's paintings are on permanent display in the recently refurbished buildings.

The Fondazione Camillo Caetani, based at Palazzo Caetani in Rome, continues to foster scholarly study of the Caetani, their lives and achievements, and to publish the results. One recent project has been the recreation of Marguerite's library, in the very salon that was once her "private refuge." There, in the cool, white room at the top of a flight of steps, where she once introduced Eugene Walter to Giorgio Bassani, her books have been brought together again, and some of her pictures rehung. This space is dedicated specifically to the study of Marguerite's

13.8
The Caetani buildings at Tor Tre Ponti, recently restored as the administrative headquarters of the Fondazione Roffredo Caetani and as home to a permanent exhibition of Lelia's paintings.

literary work, and in it the first conference dedicated to her was held in October 2013.

Standing in that space, I found it easy to imagine her, sitting quietly and thinking of writers she particularly loved. Some of the best tributes, the ones that capture her generous spirit, are those from such writers, from Conrad Aiken at one end of the alphabet to Thornton Wilder at the other, sent to her while she was still alive, and preserved today in the archives next door. Theodore Roethke assured her that "Even if I don't write, you are always present in my memory, a symbol of grace and a different life where order reigns and art matters. You deserve letters that are even more beautiful than those Rilke wrote to his Countesses ... or that Yeats wrote to Lady Gregory."[19] René Char sent her poetic fragments that he illustrated himself. One sketch of a stormy sky shows a cloud from behind which sun-rays peep, and bears a line from a poem by Luis Broder entitled "Les compagnons dans le

13.9
Marguerite's former "refuge" at Palazzo Caetani, recently transformed to hold her library and an exhibition centre.

jardin" ("The companions in the garden"): "Nôtre amitié est la nuage / blanc préferé du soleil" ("Our friendship is the white cloud / favoured by the sun"). Italo Calvino, writing from New York, reported that his travels were "already very rich of reflections and of poetical emotions" thanks to her generous support. And Robert Lowell, writing soon after *Botteghe Oscure* ended, told her: "You should be proud of your years of service – to have succeeded in bringing together so many different nationalities, to have encouraged so many young poets. Your review is part of the history of the liberation of Europe from the madness and desolation of the war."[20]

As I scanned the books that once belonged to Marguerite on the shelves of her "refuge," familiar names caught my eye: writers who contributed to *Commerce*, and to *Botteghe Oscure*, and kept writing. There are the poems of Attilio Bertolucci and the essays of Rudolf Kassner. A little farther along are volumes of short stories by Natalia Ginzburg and Ingeborg Bachmann, the novels of Elsa Morante and Ignazio Silone.

Here are the names of W.S. Merwin, Christopher Logue, and Henri Michaux, and books of poems by Jon Silken and E.J. Scovell. William Weaver's translations of Elsa Morante and Alberto Moravia jostle with the novels themselves, and with the novels of Alfred Chester, the poems of Richard Wilbur, and the novels of Marguerite's cousin Mary Britton Miller, writing as Isabel Bolton. Over there are copies of *Anabase* in five languages, the French editions of René Char's poems, and the Random House translations by Jackson Mathews, T.S. Eliot's entire published writings, and complete runs of the poetry of Theodore Roethke, Paul Valéry, Giuseppe Ungaretti, and Archibald MacLeish.

And there, where my eye falls last, are the books of Giorgio Bassani, who began as a poet, and was prodded by Marguerite to persevere with fiction. I wondered what he would say, were he to stand once again in this room. The sight of the twenty-five *quadernos* of *Botteghe Oscure* displayed here might well move him to tears, as his last visit to Ninfa, shortly before he died in April 2000, is said to have done. He of all people would remember how much the writing to be found in those twenty-five volumes owed to Marguerite: to her inspiration and her free hand, her unobtrusive generosity, her patience, her love of the unconventional, and her faith in the young and the untried. For her, as Bassani would recall, it was only a matter of time, only a few arduous steps, between the pages of *Botteghe Oscure* and the books that any writer she believed in was capable of writing.

To the hundreds of books that fill these shelves, it is only an arm's length.

NOTES

CHAPTER ONE

1 Fowlie, *Journal*, 147.

2 By her nephew the late Schuyler Chapin, Commissioner of Cultural Affairs for New York City, 1994–2001, in an interview with the author, New York, May 2007.

3 See *The Chapin Gathering: Proceedings from the Meeting of the Chapin Family in Springfield Mass., September 17, 1862*; Gilbert Warren Chapin, *The Chapin Book of Genealogical Data. With Brief Biographical Sketches of the Descendants of Deacon Samuel Chapin.* Chapin Family Association, 1924; *The First Century of the History of Springfield*, Vol. 1 (1898); account books relating to Chapin family businesses between 1787 and 1855 in the Joseph Downs Collection and the Winterthur Archives, Winterthur, Delaware; *The City of Springfield, Chicopee, Chicopee Falls and West Springfield Directory* for 1881. Six generations on from Samuel Chapin, his descendant Abigail Reed married Thomas Stearns of Springfield. This couple were the great-grandparents of the poet and critic Thomas Stearns Eliot, Marguerite Chapin's third cousin.

4 Kirkland, *Men, Cities, and Transportation*, 369. The quote is attributed to the Report of the Committee on Railroads on Matters Relating to the Boston and Albany Railroad (*Massachusetts House Documents*, 1876, no. 355, Appendix, 23–4, 65–8, 206–8; *Hartford Courant*, 24 January, 21 April, 1876).

5 Homberger, *Mrs Astor's New York*, 181.

6 Biographical material on Chester W. Chapin is drawn from the *Biographical Directory of the United States Congress*. Further information on him and on his railroad interests is drawn from a variety of sources in the public domain. The Boston and Albany later became part of the New York Central Railroad system, with its hub at Cornelius Vanderbilt's grandiose Grand Central Terminus, the name by which New York's Grand Central Station was originally known.

7 Alfred went on to become mayor of Brooklyn from 1888 to 1891, a Democratic congressman in 1891, and Railroad Commissioner of New York State from 1892 to 1897.

8 Biographical material on Chester W. Chapin, Jr, and on Alfred C. Chapin is drawn from a variety of sources in the public domain.

9 Biographical information about Abel Dexter Chapin is drawn from a variety of sources in the public domain. See also the returns of the United States Federal Census, 1870, for Springfield Ward 4, Hampden, Massachusetts.

10 "A Marriage at St Ann's," *New York Times*, 1 December 1878, reports the marriage of Lindley Hoffman Chapin and "Ellila" Maria Gibert, the misspelling of Leila's name being a reporter's error.

11 Death certificate no. 2047, Health Department of the City of New York, now held in the Municipal Archives, New York City Department of Records and Information Services, gives Leila's name as "Leila Marie Gibert Chapin."

12 Last Will and Testament of Nicholas Gibert, dated 27 July 1850, and witness statements attached to same, are held by the Commissioner of Records, Surrogates' Court, County of New York. Note that a clerk's error appears on the covering page, where "Gibert" is spelled "Gilbert."

13 The two double portraits, together with other Gibert family paintings and heirlooms, were given to the Frick Collection by Duncan G. Harris, the son of Anna Marie Gibert Harris and her husband, Richard Duncan Harris.

14 Probate of the Will of Nicholas Gibert, granted 29 May 1851.

Frederick and James presented the cases of the two girls as minors and were endorsed as their guardians and trustees. Commissioner of Records, Surrogates' Court, County of New York.

15 Schermerhorn Family Archives, available online.

16 Correspondence of Lindley Chapin with various members of his family forms part of the Cornelia Van Auken Chapin Papers (hereafter CCP), Schlesinger Library, Radcliffe Institute, Harvard University. Passenger lists of ships arriving at Boston Massachusetts, 1820–1943.

17 New York, Census records for 1890 showing the occupants of 5 West Thirty-seventh St, Manhattan.

18 Bolton, *Under Gemini*, 78–80. Bolton's descriptions of Goshen Point and other Chapin properties there give an idea of what the original Rock Lawn must have been like.

19 Fondazione Camillo Caetani, Archives, Palazzo Caetani, Via delle Botteghe Oscure 32, Rome (hereafter FCC): Marguerite to Audinet Gibert, three brief notes written between 1885 and 1888.

20 Lewis, *Edith Wharton*, 72.

CHAPTER TWO

1 Cornelia's mother, Catherine Van Auken, was the only daughter of Cornelius K. Garrison (1809–1885), who, though born in New York, made a fortune in shipbuilding in the Midwest, California, and Panama, and served a term as mayor of San Francisco in 1853–54. He was at different times the rival and associate of Cornelius Vanderbilt in the course of the latter's drive to dominate America's transport and carriage systems.

2 The correspondence between Lindley Hoffman Chapin and Cornelia Garrison Van Auken forms part of the Cornelia Van Auken Chapin Papers (CCP), held by the Schlesinger Library, Radcliffe Institute, Harvard University. Letter headed "Rock Lawn, New London. Wednesday," Box 1/6.

3 CCP: letter headed "Sunday, at sunset," Box 1/6.

4 CCP: letter headed "Thursday evening," Box 1/6.

5 *New York Times*, 19 July 1903.

6 CCP: Box 1/6.

7 An account of the wedding appeared in the *New York Times* on 15 February 1888. That Archbishop Corrigan officiated suggests that Cornelia was received into the Roman Catholic Church before, or in the course of, the marriage ceremony. This, and the fact that the archbishop later baptized the three children born to Lindley and Cornelia, may disprove the idea that Marguerite and her stepmother became estranged because of religious differences.

8 Lindley was a member of the Calumet, Fencers', Raquet, and Vaudeville clubs. He was also active in the Knights of Columbus and supported Roman Catholic charitable causes. He paid the passage from France of the first six Little Sisters of the Assumption, so that they might begin their work in Harlem, and remained actively involved with their charitable work. See *The World*, 20 April 1891.

9 Census Returns for the City of New York, 1890, for 5 West Thirty-seventh Street, Manhattan.

10 Jessie to Cornelia, November 6 1890, from London. CCP: Box 1/9.

11 See Bachman, *Illustrated History of Waterford*, 141. A black-and-white photograph of a painting of the chapel on the same page shows it as having had a little bell tower, and it is described as having been painted dark green with red trim.

12 I am grateful to Maryalice Spencer, Archivist of the LSA Family in Mission of New York City, for information about the early community and the role of "Lady Servants." Both Cornelia Chapin and Alice Gibert were childhood friends of Soeur Marie du Christ (Antoinette de Godin), the Superior of the original group of six that arrived in 1891.

13 See the *New York Times*, 9 April 1902.

14 Balsan, *Glitter and the Gold*, 16.

15 Ibid., 15.

16 Ibid.,10.

17 See the many references to the matter in the *New York Times*,

the *Chicago Tribune*, and other major American papers between September 1891 and September 1894. See also, as an example of how fast news travelled thanks to the transatlantic and other cables, the *Daily Colonist* of Victoria, British Columbia, which on 23 February 1894 reprinted the account of the duel that had appeared in the Paris papers the previous day.

18 See the *New York Times*, 17 November 1898 (which refers to Audinet's divorce as "one of the sensational episodes of some six years ago") and 9 April 1913.

19 Lindley may have been planning to bring his will up to date anyway, but the destruction of Rock Lawn must surely have impressed upon him the need to do so. Probate was granted to Cornelia on 31 January 1896, five days after his death.

20 Lindley was laid up at Rock Lawn when Paul was born in New York in December 1888. To Cornelia, he reported finding it difficult to walk, even with a cane, and wrote plaintively, "I hope the next time I am ill, that it won't be when anyone else is." CCP: Box 1/9.

21 See the *New York Times* and the *New York Daily Tribune*, both 27 January 1896.

22 Lindley Hoffman Paul Chapin would suffer the same fate, dying aged fifty in 1938.

23 A report of the accident appeared in *The Traveler*, Southold, NY, on 20 August 1897.

24 A passport application made by Marguerite in 1909 gives some of this information, while the rest comes from interviews with people who knew her (the phrase quoted was contributed by Lauro Marchetti), photographs held by the Chapin, Biddle, and Howard families, the Fondazione Camillo Caetani, the Fondazione Roffredo Caetani, and the profile portrait that accompanied the announcement of her marriage that appeared in the *New York Times* on 31 October 1911.

25 *New York Times*, 5 January 1896; 2 and 17 December 1899.

26 *New York Daily Tribune*, 4 December 1898.

27 Marguerite's transatlantic journeys, like those of her Chapin and

Gibert relations, are documented in the Ellis Island Passenger Records service, available online at www.ellisislandrecords.org.

28 Balsan, *Glitter and the Gold*, 113.

29 See McAllister, *Society as I Have Found It*, for the flavour of the social scene in the Gilded Age.

30 *New York Times*, 9 February 1900.

31 *New York Times*, 16 January 1900.

32 Balsan, *Glitter and the Gold*, 15–22.

33 *New York Times*, 9 April and 18 June 1902.

CHAPTER THREE

1 See Groom, "An American Princess and the 'Féerie bourgeoise': The Commission for Mlle Chapin, 1910–1911," in *Vuillard*, and Barolini's chapter on Marguerite in *Their Other Side*.

2 Biddle Papers: *Travel journal*, 1906. Cornelia Chapin Papers: diary entitled *Travels, 1906*.

3 In theory, Marguerite could have seen de Reszke perform in every season except that of 1892–93, which was cancelled after fire gutted the Metropolitan Opera House in August 1892.

4 Both Groom and Barolini claim that Marguerite's attendance at the de Reszke school came about because Lindley Hoffman Chapin was a friend of the singer, though neither gives a source for this assertion. Chapin had been dead for five years by the time de Reszke announced his intention to teach, though that does not rule out his having known the singer earlier.

5 In notes scribbled down during a chat with Marguerite in the mid-1950s by her assistant Eugene Walter. There are many errors of transcription, including "Alfredo" for "Roffredo," and Prince "Bovo" for "Bibesco." These notes are held in the Eugene Walter Literary and Photographic Collection, Harry Ransom Center, The University of Texas at Austin.

6 Mary Garden, the Scottish-American opera star, recorded her admiration for de Reszke in her autobiography *Mary Garden's Story* (1980): among other tributes, he was "the greatest host I have ever known," an excellent friend, "whose sense of humour

was unforgettable, and who was a constant delight at table," interested in everything and everyone. One of the many kindnesses recorded by Maggie Teyte was the experience of being one of the several "foreign" pupils who were invited by the de Reszkes to accompany them to Deauville for a well-earned holiday. See O'Connor, *The Pursuit of Perfection*, 56.

7 O'Connor, *The Pursuit of Perfection*, 50.

8 Ibid.

9 Quoted in O'Connor, *The Pursuit of Perfection*, 45.

10 Ibid.

11 In notes taken by her assistant Eugene Walter from a chat with Marguerite, as cited above.

12 She was responsible, through the Société, for the French premieres of Wagner's *Tristan und Isolde* in 1893, *Götterdämmerung* in 1902, and *Parsifal* in 1903.

13 Brandon, *Dollar Princesses*, 190.

14 Marie Anatole Louise Élisabeth, Countess Greffulhe (née Riquet de Caraman-Chimay), was a Belgian-French aristocrat, but, more importantly, a highly educated, dynamic, and capable patron and administrator. She was renowned in her own day for her beauty; in ours, she is remembered for her contribution to the musical life of Paris, and as the primary model for Marcel Proust's Duchesse de Guermantes. Proust worshipped her, and famously remarked that her silvery laugh was "like the carillon at Bruges." Gabriel Fauré dedicated his *Pavane* (1886) to her.

15 See *The Princeton Union*, 16 July 1903, 7. The photograph of the second Rock Lawn that appears on page 35 bears the following note written by Cornelia Garrison Chapin on the back: "Our New London House side view facing the sound. The stable which survived the first fire corresponds in architecture to that of the original New London House. The first house burned down in Nov. 1894. The second house (of which this is a photograph) burned down July 14th 1903."

16 Edward and Mary Harkness left "Eolia" and its grounds to the State of Connecticut. Today, as the Harkness Memorial State

Park, the mansion and gardens are open to the public and form one of the most important tourist attractions in the Waterford and New London area.

17 Marguerite continued to receive post at 44, avenue d'Ièna even after she moved into her own apartment around the beginning of March 1910. As cited in Groom, *Vuillard*, 241, n15, the art dealer Ambroise Vollard sent her an invoice there in June 1911.

18 The trip was organized around the wedding of a cousin, Esther Retallac-Garrison, to Count Francis de Casteja, on 6 July 1906, at the church of St Augustin in Paris.

19 Katherine Chapin Biddle's *Travel Journal, 1906*, cited above.

20 Cornelia Chapin's diary, entitled *Travels, 1906*, cited above.

21 Rufus Osgood Mason's works included *Telepathy and the Subliminal Self: An account of recent investigations regarding hypnotism, automatism, dreams, phantasms and related phenomena* (1897), and *Hypnotism and Suggestion in Therapeutics, Education, and Reform* (1901). Charlotte Osgood Mason extolled his achievements in *The Passing of a Prophet* (1907). Rufus Osgood Mason also taught and became the mentor of the young William Rockefeller, who with his brother John founded the Standard Oil Corporation.

22 Rampersad, *Life of Langston Hughes*, Vol. 1, describes Hughes's relationship with Mason as "Godmother," and contains a number of references to Katherine Chapin Biddle and the younger Cornelia Chapin as her assistants. See also Kellner, "White Patronage in the Harlem Renaissance," in Bloom, ed., *Harlem Renaissance*, 53–66.

23 A notebook belonging to Katherine, dating from 1930–31 when she was forty, records verbatim the conversations between Charlotte Osgood Mason as medium ("The Lady of Wisdom") and a spirit called David, and the messages conveyed through automatic writing (Katherine or the younger Cornelia Chapin acting as "holder of the pen") at these sessions. Katherine may have had a particular interest in Mason's theories at this time, since

her younger son, Garrison, had recently died, aged just seven. Her tribute to him, the poem "Bright Mariner," took its title from a message from "David": "Oh, Katherine, if you could only see the bright light that surrounds your little 'mariner,' you would rejoice." Biddle Papers: Box 14, 3.

24 See Amory, *Last Resorts*, 172–3.

25 Passenger lists, Ellis Island Foundation; *New York Times*, May 26, 1907.

26 Bernstein was born to privilege, his father being a financier and art collector. As a child he was painted by Manet. He is said to have fought thirteen duels and to have been a great dandy, at one time (according to the *New York Times* of 23 June 1912) owning 147 pairs of trousers. Despite his apparent frivolity, he tackled serious subjects, as when, in later life, he denounced anti-Semitism and Nazism. Even before 1914, the themes of his plays were often polemical, violent, or both. In 1911 his play *Après-Moi* had to be suspended after an armed royalist Catholic group known as the Camelots du Roi invaded the theatre, necessitating the intervention of the gendarmes. His works were extremely popular: it has been alleged that, between 1904 and 1914, one or more of his plays was being performed somewhere in Paris every single night.

27 He was also a cousin of Charles Ephrussi, the head of the Ephrussi Bank. This Odessa banking family has been immortalized in Edmund de Waal's *The Hare with Amber Eyes* (2010). Charles Ephrussi's Paris house was also located in the avenue d'Ièna, at number 11.

28 See Chapter 11 of Wharton, *Backward Glance*, in which the salon life of Paris is discussed.

29 See Groom, *Vuillard*, which includes chapters on his commissions for both Bernstein and the Bibescos.

30 In notes taken from a chat with Marguerite by her assistant Eugene Walter, as cited above. On the Bibescos, see Enid Bagnold's *Autobiography*; she had much to say about them after 1914,

when they were based in London. See also *Letters of Marcel Proust to Antoine Bibesco*, and the many references in Painter, *Marcel Proust.*

31 She arrived in New York on 23 May and returned via Liverpool on 21 June 1908.

32 Now in the Musée d'Orsay, Paris.

33 Three of these photos are held in the Eugene Walter Literary and Photograph Collection, Harry Ransom Center, The University of Texas at Austin, and one in the Archives of the Fondazione Camillo Caetani, Rome. Others are owned by the Fondazione Roffredo Caetani, and by the Chapin, Biddle, and Howard families.

34 This reference was found online at www.ancestry.com, in a search for Marguerite Gibert Chapin.

35 In notes taken from a chat with Marguerite by her assistant Eugene Walter, as cited above.

36 The plans are reproduced in Groom, *Vuillard*, 196. André Le Nôtre (1613–1700) was France's leading designer of formal gardens. He created many formal parks for châteaux such as Sceaux, Fontainbleau, the Tuileries, and St Germaine-en-Laye, but his best-known work remains the vast park and the gardens he designed for Louis XIV at Versailles.

37 Vuillard, Bonnard, and the Bibesco princes had travelled together by train to Spain in 1901, to study the country's architecture. The photographs documenting their journey are now in the Musée d'Orsay, Paris.

38 Vuillard, *Journal*, 11 March 1910, cited in Groom, 179–80.

39 Vuillard, see *Journal* entries cited in Groom, 180–1. The painting is now known as *Marguerite Chapin in Her Apartment with Her Dog* and hangs in the Fitzwilliam Museum, Cambridge. Through its kind permission, Vuillard's small masterpiece also appears on the cover of this book.

40 Count Harry Kessler (1868–1937), of German and English ancestry, was a diplomat, writer, librettist, promoter of modern art, and founder, in 1913, of the Cranach Press in Weimar. He is

credited with having drawn up the initial plans for the League of Nations, and was probably the greatest diarist of his age. He and Marguerite maintained friendly contact until his death in exile in France in 1937. See *Journey*, 522. His later diaries have been published as *The Diaries of a Cosmopolitan*. See also Laird M. Easton, *The Red Count: The Life and Times of Harry Kessler* (2002).

41 Kessler, *Journey*, 536–7.

42 *The Library* is now in the Musée d'Orsay, Paris.

43 Guy Cogeval, "Backward Glances," in *Edouard Vuillard*, 30.

44 *Place Vintimille: A Five-Panel Screen for Miss Marguerite Chapin* is now in the National Gallery of Art, Washington, DC.

45 Kessler, *Journey*, 542–4.

46 Ibid.

47 Ibid., 554.

48 Vuillard, *Journal*, May 1911, cited in Groom, 181.

49 In notes taken from a chat with Marguerite by her assistant Eugene Walter, as cited above.

50 Ibid.

51 Ibid.

CHAPTER FOUR

1 Roffredo's account of events appears in Chapter 5.

2 Dante held Pope Boniface responsible for the expulsion from Florence of the "White" Ghibellines, leading to the poet's exile from his native city.

3 Campitelli, "Le Residenze dei Caetani del XIII al XVIII secolo," in Fiorani, ed. *Palazzo Caetani: Storia, arte, e cultura*, 69–91.

4 The German historian Ferdinand Gregorovius regarded him as "*il più distinto rappresentante dell'indole romana non solo, ma ancora di tutt'un'epoca cittadina, che oramai con lui è scesa nella tomba*" ("the most distinguished representative not just of the Roman character but also of an entire epoch of Roman citizenry, now, however, descended with him into the tomb"). See Forni, "Il Mito di Ninfa" in Fiorani, ed. *Ninfa: Una citta, un giardino*, 322.

5 Soros and Valker, eds., *Castellani and Italian Archaeological Jewellery*, 37.

6 Until the robbery of April 2013, there was a very fine collection of such items, including a number of pieces made to the designs of Michelangelo Caetani, on display in the Augusto Castellani collection at the Villa Giulia National Etruscan Museum in Rome.

7 Alan Walker in *Franz Liszt: The Final Years* paints a dismal picture of the musical life of Rome in the 1850s, as there was no adequate hall for performance and only a minuscule music-loving public. The best concerts took place through the good offices of the Roman nobility: "The powerful Caetani family also put on concerts in their sumptuous palace; the head of the clan, Duke Michelangelo Caetani, became a personal friend of Liszt and opened many doors for him" (37).

8 Translated from the conversation with Duke Michelangelo on 7 June 1871, reported by Fr Hyacinthe Loyson in *Gratry et Loyson, 1870–1872: Letters et journaux intimes*, 1927, 187.

9 Calixta served as the model for Modeste Mignon in Balzac's *Scènes de la vie privée*, and the writer dedicated *Les parents pauvres* to Michelangelo, Duke of Sermoneta. Calixta's mother, Rosalia Rzewuska (herself a composer whose memoirs would be edited by Roffredo's sister, Giovanella, in 1939), had this to say about her daughter: "she had a facility for knowing and learning everything, of never having to vanquish difficulty in order to do so … She had a genius for music, and knew it thoroughly." (Translated from the biographical note on Ersilia Caetani, in Gorgone and Cannelle, eds., *Il salotto delle caricature: Acquerelle di Filippo Caetani*, 56.)

10 Augustus Hare, *The Story of My Life*, vol. 2, 58.

11 The case was reported in the *New York Times* on 20 September 1885, under the heading "Curious Italian Lawsuits." See also *The Letters of Harriet, Duchess of Sermoneta, to Miss Denison: 1862–1905*. London: John Murray, 1912. Digitized by the Internet Archive in 2014 and available at https://archive.org/details/lettersofharrietooserm.

12 These calculations are always inexact, but historic international currency equivalence information can be found at www.cyberussr.hcunn/gold-std.html.

13 Ersilia Lovatelli-Caetani, *Attraverso il mondo antico* (1901), *Varia* (1905), *Aurea Roma* (1915).

14 For more on Ersilia, Countess Lovatelli-Caetani, see Caterina Fiorani, "I Caetani e L'Accademia dei Lincei dal settecento al primo novecento," in Fiorani, ed., *Palazzo Caetani*, 331–45.

15 Gorgone and Cannelle, eds., *Il Costume è di rigore, 8 Febbraio 1875: Un ballo a Palazzo Caetani*, 72–7, 188–9, 208–9.

16 See Caracciolo and Pietromarchi, *The Garden of Ninfa*, 107–8.

17 Bagot, *My Italian Year*, quoted in Caracciolo and Pietromarchi, *The Garden of Ninfa*, 68.

18 Ibid.

19 Lady Walburga Paget, *Linings of Life*, 211; also quoted in Caracciolo and Pietromarchi, *The Garden of Ninfa*, 66.

20 Leone's account of the visit is cited in Caracciolo and Pietromarchi, *The Garden of Ninfa*, 62.

21 See Quest-Ritson, *Ninfa*, the introductory chapter of which brings together a number of such comments.

22 Between 1888 and 1894 Leone travelled throughout the Mediterranean basin and farther afield: first to Egypt, crossing the Sinai desert. A later trip took him through North Africa and down to the Sahara, while on a subsequent journey he explored Syria, Palestine, Turkey, and Mesopotamia. Later still, he travelled through Central Asia, and from there to Russia and to India.

23 Leone Caetani's journal recording his trip was transcribed and published only in 1999, as *In Selkirks*, translated by Danilo Aguzzi Barbagli.

24 Arthur Smith, *China in Convulsion*, vol. 2, 481; and Shirley Ann Smith, *Imperial Designs*, 82–3.

25 Franceso Tetro, "Il riccordo di Livio Caetani (1873–1915), terzogenito di Onorato VII e Ada Caetani," *Il Tempo*, 14 September 2007. During the July siege, Ada and Onorato received many letters from Ada's sister Emily, Countess

Crawford, and other members of the Lindsay family, commiserating with them on the reported death of their son. Ada's correspondence with Emily, Countess Crawford, is in the Archives of the FCC, Rome.

26 See the letter to Roffredo, written in 1958 by this devoted lady's grandson, reminding him that she was his first teacher, in Fiorani, "Roffredo Caetani, oltre il musicista," in *Roffredo Caetani: La personalitá, la cultura, la musica*, 60.

27 See Op de Coul, "Roffredo Caetani: L'evoluzione di un compositore tra ottocento e novecento," in Fiorani, ed., *Palazzo Caetani*, 407–16.

28 Ibid., 410.

29 Op de Coul, "Roffredo Caetani compositore: La formazione, le opera, il catalogo cronologico," in Fiorani, ed., *Roffredo Caetani: La personalità, la cultura, la musica*, 28, and the libretto of *Hypatia* in the same volume, 117–93.

30 Op de Coul, Ibid., 34–5.

31 Paget, *Linings*, 211, and cited in Caracciolo and Pietromarchi, *The Garden of Ninfa*, 66.

32 Fondazione Leone Caetani (hereafter FLC): file s.n., Leone to Ada. In view of the young Onorato's later physical and intellectual difficulties, it has always been assumed that he was born with them. Leone's letters to Ada during his son's early years suggest, on the contrary, that Onorato was a normal and healthy child, a "splendid little man," "always ready to laugh and play." Had he been mentally and physically afflicted from birth, it is unlikely that Leone would have commented to Ada, as he did in a letter of 2 August 1902, after describing his son's alertness, "I hope he may be something like Gelasio one day," or, in another, dated 22 September 1907, "I hope his English blood will push him to do something in life. I don't mind what it is as long as it is something useful to others too. I would like him in politics or in science. Well, who lives will see!"

33 See Vittoria Caetani, *Times Past*; also quoted in Caracciolo and Pietromarchi, *The Garden of Ninfa*, 69–70.

34 Tetro, "Il Riccordo di Livio Caetani (1873–1915)."
35 See Peele, *Gelasio Caetani*, 1936.
36 Two of Giovanella's photographs appear in Capa, ed., *Behind the Great Wall of China*. Her work was also included in an exhibition held at New York's Hallmark Gallery in 1972, entitled "Four Cameras in China: Then and Now," curated by Margaret Weiss.
37 Roffredo's Quartetto per due violini, viola e violoncello, op. 12, composed in 1905, is dedicated to "Elisabeth de Caraman Chimay Comtesse Greffulhe."
38 See Robert Croft's review, "A Modest Confutation," in Stephen Walsh, *The Second Exile: France and America, 1934-1971*, at www.naxos.com/news/default.asp.
39 A good example can be found in Caracciolo and Pietromarchi, *The Garden of Ninfa*, 63–5.

CHAPTER FIVE

1 Brandon, *Dollar Princesses*, 26.
2 Vickers, *Gladys, Duchess of Marlborough*, 94–104.
3 See "An Elgar Timeline," www.elgar.org/2time08/htm, for mention of the invitation to the composer Sir Edward Elgar and his wife, then in Rome, to visit the castle of Sermoneta by car. Accompanying Roffredo on 27 April 1908 was Countess Adelaide Spoelberch de Louwenjoul, a Belgian noblewoman who was an accomplished musician. She was also present at a dinner for Elgar and his wife the following evening at Palazzo Caetani, along with the Princesse de Polignac and the Count and Countess Greffulhe.
4 Roffredo wrote to his father on 9 August, from his chalet in Pontresina. Besides describing Marguerite's character, background, and economic situation, Roffredo told his father that he had met her "last year," and come to know her over a longer period than was in fact the case. He put great emphasis on their mutual compatibility, and stressed the high opinion of her held by everyone who knew her in Paris. All this reads as though Roffredo was

carefully constructing a counterweight to Onorato's possible disapproval of his engagement after such a short acquaintance, and of a single woman living on her own. See Caterina Fiorani, "Roffredo Caetani, oltre di musicista," in *Roffredo Caetani: La personalita, la cultura, la musica*, 57.

5 FLC: 1386, Roffredo to Leone, 14 September 1911.

6 FLC: 1417, Ada to Livio, n.d., marked "private."

7 FLC: 1417, Ada to Leone, n.d.

8 FLC: 1417, Ada to Leone, 17 September 1911.

9 FLC: 1417, Ada to Livio, n.d., marked "private."

10 FLC: 1389, Giovanella to Leone, n.d. See also a note from Countess Greffulhe, a good friend of the Caetani family, letting Leone know that she too was in Lausanne, and referring to "an event not yet official, but of which the news is imminent," which she hopes "will bring happiness and health to all the family, and to Leone's too." FLC: 1672, Countess Greffulhe to Leone (n.d., but must be August 1911).

11 FLC: 1590, Onorato to Leone, 17 September 1911. Onorato now attributed his delay in joining the family to health problems, and announced his plan to travel to St Moritz, but later altered this so as to meet the group in Aix-les-Bains.

12 FLC: 1590, Marguerite to Onorato, n.d., but marked "Friday morning."

13 FLC: 1674, Marguerite to Leone, 19 September 1911.

14 FLC: 1417, Ada to Leone, 17 September 1911. Ada divulges here that the wedding date was originally set for 15 November. She also comments that she fears her sister "the Css" (the Countess) "will be terribly upset when she hears the news. She guessed something seeing them together at the theatre, with Daisy Chanler's sister-in-law [*sic*] as chaperone." Perhaps Countess Crawford envisaged Roffredo as a husband for someone else?

15 FLC: file s.n., Leone to Ada, 19 September 1911.

16 FLC: 1386, Roffredo to Leone, 20 September 1911.

17 FLC: 1590, Onorato to Leone, 25 September 1911.

18 Kessler, *Journey*, 564.

19 Groom, *Vuillard*, 197–9.
20 Kessler, *Journey*, 564.
21 This would find expression in the compilation of *Domus Caietana*, a meticulous three-volume family genealogy, still unfinished at Gelasio's death in 1934, which brought the story up to the sixteenth century.
22 The menu is conserved in FLC: 1386.
23 Archbishop Bourne was made a cardinal in November 1911 – perhaps his availability in London determined the earlier wedding date of 30 October. It is interesting to note that he chose, as his titular church in Rome, Santa Pudenziana, where the Caetani chapel is located.
24 Vittoria Caetani, *Times Past*, contains many observations about the members of her husband's family and life at Palazzo Caetani – not all of them flattering.
25 Croce, *Due Città*, 56.
26 FCC: Marguerite to Gelasio, 24 July 1912 and 2 October 1912.
27 Ellis Island Foundation passenger lists show that "Cornelia G.V.A. Chapin and Catherine [*sic*] Chapin" arrived back in New York aboard the *George Washington* on 24 December 1912. The younger Cornelia does not seem to have accompanied them on this visit to Paris. Katherine recalled the visit in her letter to Marguerite of 4 January (n.y., but internal evidence suggests 1916), mentioned in note 35, below.
28 FCC: Marguerite to Onorato, n.d., but very likely late 1912.
29 FCC: Marguerite to Onorato, marked "Saturday," February 1913.
30 FCC: Marguerite to Onorato, 29 August 1913.
31 Hypatia was already the subject of a novel by Charles Kingsley, which served as the basis of G. Stuart Ogilvie's play *Hypatia*, staged in London in 1893 with a musical score by Hubert Parry. It is possible that Roffredo may have seen this.
32 FCC: Marguerite to Gelasio, 24 July 1912.
33 FCC: examples abound among Marguerite's letters to Onorato and Ada.
34 FCC: Marguerte to Onorato, 29 August 1913.

35 FCC: Katherine Chapin to Marguerite, 4 January (n.y. but must be 1916, as she refers to the birth of the Caetanis' son, Camillo, on 23 October 1915). Katherine had not been in touch for some time, and wondered "if baby Leila [*sic*] still has light hair and blue eyes. It seems so funny to think of a child of Roffredo's and yours *not* having brown eyes!"

36 FCC: Marguerite to Gelasio, 18 October 1913 and 9 December 1913.

37 It is often claimed that the photograph on page 120 and others of Marguerite with Lelia when tiny were taken at Villa Romaine. This cannot be the case, since Lelia, born on 4 October 1913, appears to be six to nine months old in the photographs, and the family did not move to Villa Romaine until the spring of 1920.

CHAPTER SIX

1 The arrangement created by Gelasio continues as the central collection of the Archive of the Fondazione Camillo Caetani at Palazzo Caetani, Rome.

2 Gelasio's beloved was Anna (always known as Annina), Countess Piccolomini, the wife of Count Eneas Silvio Piccolomini, whose family was a major landowner in the area around Siena and Piacenza, and claimed Pope Pius II as its most illustrious member. Gelasio's comment about marriage is quoted in Sottoriva, *Gelasio Caetani*, 27.

3 *Il Piccolo*, 29–30 January 1915.

4 Strictly speaking, the Sovereign Military Hospitaller Order of Saint John of Jerusalem, of Rhodes, and of Malta. It is a Roman Catholic lay religious order dedicated to charitable works, founded in 1113, and is the oldest order of chivalry in the world. Male members of the families who belong to it are "Knights" (today there are "Dames" too), who offer their services when disaster strikes or need arises. It also has a large number of paid medical staff, and is active today in 120 countries. The Caetani brothers were Knights of the Order.

5 FLC: 903/4, Onorato to Leone, 18 October 1915.

6 Gay and Fisher, *Public Relations of the Commission for Relief in Belgium*, document 568 and note 426. Hoover's telegram to Gelasio is dated 6 November 1914, and the Italian committee, entitled *Comitato Nazionale Italiano per i soccorsi alle vittime della guerra nel Belgio* came into being a few months later, "with Onorato Caetani, Duke of Sermoneta, as active president."

7 At the end of July, Vittoria left Palazzo Caetani and rented Villa Maria at Pallanza on Lake Maggiore. For an account of her subsequent relationship with the Futurist sculptor Umberto Boccioni, see Chia, *Una parentesi luminosa* (*The Light in Between*). Milan: Adelphi edizione, 2008.

8 FCC: Marguerite to Onorato, 15 November 1915, Friday. Unfortunately, the photograph does not survive.

9 Vittoria Caetani, *Things Past*, 242–3; and FLC: 903 (4), Onorato to Leone, 6 December 1915.

10 Gelasio Caetani, *Lettere di Guerra*, 125; and Sottoriva, *Gelasio Caetani*, 56.

11 Sottoriva, *Gelasio Caetani*, 65. See also the chapters in that book that discuss the Col di Lana exploit. After the war, Gelasio became president of the national committee to honour those who lost their lives on the Col di Lana. A monument was dedicated there on 20 August 1922.

12 FCC: Roffredo to Marguerite, 9 November 1917.

13 FCC: Roffredo to Marguerite, 16 October 1916. By the end of the year, Roffredo was "Maggiore Caetani, Direttore, Treni Ospedale, Ordine di Malta, Stagine di Ravenna" (Major Caetani, Director, Hospital Trains, Order of Malta, Ravenna Section).

14 FCC: Mary Berenson to Marguerite, 26 October 1916 and 10 November 1916.

15 FCC: correspondence between Roffredo and Marguerite for the dates mentioned, and for 10, 24, and 28 August, all 1917. For biographical information about Duke Onorato, see the entry in the *Dizionario biografico degli italiani*, vol. 16 (1973), by Piero Craveri, and obituaries in *Il Giornale d'Italia*, 3 September 1917, and *Il Messaggero*, 9 September 1917.

16 Sottoriva, *Gelasio Caetani*, 85. "I miei funerali saranno modestissimi." Onorato specified that his body was to be neither washed nor embalmed but merely wrapped in a sheet and placed in his coffin.
17 FCC: Fondo Economico 2103.
18 It is impossible to summarize the value of the Caetani lands, palaces and contents, tenancies, and various categories of seasonal income. The FCC has an extensive set of legal and financial documents, or *fondi* (as in the Fondo Economico cited in Note 17), some of which (for example, 2215 and 2943) shed light on specific areas.
19 Pre-war, the ratio of the lira against sterling was 25 to 1. By the end of 1917 the rate was 40 to 1. The rate of the lira against the US dollar was 7.51 to 1 at the end of 1917. See, among other historic conversion tools available online, www.measuringworth.com
20 Sottoriva, *Gelasio Caetani*, 203, mentions this house as "Villa Mon Rêve" at Banneville, near Blonville, Calvados. It had its own beach, and was later rented by Roffedo and Marguerite for summer holidays during the 1920s.
21 Caracciolo and Pietromarchi, *The Garden of Ninfa*, 74.
22 Quest-Ritson, *Ninfa*, 38.
23 FCC: Fondo Economico 2966.
24 FCC: Roffredo to Marguerite, 4 July 1919.
25 FCC: Fondo Economico 2741.
26 FLC: file s.n., Leone to Ada, 4 November 1919.
27 Or so Harold Acton considered her, as a member of the pre-war "tango generation": see his *Memoirs of an Aesthete*, 38.
28 FCC: Roffredo to Marguerite, 23 February 1920.
29 FCC: Roffredo to Marguerite, 30 October 1920.
30 See Sottoriva, *Gelasio Caetani*, 91–3.
31 FCC: Roffredo to Marguerite, 12 July 1921.

CHAPTER SEVEN

1 Caetani, Vittoria, *Sparkle, Distant Worlds*, 7.

2 The cataloguing and study of Marguerite's collection of artworks is ongoing. Recent research is made available at www.fondazione camillocaetani.it, and includes a listing of works by artist, image, and date acquired.

3 Some of these photographs appear in Fiorani, ed., *Palazzo Caetani: Storia, arte e cultura*, 371.

4 Fiorani, ed., *Palazzo Caetani*, 372.

5 Among them, the Abbé Mugnier, Walter Berry, Edith Wharton, Rainer Maria Rilke, André Gide, and Alice B. Toklas.

6 Op de Coul, "Roffredo Caetani compositore. La formazione, le opera, il catalogo cronologico," in Sottoriva, *Roffredo Caetani: La Personalitá, la cultura, la musica*, 30.

7 Flanner, *Paris Was Yesterday*, xv–xvi.

8 Sophie Levie, in "Marguerite Caetani, una mecenate americana in Europa," in *La rivista* Commerce *e Marguerite Caetani*, xvi, suggests that Marguerite met Paul Valéry through Nathalie Clifford Barney, and Valery Larbaud through Gaston Gallimard, the publisher of the *Nouvelle Revue Française*. As mentioned in Chapter 3, however, she may well have met Valéry earlier, at the salon of Mme Jeanne Muhlfeld in about 1909.

9 It must be emphasized that until 1922 Gelasio was a Nationalist, not a Fascist, and that his willingness to serve the Mussolini regime derived from his economic views, his experience of the Paris peace conferences, his conviction that postwar Italy required strong government, and the opportunities offered to him, first as a Nationalist deputy, then as ambassador (see Sottoriva, *Gelasio Caetani*, 91–101). But it is easy to understand why fascist ideas alarmed Marguerite and Roffredo. From the later manifesto "The Doctrine of Fascism," ghostwritten in 1932 by Giovanni Gentile for Mussolini, comes the totalitarian assertion that "for the fascist, everything is in the state, and no human or spiritual thing exists, or has any sort of value outside the state."

10 FLC: file s.n., Leone to Ada, 28 May 1922.

11 The Fondazione Leone Caetani for the study of Islam and the Arab world came into being on 6 January 1924, and given an initial endowment of 10,000 lire by Leone. Its Archive is housed within the library of the Accademia Nazionale dei Lincei at Palazzo Corsini, Rome.
12 FCC: Roffredo to Marguerite, 5 August 1922.
13 FCC: Roffredo General Correspondence 1, 16 August 1922.
14 FCC: Roffredo to Marguerite, 5 November 1922.
15 Flanner, *Paris Was Yesterday*, xvii.
16 Ibid., xviii–xix.
17 The origins of *Commerce* have been admirably explored by Sophie Levie in "Marguerite Caetani, una mecenate americana in Europa," cited in note 8 above, and in *Commerce 1924–1932: Une revue internationale moderniste*, 16.
18 The French original reads: "Vous me demandez comment Commerce a commencé. Je vais vous le dire ... Un jour Valéry dit tout à coup: Pourquoi ne continuerons-nous pas nos réunions en publiant, en revue, nos dialogues? Comme titre, je suggère 'Commerce,' commerce des idées. Cette idée enchant a tous les presents. Les directeurs (Larbaud, Valéry, Fargue) furent désignés immédiatement. Adrienne Monnier et moi-même prîmes en charge la mise en train et nous commençâmes aussitôt. Quant au résultat, c'est á vous en juger. J'ai été énormément aidée par Paulhan qui m'a permis de chercher parmi les manuscrits qu'il reçevait pour la *NRF* de même que par Alexis Léger qui choisissait les poèmes que nous avons publiés." Marguerite was replying to the question asked by Gaston Palewsky, the French ambassador to Italy, at the opening of the exhibition *Hommage à Commerce: Lettres et arts à Paris, 1920–1932*. The question appears on page 11 of the catalogue of the same title. Also quoted in Levie, *Commerce 1924–1932: Une revue internationale moderniste*, 16; and in Brown, "Guiding the 'Commerce' of Ideas," *Books Abroad* 43: 307–11.
19 They were: "We Are the Hollow Men," translated by Saint-John Perse, in Cahier III (Winter 1924), "Because I Do Not Hope to

Turn Again," translated by Jean de Menasce, in Cahier XV (Spring 1928), "Som de l'escalina," translated by Jean de Menasce, in Cahier XXI (Autumn 1929), and "Difficulties of a Statesman," translated by Georges Limbour, in Cahier XXIX (Winter 1932).

20 See Levie, *La rivista* Commerce *e il ruolo di Marguerite Caetani nella letteratura Europea, 1924–1932*, 29–30.

21 Levie, "Marguerite Caetani, una mecenate americana in Europa," in *La rivista* Commerce *e Marguerite Caetani*, xviii.

22 The French text reads: *Commerce / cahiers trimestriels publiés par / les soins de Paul Valéry, / Léon-Paul Fargue, / Valery Larbaud.*

23 It was at this lunch that Joyce – who feared dogs – had the disconcerting experience of having Beary, the Caetanis' huge and exceedingly friendly male Briard, jump up and put its paws on his shoulders. Marguerite reassured Joyce and removed the dog, but then told the assembled company how it had recently torn the seat out of a visiting plumber's trousers and forced the man to jump out of a ground-floor window. At the news that she had replaced the man's trousers, Joyce whispered to Sylvia Beach, "She's going to have to do the same for me." See Beach, *Shakespeare and Company*, 143–4.

24 The childrens' book appears in its entirety in Sottoriva, ed., *Lelia Caetani nel Centenario della Nascita*, 57–123.

CHAPTER EIGHT

1 Rainer Maria Rilke to Marguerite Caetani, 6 February 1925. Cited in Bohnenkamp and Levie, *Briefwechsel mit Deutschsprachigen autoren*, 7. The original reads "Le déjeuner d'hier était charmant dans son intimité spontanée … Et j'ai admiré votre genie de proposer á nous tous les sujets d'animations et d'activités spirituelles dont la portée surpassait les agreements de l'instant." I am grateful to Miranda Jones of Oxford for advice regarding this translation and the one cited in note 4, below.

2 Marguerite described the book as "a curious link between the two cultures that I love so much." It is interesting to find small personal

disclosures of this kind in her letters to the writers she admired, as they so seldom appear elsewhere in her correspondence.

3 Bohnenkamp and Levie, *Briefwechsel mit Deutschsprachigen autoren*, 12–13.

4 Ibid., 30. Rilke to Marguerite, 27 April 1925.

5 Ibid., 22–5.

6 Ibid., 33. Rilke to Marguerite, 21 May 1925.

7 Ibid., 21. Rilke to Marguerite, 17 March 1925.

8 Balthus was particularly known for his studies of girls and young women. In 1935 he painted the portrait of Lelia, aged twenty-two, that today belongs to the Fondazione Camillo Caetani.

9 Since Hofmannsthal was also a friend of Count Harry Kessler, with whom he had collaborated on the libretto of Richard Strauss's *Der Rosenkavalier* in 1911, it is possible that Marguerite may have met him before 1914.

10 "Voies et rencontres," which appeared in Cahier VI (Winter 1925) and "Émancipation du lyrisme français," which appeared in Cahier XX (Summer 1929).

11 For *Elektra* (1909), *Der Rosenkavalier* (1911), *Ariadne auf Naxos* (1912), *Die Frau Ohne Schatten* (1917), *Die Äegyptische Helen* (1927), and *Arabella* (1933). The years are those in which the works received their premieres. Since Hofmannsthal died in 1929, the libretto for *Arabella* must have been completed earlier.

12 See Bohnenkamp and Levie, *Briefwechsel mit Deutschsprachigen autoren*, 98.

13 Hofmannsthal to Marguerite, 2 July 1925. Ibid.,104–5.

14 *New York Herald Tribune*, 11 March 1925. The *New York Evening Journal* of the same date cited Cornelia as "one whose name was indicted in that book of life, the late Mrs Astor's visiting list. She was born and died on Fifth Avenue, and during her brilliant social career never resided an appreciable distance from that fashionable thoroughfare." It is interesting to note that in 1928 a new organ was given to St George's Episcopalian church on East Sixteenth Street, Manhattan, by Katherine and the

younger Cornelia in memory of their mother. This suggests that the three women had set Catholicism aside.

15 CCP: Journal entitled *Travels, 1925*.

16 CCP: Varied biographical notes.

17 Cassano, ed. *Marguerite Caetani e gli artisti per il teatro. Edward Gordon Craig, Fortunato Depero, Alberto Savinio* (FCC: 2013).

18 Cornelia's own relationship with Mason seems to have been free of the tendency to dominate apparent in the latter's sponsorship of Black writers. Cornelia's *Papers* contain several notes "to Godmother, from her Child," thanking her for gifts of blocks of stone to be carved, suggesting that Mason was a generous and thoughtful mentor and friend.

19 Groethuysen was one of those who linked the German cultural and art historians of the period before 1914, such as Dilthy and Wölfflin, under whom he had studied, and the movements that arose between the wars. In Paris his friends ranged across the spectrum of the French intelligentsia.

20 Edith Wharton considered that "the only completely agreeable society I have ever known is that wherein the elements are selected and blent [*sic*] by a woman of the world, instinctively alert for every shade of suitability, and whose light hand never suffers the mixture to stiffen or grow heavy" (*Backward Glance*, 290). Wharton was writing of the period before the war, and Marguerite would probably not have considered herself a "woman of the world," yet she clearly strove for the same kind of harmonious blending.

21 Valery Larbaud to Marguerite, Lar. 243, Fonds V. Larbaud, Bibliothèque Municipal de Vichy, cited in Brown, "Guiding the Commerce of Ideas," *Books Abroad* 43: 307–11.

22 Ungaretti, Introduction to *Hommage à Commerce*, 14–16.

23 Limbour, "Ode à l'Indice," in *Index to Commerce and Botteghe Oscure* (1958), 12–13.

24 Roger Fry to Helen Anrep, 11 November 1925, in Sutton, ed.,

Letters of Roger Fry, 584, and reproduced in Levie, "Marguerite Caetani, una mecenate americana in Europa," in *La rivista* Commerce *e Marguerite Caetani*, xv.

25 FCC: Roffredo to Marguerite, 17 May 1923: "he now has plenty of work – our help has brought him luck."

26 FLC: file s.n., Leone to Ada, 26 April 1925.

27 FCC: Roffredo to Marguerite, 3 December 1924.

28 FCC: Roffredo to Marguerite, 6 February 1925.

29 FCC: Roffredo to Marguerite, 2 December 1924.

30 See *Time*, 28 April 1924; *Brooklyn Daily Eagle*, 22 February 1925, 69.

31 Nazzaro, *Fascist and Anti-Fascist Propaganda*; also Chernow, *The House of Morgan*, 280.

32 See *The InTowner* (Washington, DC), March 2006.

33 *Time*, 5 May 1924.

34 See Sottoriva, *Gelasio Caetani*, for more on Gelasio's range of activities after returning from Washington. Frank Snowden's *The Conquest of Malaria: Italy 1900–1962* traces the Mussolini regime's marshland improvement project. See also Gelasio's own simplified *Redemption of the Pontine Marshes*.

35 A complete list of Gelasio's writings, collections of documents, speeches, and dispatches appears in Sottoriva, *Gelasio Caetani*, 267–8.

36 FCC: Roffredo to Marguerite, 4 December 1924.

37 See Chapter V, "Roffredo Caetani, duca di Bassiano e la nuova Villa Caetani," in Benocci, *Villa Tre Madonne*, 137–61.

38 Following the success of the Weimar production, Roffredo decided to revise *Hypatia*, this time asking the literary critic Walter Benjamin, and later, Bernard Groethuysen, to polish the translation. The work was performed again on 10 June 1927 at Dusseldorf's State Theatre, directed by Hans Balzer.

39 Marguerite to Rilke, 1 June 1926, in Bohnenkamp and Levie, *Briefwechsel mit Deutschsprachigen autoren*, 70.

40 Sylvia Beach, *Shakespeare and Company*, 122.

41 See Paul D. Lehrman, "Blast from the Past," about his restaging of Antheil's work, and its various performances, including the first, online at www.wired.com/wired/archive/7.11/ballet
42 FCC: Marguerite to Gelasio, n.d., but headed "New Year's Day"; internal evidence suggests 1 January 1924.
43 Andrea Caffi was born in St Petersburg to an Italian father and a Russian mother. He was a pupil of the German historian Theodor Mommsen and became a historian and specialist in Greek, but he also wrote and translated. Caffi worked for Milan's *Corriere della sera* and later the Italian embassy in Moscow during the Russian Revolution. According to Count Kessler, he was imprisoned by the Bolsheviks, "with people being shot in cells below his own, awful food and brutal gaolers." Count Harry Kessler, *Diaries of a Cosmopolitan*, 405–6.
44 FCC: Camillo to Marguerite, 15 September 1926.
45 Leone apparently made overtures to Roffredo about some formal declaration to this effect, but they were never given legal standing.
46 FLC: file s.n., Leone to Ada, 11 May 1928 and 16 October 1928.
47 FLC: file s.n., Leone to Ada, 11 May 1928.
48 FLC: file s.n., Leone to Ada, 16 October 1928.
49 FLC: file s.n., Leone to Ada, 26 April 1925, in which he writes of his former intention of getting out of the consortium, running Fogliano on his own, and undertaking the necessary improvements under the reclamation program. Only "when I was convinced that F. would have been taken from me, or from O. after my death, I sold. I got sent information from Italy that the Fascist government intends to put into execution a great expropriation policy in the Pontine Marshes." The area around Fogliano was apparently the focal point of this plan.
50 FLC: file s.n., Leone to Ada, 2 February 1930.
51 FCC: Ada to Michelangelo, 30 June (n.y.).
52 Levie, *Commerce, 1924–1932: Une revue internationale moderniste*, 50, n2.
53 Larbaud met Joyce through Adrienne Monnier's bookshop,

and the text of a talk given by him on the Irish author appeared in the *Nouvelle Revue Française* in 1922. Levie, *La rivista* Commerce *e Marguerite Caetani*, 78, n.10.

54 Levie, *Commerce, 1924–1932: Une revue internationale moderniste*, 226.

55 See Brown, "Guiding the Commerce of Ideas," and its Notes.

56 Cited in Origo, "Portrait of Marguerite," 83.

57 Bohnenkamp und Levie, *Briefwechsel mit Deutschsprachigen autoren*, 190.

58 Origo, "Portrait of Marguerite," 83.

59 Levie, *La rivista* Commerce, 21. The introduction to Elisabeth Förster-Nietzsche came through Count Harry Kessler.

CHAPTER NINE

1 FCC: Inventorio Analitico del Fondo Economico 2116: Giustificazioni di pagamento per lavori terreno Valle Giulia. Luglio 1925-giugno 1926. Also Fondo Economico 2954, Corrispondenza Roffredo cerca lavori di restauro e arredamento alla Villa Tre Madonne, 1929. See "Roffredo Caetani duca di Bassiano e la nuova Villa Caetani: le dofferte vicende dell'acquisito, I progetti e le opera di Pietro Aschieri, Alfredo Giannelli, Carlo Broggi e Renato Setacci," in C. Benocci, *Villa Tre Madonne*, 137–61.

2 FCC: Marguerite to Roffredo, n.d., headed "Villa Romaine."

3 FCC: Gelasio to Ada, 27 July 1927.

4 Anna Menotti Piccolomini had a son, Niccolò, who was born on 13 December 1913 and died, aged twenty-eight, in a military air crash in 1942. He was talented young man, who, against Count Enea Silvio's wishes, became an actor before joining the Italian air force and becoming a pilot. He willed the villa in Rome inherited from his mother to the Fondazione Piccolomini, created at his request to assist indigent artists and actors. A comment of Gelasio's to Ada at the time of Annina's death cites his deep sadness, "after 18 years of constant affection" – which would date the beginning of their relationship to 1912. Was Niccolò possibly

Gelasio's son? If so, the laws of inheritance made it essential that this never be divulged.

5 The dedication reads: "Cinque Liriche su parole di Antonio Rubino. Dedica alla Contessa Anna Piccolomini." Her memory also survives in connection with her former villa in Rome, the Villa del Sole, or Villa Piccolomini, on the Via Aurelia Antica, today an arts centre and residence for poor and unemployed theatrical performers.

6 FLC: Leone Caetani cart. s.n., Leone to Ada, 11 May 1928.

7 FCC: Gelasio to Ada, 7 November 1929.

8 FCC: Gelasio to Ada, 17 November 1929.

9 FCC: Gelasio to Ada, 25 September 1930.

10 FCC: Marguerite to Roffredo, n.d., headed "In the Train Tuesday."

11 FCC: Marguerite to Roffredo, n.d.

12 FCC: Marguerite to Roffredo, n.d., but headed "Mardi."

13 One of them may have been Vuillard's portrait of her, *Interior with a Lady and Her Dog*, which is described in Chapter 3 and appears on the cover of this book. It entered the collection of the judge and athlete Montague Shearman sometime before his death in 1930. The painting was later exhibited by Rex Nan Kivell, owner of London's Redfern Gallery, and bought by the diplomat Edward Maurice Berkeley Ingram. On Ingram's death in 1941, the picture passed to the Fitzwilliam Museum, Cambridge, under the terms of his will, and remains there under the title *Marguerite Chapin in Her Apartment with Her Dog*.

14 Marguerite to Valery Larbaud, headed New Year's Day (n.y., but probable date is 1931), cited as B-56 in the Fonds Larbaud, Bibliothèque Municipale, Vichy, in Brown, "Guiding the Commerce of Ideas," 307–11, n19.

15 FCC: Michelangelo to Gelasio, 4 August and 11 August 1931.

16 Skelmersdale, "The Gardens at Ninfa, Italy," 248; and Quest-Ritson, *Ninfa*, 44–5.

17 Roffredo carried out Gelasio's wishes concerning the Caetani archives by overseeing the transfer of some two hundred thousand documents to the Biblioteca Apostolica in November–December

1934. FCC: Roffredo General Correspondence 1: correspondence and item headed "Notizie sull'archivio Caetani."

18 Quest-Ritson, *Ninfa*, 46.

19 According to Frank Snowden, the houses were whitewashed inside and out, so that the mosquitos would be easy to see and kill. The farmers and their families were also taught how to eradicate potential mosquito breeding places.

20 Garrett was appointed ambassador to Italy (1929–1933) by President Herbert Hoover, "to keep an eye on Mussolini." Alice Garrett is today recalled for introducing the work of Léon Bakst and Raoul Dufy to the United States, and building up a following for both artists there. The Garretts' collections of art, porcelain, and theatre artifacts are housed in their former Baltimore home, "Evergreen," which they bequeathed to Johns Hopkins University.

21 FCC: Marguerite to Roffredo, n.d., but headed "Saturday." For a complete list of the artists and works displayed in these exhibitions, see Paola Bonani and Claudia Terenzi, "Marguerite Caetani promotrice delle arti," in *Palazzo Caetani Bollettino* 1 (2013): 30–6.

22 FCC: Marguerite to Roffredo, n.d., but headed "Venerdi."

23 FCC: small booklet entitled "Società l'Arte d'Oggi," announcing its formation and first exhibition.

24 The exhibition was reviewed very favourably by, among others, Clive Bell in the *New Statesman*, 6 June 1935. It travelled to Washington in 1939 – possibly as a result of overtures made by Marguerite during her visit to the United States in the summer of 1938.

25 The Cornelia Chapin Papers include a sketchbook and photographs of her at work dating from her time in France, but a fuller selection is held by the Smithsonian Institute's Archives of American Art in Washington, DC, and includes film footage of Chapin observing animals in various zoos, then working on sculptures in her studio. This footage can now be viewed by arrangement on the AAA's website.

26 Louis Vauxcelles, writing in the *Excelsior*, Paris, 14 June 1936. Cited in a biographical memoir of Cornelia Van Auken Chapin in the CCP.

27 Sottoriva, ed., *Lelia Caetani nel Centenario de la Nascita*, 36–7.

28 FCC: Roffredo to Marguerite, 7 May and 18 June 1934.

29 It is easy to see in this situation a parallel with Marguerite's relationship with her vivacious stepmother, Cornelia Garrison Van Auken Chapin.

30 Barjansky, *Portraits with Backgrounds*, 74–5

31 FCC: Giovanella to Roffredo, 10 September 1954. Roffredo, aged eighty-three, had written to Nella asking her for an account of their mother's death because, to his distress, he could no longer remember the event of twenty years before.

32 FCC: Fondo Economico 2969.

33 FCC: Camillo to a friend called Ruby, n.d. but clearly written soon after Gelasio's funeral.

34 Peele, *Gelasio Caetani*, 59. See also, by the same author, "Gelasio Caetani: An Appreciation," in the *Columbia University Quarterly* 27, no. 4 (December 1935): 430–5.

35 Robert Woods Bliss (1875–1962) and his wife, Mildred (1879–1969), bought the house, which they renamed Dumbarton Oaks, in 1920 and bequeathed it to the District of Columbia.

36 There are several examples of this, but the one most relevant here came in 1933, when Gelasio wrote to Roffredo to suggest swapping his own space in Palazzo Caetani for Roffredo's interest in Cisterna, which was badly in need of repair and costing more to maintain that its rents brought in. Roffredo was thus relieved of expense in return for allowing Gelasio a free hand to repair and modernize at Cisterna, and thereafter to receive any gains. This work had already been started at Gelasio's death ten months later. FCC: Fondi Economici 2966, 2968, 2969.

37 FCC: Fondo Economico 2768 includes Gelasio's will and an inventory of his possessions at all four properties, including outbuildings, machinery, and stocks and shares. The inventory was drawn up by the notary and signed by Roffredo (representing

Camillo, still a minor) and Livia as having participated in the listing of each property. They began in November 1934, and spent numerous days each month on the task until they signed the last pages on 25 January 1935.

38 FLC: Leone to Giorgio Levi Della Vida, n.d., but headed 1933; quoted in Caracciolo and Pietromarchi, *The Garden of Ninfa*, 72.

39 See www.caetaniculturalcentre.org.ca, which carries an account of Sveva's life, and interesting photographs.

40 See Giuppi Pietromarchi, "The Caetanis' Gardening Roots," in Caracciolo and Pietromarchi, *The Garden of Ninfa*, 103–26; and Quest-Ritson, *Ninfa*, 50–2.

41 Quest-Ritson, *Ninfa*, 53.

42 FCC: Camillo to Roffredo and Marguerite, 24 October 1937.

43 Interview with the late Schuyler Chapin, May 2007. Also, written notes by the late Peter Tompkins, supplied by Esme Howard.

44 FCC: Camillo to Marguerite, 6 October 1937 and 25 August 1938.

45 CCP: Biographical entry for an unnamed publication, entitled "Cornelia Van Auken Chapin."

CHAPTER TEN

1 Museo Storico della Liberazione, Roma. Archivio Centrale dello Stato. Gli Ebrei a Roma 1938–1944 (text to accompany an audiovisual presentation), and Giorgio Giannini, "La resistenza popolare a Roma durante l'occupazione nazista," in Centro Studi Difesa Civile, *La Resistenza Non Armata* (1994), 113–19.

2 See Snowden, *The Conquest of Malaria*, 143–9, 156–9.

3 See www.aeronautica.defesa.it/Organizzazione/Reparti/RepartiAddestra.

4 FCC: Fondo Economico 2010.

5 Harold Tittmann Papers, Box 4, 6: draft of his memoirs, part 1, 5.

6 FCC: Fondo Economico 2977.

7 Peter Tompkins to Esme Howard, 3 October 2006.
8 Interview with Countess Desideria Pasolini Dall'Onda, Rome, February 2007.
9 Nicholas Tucci's account of this conversation appears in Caracciolo and Pietromarchi, *The Garden of Ninfa*, 83.
10 Whitaker, *We Cannot Escape History*, 75.
11 FCC: Camillo to Marguerite, 20 September, 4 November; Camillo to Roffredo, n.d.
12 Biddle Papers: Marguerite to Katherine, 20 January 1941.
13 FCC: Eliot to Marguerite (n.d.), and quoted in Iris Origo, "Portrait of Marguerite," *Atlantic Monthly* 205 (February 1965): 81–8.
14 Harold Tittmann Papers, Box 2, 15; 8 January 1941. On 19 January, Tittmann wrote to his wife: "What a blow to the proud Caetani family. Only Onorato left to carry on the name, but the doctors seem uncertain as to whether he can even make a child. I suppose the girl could marry and give her name to her husband and their children."
15 This quote is taken from a copy of the diary of Sir D'Arcy Osborne, British ambassador to the Holy See in the Harold Tittmann Papers.
16 FCC: Michelangelo to Roffredo, 7 January 1941.
17 Roffredo's letter to Paul Chapin is included in the Katherine Biddle Papers, Box 3, Folder 1, 29. Roffredo's correspondence with the military authorities and the statements written by Camillo's fellow soldiers can be found in the FCC's file on Camillo.
18 Reference must be made to such allegations, although to date no documentary evidence that might corroborate them has come to light. Before his death in 2006, Peter Tompkins apparently told the late Schuyler Chapin and others that Marguerite had asked Francis Biddle (during the time when the latter was serving as a judge at the Nuremburg war trials and visiting Ninfa when he had a few days' respite) to find out as much as he could about Camillo's death, and that Biddle in turn had made the same request to William Donovan, Tompkins's boss as head of the OSS.

According to Tompkins, Donovan's investigations led him to the conclusion that Camillo had been deliberately killed by members of his own battalion, or exposed to extreme risk from enemy fire, on the orders of Mussolini.

19 The writings of the sixth-century philosopher Anicius Manlius Severinus Boethius (475–525), who was unjustly executed for treason by the Ostrogothic king Theodoric, strongly influenced the exiled Dante Alighieri. Written while Boethius awaited execution, *The Consolation of Philosophy* seeks answers to the injustices of the world through the device of debates with "Lady Philosophy," who leads him to higher understanding and the acceptance of the workings of an all-just Providence, though this entity is not specifically Christian.

20 In June 1941, Harold Tittmann reported to his wife, somewhat irritably, that Marguerite was "pestering him to death" to take her over to Osborne's Vatican office, which suggests that special permission may have been required. He declared to Eleanor, "I shall not do it as I daren't jeopardize my position by getting myself on the police blotter as accompanying an anti-Fascist to the British Ministry apartment at Santa Marta." Harold Tittmann Papers, 17 June 1941, Box 2, 24.

21 From the copy of the diary of Sir D'Arcy Osborne in the Harold Tittmann Papers comes the following entry, which indicates that Tittmann finally capitulated: "October 21, 1941. Tittmann called with Marguerite Bassiano, who brought gifts to D'Arcy." In his diary, Osborne habitually referred to himself in the third person.

22 On a website dedicated to Monsignor Hugh O'Flaherty, Sam Derry, author of *The Rome Escape Line*, described the REO as an initiative "in which soldiers and priests, diplomats and communists, noblemen and humble working-folk, were all operating in concord with a single aim, yet without any clearly defined pyramid of authority," www.hughoflaherty.com/index.cfm/page/cast. Sir D'Arcy Osborne inherited a dukedom from a distant relative after the war and became the 12th and last Duke of Leeds. For

his role in the REO, see Steven Walker, *Hide and Seek* (2011). He used his own funds to supply the REO, and in 1940 had been involved in the plot devised by a number of German generals and the Pope to overthrow Hitler.

23 Harold Tittmann Papers, Box 2, 29, 17 January 1942.

24 Harold Tittmann Papers, Box 2, 32, 28 January 1942.

25 Biddle Papers, Samuel Barber to Katherine, 22 March 1942.

26 The answer may lie in the partial copy of a letter dated 3 February 1950 (FCC: Roffredo General Correspondence 1) from Roffredo to a banking official in New York, one W. Grossenbacher, in which he mentions an earlier request to add the names of Giovanella Grenier (based in Madrid) and Paz Larrain de Subercaseaux (the wife of the Chilean Consul in London, and the friend to whom Roffredo had dedicated his "La commedia d'un musicista per pianoforte" in 1937) to his own and Marguerite's as signatories for the Caetanis' joint bank account. He gives no date for this request, but Spain and Chile were nominally neutral during the war, and so these two trusted women might have been able to facilitate the transfer of funds.

27 Harold Tittmann Papers, as cited above: Box 2, 41, 12 February 1943.

28 See Peter Tompkins, *A Spy in Rome*, 1962. Also two interviews with Tompkins's widow, Maria Luisa Fiorenza Tompkins, February 2007 and February 2009.

29 FCC: Marguerite to Roffredo, several undated letters.

30 FCC: Roffredo General Correspondence 1, copy of a fragment of a letter dated 3 February 1950.

31 Sottoriva, *Cronache da due fronti*, 216.

32 Dorothy McCardle reviewed Lelia's exhibition of paintings in the *Washington Post*, 22 March 1954.

33 Harold Tittmann Papers, Box 4, 25, draft of Tittmann's memoirs, 15.

34 British Parliamentary Papers (*Hansard*), 1 August 1944, vol. 402, c1157: "Italy (Enemy Vandalism)."

35 See Snowden, *Conquest of Malaria*, 187–98.
36 Biddle Papers, Marguerite to Katherine, 18 June 1944.
37 Quoted in Jackson, *The Battle for Rome*, 206.
38 See Peter Tompkins, *A Spy in Rome*, concerning the liberation of the city in June 1944.
39 Interview with Countess Desideria Pasolini Dall'Onda, February 2007.
40 Biddle Papers, Marguerite to Katherine, 30 June 1944.
41 Vittoria's account of her narrow escapes during the German Occupation also mention Cora's, and are described in *Sparkle, Distant Worlds*, 250–65.
42 FCC: Fondo Economico 2909.
43 FCC: Fondo Economico 2909, document dated 14 August 1946.
44 Biddle Papers, Marguerite to Katherine, August (n.y. but very likely 1945).

CHAPTER ELEVEN

1 Elena Croce, *Due Città* (2004), 40.
2 FCC: T.S. Eliot to Marguerite, 5 February 1945.
3 FCC: T.S. Eliot to Marguerite, 22 May 1945.
4 Jean Paulhan to Marguerite, 23 May 1945. In Risset, gen. ed., *La rivista* Botteghe Oscure *e Marguerite Caetani: La corrispondenza con gli autori stranieri, 1948–1960*. Laura Santone and Paola Tamassia, eds., I. Sezione francese. FCC: 3.
5 Biddle Papers, Marguerite to Katherine, 12 April (n.y., but must be 1947, since it belongs to a series of letters written between September 1946 and April 1947, the order of which can be determined by internal evidence). This series can be found in Box 3.1.18.
6 *Quaderno* ("notebook") recalls the term *cahier* given to successive numbers of *Commerce*.
7 Marguerite liked Bassani's poems, but soon encouraged him to write more fiction. She backed up her words by publishing, in Quadernos I, VII, X, and XV, four of the five stories later brought together as *Cinque Storie Ferrarese*, which won the

Strega Prize in 1956. He remains best known today for the novel *Il Giardino dei Finzi-Contini*, inspired by Ninfa, which won the Viareggio Prize in 1962.

8 Elena Croce, "Nasce una rivista a Roma liberata," *La Stampa*, 5 January 1975.

9 There are various versions of this exchange, the most often cited being that of Guglielmo Petroni, to whom Marguerite alleged that "we've been living here for 1,000 years." This may have been amusing, but it was not strictly speaking true: the Caetani had owned the building since the mid-eighteenth century but had only lived in it since the beginning of the nineteenth. In any case, their presence in the Via delle Botteghe Oscure certainly predated that of the Communist Party.

10 Giambattista Bodoni, who designed the typeface named for him, claimed that "Letters do not achieve their true beauty when done in haste and discomfort, nor when done with diligence and pain, but only when they are created with love and passion." Quoted in Simon Garfield, *Just My Type: A Book about Fonts*, 204.

11 See the correspondence between Marguerite and Ricciardi, in Valli, ed., *La rivista* Botteghe Oscure *e Marguerite Caetani: La correspondenza con gli autori italiani, 1948–1960*, 223–33.

12 Attilio Bertolucci was also the father of film directors Bernardo and Guiseppe Bertolucci.

13 Elena Croce to Marguerite, "summer 1948," in Valli, ed., *La rivista* Botteghe Oscure *e Marguerite Caetani*, 138–9.

14 Laura Santone, "Introduzione," in Risset, gen. ed. *La rivista* Botteghe Oscure *e Marguerite Caetani*, xxxiii, cites a letter from Ungaretti to Paulhan of 28 December 1948. Ungaretti erred in attributing any role in *Botteghe Oscure* to "the Croce-Craveri group," perhaps because, as Santone points out, he assumed that Marguerite's friendship with Elena Croce, begun through Il Ritrovo, must involve the latter's active participation in the review.

15 Jean Paulhan to Marguerite, 13 January [1949], in Santone and Tamassia, *La rivista* Botteghe Oscure, 13.

16 Marguerite to Elena Croce Craveri, 22 July 1948. Instituto Italiano per gli Studi Storici, Biblioteca Benedetto Croce, Naples.
17 See De Luca's letters to Marguerite in Valli, *La rivista* Botteghe Oscure *e Marguerite Caetani*, 189–93. The courtesy and professionalism that made working with De Luca a pleasure are evident in these few letters. Interview with Benedetta Origo, February 2007.
18 The poems by Scotellaro published by Marguerite in Quadernos II, III, V, VIII, IX, and XI were the only ones to appear in his lifetime, as he died at the tragically early age of thirty in 1953.
19 Katherine Garrison Chapin Biddle, *The Tapestry of the Duchess* (1925), *Outside of the World* (1930), *Bright Mariner* (1933), *Time Has No Shadow* (1936), *Plain-chant for America* (1942), *Harbor Night* (1945), *Sojourner Truth* (1948), and later volumes. Several of her poems were set to music.
20 Biddle Papers. In the letter of 12 April 1947 cited above, Marguerite goes on to ask: "What would you and Alexis and Archie say? and [*sic*] would you send me manuscripts?"
21 Biddle Papers, Marguerite to Katherine, 17 February 1947.
22 Biddle Papers, Marguerite to Katherine, 29 March 1947.
23 According to the catalogue of Roffredo's compositions prepared by Paul Op de Coul, in Mariantonietta Caroprese, ed., *Roffredo Caetani, un musicista aristocratico*, 115–23, he wrote only two after Camillo's death: a five-part suite for piano called "Le Marionette per pianoforte," dated 1944–45, and "The Night Ramblers," for contralto voices and instrumental ensemble, sometime in the 1950s.
24 Interview with Dott. Piero Craveri (the son of Raimondo and Elena Croce Craveri), February 2007. Roffredo told the then-ten-year-old Piero that he kept the vast tome open on a shelf of his wardrobe, and read a page of it while dressing and preparing for the day.
25 Giuppi Pietromarchi, "The Caetanis' Gardening Roots," in Caracciolo and Pietromarchi, *The Garden of Ninfa*, 109.

26 Ibid., 110–11.
27 Ibid.
28 Interview with Benedetta Origo, 22 February 2007.
29 Gioconda de Vito, the great classical violinist, was a friend of the Caetanis. Marguerite's letter to Katherine of 17 February 1947 contains the request that her sister send, via their mutual friend Raffaele Matteoli, who was on a visit to the United States, a list of items impossible to obtain in postwar Italy: toothbrushes and toothpaste, lisle stockings, Pond's cold cream, and strings for de Vito's violin. In her letter of 12 April 1947 (Matteoli having returned and delivered the items), Marguerite asked Katherine to send horsehair for de Vito's bow.
30 Barolini, *Their Other Side*, 209–10, cites (but does not give a source for) Francis Biddle's impression that Marguerite avoided being alone with him – or with anyone – so as to avoid any possible mention of Camillo, or of how she was feeling. She did this by entertaining constantly: "She draws in on herself and faces no intimacy."
31 Roffredo and Marguerite were less than pleased to learn of Topazia's marriage, unbeknownst to them, to the conductor Igor Markevitch on 23 July 1947. Markevitch moved to Rome early in 1947, having divorced his first wife, Kyra Nijinsky, and obtained Italian citizenship. It is likely that he met Topazia at Ninfa, where he was welcomed as a friend of Bernard Berenson's, and of Marguerite's, though it is possible that they met in Florence, where the conductor was the guest of "BB" when he was the director of the Maggio Musicale, and Topazia a frequent visitor to her Antinori relatives. Topazia wrote to "Zio Roffredo" nearly nine months after her elopement to beg his forgiveness, admitting that "knowing your ideas about the family in general, and Igor in particular," she had not had the courage to tell him of her intentions face to face. FCC, Topazia to Roffredo, 15 May 1948.
32 Howard, *Virtues and Vanities*, 81.
33 FCC: Marguerite to Roffredo, 4 August 1947. Marguerite was

initially nervous about driving on the left, but Lelia, as the driver, rose to the challenge with her usual quiet practicality. Marguerite herself never learned to drive.

34 Howard, *Virtues and Vanities*, 177, describes how his eight-year-old brother Johnny managed to tip Roffredo from a rowing boat into the river on one such occasion, but was graciously forgiven.

35 Coincidentally, Hubert's parents had also held their wedding reception at Tetton.

36 Biddle Papers, Katherine to Marguerite, 24 September 1951.

37 Biddle Papers, Katherine to Marguerite, 18 April 1951.

38 FCC: Niccolò Tucci to Marguerite Caetani (n.d., but cat. as August 1951).

39 See Marguerite's letter to Paulhan, 6 Dec 1951, and the accompanying notes, in Santone and Tamassia, *La rivista* Botteghe Oscure *e Marguerite Caetani*, 334. The situation may have been complicated by an earlier disagreement between Paulhan and Char.

40 Promotional flyer, n.d., but probably 1949, since it shows the tables of contents for Quadernos I and II. FCC, file containing Marguerite's correspondence with the Gotham Book Mart, 1950–58.

41 James Laughlin's comments appear in "The Art of Publishing, Part 1," in the *Paris Review* 89 (Fall 1983).

42 Biddle Papers, Katherine to Marguerite, 25 February 1949. Francis had received the first package and sent the copies personally to a list of likely contacts, including Thornton Wilder, Donald Adams of the *New York Times*, Lionel Trilling, and Louise Bogan at the *New Yorker*.

43 Katherine was not only a great support to Marguerite; she and Francis were generous hosts to a number of European writers who arrived in the US friendless and all but destitute after the war. Herbert Steiner, who by 1950 was teaching at Penn State and the Quaker College in Flushing, New York, commented to Marguerite, of Katherine, that "For me she is one of the gifts of

life I owe America" (a sentiment echoed by Alexis Léger). FCC: Herbert Steiner to Marguerite, 15 January 1950.

44 Edwin Muir, "The Italian Spirit," the *Observer*, 4 February 1951.

45 Margaret Bottrall, "From the Dark Shops," *Statesman and Nation*, 3 March 1951.

46 This fuller correspondence file, which apparently came to light in the basement of the GBM Gallery in the 1970s, is held by the Harry Ransom Center at the University of Texas at Austin. It provides a good overview of the working relationship between Marguerite and Frances Steloff and the promotion of *Botteghe Oscure* in the United States.

47 Suspicion reigned in the postwar atmosphere: to enter the United States, foreign publications had to be individually stamped so as to make clear where they were printed, and such stamping could take place only at the port of departure (which meant packing up copies in Rome, then unpacking them for stamping at the port, then repacking them, under supervision); on arrival, all this had to be done again for the American customs authorities. Packages could contain only a certain number of copies; costs for overweight were high, and if multiple, identical packages were sent at the same time, each package had to be accompanied by a separate set of customs documents. Evidence of copyright permission for every piece of writing in a given volume was also needed.

48 See Tortora, ed., *Giorgio Bassani – Marguerite Caetani: Sarà un bellissimo numero, Carteggio, 1948–1960*.

49 Valli, *La rivista* Botteghe Oscure, 47.

50 Ibid., 140–87. See the correspondence between Marguerite and Elsa Dallolio.

51 Weaver's comments appear in "The Art of Translation, Part 3" (interview by Willard Spiegelman), *Paris Review* (Spring 2002).

52 Croce, *Due Città*, 57.

53 FCC: Dylan Thomas to Marguerite, 2 November 1949.

54 FCC: Dylan Thomas to Marguerite, 24 November 1949; n.d., but probably summer 1950; 17 May 1951.

55 FCC: Katherine to Marguerite, 8 April 1950.
56 FCC: Dylan Thomas to Marguerite, October 1951, in which he described the plot and characters of *Llareggub* at length and pleaded to be paid in advance for the whole work, even though it was only half-written, which would allow him to finish it; FCC: David Higham of Pearn, Pollinger & Higham, Ltd, Authors' Agents, to Marguerite, 26 January 1954 and 4 February 1954.
57 Louise Bogan, reviewing the *Anthology* in the *New Yorker* on 18 November 1950, called Petroni's hundred-page story "a minor masterpiece in the type of symbolic realism we have come to associate with the best Italian films."
58 Valli, *La rivista* Botteghe Oscure, 282–8.
59 FCC, Niccolò Tucci to Marguerite (n.d., but cat. as 1953–54).

CHAPTER TWELVE

1 Judith Jones, in her memoir *The Tenth Muse*, relates how she and Paul Chapin started offering cheap home-cooked meals in the apartment to fellow Americans and other lonely young souls living in Paris, which worked well until the concierge told Marguerite!
2 Walter, *Milking the Moon*, 131.
3 Ibid., 135.
4 HRC, Eugene Walter Collection: Box 1 item 9.
5 Walter, *Milking the Moon*, 166–7.
6 Ibid., 136–7.
7 Despite the distractions of life in Paris, Eugene managed to finish a novel begun before he left New York. *The Untidy Pilgrim* won the Lippincott Prize in 1954.
8 HRC, Eugene Walter Collection: "Letters to EW 1956," Marguerite to Eugene (n.d.), item 81.
9 HRC, Alfred Chester Papers: Marguerite to Alfred Chester, 8 February (n.y.)
10 HRC, Alfred Chester Papers: Marguerite to Alfred Chester, 2 June 1954. She added the comment: "What fools all Publishers

are – really timid fools. They sell books as if they were buttons or some similar commodity."

11 HRC, Alfred Chester Papers: Marguerite to Alfred Chester, 20 December 1953. Chester published his first collection of stories, *Here Be Dragons*, in 1955, and his first novel, *Jamie Is My Heart's Desire*, in 1956. Marguerite was instrumental in obtaining for him the Guggenheim Fellowship in 1957 that enabled him to produce *The Exquisite Corpse* (1960). His short stories were published in many leading American magazines during the 1960s.

12 HRC, Eugene Walter Collection: "Letters to EW 1954," Marguerite to Eugene (n.d.), item 56.

13 Camus's essay "René Char" was included in Marguerite's publication, *René Char's Poetry: Studies* (1956).

14 See Cassano, ed., *Marguerite Caetani e gli artisit per il teatro.*

15 HRC, Gotham Book Mart Papers: "Caetani correspondence," Marguerite to Frances Steloff, 20 February and 3 August 1951.

16 For a detailed study, see Lorenzo Salvagni, "The Caetani-Mathews Papers: Introducing René Char to the American Readership" in <<altrelettere>>, 28.5.2014, DOI: 10.5903/al_uzh-20.

17 Char's biographer Laurent Greilsamer, in *L'éclair au front: La vie de René Char*, 268–9, claims that the poet charged clothing to a department-store account paid for by Marguerite. If this was the case, it would not be out of keeping with her generosity, but to allege that such kindness implies an extramarital relationship, as Greilsamer goes on to do, not only misunderstands Marguerite, but also sets aside the obvious: in 1950 when she began to promote Char, she was seventy and Char was forty-three and deeply involved with someone else. She was his admiring patron and friend, not his lover. See also Bruno Toscano, "René e Marguerite," in *I pensieri dell'instante. Scritti per Jacqueline Risset* (2012), 511–21.

18 Biddle Papers: Susan Revere Chapin to Katherine, 17 February and 12 April 1954.

19 FCC: Katherine to Marguerite, 19 March 1954; Biddle Papers: Lelia to Katherine, 4 and 27 February 1954.
20 FCC: Material in Roffredo General Correspondence 2 resuming the earlier petition, and drafts of a letter Roffredo proposed to send to the king in 1955 – having forgotten that the king and the royal family had been exiled in 1947. His correspondence with Hubert reveals the trust and closeness he felt for his son-in-law. See also the Constitution of the Fondazione Camillo Caetani, 10 May 1956.
21 As in the case of Guglielmo Petroni, she promoted Giorgio Bassani strongly to the American publisher Blanche Knopf. See the correspondence between Marguerite and Bassani during 1956 and 1957 in Valli, *La rivista* Botteghe Oscure, 98–100.
22 Tortora, ed., *Sará un bellissimo numero*, 154–5.
23 Walter, *Milking the Moon*, 186–8. Eugene Walter was an entertaining – but not always truthful or accurate – narrator, and readers of his memoir will do well to seek corroboration for his versions of events.
24 In the event that Marguerite wished to invite someone to lunch for whom she had no current details, Walter was dispatched to the relevant embassy in Rome to try to track the person down.
25 Marguerite had a high opinion of Walters's aesthetic sense: "Dearest Eugene, You really are a treasure ... I find the new cover *beautiful* and everyone does who has seen it." HRC, Eugene Walter Collection: "Letters to EW 1956," Marguerite to Eugene, item 28.
26 FCC, Marguerite to Eugene, n.d., but headed "Friday, Ninfa" and very likely from the summer of 1956, since the specific travel instructions suggest that this was Eugene's first journey to Ninfa.
27 Walter, *Milking the Moon*, 189–91.
28 Interviews with Esme Howard, Benedetta Origo, and Lauro Marchetti, all February 2007. Walter's notes are held by the FLC.
29 *Botteghe Oscure*, Quaderno XX (Autumn 1957): 11–15.
30 HRC, Eugene Walter Collection: loose item, Marguerite to

Eugene (n.d., but headed "Friday"; internal evidence suggests summer 1957).

31 Marguerite's concern about money is at least proof that *Botteghe Oscure* was not funded by the CIA, unlike – as has been admitted in recent years – the *Paris Review*, *Encounter*, and other contemporary European publications.

32 Published in 1958 as *Commerce, Index: 1924–1932 and Botteghe Oscure, Index: 1948–1957*. Preface by Archibald MacLeish; introductions by Georges Limbour, Alan Pryce-Jones, and Guglielmo Petroni.

33 It also contains brief tributes to *Commerce* by Palewski and by Marguerite's old friend, the poet Giuseppe Ungaretti. Walter, *Milking the Moon*, 204, alleges that the ambassador's original aim was to honour *Botteghe Oscure* on the occasion of its tenth anniversary, but that lingering anti-German sentiment made *Commerce* the safer choice.

34 Rudolf Kassner to Marguerite, 29 January 1957, in Bohnenkamp and Levie, *Briefwechsel mit Deutschsprachigen autoren*, 128–9.

35 Interview with Lauro Marchetti, February 2008.

36 Biddle Papers: Allen Tate to Katherine, 14 August 1956.

37 Biddle Papers: Allen Tate to Katherine, 5 February 1957.

38 Biddle Papers: Allen Tate to Katherine, 2 April 1957.

39 Biddle Papers: Allen Tate to Katherine, 14 February 1958.

40 Walter, *Milking the Moon*, 207.

41 HRC, Eugene Walter Collection: loose item, Marguerite to Eugene, (n.d., but headed "Thursday").

42 Interview with Florence Hammond, May 2007.

43 Interview with the late Gore Vidal, February 2009.

44 Biddle Papers: Eliot to Katherine, 15 July 1959; Katherine to Eliot, 19 July 1959.

45 Biddle Papers: Eliot to Katherine, 4 August 1959.

46 American friends had purchased this house for Léger, and from 1957 onwards, he spent six months of the year there. Biddle Papers: note from René Char to Alexis Léger, transcribed by Francis Biddle, 30 September (n.y., but must be 1959).

47 Biddle Papers: Léger to Katherine, 10 August 1959.
48 Biddle Papers: Allen Tate to Katherine, 11 February 1960.
49 Interview with Benedetta Origo, February 2008. Biddle Papers: Marguerite to Katherine, 1 March 1960.
50 Garrett, ed., *Botteghe Oscure Reader*, xvi–xvii.
51 Ibid.

CHAPTER THIRTEEN

1 Biddle Papers: Hélène Sardeau Biddle to Katherine, 2 May 1960.
2 Biddle Papers: Allen Tate to Katherine, 21 November 1960.
3 There seem to have been no major obituaries for Roffredo, and appreciations of his music have only begun to appear relatively recently, mainly in the publications of the Caetani foundations. For a concise biography, see Benedetta Origo, "Roffredo Caetani" in *Dizionario biografico degli italiani*, vol. 16 (1973), 224–6, available online.
4 Biddle Papers: Allen Tate to Katherine, 5 May 1961.
5 Biddle Papers: Hubert Howard to Katherine, 22 November 1962 and Christmas 1962.
6 Biddle Papers: Kathleen Raine to Katherine, 27 September 1967. In the same letter, Raine commented that, on a later visit to Ninfa, Lelia had given her Marguerite's room, "and I wrote at her desk – I hope with her blessing on what I wrote there." This may have been the occasion on which Raine wrote the poem "Ninfa Revisited."
7 See Caetani, Sveva, *Recapitulation: A Journey*, edited by Thompson, Peart, and Butler. See also the website of the Caetani Cultural Centre, www.caetaniculturalcentre.org.ca, located in the house left by Sveva to the town of Vernon, British Columbia. *Recapitulation* can be viewed at the Alberta Arts Centre in Edmonton, Alberta.
8 On the death certificate issued by the Commune di Latina, dated 1 Feb. 1964, it is interesting to note that Marguerite's residence is given as Paris, probably because her apartment there was registered in her own name.

9 Biddle Papers: Lelia to Katherine, 20 December and 26 December 1963, 1 January 1964.
10 Biddle Papers: Lelia to Katherine, 13 February 1965.
11 FCC: Fondo Economico 2759/10.
12 Biddle Papers: Cornelia Chapin to Marguerite Young, 21 January 1964, copied to Katherine; the copy can be found in Box 3.1.22. Young's story was an excerpt from the novel that took her eighteen years to write, *Miss Mackintosh, My Darling* (1965), which has since become a cult classic.
13 Petroni, Guglielmo. "Incontri con Marguerite Caetani," in Fiorani, ed., *Ninfa, una città, un giardino*, 330.
14 The Italian writer Nina Ruffini had been a friend of both Marguerite and Iris Origo since the days of Il Ritrovo. Her translation, "Ritratto di Marguerite" appeared in the Italian review *Tempo Presente*, vol. 10, no. 3 (March 1965): 21–35. See also Umberto Morra's "La Principessa Caetani," in *La Nazione*, 23 January 1964.
15 See MacLeish, "Requiem for a Literary Haven," *Saturday Review*, 26 November 1960, and "Reader to Readers: A Parenthesis," in *Index: Botteghe Oscure, 1948–1960*.
16 Biddle Papers: Kathleen Raine to Katherine, 27 September 1967.
17 Garrett, ed., "Introduction," *Botteghe Oscure Reader*, xiv.
18 Skelmersdale, "The Gardens at Ninfa, Italy," *Journal of the Royal Horticultural Society*, 1969.
19 FCC: Theodore Roethke to Marguerite (n.d.); quoted in Caracciolo and Pietromarchi, *The Garden of Ninfa*, 84.
20 FCC: Robert Lowell to Marguerite (n.d.); quoted in Caracciolo and Pietromarchi, The *Garden of Ninfa*, 85.

SELECT BIBLIOGRAPHY

Acton, Harold. *Memoirs of an Aesthete*. London: Hamish Hamilton, 1984.

Amory, Cleveland. *The Last Resorts*. New York: Harper & Brothers, 1952.

Bachman, Robert. *An Illustrated History of Waterford, Connecticut*. Waterford: Bicentennial Committee, 2000.

Bagnold, Enid. *Autobiography*. London: Pimlico Paperback, 1985.

Bagot, Richard. *My Italian Year*. London: Mills and Boon, 1911.

Balsan, Consuelo Vanderbilt. *The Glitter and the Gold*. London: William Heinemann, 1953.

Barjansky, Catherine. *Portraits with Backgrounds*. London: The Macmillan Company, 1947.

Barolini, Helen. *Their Other Side: Six American Women and the Lure of Italy*. New York: Fordham University Press, 2006.

– "The Shadowy Lady of the Street of the Dark Shops." *Virginia Quarterly Review*, Spring 1998.

Beach, Sylvia. *Shakespeare and Company*. New York: Harcourt Brace, 1956.

Benocci, C. *Villa Tre Madonne: L'Ambasciata del Belgio presso la Santa Sede e l'eredità spirituale di Giulio III, papa toscano*. Rome: Artemide edizione, 2010.

Biddle, Francis. *In Brief Authority*. New York: Doubleday, 1962.

Biddle, George. *An American Artist's Story*. Boston: Little, Brown & Co.,1939.

Biddle, Katherine. Papers. Booth Family Center for Special Collections, Joseph Mark Lauinger Memorial Library, Georgetown University, Washington, DC.

Blanchot, Maurice, et al. *René Char's Poetry: Studies.* Translated by Robert Fitzgerald and David Paul. Rome: Botteghe Oscure, 1956.

Bohnenkamp, Klaus, and Sophie Levie. *Briefwechsel mit Deutschsprachigen autoren.* (correspondence between Marguerite Caetani and German authors). Rome: FCC, 2012.

Bolton, Isabel. *Under Gemini.* New York: Harcourt, Brace & World, 1966.

Bottrall, Margaret. "'From the Dark Shops': Review of *An Anthology of New Italian Writing*, edited by Marguerite Caetani." *Statesman and Nation*, 3 March 1951, 135–6.

Bradbury, Malcolm. *Dangerous Pilgrimages: Trans-Atlantic Mythologies and the Novel.* London: Penguin, 1993.

Brandon, Ruth. *The Dollar Princesses. Sagas of Upward Mobility, 1870–1914.* New York: Knopf, 1980.

British Parliamentary Papers (*Hansard*), 1 August 1944, vol. 402, c1157: "Italy (Enemy Vandalism)."

Brown, John. "Guiding the 'Commerce' of Ideas." *Books Abroad* 43 (1973): 307–11.

Caetani, Gelasio. *Col di Lana, Col di Sangue. Battaglia dell'ottobre 1915: Diario di un capitano austriaco, Lettere di un Ufficiale italiano.* Perugia: Unione Tipografico Cooperativa, 1920.

– *Lettere di Guerra di un Ufficiale del Genio, dal 2 agosto 1915 al 17 agosto 1918.* Perugia: Unione Tipografico Cooperativa, 1919.

– *Redemption of the Pontine Marshes: By Draining the Malarial Wastes around Rome, Italy Has Created a Promised Land.* Washington: National Geographical Society, 1934.

Caetani; Lelia and Camillo. *Piski, Poska e Piska.* In *Lelia Caetani nel centenario della nascita*, edited by Pier Giacomo Sottoriva. Quaderni di Ninfa/Documenti/2. Fondazione Roffredo Caetani, Sermoneta, 57–123.

Caetani, Leone. *In Selkirks.* Transcribed and translated by Danilo Aguzzi Barbagli, 1999.

– Papers. Fondazione Leone Caetani, Accademia Nazionale dei Lincei, Palazzo Corsini, Rome.

Caetani, Marguerite, ed. *An Anthology of New Italian Writers.* Rome: Botteghe Oscure, 1950.
– ed. *Botteghe Oscure.* Naples: Riccardo Ricciardi, 1948.
– ed. *Botteghe Oscure.* Rome: Istituto Grafico Tiberino, 1948–1960.
– ed. *Commerce. Cahiers trimestriels publiés par les soins de Paul Valéry, Léon-Paul Fargue, Valery Larbaud.* Paris: 1924–1932.
Caetani, Roffredo. *Hypatia: Azione lirica in tre atti.* With an introduction by Claudia Borsari. In Comitato Roffredo Caetani, ed. *Roffredo Caetani: La personalità, la cultura, la musica.* Latina: FRC, Quaderni di Ninfa/3, 2011, 107–95.
Caetani, Sveva. *Recapitulation: A Journey.* Edited by Heidi Thompson, Angela Gibbs Peart, and Dennis Butler. Vernon, British Columbia: Coldstream Press, 1995.
Caetani, Vittoria. *Things Past.* London: Hutchinson & Co., 1929.
– *Sparkle, Distant Worlds.* London and New York: Hutchinson, 1949.
Campitelli, Alberto. "*Le Residenze dei Caetani del XIII al XVIII secolo.*" In *Palazzo Caetani: Storia, arte e cultura*, edited by Luigi Fiorani, 69–91. Rome: FCC, 2007.
Capa, Cornell, ed., *Behind the Great Wall of China: Photographs from 1870 to the Present.* (With an introduction by Weston J. Naef.) New York: Metropolitan Museum Publications, 1972.
Caracciolo, Marella, and Giuppi Pietromarchi. *The Garden of Ninfa.* (With photographs by Marella Agnelli.) Turin: Umberto Allemandi, 1995.
Caroprese, Mariantonietta, ed. *Roffredo Caetani, un musicista aristocratico.* Atti della giornata di studio, Latina, 23 Novembre 2012. Rome: Libreria Musicale Italiana, 2014.
Cassano, Rita, ed. *Marguerite Caetai e gli artisti per il teatro: Edward Gordon Craig, Fortunato Depero, Alberto Savinio.* With essays by Paola Bonani, Giafranco Pedullà, and Claudia Terenzi. Prepared for the international conference *Il Novecento di Marguerite Caetani*, Rome, 24–25 October 2013. Rome: FCC, 2013.

Chapin, Cornelia Van Auken. Papers. Schlesinger Library, Radcliffe Institute, Harvard University, Cambridge, Massachusetts.

The Chapin Gathering: Proceedings from the Meeting of the Chapin Family in Springfield Mass., September 17, 1862. Springfield: n.p., 1862.

Chapin, Gilbert Warren. *The Chapin Book of Genealogical Data.* With Brief Biographical Sketches of the Descendants of Deacon Samuel Chapin. Chapin Family Association, 1924.

Char, René. *Hypnos Waking: Poems and Prose*. Translated by Jackson Mathews. New York: Random House, 1956.

Chernow, Ron. *The House of Morgan: An American Banking Dynasty and the Rise of Modern Finance*. New York: Atlantic Monthly Press, 2010.

Chester, Alfred. Papers. Harry Ransom Center for the Study of the Humanities, University of Texas at Austin.

Chia, Marella Caracciolo. *Una parentesi luminosa*. Milan: Adelphi edizioni, 2008. Translated by Howard Curtis as *The Light in Between*. London: Pushkin Press, 2010.

The City of Springfield, Chicopee, Chicopee Falls, and West Springfield Directory for 1881. Springfield: Springfield Publishing Company, 1881.

Cogeval, Guy, gen. ed. "Backward Glances," in *Edouard Vuillard: Catalogue of an Exhibition Organised by the National Gallery of Art, Washington, the Montreal Museum of Fine Arts, the Musée d'Orsay, Paris, and the Royal Academy of Arts, London, 2003–2004*. New Haven: Yale University Press, 2003.

Commerce. Cahiers trimestriels publiés par les soins de Paul Valéry, Léon-Paul Fargue, Valery Larbaud, nos. I–XXIX. Paris: Levé, 1924–32. Reprinted by Kraus Reprint, Liechtenstein, New York, 1969.

Craveri, Piero. "Onorato Caetani." *Dizionario biografico degli italiani*, vol. 16 (1973), 209–12.

Croce, Elena. *Due Città*. Milan: Adelphi Edizione, 1985.

– "Nasce una rivista a Roma liberata," *La Stampa*, 5 January 1975.

– "Un punto di ritrovo." *Il Mondo*, 21 January 1964, 7–8.

Croce, Elena. Papers. Instituto Italiano per gli Studi Storici, Biblioteca Benedetto Croce, Naples.

Croft, Robert. "A Modest Confutation." In Stephen Walsh, *The Second Exile: France and America, 1934–1971*, at www.naxos.com/news/default.asp.

Derry, Sam. *The Rome Escape Line*. London, Toronto, Wellington, Sydney: George Harrap & Co., 1960.

Easton, Laird M. *The Red Count: The Life and Times of Harry Kessler*. Oakland: University of California Press, 2006.

An Elgar Timeline, www.elgar.org/2time08/htm.

Ellis, Harriet. *Alcuni ricordi di Michelangelo Caetani duca di Sermoneta raccolti dalla sua vedova. 1804–1882*. Edited and with an introduction by Guiseppe Monsagrato. Rome: L'Erma di Bretschneider, 2005.

– *Letters of Harriet, Duchess of Sermoneta, to Miss Dennison: 1862–1905*. London: John Murray, 1912.

Ellis Island Passenger Records service, www.ellisislandrecords.org.

Engle, Paul, "Literary Light from the Roman Street of Dark Shops," *New York Times Book Review*, 2 June 1957, 245.

Ferris, Paul. *Dylan Thomas: The Biography*. Washington, DC: Counterpoint Press, 2000.

Fiorani, Caterina. "I Caetani e L'Accademia dei Lincei dal settecento al primo novecento." In *Palazzo Caetani, storia, arte e cultura*, edited by Luigi Fiorani, 331–45. Rome: FCC, 2007.

– "Roffredo Caetani, oltre il musicista." In Comitato Roffredo Caetani, *Roffredo Caetani: La personalitá, la cultura, la musica*. Quaderno di Ninfa 3, 55–68. Latina: FRC, 2011.

Fiorani, Luigi, ed. *Ninfa: Una città, un giardino*. Atti del Colloquio della Fondazione Camillo Caetani, Roma, Sermoneta, Ninfa, 7–9 Ottobre 1988. Rome: L'Erma di Bretscheider, 1990.

– ed. *Palazzo Caetani: Storia, arte e cultura*. Rome: FCC, 2007.

The First Century of the History of Springfield. Springfield. H.M. Burt, 1899.

Fitch, Noel Riley. *Sylvia Beach and the Lost Generation*. New York: W.W. Norton, 1983.

Flanner, Janet. *Paris Was Yesterday, 1925–1939*. Edited by Irving Drutman, with a foreword by James Campbell. London: Virago, 2003.

Floyd, Juanita Helm. *Women in the Life of Balzac*. New York: Henry Holt, 1921.

Fondazione Camillo Caetani. *Il salotto delle caricature: Acquarelli di Filippo Caetani, 1830–1860*. Rome: FCC, 1999.

– Fondi Economici 2010, 2103, 2116, 2215, 2741, 2759/10, 2909, 2943, 2954, 2966, 2968, 2969, 2977.

– *Archivio Leone Caetani all'Accademia dei Lincei*. Rome: L'Erma di Bretschneider, 2007.

– *Bollettino della Fondazione Camillo Caetani*. Vol. 1 (2013); Vol. 2 (2014). Rome: Edizioni di Storia e Letteratura, 2014.

Forni, Alberto. "Il Mito di Ninfa." In *Ninfa: Una città, un giardino*. Atti del Colloquio della Fondazione Camillo Caetani, Roma-Sermoneta-Ninfa, 7-9 ottobre 1988, edited by Luigi Fiorani, 313–25. Rome: L'Erma di Bretschneider, 1990.

Fowlie, Wallace. *Journal of Rehearsals: A Memoir*. Durham: Duke University Press, 1977.

Fry, Roger. *Letters of Roger Fry*. Edited and with an introduction by Denys Sutton. London: Chatto and Windus, 1972.

Garden, Mary. *Mary Garden's Story*. New York: Ayer Publishing Company, 1980.

Garfield, Simon. *Just My Type: A Book about Fonts*. London: Profile Books, 2010.

Garrett, George, ed. *Botteghe Oscure Reader*. Middletown Connecticut: Wesleyan University Press, 1974.

Gay, G.I., and H.H. Fisher. *Public Relations of the Commission for Relief in Belgium*. (2 vols.) Stanford: Stanford University Press, 1929.

Giannini, Giorgio. "La resistenza popolare a Roma durante l'occupazione nazista." In Centro Studi Difesa Civile, *La Resistenza Non Armata*, 113–19. Rome: Simos Editrice, 1995.

Gorgone, Giulia, and Cristina Cannelle, eds. *Il salotto delle caricature: Acquerelli di Filippo Caetani, 1830–1860*. Rome: Fondazione Camillo Caetani, 1999.

– *Il Costume è Di Rigore, 8 Febbraio 1875: Un Ballo a Palazzo*

Caetani. Fotografie romane di un appuntamento mondano. Rome: L'Erma di Bretschneider, 2002.

Gotham Book Mart Papers. Correspondence between Frances Steloff and Marguerite Caetani concerning *Botteghe Oscure*. Harry Ransom Center for the Study of the Humanities, University of Texas at Austin.

Greilsamer, Laurent. *L'éclair au front: La vie de René Char*. Paris: Fayard, 2004.

Grenier, Giovanella Caetani. *The Last Caetani*. Rome: privately printed, 1965.

Groom, Gloria. *Edouard Vuillard, Painter-Decorator: Patrons and Projects, 1892–1912*. New York: Yale University Press, 1994.

Hare, Augustus. *The Story of My Life*. London: George Allen, 1900.

Homberger, Eric. *Mrs Astor's New York: Money and Power in the Gilded Age*. New York: Yale University Press, 2004.

Howard, Esme. *Virtues and Vanities: Family Chronicles*. Bodmin and King's Lynn: MPG Books Group, 2013.

Jackson, W.G.F. *The Battle for Rome*. London: B.T. Batsford, 1969.

Jones, Judith. *The Tenth Muse: My Life in Food*. New York, Alfred Knopf & Co., 2007.

Kellner, Bruce. "'Refined Racism': White Patronage in the Harlem Renaissance." In *The Harlem Renaissance*, edited by Harold Bloom, 53–66. New York: Chelsea House Publishers, 2004.

Kessler, Harry. *Journey to the Abyss: The Diaries of Count Harry Kessler, 1880–1918*. Edited, translated, and introduced by Laird M. Easton. New York: Alfred Knopf & Co., 2011.

– *The Diaries of a Cosmopolitan, 1919–1937*. Translated and edited by Charles Kercher and introduced by Ian Buruma. London: Weidenfeld & Nicholson, 2000.

Kirkland, Edward Chase. *Men, Cities, and Transportation: A Study in New England History, 1820–1943*. Cambridge: Harvard University Press, 1948.

Kolocotroni, Vassiliki, Jane Goldman, and Olga Taxidou, eds. *Modernism: An Anthology of Sources and Documents*. Edinburgh: Edinburgh University Press, 1998.

Larbaud, Valery. Fonds V. Larbaud, Bibliothèque Municipal de Vichy, Vichy, France.

Laughlin, James. Interviewed by Richard Ziegfield for "The Art of Publishing, Part 1." *Paris Review*, no. 89 (Fall 1983).

Lehrman, Paul D. "Blast from the Past," www.wired.com/wired/archive/7.11/ballet.

Levie, Sophie. *La rivista* Commerce *e il ruolo di Marguerite Caetani nella letteratura europea, 1924–1932*. Rome: FCC, 1985.

– *Commerce, 1924–1932: Une revue internationale moderniste*. Rome: FCC, 1989.

– "Marguerite Caetani: Una mecenate americana in Europa." In *La rivista* Commerce *e Marguerite Caetani*. Rome: Edizioni di Storia e Letteratura, 2012.

Lewis, R.W.B. *Edith Wharton: A Biography*. New York: Fromm International, 1975.

Limbour, Georges. "Ode à l'Indice." Introduction to *Commerce Index: 1924–1932*, in *Commerce Index: 1924–1932 and Botteghe Oscure Index: 1948–1957*. Rome: Botteghe Oscure, 1958, 11–14.

McAllister, Ward. *Society as I Have Found It*. New York: Cassell and Co., 1890.

MacLeish, Archibald, "Reader to Reader: A Parenthesis." Preface to *Commerce Index: 1924–1932 and Botteghe Oscure Index: 1948–1957*. Rome: Botteghe Oscure, 1958, 7–10.

Muir, Edwin. "'The Italian Spirit.' Review of *An Anthology of New Italian Writers*, edited by Marguerite Caetani." *The Observer*, 4 February 1951, 100.

Museo Storico della Liberazione, Roma. Archivo Centrale dello Stato. "Gli Ebrei a Roma, 1938–1944." An exhibition and audiovisual presentation based on interviews made by the survivors of the Shoah Visual History Foundation, Los Angeles.

Nazzaro, Pellegrino. *Fascist and Anti-Fascist Propaganda in America: The Dispatches of Italian Ambassador Gelasio Caetani*. Amherst: Cambria Press, 2009.

O'Connor, Gary. *The Pursuit of Perfection: A Life of Maggie Teyte*. London: Victor Gollanz, 1979.

O'Flaherty, (Mons.) Hugh. www.hughoflaherty.com/index.cfm/page/cast.

Op de Coul, Paul. "Roffredo Caetani: L'evoluzione di un compositore tra ottocento e Novecento." In *Palazzo Caetani: Storia, arte e cultura*, edited by Luigi Fiorani, 407–16. Rome: Libreria dello Stato, 2007.

– "Roffredo Caetani compositore: La formazione, le opera, il catalogo cronologico." In Pier Giacomo Sottoriva, ed., *Roffredo Caetani: La personalità, la cultura, la musica*, 19–41. Quaderno di Ninfa 3. Sermoneta: Fondazione Roffredo Caetani, 2011.

Origo, Benedetta. "Roffredo Caetani." In *Dizionario biografico degli italiani*, vol. 16 (1973), 224–6.

Origo, Iris. "Portrait of Marguerite." *Atlantic Monthly* (February 1965): 81–8.

Osborne, D'Arcy. "Diary of Sir D'Arcy Osborne, British Ambassador to the Holy See." In Harold Tittmann Papers, Georgetown University Library Special Collections Research Center.

Osgood Mason, Charlotte. "The Passing of a Prophet." *The North American Review*, August 16, 1907: 869–79.

Osgood Mason, Rufus. *Telepathy and the Subliminal Self: An account of recent investigations regarding hypnotism, automatism, dreams, phantasms, and related phenomena*. New York: Henry Holt and Co., 1897.

– *Hypnotism and Suggestion in Therapeutics, Education, and Reform*. New York: Henry Holt and Co., 1901.

Paget, Walburga. *The Linings of Life*. London: Hurst & Blackett, 1928.

Painter, George. *Marcel Proust: A Biography*. New York: Random House, 1989.

Peele, Robert. *Gelasio Caetani: A Biographical Memoir*. New York: privately printed, 1936.

Petroni, Guglielmo. "La Coda di Due Comete." Introduction to a list of books and pamphlets published by the review *Botteghe Oscure* in *Commerce Index: 1924–1932 and Botteghe Oscure Index: 1948–1957*, 119–21. Rome: Botteghe Oscure, 1958.

Pietromarchi, Giuppi. "The Caetanis' Gardening Roots." In Caracciolo and Pietromarchi, *The Garden of Ninfa*, 103–26. Turin: Umberto Allemandi, 1995.

Proust, Marcel. *Letters of Marcel Proust to Antoine Bibesco*. Translated by Gerard Hopkins. London: Thames and Hudson, 1953.

Quest-Ritson, Charles. *Ninfa: The Most Romantic Garden in the World*. London: Frances Lincoln Publishers, 2009.

Pryce-Jones, Alan. "Twentieth-Century Writing." An introduction to *Botteghe Oscure Index: 1948–1957* in *Commerce Index: 1924–1932 and Botteghe Oscure Index: 1948–1957*, 33–7. Rome: Botteghe Oscure, 1958.

Rampersad, Arnold. *The Life of Langston Hughes*. Vol. 1: 1902–1941. New York: Oxford University Press, 1986.

Risset, Jacqueline, gen. ed. *La rivista* Botteghe Oscure *e Marguerite Caetani: La corrispondenza con gli autori stranieri, 1948–1960*. (Various titles.) Rome: L'Erma di Bretschneider.

Saint-John Perse (pseudonym of Alexis Saint-Léger Léger). *Anabasis*. Translated by T.S. Eliot. London: Faber and Faber, 1930.

Salvagni, Lorenzo. "The Caetani-Mathews Papers: Introducing René Char to the American Readership." <<altrelettere>>, 28.5.2014, DOI: 10.5903/al_uzh-20.

Santone, Laura, and Paolo Tamassia, eds. I. Sezione francese: *La rivista* Botteghe Oscure *e Marguerite Caetani: La corrispondenza con gli autori stranieri, 1948–1960*, gen. ed. Jacqueline Risset. Rome: L'Erma di Bretschneider, 2007.

Skelmersdale, Lionel. "The Gardens at Ninfa, Italy," *Journal of the Royal Horticultural Society*, 1969.

Smith, Arthur H. *China in Convulsion*. 2 vols. New York, Chicago: H. Revel, 1901.

Smith, Shirley Ann. *Imperial Designs: Italians in China, 1900–1947*. Lanham, MD: Rowman & Littlefield, 2012.

Snowden, Frank M. *The Conquest of Malaria: Italy, 1900–1962*. New Haven: Yale University Press, 2005.

Soros, Susan Weber, and Stephanie Walker, eds., *Castellani and Italian*

Archaeological Jewellery. New York: Bard Graduate Center for Decorative Arts, Design History, Material Culture, 2004.

Sottoriva, PierGiacomo. *Cronache da due fronti*. Latina: Editrice Il Gabbiano, 2004.

– *Gelasio Caetani (1877–1934): Il Realismo dell'Utopia*. Appunti per una biografia. Rome: Palombi Editori, 2014.

– ed. *Lelia Caetani nel centenario de la nascita*. Quaderni di Ninfa/ Documenti 2. Sermoneta: Fondazione Roffredo Caetani, 2013.

Tetro, Francesco. "Il Riccordo di Livio Caetani (1873–1915), terzogenito di Onorato VII e Ada Caetani." *Il Tempo*, 14 September 2007.

Tittmann, Harold. Papers. Georgetown University Library Special Collections Research Center.

Tompkins, Peter, *A Spy in Rome*. New York: Simon & Schuster, 1962.

Tortora, Massimilliano, ed. *Giorgio Bassani-Marguerite Caetani: "Sarà un bellissimo numero." Carteggio 1948-1959*. Rome: FCC, 2011.

Toscano, Bruno. "René e Marguerite." In *I pensieri dell'instante: Scritti per Jacqueline Risset*, 511–21. Rome: Editori Internazionale Reuniti, 2012.

Ungaretti, Giuseppe. "Introduction." In *Hommage à Commerce: Lettres et arts à Paris, 1920–1935*, 14–16. Rome: Botteghe Oscure, 1958.

– "La Rivista 'Commerce.'" In *Vita d'un uomo: Saggi e interventi*. Milan: Mondadori, 1974.

– *Lettere a Marguerite Caetani*. Sophie Levie e Massimilliano Tortora, eds. Rome: Edizioni di Storia e Letteratura, 2012. The Letters to Marguerite!

Valli, Stefania, ed. *La rivista* Botteghe Oscure *e Marguerite Caetani: La corrispondenza con gli autori italiani, 1948–1960*. (Unnumbered volume in series edited by Jacquline Risset.) Rome: L'Erma di Bretschneider, 1999.

Vickers, Hugo. *Gladys, Duchess of Marlborough*. London: Weidenfeld and Nicholson, 1979.

Walker, Alan. *Franz Liszt: The Final Years*. Ithaca: Cornell University Press, 1996.

Walker, Steven. *Hide and Seek. A Dramatic True Story of Rivalry, Survival, and Forgiveness During WWII*. London and New York: Collins, 2011.

Wharton, Edith. *A Backward Glance Over Travelled Roads*. New York and London: D. Appleton Century Company, 1934.

Walter, Eugene. *Literary and Photographic Collection*. Harry Ransom Research Center for the Study of the Humanities, University of Texas at Austin.

Walter, Eugene. *Milking the Moon: A Southerner's Story of Life on This Planet, as Told to Katherine Clark*. Foreword by George Plimpton. New York: Crown Publishers, 2001. (Now out of print, but available as an ebook from Untreed Reads at www.store.untreedreads.com.)

Weaver, William F. "The Art of Translation No. 3" (interview by Willard Spiegelman). *The Paris Review*, no. 161 (Spring 2002).

Weaver, William F. *Open City: Seven Writers in Postwar Rome – Ignazio Silone, Giorgio Bassani, Alberto Moravia, Elsa Morante, Natalia Ginzburg, Carlo Levi, Carlo Emiliano Gadda*. Hanover, NH: Zoland Books, 1999.

Whitaker, John T. *We Cannot Escape History*. New York: Macmillan, 1943.

IMAGE CREDITS

Every effort has been made to identify, credit, and obtain publication rights from copyright holders of illustrations in this book. Notice of any errors or omissions in this regard will be gratefully received and corrections will be made in any subsequent editions.

Images courtesy of:

Fitzwilliam Museum, Cambridge	Front cover, Édouard Vuillard's *Marguerite Chapin in Her Apartment with Her Dog*, 1910
Imperial War Museum, London	10.3
Vernon Museum, Vernon, BC	6.4
Fondazione Camillo Caetani	3.3, 4.1, 4.2, 4.3, 4.4, 4.6, 4.7, 5.1, 5.3, 5.4, 6.1, 7.1*, 7.2*, 7.3, 7.4, 7.5, 7.6, 8.1, 8.2, 8.4, 8.6, 9.1, 9.3, 9.8, 10.6, 11.2.a, 11.3.b, 11.5.b, 11.7.a, 11.7.b, 11.9, 12.1, 12.2, 12.3, 12.5, 12.6, 12.7, 12.8.a, 12.8.b, 12.8.c, 12.8.d, 13.1, 13.9

Fondazione Roffredo Caetani	3.4, 8.3, 8.5, 11.1.a, 11.2.b, 11.4.a, 11.4.b, 11.4.c, 11.5.a, 13.8
Stephen G. Biddle	1.4, 2.2, 3.2, 6.3, 9.4, 9.6, 9.7, 9.9, 10.2, 11.8, 13.5
Giovanella Caetani Diaries, 1965	5.2
The Chapin family	1.1, 1.2, 1.3, 1.5, 2.1, 2.3, 6.2
E. Fisher, *Cassino to the Alps*	10.1
Howard Family Archives	11.6, 12.4, 13.7.a, 13.7.b
Charles Quest-Ritson	4.5, 13.6**
Pier Giacomo Sottoriva	10.5
Heidi Thompson	13.4
James Carbone	11.1.b
Anne Fraser	9.5, 11.3.a
Edmund Howard	9.2, 10.4, 13.2, 13.3
Opera Magazine	3.1

Notes:

*Photographs by Lino Ricci

**Original photograph by Lelia's cousin, Lionel, Lord Skelmersdale, 1968

INDEX

abstraction, 290
Abyssinia, 95, 212
Accademia Nazionale dei Lincei, 78, 94, 151, 212–13, 356n11
Adamovich, Georgii, 190
Adams, Donald, 374n42
African art, 57
Agee, James, 268
Agro Pontino, 202, 232, 236, 330. *See also* Pontine Marshes
Aitken, Conrad, 251, 315, 331
Albania, 223, 225, 228, 316
Aldington, Richard, 186
Aldobrandini family, 172
Allied Control Commission, 238–9
Allied forces: American Fifth Army, 233–5, 237–8; British Eighth Army, 237–8
Amis de l'Art Contemporain, Les, 203–5
Amnesty International, 314
Anabase, 188–90 (poem and translations), 268, 333. *See also* Léger, Alexis Saint-Léger
Anatolio of Gaeta, 71
Andrews, Catherine (Van Auken, née Garrison), 24, 29, 337n1
Andrews, George Pierce, 29
Anglo-Saxon epics, 36
Antheil, George, 176–7, 361n41
Anthology of New Italian Writers, An, 271–3, 279, 286
Antinori, Cora, 136. *See also* Caetani, Cora
Antinori, Count Piero, 136
Apollinaire, Guillaume, 133
"Appeasement," 1938: German annexation of Austria, 221; Munich conference, 222
Aragon, Louis, 184–5
Arethusa (review), 286
Aristotle, 36
Artaud, Antonin, 185, 286
art nouveau, 44
Astor, Caroline (née Schermerhorn), 17, 22, 40
Astor, John Jacob, 17
Auden, W.H., 251
Audinet, Catherine, 15, 154

Bacchelli, Riccardo, 186
Bachmann, Ingeborg, 292, 332
Badoglio, Marshal Pietro, 231
Balla, Giacomo, 168
Ballet Mécanique, 176–8
Ballets Russes, 5, 97, 118
Balthus (Balthasar Klossowski), 162, 281, 358n8
Balzac, Honoré de, 74–5, 346n9
Banneville, Calvados (Normandy), 133, 144, 151, 184, 354n20
Barber, Samuel, 230
Barilli, Bruno, 186
Barjansky, Alexandre, 208
Barjansky, Catherine, 208–9
Barker, George, 268
Barnard, Tristan, 59, 64
Barney, Natalie Clifford, 60, 284
Bassani, Giorgio, 246–51, 268, 270, 272, 274, 276, 285, 293 (12.2), 294–5, 306, 309, 325, 330–1, 333, 378n21; "Congedo," 311–13; *The Garden of the Finzi-Continis*, 316, 318; *The Leopard*, 303–5
Bassiano (hill town), 70–1, 114, 212. For Prince and Princess di Bassiano, *see* Caetani, Roffredo *and* Caetani, Marguerite

Bataille, Georges, 268, 281
Bayreuth, 90, 96, 299
Beach, Sylvia, 149, 154, 158, 176, 216
Bell, Clive, 364n24
Bellaigue, Camille, 48
Benjamin, Walter, 189
Bennett, James Gordon, 9
Benzoni, Giuliana, 239, 260
Berenson, Bernard, 98, 127–8, 154, 229, 246, 260, 373n31
Berenson, Mary, 98, 127–8, 154
Bergson, Henri, 50
Berlioz, Hector, 49
Bernhardt, Sarah, 49
Bernheim, Gaston, 57, 64
Bernheim, Joss, 57, 64
Bernheim Jeune, 57
Bernstein, Henri, 55–7, 62, 65, 343n26, 343n27, 343n29
Berry, Walter, 154
Bertolucci, Attilio, 249, 332
Biarritz, 151–2
Bibesco, Prince Antoine, 56–8, 60–2, 66–8, 97, 340n5, 343–4n30, 344n37
Bibesco, Prince Emmanuel, 56–8, 62, 340n5, 343–4n30, 344n37
Bibesco, Princess Hélène, 56
Biddle, Francis, 128, 168, 193, 218, 221, 229, 235 (10.2), 265, 271 (11.8) 310, 315, 320–1, 321 (13.5), 373n30; Camillo's death, 367–8n18; visits Ninfa during Nuremburg trials, 262
Biddle, Garrison, 168, 193, 342n23
Biddle, George, 262, 315
Biddle, Katherine (née Chapin), 168, 193, 216, 218, 221, 229–30, 238–40, 244, 252, 255, 262, 265, 270–1, 271 (11.8), 289–90, 310–11, 315, 320–1, 321 (13.5), 324, 342n22, 342–3n23, 374–5n3, 372n19. *See also* Chapin, Katherine Garrison
Biddle, Randolph, 168, 221
Binford, Lawrence, 204
Blake, William, 162, 188
Blanche, Jacques-Émile, 59
Bliss, Mildred, 211–12
Bliss, Robert Woods, 211–12
Blixen, Baroness Karen (Isak Dinesen), 296–7, 300
Boas, Franz, 54, 128
Boccioni, Umberto, 353n7
Boethius, Anicius Manlius Severinus, 229, 368n19
Bogan, Louise, 374n42, 376n57
Boldoni, Giovanni, 117
Böll, Heinrich, 292, 300
Bolshevism, 135, 137, 174
Bonnard, Pierre, 56–8, 62–3, 109, 204, 250
Bonnefoy, Yves, 268
Bootle-Wilbraham, Edward William (3rd Earl of Lathom, 4th Baron Skelmersdale), 112
Bootle-Wilbraham, Emily, 97, 101, 112. *See also* Lindsay, Emily
Bootle-Wilbraham, Evelyn, 111
Bootle-Wilbraham, (Major) Lionel, 111–12
Bootle-Wilbraham family, 79–80, 265; and Lathom Park, 80, 112; and Rode Hall, 79–80, 112
Boston and Albany Railroad Company, 8–10
Botteghe Oscure, 3, 4, 247–9, 251-2, 261, 266–77, 267 (11.7.a and b), 268–76, 279–81, 284–9, 291–4, 299–301, 305–6, 308–9, 311–16, 323–4, 331–3, 374n42, 375nn46–7; *Anthology*, 271–3; authors, 275–84; cash flow, 300–1; design and production, Quaderno I, 248; end and legacy, 311–16; German and Spanish sections, 292; index to, 301; *The Leopard*, 305; MC's quarrel with Paulhan, 268–9 (*see also* Char, René); MC cited as editor-in-chief, 269; office, 293–4; and the *Paris Review*, 273–6, 281–2; payment of authors, 276, 279; production, 285 (*see also* Walter, Eugene); Quadernos II and III, 251–2; reception, 249; and René Char, 286–9, 291; reviews, statistics, 300; tenth anniversary, 300–1; title, 247; tributes, 331–2; US market, 288–9
Botteghe Oscure Reader, The, 324–5
Bottrall, Margaret, 272
Bottrall, Ronald, 272
Bourne, Francis, Cardinal Archbishop of Westminster, 111, 351n23
Boxer Rebellion, 88, 112, 347–8n25
Bracco, Federico, 275, 293, 295
Brahms, Johannes, 91, 299
Braque, Georges, 57, 168
Brecht, Bertholt, 266
Breton, André, 164, 168, 185, 286
Broder, Luiș, 331–2
Broughton, James, 284

Browne, Sir Thomas, 185–6
Browning, Robert, 36
Büchner, Georg, 164, 186, 197–8

Cadwalader, Wickersham, and Taft, 35, 100, 103, 106
Caetani, Ada, 14th Duchess of Sermoneta (née Bootle-Wilbraham), 79–85, 89, 93, 96–7, 101–5, 107–12, 114–16, 119–21, 124–5, 130–1, 133–4, 136, 138, 150–2, 172, 175, 179–81, 192–5, 198–200, 209–10, 213, 263, 365n31; character, 79–82, 102–3; children, 80–1, 83–4, 84 (4.3); death and influence, 209–10; and gardening, 80–1, 85, 114–16; marriage, 80–3,108; Ninfa, 96; social attitudes, 104–5, 121; stud farm, 82, 114
Caetani, Benedetto (Pope Boniface VIII), 71, 75, 83, 345n2
Caetani, Calixta, 13th Duchess of Sermoneta (née Rzewuska), 75–6, 120, 346n9
Caetani, Camillo, 124–5, 127, 136–7, 144, 147, 159, 164, 168, 171–2, 175, 178, 181, 184 (8.6), 196, 199–200, 210–1, 218–19, 219 (9.8), 221, 223–4, 225–8, 232, 239, 256, 260, 287, 290, 316, 367nn17–18, 373n30; death and effect on family, 225–8; enlists, 223–4; visits the US, 218–19
Caetani, Cora (née Antinori), 137–9, 176, 224, 238, 263
Caetani, Filippo ("Don Pippo"), 73, 199, 346n9
Caetani, Francesco, 11th Duke of Sermoneta, 73
Caetani, Gelasio, 70, 81–2, 85–91, 87 (4.6), 93, 95, 110, 115–16, 116 (5.3), 119–23, 125–6, 131, 133, 135–7, 150, 152, 159, 173–4, 176, 181, 193–4, 198–9, 207–14, 224, 227, 255, 263, 291, 316; 85 ambassador to US, 152; Col di Lana, 125–6, 126 (6.1); death and tributes, 210–13; engineering, 89; enters politics, 137–8; genealogy, 89, 95–6, 123, 201–2; health, takes up sculpture, 163 (9.1), 193–4; made a senator, 208; marshland drainage, 202; and Ninfa, 85, 95–6, 123, 134, 150, 175, 200–1, 201(9.2), 214; returns to Italy, honours, 174; travels and work in US, 95–6
Caetani, Giovanella, 80–1, 83, 86, 89, 91–2, 92 (4.7), 116 (5.3). *See also* Grenier, Giovanella
Caetani, Lelia, 119–22, 124, 127, 136–7, 144, 147, 159, 164, 168, 171–2, 178, 181, 184, 195–6, 199–200, 204–5, 207–8, 211, 216, 221–2, 226–7, 232–4, 239, 250, 254 (11.2.a, 11.2.b), 255, 257–8 (11.4.a, b, and c), 259, 263, 265 (11.6), 274, 289–90, 304, 317, 320–2, 325, 328 (13.7.a), 352n35 and n37; begins to paint, tutored by Vuillard, 172, 195; conservation at Ninfa and Sermoneta, 324–8; creates Caetani foundations, 290–1, 317; death, 328; and Lauro Marchetti, 304–5; meets and marries Hubert Howard, 263–5; painter and gardener, 250–8; US exhibitions, 289–90; visits US, 221–2
Caetani, Leone, 15th Duke of Sermoneta, 70, 80, 84 (4.3,4.4), 85–91, 93–4, 96–7, 99, 105–8, 110–2, 116 (5.3), 122–4, 131, 134–6, 138, 139 (6.4), 151, 159, 172, 179–81, 192–4, 199, 210–14, 317, 347nn22–3, 361n49; Fogliano, 361n49; Islamic studies, 86–8, 92–4, 114; marriage, 93; moves to Vernon, British Columbia, 138; new family, becomes 15th Duke, 134–5; political disillusion, loses Fogliano, 136; travels, 87–9; Wall Street Crash, 192–3
Caetani, Livio, 80, 84(4.3, 4.4), 88–91, 95, 102–3, 108, 110, 112, 116 (5.3), 122–3, 125, 131, 142, 347nn24–5
Caetani, Marguerite, Princess di Bassiano, later 17th Duchess of Sermoneta, 110–12, 117–19 (5.4), 120–4, 126–7, 130–1, 136–8, 141–3, 150–60, 164, 168, 170, 173, 176, 182–3, 185–8, 192–211, 213, 219, 221–32, 234–5, 239, 241, 243, 246–7, 250–2, 254–5, 258–63, 265–6, 269, 271, 276–84, 286–7, 292, 299, 301, 305–8, 311, 315–17, 320–1, 330–1. *See also* Chapin, Marguerite
– and art: 142–3, 168, 170–1,173, 191–2, 203–6
– biographical: and Ada, 210; becomes Duchess of Sermoneta, 243; birth of Camillo, 123–4; birth of Lelia, 117–8; Crash, 195; death, 320; death of

Camillo, 225–9; death of Roffredo, 316; as enemy alien, 229; health, 171; languages, 148; marriage 110–12; move to Rome, 199–201
– and *Commerce*, 154–92: aim to be international, 186–8; authors, 186; circulation, 182; cross-fertilization, 188–9; direction and funding, 157–8, 164, 182; old and new content, 185–6; payment of authors, 183; translation, 157, 182–3, 186–7. See also *Commerce*
– and *Botteghe Oscure* (*see also* entries for *Botteghe Oscure*; Bassani, Giorgio; Biddle, Katherine; Char, René; Paulhan, Jean): aim of, 244–6, 269; and Allen Tate, 271 (11.8), 286, 306–7, 316; *Anthology of New Italian Writers*, 270–3; beginnings, 244–7; *Botteghe Oscure Reader*, 324–5; decision to end, 311; and Dylan Thomas, 276–9; editorial restraint in, 266–9, 311–12; and Elena Croce Craveri, 246–50, 276; and Elsa Dallolio, 274–5, 293; empathy with writers, 275–80; and Eugene Walter, 282–5, 294–9, 302, 307–9; failing sight affects work on, 309–10; and Federico Bracco, 275, 293; and Guglielmo Petroni, 248–9, 279 (11.9), 306, 322, 371n9, 376n57; hospitality, 260–3; index to, 323–4; and last quaderno, 311–3 (12.8.a,b, c,d); and Luigi De Luca, 251, 285, 311; MC's name and title given as owner-editor, 269; name of, 247–8; new writing in US, 251–2; office, 294; production of, 273–6, 285–9, 293–4; and René Char, 268–9, 285–8 (12.1), 289, 291–2; reviews of, 299–300; and Riccardo Ricciardi, 248, 250–1; and statistics, 300, 313; tenth anniversary of, 299–301; translation in, 245–6, 266, 270, 292; tributes to, 322–5, 331–2; and T.S. Eliot, 244, 251, 310; and US market, 273
– and Ninfa: 150, 200–1, 214–16, 222, 232–7, 239–40, 250–63, 266, 275–6, 279, 281, 295–6, 301–2, 305
Caetani, Michelangelo, 86, 91, 102–3, 110, 112, 116 (5.3), 123, 125, 131, 135–8, 151–2, 172, 175, 192, 195, 198–9, 208–9, 211, 219, 227–8; courage and resilience, 208–9; diagnosis of tubercular illness, 152; marriage, 37
Caetani, Michelangelo, 13th Duke of Sermoneta, 73–7, 77 (4.1), 80, 86, 89, 123, 199, 227, 298 (12.5), 345–6n4, 346nn6–11
Caetani, Onorato, 1st Duke of Sermoneta, 72
Caetani, Onorato, 14th Duke of Sermoneta, 70, 76–8, 78 (4.2), 79–89, 91, 101–3, 106–8, 110–12, 116 (5.3), 116–17, 119, 121, 123–5, 130–1, 133, 193, 263, 346n11; caution in accepting Marguerite, then won over, 100–8; creates garden at Fogliano, 181–2; death, will, 130–1; lawsuit, 76–7; marriage and family, 79–85; Ninfa, 84–5; political life, 79–80
Caetani, Onorato ("Onoratino"), 16th Duke of Sermoneta, 93–5, 112, 116 (5.3), 124, 135, 152, 178–9, 179 (8.4), 194, 211, 213–14, 227, 243, 290, 348n32
Caetani, Roffredo, Prince of Bassiano, later 17th Duke of Sermoneta, 3, 4, 67 (3.4), 68–70, 72–3, 80, 84 (4.3, 4.4), 85, 89, 93, 96–9, 100–12, 114–15 (5.2), 116 (5.3), 117–24, 126–7, 130–3, 135–8, 141–2, 150–4, 159, 161–4, 170–3, 176, 177 (8.3), 178, 181, 191–2, 195–8, 208, 211, 213, 215, 219, 222–3, 225–7, 230, 243, 256–8, 265, 290, 297–9, 303–4, 309, 315–16, 322; becomes 17th Duke, 243; compositions performed, 90–6; Crash, financial worries, move to Rome, 191–8; death, 316, 380n3; death of Camillo, 225–8; Fondazione Camillo Caetani, 290–1; Fondazione Roffredo Caetani, 326; *Hypatia*, 97, 106, 116, 118, 133, 138, 149, 153, 159, 161–3, 169, 171–3, 304, 348nn26–7, 348n29, 349n37, 351n31, 360n38, 369n26, 372n23; influences on composition, 90–1; marriage, 110; meets Marguerite, 99; musical education, 89–91; specific contributions to Ninfa, 214–15, 252–7; Villa delle Tre Madonne, 150, 159, 175, 191, 198–9
Caetani, Sveva, 135, 138, 139 (6.4), 179–80, 180 (8.5), 181, 192, 213, 227, 317–20, 319 (13.4)
Caetani, Topazia, 139, 176, 227, 238, 263, 373n31
Caetani, Vittoria (née Colonna), 93–5,

107, 110, 112, 123–5, 135, 140–1, 152, 176, 192–3, 198–9, 213, 238, 263
Caetani chapel, Santa Pudenziana, Rome, 113, 225, 351n23
Caetani estates, 70–2, 81–5, 91, 114–15, 175, 191–2, 223, 238; Cisterna, 82–3, 92, 114, 131, 135, 199, 212, 223, 235 (10.3), 238–9, 263, 365n36; Fogliano, 81, 83, 89, 96, 114–15 (5.2), 116, 131, 133–5, 138, 361n49; Friends of Ninfa, 330; and Gelasio, 95–6, 115, 123, 131, 134, 150, 174–5, 200–1 (9.2), 202; and Giorgio Bassani, 316, 318 (13.3), 333; history, 83–5; and Lelia, 216, 234–5, 257–8, 325–8 (13.7.a); and Marguerite, 115, 214–15, 234–5, 258–63, 288 (12.1), 295–6 (12.3); microclimate, 214, 326–7; nightingales, 250, 263; Ninfa, 83–5 (4.5), 93, 95–6, 115, 123, 131, 134, 138, 150, 174–5, 199, 200–1 (9.2), 210–12, 222, 228, 230–2, 236–9, 252–3 (11.1.a, 11.1.b), 254 (11.2.a, 11.2.b), 255–63, 279, 296–7, 311, 327 (13.6), 329–30, 333; opening to visitors, 325–6, 330; Pantanello, 330; protection, 325–30; and Roffredo, 214–15, 256–7; Sermoneta, 70–3, 83, 85, 114–15, 123, 181, 199, 212, 228, 232–6, 236 (10.4), 239 (10.6), 243, 259, 325–30; Tor Tre Ponte, 223, 330–2, 331 (13.8); Visitors' Book, 260–1 (11.5.a), 262–3
Caetani family, 70–2, 75, 80–1, 83–6, 93–4, 114–15, 119, 139–41, 210–11, 262, 290–1
Caetani genealogy, 70, 110, 123, 175, 201–2, 291
Caetani mausoleum (Campo Verano cemetery, Rome, 131, 228–9, 316, 329
Caetani residences (Rome), 72–3; Palazzo Caetani, 73–4, 78, 80, 93–4, 109, 112–13, 116, 123–4, 130–2, 193, 195–6, 199, 208–10, 212, 228, 231–2, 238, 247, 264, 266, 269, 281, 290–1, 294, 296, 299, 311, 330–1, 372n9; Villa delle Tre Madonne, 150, 159, 175, 191–2, 195, 198–9
Caffi, Andrea, 178, 181, 196–7, 361n43
Cagli, Corrado, 204
Cahiers du Pleïade (review), 252. *See also* Paulhan, Jean
Calvino, Italo, 268, 300, 332
Campbell, Roy, 186
Campus Internazionale di Musica di Latina, 326
Camus, Albert, 268, 286
Cancogni, Manlio, 249
Capote, Truman, 268, 294
Cardinale, Claudia, 305
Carlos I (King of Portugal), 49
Carnegie, Andrew, 9
Carruth, Hayden, 251
Casati, Marchesa Luisa, 117
Castellane, Count Boni de, 163
Castellani, Fortunato Pio, 74, 346nn5–6
Cavour, Count Camillo, 75
Cecchi, Emilio, 186
Celan, Paul, 292
Cerasoli, Giulia de Cousandier, 89
Cézanne, Paul, 50, 56–7
Chapin, Abel Dexter, 11–12, 35, 336n9
Chapin, Adèle (née Le Bourgeois), 26, 39, 51, 110–12
Chapin, Alfred Clark, 11, 336nn7–8
Chapin, Chester William, 7–8, 8 (1.1), 9–11, 13, 20; and "The Puritan," 10; and railroads, 8–11, 336n6
Chapin, Chester William II, 11, 336n8
Chapin, Cornelia (née Van Auken), 24–30, 28 (2.1), 33–8, 42–3, 51–2 (3.2), 53, 117, 127–8, 130, 166, 337nn1–2, 338n7, 338n12, 358–9n14
Chapin, Cornelia Van Auken, 29–30, 34, 43, 51–2, 52 (3.2), 53–4, 166, 168, 171–2, 206 (9.4), 207, 216–17, 220 (9.9), 221, 226, 289–90, 322, 324, 342n22, 359n18, 364n25
Chapin, Dorcas, 11
Chapin, Henry Bainbridge, 18, 110, 289–90
Chapin, John, 168, 221
Chapin, Julia Clark, 12–14, 18, 26, 34, 38
Chapin, Julia Irene, 14
Chapin, Katherine Garrison, 29–30, 34, 43, 51–2, 52 (3.2), 53–4, 117, 127–9, 166, 342–3nn22–3. *See also* Biddle, Katherine
Chapin, Leila (née Burden), 168, 221
Chapin, Leila Marie (née Gibert), 12–15, 17, 35, 55, 119, 336nn10–11
Chapin, Lindley Hoffman, 12–13, 13 (1.3), 14, 18–21, 23–8, 28 (2.1), 33–5, 54, 336n10, 337nn16 and 2, 338n8, 339nn19–20

Chapin, Lindley Hoffman Paul, 29–30, 34, 53, 127–8, 129 (6.2), 168, 218, 339n22
Chapin, Marguerite Gibert, 3–6, 11, 14–15, 17–19, 19 (1.4), 20–31, 31 (2.2), 32–8, 41, 55, 58, 60 (3.3), 60–1, 63–5, 99–112; appearance, 37, 41, 55, 58, 60–1, 63–5, 104–5; birth, 3, 14; character, 4–5, 14, 23, 27–8, 31, 104–5, 108; childhood, 18–21, 25–30; debut, 38; education and reading, 30–2, 36, 44, 50, 105, 107; French language and culture, 14–15, 18–19, 39, 41, 43–4, 48; inheritance, 15, 17, 34–5, 42, 100; interest in gardening, 3–4, 63, 65, 214–16; interest in music, 36, 43–4, 46, 48, 51, 66, 105, 107–8; interest in painting, 56–8, 62–6; moves to Paris, 42–3; and religion, 15, 25, 27, 29, 34, 36, 54; travels, 18, 39, 43, 54–5, 60–1, 339–40n27. *See also* Caetani, Marguerite
Chapin, Paul, 168, 221, 227, 281, 367n17, 376n1
Chapin, Robert Williams, 12, 20, 26, 35, 39, 51, 110–12
Chapin, Samuel, 6–7, 10 (1.2), 13, 335n3; "The Puritan," 10
Chapin, Schuyler, 168, 219, 221, 289–90, 335n2, 367n18
Chapin, Susan (née Revere), 289–90
Chapin family, 6–7, 11–13, 18, 20–1, 23, 36, 263, 335n3, 336nn6–9
Chapin Library of Rare Books, Williams College, 11
Char, René, 252, 268–9, 281, 288 (12.1), 292, 306–7, 310, 331–33, 377n17; *Feuillets d'Hypnos*, 286–7, 291; *Hypnos Waking*, 289; *Lettera Amorosa*, 291; *Une Serenité Crispée*, 287–8
Chastel, Roger, 204
Chester, Alfred, 333, 377n11; "Silence in Heaven," "Rapunzel, Rapunzel," and "Head of a Sad Angel," 284–5.
Christie, Agatha, 261
Ciano, Count Galeazzo, 224
Clancy, Kate, 19
Clark, Edith, 26, 41–2
Clark, George, 26
Clark, Julia, 26, 41–2
Clark, Gen. Mark, 235
Claudel, Paul, 59–60, 164, 185, 197
Clerici, Gino, 135, 138
Codex Caetani (of Dante Alighieri's *La Divina Commedia*), 298 (12.5), 372n24
Coindreau, Maurice-Edgar, 198
Col di Lana, 125–6, 353n11. *See also* Caetani, Gelasio
Cold War, 314
colonie di bambini, 239, 240 (10.6)
Colonna, Prince Marc'Antonio, 93
Colonna, Vittoria. *See* Caetani, Vittoria
Colonna family, 71–2
Commerce, 155–7, 159–64, 166, 170–1, 173, 185–9, 197–8, 244, 269, 301–3, 323, 332, 355n8, 356nn17–18, 357n23; authors, 184–6; beginning and name, 155–6; eclecticism, 170–1; ends, 198; ethos, 157; finance, 157–8; financial burden, 197–8; first cahiers, 159; and modernism, 188–9; international scope, 185; and translation, 186–7
Commission for Relief in Belgium, 123–4, 353n6
Connaught, Duke of, 49
Copeland, Aaron, 177
Corbett, Gail Sherman, 168
Corrigan, Michael (Roman Catholic Archbishop of New York), 26, 29, 34, 338n7
Courtin, Bernard, 268
Craig, Edward Gordon, 143 (7.1)
Cranach Press, 143 (7.1), 189, 344n40. *See also* Kessler, Count Harry
Craveri, Elena (née Croce), 240–1, 248–50, 260, 371n1; *The Leopard*, 305; title of *Botteghe Oscure*, 247–8
Craveri, Piero, 353n15, 372n24
Craveri, Raimondo, 246, 260
Crawford, Earls of. *See* Lindsay, James
Criterion, The (review), 156, 185
Cubism, 57
Cummings, E.E., 149, 251, 299
Cutting, Lady Sybil, 128

Dadaism, 142
Dallolio, Elsa, 239–40, 274–5, 293
D'Annunzio, Gabriele, 65–6, 117, 133
Dante Alighieri, 71, 74, 77, 211–12, 228–9, 298, 319, 368n19; *La Divina Commedia* (*The Divine Comedy*), 74, 77, 256, 298 (12.5), 319
Davies, Ronald, 164

Dawes Plan, 192
Day-Lewis, Cecil, 251
Deacon, Gladys, 100
Debussy, Claude, 49, 56, 299
De Chirico, Giorgio, 168, 171, 173
Delacroix, Eugene, 299
De La Mare, Walter, 251
De La Tour, Georges, 286–7
De Luca, Luigi, 251, 274–5, 277, 285, 311, 372n17
De Reszke, Edouard, 46
De Reszke, Jean, 27, 47 (3.1), 117, 133, 221, 340nn3–4, 340–1n6; school and training, 43, 45–51
De Reszke, (Countess) Marie (née Goulaine), 46–7, 117, 133
De Sanctis, Cesare, 90
De Staël, Mme Anne Louise (née Necker), 155
Delon, Alain, 305
Deparo, Fortunato, 143
Derain, André, 154, 168, 171, 204
Despiau, Charles, 204
Dessí, Guiseppe, 268
Deutsch, Babette, 267
Devlin, Dennis, 286–7
Dhôtel, André, 268
Diaghilev, Sergei, 5, 97, 118
D'Indy, Vincent, 50
Dinesen, Isak. *See* Blixen, Baroness Karen
Divisionism, 142
Donne, John, 36
Donovan, William ("Wild Bill"), 231–2, 367n18
Dos Passos, John, 149
Dreyfus affair, 56
Dufy, Raoul, 204
Dukas, Paul, 50
Duke, James, 9
Dunoyer de Segonzac, André, 154, 157, 168, 171, 204
Du Pré, Jacqueline, 326
Durazzo, Count Francesco, 211
Durazzo, Livia (née Grenier), 211–12, 227, 365–6n37
Duse, Eleanora, 174

Eastman, Max, 128
Eberhart, Richard, 251, 270
Eckhart, Meister, 169, 185
Elgar, Sir Edward, 349n3
Eliot, T.S., 156, 164, 171, 177–8, 185–6, 198, 244, 251, 296–7, 297 (12.4), 333, 335n3, 379nn44–5; Camillo's death, 226; poems in *Commerce*, 356–7n19; translation of *Anabase*, 189; *The Waste Land*, 154
Eliot, Valerie, 296
Elizabethan poets, 36
Ellis, Harriet, 76, 346n11
Eluard, Paul, 286
Enaudi (publisher), 305
Enesco, Georges, 56
Engle, Paul, 299–300
"Eolia." *See* Waterford, Connecticut
Ephrussi, Charles, 343n27
Europa Nostra, 327

Fabiani, Ofelia, 134–6, 138–9 (6.4), 181, 192, 213, 317, 320
Fantin-Latour, Henri, 56
Fargue, Léon-Paul, 59, 149, 154–6, 158, 160–1, 163–4, 183
Farrar, Strauss (publisher and distributor), 273, 301
fascism, 122, 200, 203, 223–4, 242, 246–7, 355n9
Faulkner, William, 186, 284; and "A Rose for Emily," 198
Fauré, Gabriel, 50, 56, 299, 341n14
Fauves, 57
Fazzini, Pericle, 204
Fellini, Federico, 308
Feltrellini (publisher), 293
Feuillets d'Hypnos, 287, 291. *See also* Char, René
Ficino, Marsilio, 74, 256, 298 (12.5). See also *Codex Caetani*; Dante Alighieri
Filippini sisters, 231
First World War, 121, 132–3, 140–2, 188
Fitzgerald, F. Scott, 149
Fitzgerald, Robert, 291–2, 306–7
Flanner, Janet, 149, 154
Fondazione Camillo Caetani, 291, 331–3, multiple entries in Select Bibliography
Fondazione Leone Caetani, 151, 156, 356n11
Fondazione Roffredo Caetani, 326, 329–31 (13.8), multiple entries in Select Bibliography
Förster-Nietzsche, Elisabeth, 187
Fowlie, Wallace, 3, 4, 284
Francavilla, Marchesa Giovanna Maria Colonna, 112

France, Anatole, 56
Franco-Italian Exhibition, 206, 364n24
Frangipane family, 72
Freud, Sigmund, 187
Friends of Ninfa, 330
Fritsch, Hugo Gibert de, 32, 44, 51–2
Fritsch, (Chevalier) Hugo Otto de, 17, 32
Fritsch, Marie Joséphine de (née Gibert) ("Cousin Minnie"), 16–17, 32–3, 39, 44–5, 51–2, 59
Fry, Roger, 170–1
Fuentes, Carlos, 292
Fuller, Roy, 267
Futurism, 142

"Gaetani," 70
Gaetani dell'Aquila d'Aragona family, 71
Gallimard (publisher), 273, 288, 291
Gallimard, Gaston, 148, 288
Garampon, Georges, 198
García Lorca, Federico, 182
Garden, Mary, 340–1n6
Garrett, Alice Warder, 203–4, 364n20
Garrett, George, 324. See also *Botteghe Oscure Reader*
Garrett, John Work, 203, 364n20
Garrigue, Jean, 284
German culture, 91
German Occupation of Italy: in Rome, 229; reprisals, 231–3, 236–8 (10.5)
Gibert, Alice (née Reed), 21, 33, 51, 110, 338n12
Gibert, Annie (née Reed), 21, 32, 338–9nn17–18
Gibert, Frédéric Edouard (Frederick Edward), 12, 16–18, 21, 28–9, 33, 51, 110, 336–7n14
Gibert, Jean-Jacques (Dr James Thevigny), 16–17, 336–7n14
Gibert, Joseph, 18, 50
Gibert, Julia, 17
Gibert, Margaret (née MacLaren), 33, 110, 127
Gibert, Margaret (née Reynolds), 17–18, 21, 28, 32–3, 39, 44, 51, 53
Gibert, Nicholas, 15–18, 336nn12 and 14
Gibert, Nicholas Audinet, 12, 17–18, 21, 28–9, 32–3, 39, 44, 110, 127, 322, 337n19, 338–9nn17–18
Gibert, William Nicholas, 16–17
Gibert family, 15–18, 21–3, 28–9, 44, 51, 54–5, 336n13
Gide, André, 59, 148–9, 154, 185, 355n5
Gil Blas (newspaper), 109
Ginsberg, Allen, 296
Ginzburg, Natalia, 332
Giono, Jean, 185
Giordano, Umberto, 90, 173
Glennie, Arthur, 85 (4.5)
Gold, Herbert, 299
Gotham Book Mart, 273–87
Gould, Jay, 9
Gounod, Charles, 46, 56
Greffulhe, Elaine, 97
Greffulhe, Countess Elisabeth, 49–50, 56, 96–7, 118, 341nn12 and 14, 350n10
Gregorovius, Ferdinand, 74
Grenier, Baron Albéric, 93–4, 96, 115 (5.2), 133
Grenier, Eric, 93, 96, 115 (5.2), 116 (5.3), 133, 139
Grenier, Giovanella (née Caetani), 93–4, 101–6, 108, 110–12, 115–16, 123–5, 131, 133, 150–1, 194, 207, 211, 263, 316, 349n36, 369n26; photography, 96. *See also* Caetani, Giovanella
Grenier, Livia, 96, 116 (5.3), 152. *See also* Durazzo, Livia
Greystoke Castle, 264
Groethuysen, Bernard, 169, 170–1, 185–6, 189, 198, 244, 250, 359n19, 360n38
Guidi, Augusto, 249
Guimard, Hector, 44
Guïraldes, Ricardo, 183
Gunn, Thom, 283

Hackett, Dr Lewis, 255
Hahn, Reynaldo, 46, 50, 154, 299
Hall, Donald, 281
Hamburger, Michael, 268
Hamilton, Jamie, 273
Hamish Hamilton (publisher), 273
Hammond, Florence, 308–9
Hammond, Mason, 260, 308
Harcourt, Brace (publisher), 287
Hardy, Thomas, 186
Hare, Augustus, 76
Harkness, Edward, 51, 341n15, 341–2n16
Harlem Renaissance, 54, 342n22
Haussmann, Baron Georges-Eugène, 45

Hawthorne, Nathaniel, 36, 183, 186
Head, Henry, 221
Heap, Jane, 154
Heath-Stubbs, John, 267
Heifetz, Jascha, 289
Hemingway, Ernest, 149
Heraclitus, 155
Hernández, Mateo, 206 (9.4), 207, 216–17 (9.6, 9.7)
Herodotus, 178
Herrick, Robert, 183
Higham, David, 278–9
Hill, Pati, 284
Hilliard & Sons, 260
Hofmannsthal, Christiane von, 162–3
Hofmannsthal, Gertrude von, 164
Hofmannsthal, Hugo von, 11, 13, 162–5 (8.1), 176, 185–6, 189, 292, 299, 358nn9
Hölderlin, Friedrich, 186, 292
Hommage à Commerce: Lettres et Arts à Paris, 1920–1935 (exhibition), 301–4, 307 (12.6, 12.7), 379n33
Hoover, Herbert, 124, 364n20
Hotel Engadiner Kulm (Kulm Hotel), 101–3, 108
Howard, Adèle (née Le Bourgeois Alsop), 263
Howard, Cécile (née Geoffroy-Dechaume), 264–5
Howard, Edmund, 264–5
Howard, Esme, 265, 316
Howard, Sir Esme, 1st Baron Howard of Penrith, 263–5
Howard, Lady Isabella (née Guistiniani Bandini), 263, 265, 289
Howard, Henry, 263
Howard, Hubert, 263–5, 264 (11.6), 289–91, 304–5, 316, 321–2, 325–8, 329 (13.7.b); marriage, 264–6
Howard, John, 374n34
Hughes, Langston, 54, 342n22
Hugo, Victor, 50
Humes, Harold ("Doc"), 281
Hurston, Zora Neale, 54
Hypatia (philosopher), 97
Hypatia (opera). *See* Caetani, Roffredo: compositions performed
Hypnos Waking: Prose and Poems, 291–2. *See also* Char, René; Mathews, Jackson

Ibert, Jacques, 262
Impressionists, 57
influenza pandemic ("Spanish flu"), 132–3
Istituto Grafico Tiburino, 251
Italian Communist Party, 248
Italian embassy, Washington, DC, 174
Italy, 1914–22: Abyssinia, 95, 212; alliances, 1914–18, 121–2, battle of Caporetto, 132; colonial ambitions, 122, 124, 212; communists and anarchists, 150; effects of 1914–18 war on, 132; fascism, 122, 150; Libya, 124; Nationalist Party, 134, 136–7, 150, 152; reparations, 174; and Treaty of London, 122, 133
Italy, 1922–40: Bonifiche integrale scheme, 222; Fascist doctrine, 355n9; March on Rome, 152; and Benito Mussolini, 122, 137, 150, 152, 173, 196, 212–13, 228, 231, 246–7; National Fascist Party, 137, 150, 152, 191, 196; new towns, 222, 230, 232, 239; Pontine Marshes drainage scheme, 174–5; racial laws, 223; and reprisals against Leone Caetani, 212–13
Italy, 1940–45: declares war on the Allies, 224; declares war on the US, 229; military reversals, 231; "Pact of Steel," 224; removal of Mussolini, 231; sends troops to Albania and Libya, 224; surrenders to Allies, 231; war with Germany, 231
Ivanov, Georgii, 190

Jaccottet, Phillipe, 268
Jacob, Max, 164, 185
James, Henry, 299
Jammes, Francis, 185
Jarrell, Randall, 268, 299
Jones, Judith, 281, 376n1
Jouhandreau, Marcel, 185
Joyce, James, 154–5, 158, 164, 177, 183, 186, 357n23; *Ulysses*, 154–5, 158, 183, 187
J.P. Morgan and Company, 173–4
Jüll, Miss, 138, 213, 319

Kafka, Franz, 169, 186
Kandinsky, Wassily, 287
Kassner, Rudolf, 176, 183, 185–6, 198, 252, 292, 304, 332

Keats, John, 266
Kessler, Count Harry, 63–6, 105, 108–9, 143 (7.1), 176, 189, 202, 344–5n40. *See also* Cranach Press
Kierkegaard, Søren, 186
Kirkland, Edward Chase, 8–9, 11
Klossowska, Baladine, 162
Klossowski, Balthasar. *See* Balthus
Knight, Margaret, 76
Knopf, Blanche, 279, 378n21
Knox, Monsignor Ronald, 265
Kootenay Lake, 88
Kutune Shirka (Ainu epic), 292

Lancaster, Burt, 305
Larbaud, Valery, 59, 149, 154, 158, 164, 169–71, 185–6, 197, 302; contribution to *Commerce*, 182–3
La Scala (opera house), Milan, 173, 299
Latina (formerly Littoria), 222, 230, 232, 239, 296; and music, 326
Laughlin, James, 252, 270
Lazio, 326–7, 330
Lear, Edward, 85
Léger, Alexis Saint-Léger ("Saint-John Perse"), 60, 154–6, 158, 160, 163–4, 222, 252, 268, 310, 333, 372n20; *Anabase*, 188–90
Légion d'Honneur, 301–4 (12.7)
Lehmann, John, 251–2, 261, 271
Lemaître, Jules, 56
Leoncavallo, Ruggiero, 90
Leopard, The, 305
Leopardi, Giacomo, 185–6
Lepini mountains, 5, 83, 259 (11.4.a)
Levi, Carlo, 261, 268
Levi della Vida, Giorgio, 87
Libero, Libero di, 251
Libya, 212, 223
Limbour, Georges, 170, 185–6, 198, 252, 268
Lindbergh, Charles, 130
Lindsay, Emily (née Bootle-Wilbraham), Countess Crawford, 97, 101, 110–12, 176, 265, 347–8n25
Lindsay, James (26th Earl of Crawford), 97–8, 110–12, 176, 265
Liszt, Abbé Franz, 74, 89–90, 97, 199, 256, 346n7
Little Review, The, 154
Little Sisters of the Assumption, 338n8, 338n12
Locke, Alain, 54
Logue, Christopher, 333
London: Green Park, 110; 34 Kensington Square, 112; Lefevre Gallery, 258; Queen's chapel, St James's Palace, 109, 111; Redfern Gallery, 363n13; Ritz Hotel, 110; Royal Opera House, Covent Garden, 46, 299; Wertheim Gallery, 206
Longhi, Roberto, 246, 293
Lord and Hewlett, architects, 51
"Lost Generation, The," 149
Loti, Pierre, 56
Lovatelli, Ersilia (née Caetani), 76–9, 86, 112, 118, 152, 172
Lovatelli, Giacomo, 77
Lovatelli Caetani, Calixta, 77
Lovatelli Caetani, Filippo, 77, 172, 180 (8.5), 360n25
Lowell, Robert, 287, 299, 332
Lysy, Alberto, 326
Lyulph's Tower, 264, 290, 328 (13.7.b)

MacDiarmid, Hugh, 267
Maclean, Fitzroy, 261
MacLeish, Archibald, 149, 186, 252, 284, 296, 299–300, 313, 323–4, 333, 372n20
MacNiece, Louis, 267
Magaloff, Nikita, 262, 326
Maillol, Aristide, 56, 154, 204
malaria, 82, 114, 173, 210, 224, 252–5, 360n34, 364n19; effects of German reprisals, 236–7
Mallarmé, Stéphane, 36, 148
Malraux, André, 185
Mandelstam, Osip, 186
Marchetti, Lauro, 304–5, 327, 329, 339n24, 378n28
Marchetti, Sante, 304
March on Rome, 152
Margherita, Queen of Italy, 80
Mariano, Nicky, 260
Marie José (of Belgium), Princess of Piedmont, 205, 262
Markevitch, Igor, 262, 373n31
Martucci, Guiseppe, 90
Mascagni, Pietro, 90, 96
Massenet, Jules, 56
Massignon, Louis, 185
Masson, André, 168, 171, 204
Mathews, Jackson, 286–8, 292, 307, 333; *Hypnos Waking*, 291. *See also* Char, René

Matisse, Henri, 50
Matteoli, Raffaele, 373n29
Matthiessen, Peter, 281, 284
Mauron, Charles, 188
McAllister, Ward, 40, 340n29
McCullers, Carson, 284, 296
Mead, Frank, 128
Melville, Herman, 36
Ménard, René, 268, 291–2
Mendelssohn, Felix, 90
Menotti, Gian Carlo, 262
Menuhin, Yehudi, 326
Meredith, George, 186
Merwin, W.S., 333
Messager, André, 117
Michaux, Henri, 185, 198, 268, 300, 333
Miller, Grace, 20, 36
Miller, Mary Britton ("Isabel Bolton"), 20–1, 36–7, 270, 333, 337n18
Milton, John, 36
Ministry of Public Works, 238–9
Miró, Joan, 287
Mirsky, D.S., 185
"modernism," 188–9
Mommsen, Theodor, 74
Mondadori (publisher), 273, 305
Monet, Claude, 56
Monnier, Adrienne, 148–9, 156, 164, 216
"Mon Rêve." *See* Banneville, Calvados
Montale, Eugenio, 248
Monte Cassino, 234
Montesquieu, Count Robert de, 56
Moore, Marianne, 251, 300
Morandi, Giorgio, 204
Morante, Elsa, 261, 332–3
Moravia, Alberto, 261, 285, 333
Morel, Auguste, 158, 183
Morgan, John Pierpoint, 9; Morgan Library, 26. *See also* J.P. Morgan and Company
Morra di Lavriano, Count Umberto, 260, 381n14
Mugnier, Abbé, 154
Muhlfeld, Jeanne, 57, 64
Muhlfeld, Lucien, 59
Murat, Princess Lucien (née Marie de Rohan-Chabot, Countess of Chambrun), 60, 64
Muir, Edwin, 271–2

Nabis, 57, 62
Natanson, Thadée, 59
National Trust, 291
New Directions (publisher), 252, 270–1
New London, Connecticut, 10, 14, 20, 35, 42, 61. *See also* Waterford, Connecticut
Newport, Rhode Island, 15–16, 54–5
New Writing, 252. *See also* Lehmann, John
New York: Academy of Music, 22; Fifth Avenue, 13–14, 17, 21–2, 24, 26, 358n14; Grand Central Terminus (later Grand Central Station), 26, 35; Gotham Book Mart, 274, 287, 374n40; Greenwich Village, 270; Harlem, 338n8; Hugo Gallery, 290; Metropolitan Museum of Art, 32, 168; Metropolitan Opera House, 22, 26–7, 43, 46, 221; Murray Hill, 26; Times Square, 221
New Yorker, The, 266, 270, 374n42, 376n57
New York Herald Tribune, 252, 358n14
New York Times, 270, 374n42, and the many references cited
Nietzsche, Friedrich, 58, 186
Noailles, Anna de, 60
Noonday Press, 301
Norba (hill town), 114
Norma (hill town), 71, 114–15, 212
Nouvelle Revue Française, 148, 154–5, 189, 252. *See also* Paulhan, Jean
Noventa, Giacomo, 251
Nuremburg trials, 262

Observer, The, 270–2
O'Criadain, Sean, 309
Office of Strategic Services (OSS), 231–2
O'Flaherty, Monsignor Hugh, 229
O'Flaherty, Liam, 186
Order of Malta, 123, 133, 352n4
Origo, Marchese Antonio, 128, 240, 260, 311
Origo, Benedetta, 260
Origo, Donata, 260
Origo, Marchesa Iris (née Cutting), 128–9, 229, 240, 260, 274, 311, 322–3
Orsini family, 72
Ortega y Gasset, José, 182
Osborne, Sir Francis D'Arcy Godolphin, 195, 227, 229, 232, 260, 368nn21–23
Osgood Mason, Charlotte (née Van der Veer Quick), 53–4, 128–9, 168–9, 342nn21–23, 359n18

Osgood Mason, Rufus, 53–4, 342n21
Ozick, Cynthia, 296

Pacht, Paola (née Bassani), 294–5
Paget, Lady Walpurga, 82
Palewski, Gaston, 301–3, 303 (12.7)
Palomar Apartments, 128, 130 (6.3)
Papal States, 72, 75, 114, 291
Paragone, 293. *See also* Bassani, Giorgio
Paris Review, The, 281–2, 284, 379n31
Pasolini, Pier Paolo, 268
Pasolini Dall'Onda, Countess Desideria, 260
Pasolini Dall'Onda, Countess Ginevra, 260
Pasternak, Boris, 186
Paulhan, Jean, 154, 156, 162–4, 169–70, 176, 182, 186, 216, 244, 249–50, 252, 268–9, 289, 307
Paulhan, Germaine, 154, 176, 250, 268
Paz, Octavio, 292
PEN, 314
Penna, Sandro, 249
Perse, Saint-John. *See* Léger, Alexis Saint-Léger
Petroni, Guglielmo, 248–9, 279 (11.9), 306, 322, 371n9, 376n57
Petroni, Puci, 279
Philip IV (King of France), 71
Phillips, William (Bill), 229, 260
Picasso, Pablo Rúiz y, 50, 57, 168
Piccolomini, Countess Anna ("Annina," née Menotti), 176, 194, 201, 210, 362n4, 363n5
Piccolomini, Count Enea Silvio, 194, 363n5
Piccolomini, Niccolò, 363n5
"Pio Nono's curse," 75, 93, 227
Plato, 36
Plimpton, George, 281–2, 284. See also *Paris Review*, *The*
Poe, Edgar Allen, 36, 186, 322
Pointillists, 57
Polignac, Princesse de (née Winnaretta Singer), 49, 96–7, 163, 349n3
Ponchielli, Amilcare, 90
Ponge, Francis, 185, 252, 268
Pontine Marshes, 70, 72, 81, 84, 96, 113–14, 150, 173, 199–202, 211, 263, 330. See also *Agro Pontino*
Pontine Music Festival, 326
Pontresina, 102, 230
Popes: Alexander VI (Rodrigo Borgia), 72; Boniface VIII (Benedetto Caetani), 71; Gelasius II (Giovanni Caetani), 71; Julius II (Giuliano Della Rovere), 72; Pius IX (Giovanni Mastai-Ferretti) ("Pio Nono"), 75; Sixtus V (Felice Peretti di Montalto), 72
Pound, Ezra, 149, 155, 171, 177
Powys, T.F., 186
Praetorius, Ernst, 176–7 (8.3)
Pratolini, Vasco, 268
Prévert, Jacques, 185
Proust, Marcel, 56–7, 154, 341n14
Psellos, Michael, 186
Pushkin, Alexander, 186

railroad development, 7–9, 335n4
Raine, Kathleen, 251, 216–17, 324, 380n6
Randall, Julia, 284
Random House (publisher), 287–8, 291–2, 306, 333
Recapitulation, 319–20, 380n7
Redon, Odilon, 56
Reed, Edgar, 21
Reinhardt, Max, 163
Renoir, Auguste, 56
Resistance, 233, 249, 286, 366n1
Respighi, Ottorino, 194, 363n5
Reverdy, Pierre, 268
revolutions of 1848, 75
Revue Blanche, La, 59
Reyes, Alfonso, 183
Ricciardi, Riccardo, 248, 250–1, 371n10
Rilke, Rainer Maria, 154, 160–4, 176, 185–6, 189, 292, 331
"Risorgimento," 74–5, 305
"Ritrovo, Il," 240–3
Rivière, Jacques, 148, 182
"robber barons," 9
Rockefeller, John D., 9
Rockefeller, William, 342n21
Rockefeller Foundation, 173, 252, 255, 342n21
Rocky Mountains, 88, 138
Roditi, George, 198
Roethke, Theodore, 251, 275, 296, 299, 331, 333
Roffman, Ludwig, 177 (8.3)
Romaine, Jules, 149
Roman balance, 166, 302 (12.6)
Roman Jubilee, 71
Rome, 70–2, 79, 80, 90, 196–7, 229, 241–2, 245–7; Acqua Santa Golf

Club, 224; ancient monuments, 113; Archivio Segreto, 202; atmosphere under fascism, 196–7, 200; atmosphere post-1945, 241–2, 245–7; Biblioteca Apostolica, 202, 363–4n17; Campo Verano cemetery, 131, 228–9, 316, 329; Capitoline Hill, 238; Circus Flaminius, 247; German Occupation, 229; Isola di Mattei, 73; Liceo Municipale, 89–90; Palazzo Lovatelli-Caetani, 112, 231, 232, 238; Palazzo Orsini (Orsini Palace), 135, 198, 213, 238, 240; Palazzo Primoli, 301–2 (12.6); Palazzo Quirinale (Quirinal Palace), 113, 258; Piazza Venezia, 238; Society of Jesus (Jesuit) Mother House, 248; Stazione Termini, 192; Teatro Communale Argentina, 97; Teatro di Marcello, 135; Vatican, 74, 202, 229, 232, 234; Via Appia Antica 114; Via delle Botteghe Oscure. *See also* Caetani residences: Palazzo Caetani
Rome Escape Organization, 229
Roosevelt, Franklin Delano, 227, 234, 235
Ross, Janet, 128
Rostand, Edmund, 133
Rouault, Georges, 168, 204
Roussel, Annette, 64
Ruffini, Nina, 260, 323
Rzewuska, Lela and Toutou, 232
Rzewuski, Wenceslas Severin, 75, 86
Rzewuski family, 75

Saba, Umberto, 268
Saint-Gaudens, Augustus, 10
Saint-Saens, Camille, 56
Salic Law, 99
salons, 56, 59, 74, 97, 359n20
Salzburg Music Festival, 163–4, 195
San Donato (hill town), 71
Sardeau, Hélène, 262–3, 315
Satie, Erik, 154
Schalk, Franz, 173
Schermerhorn, Caroline. *See* Astor, Caroline
Schermerhorn, Elizabeth, 16–17, 337n15
Schermerhorn, George Stevens, 17, 337n15
Schlumberger, Jean, 148–9
Schoenberg, Arnold, 118
Schott (music publisher), 90, 153
Schubert, Franz, 299
Schumann, Robert, 90
Scotellaro, Rocco, 251, 372n18
Scott, Sir Walter, 74
Scovell, E.J., 333
Second World War, 224, 231–40, 233 (10.1), 234 (10.2), 235 (10.3), 236 (10.4), 237 (10.5), 240 (10.6), 249
Segantini, Giovanni, 168
Seligman, William, 56
Serbelloni family, 73
Sert, José Maria, 109
Severini, Gino, 205 (9.3)
Sgambati, Giovanni, 89–90
Shakespeare and Company (book), 357n23
Shakespeare and Company (bookshop), 149
Shapiro, Karl, 251, 299
Shattuck, Roger, 300
Shelley, Percy Bysshe, 296
Sickert, Walter, 204
Signac, Paul, 56
Silkin, Jon, 300, 333
Silone, Ignazio, 268, 332
Sils Maria, 58–60
Simpson, Wallis, 130
Singer, Winnaretta. *See* Polignac, Princesse de
Sitwell, Edith, 171, 186, 251
Smith, William Jay, 251
Società Bonifiche Pontine, 135, 138, 200
Società l'Arte d'Oggi, 205–6
Société des Amis du Luxembourg, 207
Société des Grands Auditions Musicales, 49–50
Soldati, Mario, 251
Sonnino (hill town), 234
Sorbonne, 18, 50
Spark, Muriel, 296
Spender, Stephen, 267
Spettatore Italiano, Lo (review), 246. *See also* Craveri, Elena; Craveri, Raimondo
Spiritualism, 53–4, 342n21, 342–3n23
Spoelberch de Louwenjoul, Countess Adelaide, 100, 102, 349n3
Springfield, Massachusetts, 14, 18, 20, 34, 42, 191, 335n3, 336n9; Chapin family seat, 11–13; origins and development, 6–9; "The Puritan," 10
Standard Oil Company, 51, 342n21
Statesman and Nation, 270
Stein, Gertrude, 50, 149